Mobile Information Device Profile for Java 2 MicroEdition

C. Enrique Ortiz

Eric Giguère

Wiley Computer Publishing

John Wiley & Sons, Inc.

NEW YORK • CHICHESTER • WEINHEIM • BRISBANE • SINGAPORE • TORONTO

Publisher: Robert Ipsen
Editor: Carol A. Long
Assistant Editor: Adaobi Obi
Managing Editor: John Atkins
Associate New Media Editor: Brian Snapp
Text Design & Composition: D&G Limited, LLC

This book is printed on acid-free paper. ♾

Published by John Wiley & Sons, Inc.

Published simultaneously in Canada.

Library of Congress Cataloging-in-Publication Data:

Ortiz, Enrique, 1965–
Mobile information device profile for Java 2 MicroEdition : professional developer's guide / Enrique Ortiz, Eric Giguere.
p. cm. — (Professional developer's guide series)
ISBN 0-471-03465-7 (pbk. : alk. paper)
1. Java (Computer program language) I. Giguère, Eric, 1967– II. Title. III. Series.

QA76.73.J38 O825 2001
005.13'3—dc21

2001046612

Printed in the United States of America.

10 9 8 7 6 5 4 3 2 1

To our wives, Sarylda and Lisa,
who are always in our hearts.
And to our children, our gems,
Damián, Sarylda, Diana, and Victoria.

Professional Developer's Guide Series

Other titles in series:

GPRS and 3G Wireless Applications by Christoffer Andersson, ISBN 0-471-41405-0

Constructing Intelligent Agents Using Java by Joseph P. Bigus and Jennifer Bigus, ISBN 0-471-39601-X

Advanced Palm Programming by Steve Mann and Ray Rischpater, ISBN 0-471-39087-9

WAP Servlets by John L. Cook, III, ISBN 0-471-39307-X

Java 2 Micro Edition by Eric Giguère, ISBN 0-471-39065-8

Scripting XML and WMI for Microsoft® SQL Server™ 2000 by Tobias Martinsson, ISBN 0-471-39951-5

Contents

Preface

This book has been my introduction to the world of publishing and I have to admit that this particular project has been more involved than expected and took many sacrifices. Now I know better . . .

To make this book happen I had the help from many people, both directly and indirectly. First I must thank my family—my wife Sarylda, and children Damián, Sarylda, and Diana, who patiently endured the writing of this book. I must thank Carol Long from Wiley for giving me this unique opportunity and for helping make this book happen. Carol, you are the nicest person. . . . I want to thank Carole McClendon, my agent, for helping me take care of all those little details that I had no idea how to take care of. I want to really thank Eric, my colleague in this project and mentor throughout this book, and the AGEA Corporation (formerly agentGO), my company, for their patience during the writing of this book.

I dedicate this book to my family, friends, and colleagues and to everyone who helped me in one way or another over the years. And to those who have helped make or are making mobile/pervasive computing into a reality.

C. Enrique Ortiz
November 2001

This is my third book and my first with a co-author. Writing with someone else poses its unique challenges, especially when both of you are busy people with families and full-time jobs. Enrique really wanted to do it, though, and I think having two heads working together has made for a better book. I certainly hope you think so!

In many ways this book is a follow-on to *Java 2 Micro Edition: Professional Developer's Guide*, which turned out to be the first (and for a while, the only) book on J2ME available anywhere. In the year since I finished that manuscript, though, many things have changed. For one thing, the Mobile Information Device Profile was finalized and actual devices with MIDP support have been shipped. Tools are becoming available, and other J2ME profiles are finally being released as well. These events have made it possible to write a much more focused book, one that explores MIDP programming in depth.

As always, I have to thank the people directly or indirectly involved in the creation of this book. Enrique was the inspiration for this book and had a lot of ideas and energy to share, which was great. Carol Long, our editor, put up with our lateness—you'd think I'd learn to submit a book on time by now, this being my third . . . Ed Ort at Sun for letting me use some material I wrote for him. The kind folks at Motorola who let me use an i85s for some testing—it's always great to have a real MIDP device to play with. The company I work for, iAnywhere Solutions, deserves mention because they provide me with a wonderful working environment. Last, but certainly not least, I'd like to thank my wife Lisa, who generally puts up with me whether I'm writing a book or not, for which I'm always grateful. She, our daughter Victoria, and our two dogs (Dino and Taffy), make me look forward to spending time at home. I like my family, and I'm glad to have them!

Eric Giguère
November 2001

Introduction

Only recently have mass-produced, low-cost wireless devices—pagers and cellular telephones being the prime examples—evolved beyond being closed devices with fixed sets of features and services. The development of Wireless Access Protocol (WAP) and related technologies—specifically, markup languages such as Wireless Markup Language (WML) and its predecessor, HDML, as well as newer technologies such as XHTML Basic, and XForms—make it possible to browse the Internet (or a controlled subset) directly on the devices. These devices can run thin-client applications—server-based applications where the user interface consists of pages of markup that are downloaded to the client and displayed by using a built-in browser application, but where the application logic is executed on the server. The biggest advantage to deploying thin-client applications is that because they really run on the server and not on the client, they can be updated at any time and can make use of server-side facilities that are not available to individual clients.

Still, thin-client programming has its disadvantages. With today's slow-speed wireless networks, for example, there is a noticeable delay when the application accesses the server to get the next set of pages to display. Faster networks are in development and will reduce or eliminate this problem, of course, but there is still a fundamental problem with thin-client applications: They require a connection to the server. If the device goes out of wireless coverage, it loses the capability to run those applications. Thin-client applications not only place a lot of strain on the network but also on the servers, because almost every operation involves the server—sometimes even for simple validation of user input. As well, the server must maintain session information for each active application instance, and session tracking itself can be non-trivial when dealing with certain wireless devices and gateways.

The new trend in wireless technology is to build "thicker" or "fatter" thin-client applications. In other words, instead of doing all the computing on the server, do some on the client. This method is not necessarily a return to the traditional client-server programming model but rather an acknowledgement that some things are best done locally instead of remotely. This augmented thin-client model is referred to as the *smart-client* programming model: The client is "smarter" because it can execute logic right on the device instead of depending entirely on the server. A smart-client application lies somewhere between a pure client-server application and a pure thin-client application.

Smart-client applications reduce the load on the server and the network and can usually work—albeit with limitations—when the server is not available; these are occasionally connected clients. They leverage technologies such as HTTP, XML, data synchronization, messaging, end-to-end security, Web services, servlets, JavaServer Pages, and Enterprise JavaBeans to bring the power of the enterprise—the business logic and data sources that are so critical to an organization—to small, handheld devices. Instead of being tethered to a computer, the end users are free to roam wherever business needs take them.

To build a smart-client application, of course, the device must support a more conventional programming model. More recent WAP-based clients can run scripts written in WMLScript. Similarly, products such as AvantGo or AppForge enable you to build more sophisticated applications with local code execution. And now there is also Java, or more specifically Java 2 Micro Edition (J2ME) and the Mobile Information Device Profile (MIDP).

The ability to run Java applications on handheld and wireless devices such as cellphones, pagers and low-end personal digital assistants (PDAs) by using the MIDP opens an exciting new world for software developers. Just as Java has become the dominant development platform for server and enterprise programming, J2ME and its profiles extend the platform to wireless and handheld devices. Only time will tell whether Java proves as successful on these devices as it has on the server. J2ME and the MIDP are new yet familiar technologies that make smart-client programming simpler. As a comprehensive programming and reference guide to the MIDP, this book gets you started in this exciting new area.

Wireless Java: An Evolving Technology

Java is a technology that has taken a life of its own—a technology that has gone through several phases of evolution. During the early 1990s, Sun worked on a secret project, known as the Green project, that created an object-oriented, machine-independent programming language and environment called Oak. This new language enabled you to write software that ran on different devices without modification; the idea of "write once, run anywhere." Oak was originally targeted at electronic devices for the consumer space.

Oak, which was loosely based on C++, was designed to run on constrained devices (devices with minimal resources) and to run by using an interpreter. By 1992, the first prototype of Oak was ready. It included the Oak language, an operating system, a graphical user interface (GUI), and a handheld device code-named the Star Seven (*7), shown in Figure I.1, that was ahead of its time.

The market was not ready for Oak, and attempts to apply the technology to embedded devices failed. In 1995, Oak was revamped and renamed and Java was made available for free, together with HotJava, a Java-based Web browser. Different versions and variations of Java have been released since then, including EmbeddedJava, PersonalJava, and the

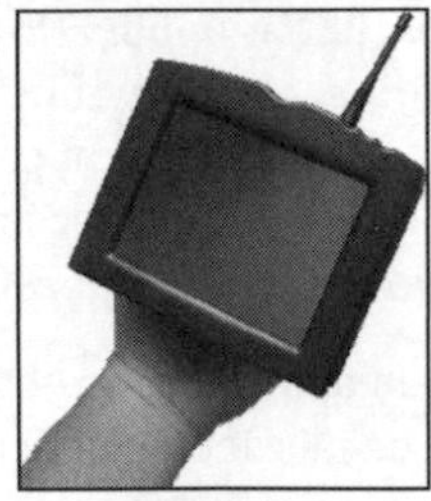

Figure I.1 The Star Seven (*7) handheld.

	High-end devices	Cellphones, pagers, low-end PDAs	Smartcards
Profiles	Foundation, Personal, . . .	MID, PDA	GSM, Open Platform
Configurations	CDC	CLDC	JavaCard API
Virtual Machine	JVM	KVM	JavaCard VM

Figure I.2 J2ME configurations and profiles.

different editions of what is now called Java 2. Chapter 1, "Java 2 Micro Edition Basics," discusses the evolution of Java and how J2ME came to be.

Not only is Java in general continually evolving, but Java for handheld and embedded devices is also evolving. The concepts of profiles and configurations, also discussed in Chapter 1, address how to make Java work on a wide range of electronic devices from set-top boxes to cell phones. One of these profiles is the Mobile Information Device Profile (MIDP), discussed in detail throughout this book, but there are also other profiles of interest and also related smart-card technologies (JavaCard). Together, these various configurations and profiles work together, as shown in Figure I.2, to provide support for Java on a wide variety of devices.

The Case for J2ME/MIDP

Why use J2ME? The answer is simple: To build smart-client applications for resource-constrained devices. Specifically, the resources required to run MIDP-based applications are fairly minimal and certainly within the realm of possibility for most device manufacturers. With J2ME/MIDP, you can build sophisticated applications by using a familiar development platform and deploy it across many different mobile devices. There are non-Java alternatives to J2ME, of course, and often such applications run faster and have access to more device capabilities. J2ME applications are portable, however, and the performance issues are being worked on. Only time will tell how successful J2ME will be, but it is encouraging to note that most major cell phone, pager, and PDA manufacturers have pledged support for J2ME, whether it is MIDP support or PersonalJava (which is being redefined to fit within the J2ME umbrella; see Chapter 1) support.

What features do smart-client applications require? Smart-client applications can be fairly sophisticated and can also be mission-critical applications with high expectations on the user's part. Table I.1 lists common features expected of mission-critical enterprise mobile applications; the MIDP allows for most of these, demonstrating why MIDP is a good choice for building smart-client applications.

Another compelling reason to support J2ME is that it is an industry standard. J2ME is defined by the development community and supported by major device vendors. It has a built-in developer base consisting of several million Java developers worldwide.

Let's summarize the benefits and weaknesses of J2ME and the MIDP. The strengths include the following:

- The MIDP is a portable platform enabling "write once, deploy anywhere" application development, decreasing development and ownership costs.
- J2ME is industry-supported: Motorola, RIM, Ericsson, Nokia, Panasonic, Nextel, BT Cellnet, and others are example supporters.

Table I.1 Smart-Client Application Features

FEATURE	CHARACTERISTICS	EXAMPLES
Local application	*Small footprint versions of application logic and local processing: thick, intelligent client/server applications	*Local, standalone applications (offline)
	*Applications can run on devices without network coverage.	*Wireless IT applications; better use of wireless bandwidth
	*Better use of wireless bandwidth	
Rich user interface	*High- and low-level UI APIs allow for simple but rich user interfaces for business applications and games.	*Intelligent UI, navigations, and graphics
Network aware	*Support for HTTP and optionally datagrams	
	*Distributed applications: Applications run on multiple devices without a server.	*Server and server-less network-based applications

Table I.1 Continued

FEATURE	CHARACTERISTICS	EXAMPLES
Network aware	*Peer-to-peer: Direct device-to-device network communications *Easy integration by leveraging HTTP and XML	*Instant messaging and information sharing
Reliable messaging	*Guaranteed message delivery can be implemented to ensure that transactions are not lost due to a loss of network coverage.	*Mission-critical wireless IT applications that work even under disconnected situations
Local persistence	*Local data store enables persistence at the device. Key to offline functionality and guaranteed message delivery and better utilization of wireless bandwidth	* Keep important information on the device itself and synchronize with corporate serves only when needed.
End-to-end security	*Support for HTTPS and alternative cryptosystems enables end-to-end security without translations at the network provider.	*Secure access to corporate servers behind the firewall
Data synchronization	*Synchronize data when/as needed.	*Data synchronization with corporate servers behind the firewall
Alerts	*Real-time notifications	*Salesperson on the road gets notifications about sales leads in his or her region
Multi-language support	*Target your application to different languages.	*Deploy an IT application in different countries with minimal changes.
Cross platform and low cost of development and ownership	*Develop 'once' to deploy to any J2ME device with an appropriate profile.	*Develop the application once and deploy on company-supplied cell phones, two-way pagers, and PDAs.
Access to corporate servers	*Integrate and interoperate with existing corporate servers. *Easy integration by levering HTTP and XML	*Access to Exchange/ Notes servers and/or ERP and CRM servers

- J2ME supports standalone, offline, smart-client and network-aware applications.
- You can add enhanced services such as end-to-end security, data synchronization, and access to Web services.
- J2ME is supported by the Java developer community and is based on open standards.

Nothing is perfect, though, and here are some current weaknesses:

- The MIDP is new technology (still in the early-adoption phase).
- There are few J2ME-enabled devices on the market.
- Support for network security is minimal at this stage.
- J2ME applications do not normally have access to native device functionality.
- The MIDP user interface, although sufficient for many applications, is primitive.
- There is no support for pushing data from a server to the client.

You will need to carefully weigh these pros and cons and decide for yourself whether J2ME, and the MIDP specifically, is an appropriate development platform for you.

About This Book

This book is about programming Java-enabled devices that support the Mobile Information Device Profile. This profile and its associated configuration—again, profiles and configurations are described in detail in Chapter 1—provide a minimal Java runtime environment that can run on devices that are much more limited than the typical desktop or server computers that are used for Java-based computing. Included with the MIDP are classes for building simple user interfaces, persisting data locally, and communicating with external devices. These enable you to build small but complete Java applications that can be run on MIDP-compatible devices from Motorola, Research in Motion, Nokia, Palm, and others—all participants in the process that defined the profile. At this writing, only a few of these devices are currently available to the general public, but more appear or are announced each month. This book covers *all* of these devices; you will be able to write applications for any device that complies with the MIDP 1.0 specification covered here. Even more powerful devices such as the Nokia Communicator that can actually run more conventional Java applications (based on PersonalJava or even Java 2 Standard Edition) also include MIDP support, which broadens the deployment base even further. Please note that this book does not cover proprietary extensions to the MIDP that specific devices might offer or specific instructions for installing the applications on the device; you will still need to consult your device's documentation for that information.

We assume that you already have experience with Java programming in a desktop or server environment. Access to an MIDP-compatible device is not a requirement, but it is certainly desirable. Testing with a real device is important before distributing your MIDP applications.

Chapter Summary

This book is organized into 11 chapters and two appendices and serves as a complete guide to MIDP programming.

Chapter 1, "Java 2 Micro Edition Basics," introduces you to J2ME. It discusses how J2ME evolved and presents the concepts of configurations and profiles. It finishes with an overview of the Connected Limited Device Configuration (CLDC), the configuration that determines the core capabilities of the Java runtime environment used in MIDP-enabled devices. (For more detailed information on J2ME in general, refer to Eric Giguère's *Java 2 Micro Edition: Professional Developer's Guide*, also published by John Wiley & Sons.)

Chapter 2, "The Mobile Information Device Profile," introduces you to the Mobile Information Device Profile, version 1.0. It includes a discussion of over-the-air provisioning and what to expect from the next release of the MIDP specification already in development.

Chapter 3, "The MIDlet Lifecycle," describes how to build and run MIDP applications, which are referred to as MIDlets for short. A MIDlet resembles a Java applet, but it has different behavior and different requirements. Included in this chapter are all the steps required to build and package MIDlets by hand or with a development tool as well as a discussion of how MIDlets behave and what kind of programming errors to avoid.

Chapter 4, "User Interface Basics," describes the MIDP user interface model and how to use the new user interface (UI) classes that the MIDP defines, which are different from the Abstract Windowing Toolkit (AWT) or Swing classes that you already know. The MIDP defines high-level and low-level UI abstractions, both of which are covered here. Each user interface component is covered in detail.

Chapter 5, "User Interface Examples," takes you step-by-step through MIDP programming examples that demonstrate how to combine the user interface classes described in Chapter 4 to build complete user interfaces.

Chapter 6, "Network Communication," describes how MIDlets can communicate with external servers by using HTTP and other protocols. It starts with a detailed explanation of the CLDC's Generic Connection Framework, first introduced in Chapter 1. It then proceeds to show you how you can use HTTP as a way to exchange data with servers on the Internet.

Chapter 7, "The Record Management System," describes the MIDP's persistence mechanism. The Record Management System (RMS) lets you store arbitrary data locally on the device without involving a server.

Chapter 8, "Security," describes how MIDlets can securely exchange data and authenticate users. Security is always important but is especially so on wireless devices. MIDP security is still in its infancy and is quite limited, but it warrants a separate discussion.

Chapter 9, "Using XML In MIDP Applications," demonstrates how XML can be used to communicate with servers to exchange data and invoke Web services. Although XML is not part of the MIDP specification, there are MIDP-compatible XML parsers available that you can include in your applications. Besides explaining what XML is and how XML documents are created and parsed, this chapter also demonstrates how to invoke Web services by using the XML-based Simple Object Access Protocol (SOAP).

Chapter 10, "Techniques for Writing Better MIDP Applications," describes how to avoid potential pitfalls and how to make your MIDP applications more portable and more efficient.

Chapter 11, "Final Thoughts," wraps up our discussion of MIDP programming and describes alternatives and future directions.

Appendix A, "MIDP/CLDC Quick Reference," is a complete reference guide to all the classes defined by the MIDP 1.0 and CLDC 1.0 specifications.

Appendix B, "Resources," lists J2ME and MIDP programming resources.

Companion Web Site

A companion Web site for the book, `www.wiley.com/compbooks/ortiz`, updates the material in this book and provides additional examples and resources as well as current links to the various specifications and toolkits mentioned throughout the book. Included on the site is a password-protected section solely for the readers of this book—see the site for instructions on how to access the protected area.

Be sure to check the Web site regularly as well as the Web sites listed in Appendix B for updates and news about Java 2 Micro Edition and the Mobile Information Device Profile.

CHAPTER 1

Java 2 Micro Edition Basics

The Mobile Information Device Profile (MIDP) is just one part of a larger initiative to make Java work on small computing devices, the Java 2 Micro Edition (J2ME). Before starting our exploration of the MIDP, we need to step back and understand what J2ME is and how it evolved. This chapter provides you with a broad overview of J2ME and the MIDP's place in it, including the Connected Limited Device Configuration on which it is based. For a more comprehensive look at J2ME, refer to Eric Giguère's *Java 2 Micro Edition*, also part of John Wiley & Sons' Professional Developer's Guide series.

A Very Brief History of Java

Java's first incarnation was Oak, a language developed at Sun Microsystems for programming consumer devices. You can still find information about Oak on Sun's Web site by searching for references to the Green Project. Oak was ahead of its time, however, and instead became the more general-purpose language we now know as Java.

The Architecture of Java

Architecturally, Java has not changed much since its first release. A Java compiler transforms the Java programming language into a set of Java *bytecodes*. Bytecodes are instructions for an abstract computing machine referred to as a *virtual machine*, or VM for short. A Java VM, sometimes referred to as a JVM, interprets the Java bytecodes in order to run a Java program. A Java VM is thus often called an *interpreter*, although Java code can also be compiled straight into native machine binary code. Whether interpreted or compiled, Java bytecode execution must follow the steps and semantics described in *The*

Java Virtual Machine Specification (JVMS), or else you cannot call it Java. (Java is a trademark of Sun Microsystems, and anyone wishing to implement a Java runtime environment and call it such must obtain permission from Sun and pass a comprehensive set of compatibility tests.) The syntax and semantics of the Java language itself are described in a separate document entitled *The Java Language Specification* (JLS).

One of Java's inherent strengths is its portability—the capability to take a Java program and execute it on various operating systems without having to recompile or otherwise retarget the program for each operating system. This portability is achieved in several ways. First, both the JLS and the JVMS ensure that the types, bytecodes, and encodings used in Java are defined independently of the underlying operating system. Second, the binary encoding of a Java class—how the bytecodes are packaged at a class level—is defined by the JVMS, also in a machine-independent fashion. Third, a core set of runtime classes (and an associated set of platform-specific native code) abstract the interface between a Java program and the underlying operating system.

Java is also known for its security infrastructure. From the verification of class files to ensure the integrity of the generated bytecode to the use of class loaders and security managers, Java makes it possible to securely and safely download and execute third-party code of untrusted origin. This capability to download code across a network was arguably Java's most important feature when it was first developed and is being re-emphasized today with initiatives such as J2ME and Jini.

Unless the operating system is written in Java, of course, there has to be a way for Java programs to access the features of the native operating system. Java programs can call native code in a controlled manner through a native code interface. The current form of the native code interface is referred to as the Java Native Interface, or JNI for short. User-developed native code is rarely found, however, and can hamper portability and security.

Early Java

The first official release of Java outside Sun was called Java 1.0.2. The 1.0.2 actually refers to the version of the *Java Development Kit* (JDK) that included everything needed to develop and run Java programs on the Windows and Solaris operating systems. Even today, you will still refer to Java by the JDK version, although Sun now refers to it as the *Java Software Development Kit* (JSDK) and has separated the runtime-only portions of

Reading the Specifications Online

Although they are available in hard copy as well, both *The Java Language Specification* and *The Java Virtual Machine Specification* can be read online from Sun's Web site. The JVMS is at `http://java.sun.com/docs/books/vmspec/index.html`**, and the JLS is at** `http://java.sun.com/docs/books/jls/index.html`**.**

the JDK into a separate *Java Run-Time Environment* (JRE). Although strictly speaking, the JRE did not actually appear until version 1.1 of the JDK was released, we will use the term generically to refer to the runtime part of any Java platform.

Java 1.0.2 was notable primarily for two things. First, it defined an *Abstract Windowing Toolkit* (AWT) for the creation of portable *graphical user interfaces* (GUIs). Second, it defined *applets,* a way in which Web browsers use an embedded Java VM to safely run applications downloaded on the fly from untrusted Web sites.

While 1.0.2 was a good first attempt, it had a number of deficiencies, such as limited control over the user interface, a lack of internationalization and localization capabilities, and a restrictive security model. The next major release, Java 1.1, addressed a number of these issues and added many new features. The new features included a listener-based event model, object serialization, *remote method invocation* (RMI), *just-in-time* (JIT) compiling, and inner classes. There were also some optional pieces, like a new user interface toolkit called Swing (a set of enhanced AWT components) and a set of collections classes with more advanced data structures than those found in the `java.util` package.

Java 2

As work progressed within Sun Microsystems on Java 1.2, a decision was made to rebrand Java and to make major changes in the way Java was packaged and licensed. Java 1.2 became simply Java 2, although the JDK and JRE versions remained at 1.2. More importantly, however, the Java platform was split into three editions:

- *Java 2 Standard Edition* (J2SE) is for conventional desktop application development. Swing has been folded into the core Java classes, and a number of new classes have been added to enhance application development even more than what Java 1.1 offered.
- *Java 2 Enterprise Edition* (J2EE) is a superset of J2SE that is geared toward enterprise programming with an emphasis on server-side development using *Enterprise JavaBeans* (EJBs), web applications (servlets and JavaServer Pages), CORBA, and *Extensible Markup Language* (XML).
- *Java 2 Micro Edition* (J2ME) is a subset of J2SE that is geared toward embedded and handheld devices that cannot support a full J2SE implementation.

Although there is a certain amount of overlap, each edition targets a different kind of application developer. The sheer number of classes available to J2EE programmers—and the complexities of using those classes—stands in stark contrast to the much smaller set of classes available to J2ME programmers. On the other hand, J2ME programmers have severe memory and resource constraints to handle. Splitting Java 2 into three editions makes it possible for Java to evolve in different directions while staying true to the spirit of the language.

The Java Community Process

Although Sun is the ultimate authority for the Java platform, much of its work in defining and extending the platform is done through the auspices of the *Java Community*

Process (JCP). The JCP enables corporations and individuals to participate in the definition and revision of different parts of the Java platform. The process is fairly simple: A specification request (known as a JSR) is submitted with a specific proposal to extend the Java platform. If the JSR is accepted for development, an *Expert Group* (EG) is formed to define a formal specification for the JSR. The Expert Group consists of JCP members who have expertise in the area covered by the JSR and who volunteer their time and effort to develop the proposal with the interests of the larger Java community in mind. When ready, the specification is published for review by other JCP members and by the general public. The specification is revised based on reviewer comments before being voted on and accepted as a formal Java standard.

All J2ME standards are defined by using the Java Community Process. For more information about the JCP, see the JCP Web site at `www.jcp.org`. From there, you can get a list of all the JSRs that have been defined or are in the process of being defined, including the ones mentioned in this book.

Java 2 Micro Edition

J2ME enables Java applications to run on small, resource-constrained computing devices. It does not define a new language; rather, it adapts existing Java technology for handheld and embedded devices. Compatibility with J2SE is maintained wherever feasible. In fact, J2ME removes the parts of J2SE that are not applicable to constrained devices, such as AWT and other features. In this section, we briefly describe the key components of J2ME: configurations and profiles.

Configurations

A *configuration* defines the basic J2ME runtime environment. This environment includes the virtual machine, which can be more limited than the VM used by J2SE, and a set of core classes derived primarily from J2SE. The key point is that each configuration is geared toward a specific family of devices with similar capabilities.

Currently, two configurations are defined: the *Connected Device Configuration* (CDC) and the *Connected Limited Device Configuration* (CLDC). Both target connected devices—devices with network connectivity—whether it is a high-speed fixed link or a slow-speed wireless link. The CLDC targets the really small devices: cellular telephones, *personal digital assistants* (PDAs), and interactive pagers. As a group, these devices have important power, memory, and network bandwidth restrictions that directly affect the kind of Java applications that they can support. The CDC, on the other hand, targets devices that are less restricted, such as set-top boxes (devices that provide network-based computing features through a television) and car navigation systems. The line between the CDC and the CLDC is not distinct, because some high-end cellular telephones and PDAs can meet the requirements of the CDC—forcing the device manufacturer (the most likely provider of a Java runtime environment) to decide which configuration to support.

Note that the CDC is a superset of the CLDC: The CDC includes all of the classes defined by the CLDC, including any new ones that are not part of J2SE. The CDC includes many more core J2SE classes than the CLDC, however, which makes the CDC a more familiar and comfortable environment for experienced Java programmers. For the purposes of this book, though, you will have to learn to live within the restrictions imposed by the CLDC.

Perhaps the biggest difference between the CDC and the CLDC is that the former requires a full-featured Java virtual machine that is compliant with the one in J2SE. In other words, the CDC VM must support all the advanced features of a J2SE VM, including low-level debugging and native programming interfaces. Sun has released a new Java VM, the *Compact VM* (CVM), for this purpose—it is more portable and efficient than the standard VM.

Profiles

A *profile* extends a configuration, adding domain-specific classes to the core set of classes. In other words, profiles provide classes that are geared toward specific uses of devices and that provide functionality missing from the base configuration—things such as user interface classes, persistence mechanisms, and so on. Profiles are the double-edged sword of J2ME: While they provide important and necessary functionality, not every device will support every profile. In Japan, for example, NTT DoCoMo has released a number of Java-enabled cellular telephones based on the CLDC but with their own proprietary profile. Applications written for these devices will not work on cellular telephones that support the MIDP.

A number of profiles are defined or are in development. Besides the MIDP, which is based on the CLDC (we will discuss this topic in detail in the next chapter), the following profiles are or will be available:

- A *Personal Digital Assistant Profile* (PDAP) that extends the CLDC to take advantage of the extended capabilities of PDAs when compared to the simpler devices targeted by the MIDP.
- A *Foundation Profile* that adds additional J2SE classes to the CDC but no user interface classes. It acts as a foundation for building other profiles.

What about Java Card and EmbeddedJava?

J2ME is not Sun's first foray into the handheld and embedded device space. Although PersonalJava is being folded into J2ME as a CDC profile, what happens to Java Card and EmbeddedJava? Nothing; they remain as they are. Java Card adapts Java for use on smart cards, a very specialized environment that is not suitable for general-purpose programming. EmbeddedJava is more about licensing than defining a portable Java subset: EmbeddedJava licensees can pretty much choose which features of Java they want to support in their devices. The catch is that they cannot expose those features for use by a third party—only their own developers can write the applications that run on the device.

- A *Personal Profile* that redefines PersonalJava as a J2ME profile. The Personal Profile extends the Foundation Profile.
- An *RMI Profile* that adds RMI support to the CDC.

Multiple profiles can exist within the same configuration. Profiles can also build on each other—for example, the Personal Profile is an extension of the Foundation Profile. Expect more profiles to be developed as J2ME evolves.

The Connected Limited Device Configuration

To understand the MIDP, you must first understand the CLDC, the most minimalist of the J2ME implementations. The CLDC is defined by JSR-30 in the Java Community Process. For more information on the CLDC, refer to Sun's Web site at `http://java.sun.com/products/cldc`.

Requirements

The CLDC does not require many resources. It is meant to run on devices with 128K or more of non-volatile (persistent) memory and 32K or more of volatile memory. CLDC devices are required to have some kind of network connection (hence the term *connected device*), although it might be an intermittent, slow-speed connection. The configuration is for *limited* devices (devices that have severe limits on their computational power and battery life).

The CLDC defines a number of requirements for the Java environment. The first requirement is for full support of the Java language, except for a few differences. These differences are as follows:

- **No floating point support.** Floating point types or constants are not supported, and neither are the core J2SE classes that deal specifically with floating point values—classes such as `java.lang.Float` and `java.lang.Double`. Methods taking or returning floating point values are removed from all classes.
- **No object finalization.** To simplify the garbage collector's task, the `finalize` method is removed from `java.lang.Object`. The garbage collector will simply reclaim any unreferenced object. This action prevents unreferenced objects from "resurrecting" themselves and causing extra bookkeeping work for the garbage collector.
- **Runtime errors are handled in an implementation-dependent fashion.** Runtime errors are exceptions that are subclasses of `java.lang.Error` thrown by the virtual machine itself. The CLDC only defines three of these error classes: `java.lang.Error`, `java.lang.OutOfMemoryError`, and `java.lang.VirtualMachineError`. Any other error condition is handled by the VM in an

implementation-dependent manner, which usually means terminating the application.

The second requirement is for full virtual machine support, except for these few differences:

- **No floating point support.** CLDC devices might have no native support for floating point operations. As such, the VM does not support floating point constants or any of the bytecodes that involve floating point types.
- **No finalization and no weak references.** These are left out to simplify the garbage-collection algorithms.
- **No support for JNI or reflection or any low-level interfaces that depend on them.** In particular, there is no support for object serialization in the CLDC. Note that a VM *can* have a native interface, a debugging interface, or a profiling interface, but it is not required and it does not have to be a standard J2SE interface.
- **No thread groups or dameon thread.** Threads are supported, but thread groups or dameon threads are not. The VM can choose to implement threads by relying on the operating system or by performing its own context switching.
- **No application-defined class loaders.** An application cannot influence how classes are loaded. Only the runtime system can define and provide class loaders.
- **Implementation-defined error handling.** As mentioned, any runtime errors that are not specifically defined by the CLDC are handled in an implementation-specific manner.
- **Class verification is done differently.** The standard class verification process is too computationally expensive, so an alternate process was defined. The alternate process moves most of the verification work to a separate *preverification* step that occurs on a desktop or server computer and not on the device. The preverified class files are then processed on the device using a second, much simpler kind of verification that merely validates the results of the preverification step.

The third requirement is that any classes that are drawn or "inherited" from J2SE must be subsets of the J2SE 1.3 classes. Methods can be omitted, but no new public methods or data members can be added. Upward compatibility is of paramount importance.

The fourth requirement is that classes defined by the CLDC and its profiles are in the `javax.microedition` package or its subpackages, which makes it easy to identify the classes that are specific to the CLDC.

The final requirement is for minimal internationalization support. The CLDC provides basic support for converting byte streams to Unicode and back by using at least one character encoding. The CLDC does not address localization issues, such as how to display dates, times, currencies, and other locale-specific behaviors.

Supported J2SE Classes

The CLDC includes classes and interfaces drawn from these three J2SE packages:

- `java.lang`
- `java.io`
- `java.util`

As you can see, most J2SE classes are excluded, including those from useful packages such as `java.awt`, `java.net`, and `java.sql`. Even the packages that are included are missing classes, and many of those classes are missing methods. A listing of supported non-exception classes is found in Table 1.1. For a complete list of what is actually included in each class and which exceptions are available, refer to the class reference in Appendix A.

Table 1.1 Non-Exception J2SE 1.3 Classes Included in the CLDC

PACKAGE	CLASS
java.lang	Boolean
	Byte
	Character
	Class
	Integer
	Long
	Math
	Object
	Runnable
	Runtime
	String
	StringBuffer
	System
	Thread
	Throwable
java.io	ByteArrayInputStream
	ByteArrayOutputStream
	DataInput
	DataInputStream
	DataOutput
	DataOutputStream
	InputStream

Table 1.1 Continued

PACKAGE	CLASS
	InputStreamReader
	OutputStream
	OutputStreamWriter
	PrintStream
	Reader
	Writer
java.util	Calendar
	Date
	Enumeration
	Hashtable
	Random
	Stack
	Time
	Vector

The Generic Connection Framework

Apart from the classes discussed, the only other classes defined by the CLDC are the classes that make up the Generic Connection Framework, or GCF for short. The GCF abstracts the concepts of files, sockets, HTTP requests and other input/output mechanisms into a simpler set of classes than those defined by J2SE. In other words, the GCF is meant to provide the same functionality as classes from the `java.io` and `java.net` packages without requiring specific capabilities from a device. Note that the CLDC does, in fact, include some classes from the `java.io` package, but only the classes that do not depend on the capabilities of the underlying operating system. The GCF does not replace these basic input/output classes and depends on and uses classes such as `java.io.InputStream` and `java.io.OutputStream`. One way to look at the GCF is as a framework for building communications drivers, much like JDBC in J2SE is a framework for building database drivers.

With the GCF, all communication is abstracted through a set of well-defined interfaces. Instead of creating a specific class of communication objects like `java.io.File` or `java.net.Socket`, the application asks the GCF to create a connection that uses a specific protocol. The protocol can be a formal protocol, such as *Hypertext Transfer Protocol* (HTTP), or a reference to a low-level storage or communication facility like a filesystem or a wireless packet transceiver. The protocol is passed in as part of a *Universal Resource Identifier* (URI) that specifies other important information that is relevant to the protocol, such as the name of a host to connect to or the name of a file on the filesystem. The GCF then determines whether the implementation supports that protocol and returns an appropriate interface if it does. The application then uses this interface to interact with the implementation in sending or receiving data.

The classes defined by the GCF are listed in Table 1.2. All the classes are defined as part of the `javax.microedition.io` package. An application uses one of the static `Connector.open` methods to obtain an object that implements the `Connection` interface or one of its subinterfaces. The application then uses the methods defined by the interface to read and/or write data. Most of the interfaces work on stream-based data and therefore expose input or output streams.

All told, there are six subinterfaces of `Connection` defined. The `Input-Conection` and `OutputConnection` interfaces are for one-way stream connections. The `StreamConnection` interface is for two-way stream connections—it extends both `InputConnection` and `OutputConnection`. The `Content-Connection` interface extends `StreamConnection` with methods for determining information about the content itself such as its type and length. The `DatagramConnection` interface is for sending and receiving packet data. Finally, the `StreamConnectionNotifier` interface is for implementing server-side connections where the application must wait for a client to connect to it. The interface hierarchy is shown in Figure 1.1.

Note that while the CLDC defines the Generic Connection Framework, *it does not mandate support for any particular protocol.* This concept has confused more than one novice J2ME programmer, because there is a reference implementation of the CLDC available from Sun Microsystems that includes support for a number of communication protocols. Those protocols are there strictly as examples, though. Protocol support is defined at the profile level or as device-specific extensions.

We will look at the GCF in more detail in Chapter 6, "Network Communication," when we discuss networking and the MIDP.

Table 1.2 Generic Connection Framework

PACKAGE	CLASSES/INTERFACES
javax.microedition.io	Connection
	ConnectionNotFoundException
	Connector
	ContentConnection
	Datagram
	DatagramConnection
	InputConnection
	OutputConnection
	StreamConnection
	StreamConnectionNotifier

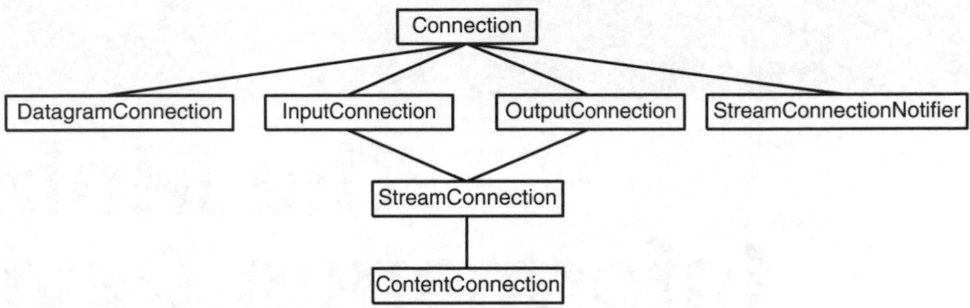

Figure 1.1 The GCF connection hierarchy.

Summary

In this chapter, we have taken a short history lesson on Java and learned about Java 2 Micro Edition in general and the Connected Limited Device Configuration more specifically. We are now ready to take our first look at the Mobile Information Device Profile.

CHAPTER 2

The Mobile Information Device Profile

Armed with a basic understanding of Java 2 Micro Edition (J2ME), we can start our exploration of the first J2ME profile and the focus of this book: the *Mobile Information Device Profile*, or MIDP for short. The MIDP is a CLDC-based profile for devices such as cellular telephones, interactive pagers, and low-end PDAs. In this chapter, we explore what a mobile information device is and discuss the features and limitations of the MIDP.

MIDP Specifications

Like all standards, the MIDP has a formal specification, known simply as the *Mobile Information Device Profile (JSR-37)*, which is downloadable from the JCP Web site. There are also related specifications of interest to MIDP programmers. Although this book provides you with all the information you need, you might still want to sit down and read through each of these specifications.

The first specification to read and understand is that of the Connected Limited Device Configuration (CLDC), which we discussed in Chapter 1. Configurations place absolute limits on what profiles can and cannot do, and the CLDC has strict constraints in order to target the smallest devices.

The next specification to read is the MIDP specification itself. This book is based on version 1.0 of that specification. At first glance, the MIDP specification seems much larger than the CLDC specification, but that is only because the former includes an appendix with detailed descriptions of each class and interface while the latter presents detailed information about its classes and interfaces in a separate document. The core of each specification is about 50 pages, not counting the table of contents and other preface material. Note that the next version of the MIDP specification is in development. We will explore this more at the end of this chapter.

A third specification is an addendum to the MIDP specification called *Over the Air User Initiated Provisioning Recommended Practice*, which describes in some detail how the MIDP Expert Group expects MIDP-based devices to support the downloading and installation of applications (referred to as *provisioning*) by using wireless networks (hence the term "over the air," or OTA for short) as opposed to using a direct serial or other connection to special software running on a desktop computer. We will refer to this document as the OTA specification, although it is not really a formal specification like the MIDP and CLDC specifications are.

The latest versions of the specifications are available for download from Sun's Web site from the main MIDP Web page at `http://java.sun.com/products/midp` or from the main CLDC Web page at `http://java.sun.com/products/cldc`. On those pages, you will also find links to other related specifications and additional documentation. All specifications published through the Java Community Process are available from `www.jcp.org`.

Mobile Information Devices

The MIDP specification deals with a class of devices referred to as *mobile information devices*, or MIDs, which are small, hand-held devices with very limited capabilities but with user interaction as a key focus.

Hardware Requirements

The hardware requirements for MIDs are fairly simple:

- A monochrome or color display screen with a minimum size of 96 pixels wide by 54 pixels high and a 1:1 aspect ratio
- One of the following input mechanisms: a telephone keypad, a QWERTY keyboard, or a touch screen
- Two-way wireless networking capability
- At least 128K of non-volatile (persistent—such as flash or ROM) memory for the MIDP software, 8K of non-volatile memory for application-defined storage, and 32K of volatile (RAM) memory for the Java run-time heap. The amount of non-volatile memory required is in addition to that required for the CLDC software and any vendor-specific software.

Note that the specification describes a telephone keypad as a "one-handed keyboard" and a QWERTY keyboard as a "two-handed keyboard," which reflects the way a user typically holds the device in order to use the keypad/keyboard. Two things should be apparent from the input mechanism requirements, though: First, a pointing device is not required and all input can occur exclusively through the keypad or keyboard; and second, text entry can be non-trivial if a QWERTY keyboard is unavailable. Cellular telephones, for example, must provide a way to map the 12 buttons in a telephone keypad into alphabetic and punctuation characters as well as numbers, usually by assigning multiple characters to each button and letting the user cycle through the character mappings by pressing the button several times in succession.

Software Requirements

The MIDP specification makes some assumptions about the *system software*—the device's operating system and related applications and utilities—that the Java VM and the CLDC and MIDP classes must use. In particular, the software must:

- Manage the underlying hardware and provide a *schedulable entity* (thread) on which to run the Java VM.
- Provide ways to read and write to non-volatile memory, access the device's wireless networking capability, write to the display, and keep track of elapsed time.
- Convert button presses and/or screen strokes into appropriate input events.
- Manage the *lifecycle*—installation, selection, launching, shutdown, and removal—of MIDP applications.

You should note two important things here. First, the number of threads that a MIDP application can create is not limited by the number of threads supported by the device, even if the device can only supply a single thread to run the Java VM. The VM can perform the appropriate context switching itself as it runs the application, switching from one Java "thread" to another all within the context of a single operating system thread.

The second thing to note is that the *application management software*—the software that manages application lifecycles—is not actually defined by the MIDP specification. This issue has been the cause of some confusion and contention in the MIDP development community, so we will explore application lifecycle issues in the next chapter.

Typical Devices

The most typical mobile information devices are cellular telephones and interactive (two-way) pagers, as shown in Figures 2.1 and 2.2, respectively. Such devices are small and tend to have tiny screens. The input methods differ, of course. The cellular telephone augments the standard telephone keypad with a number of buttons for different tasks. Some of these buttons are programmable; the labels and functions associated with them are determined by the application that is currently active and so are referred to as *soft* buttons. Non-programmable buttons are referred to as *hard* buttons.

Figure 2.1 A cellular telephone.

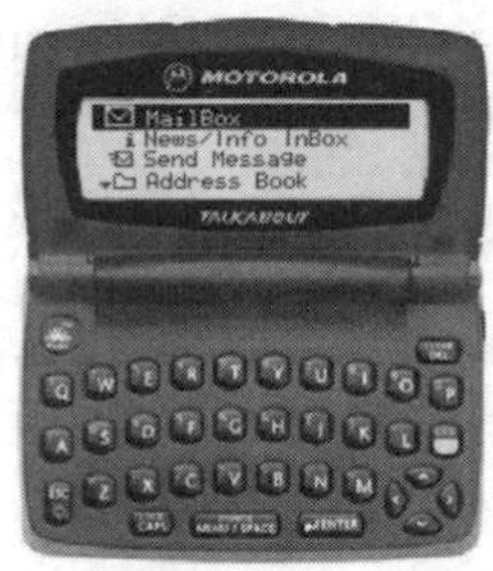

Figure 2.2 An interactive pager.

The interactive pager uses a minimized but fully functional QWERTY keyboard for input. As with the cellular telephone, it might also have additional buttons for device-specific tasks.

PDAs as MIDs

Is a personal digital assistant (PDA) a mobile information device? If you ignore the requirement for wireless network connectivity, the answer is definitely yes, because a PDA fulfills all the other hardware and software requirements. In fact, a PDA will typically have a larger screen, much more memory, and many more built-in features than a cellular telephone, although more cellular telephone models are being upgraded to PDA status (such as the Kyocera Smartphone or the Nokia Communicator). An example PDA is shown in Figure 2.3.

Of course, wireless connectivity is what makes a mobile information device truly mobile, so we cannot ignore this function. Some PDAs, such as the Palm VII, do have built-in wireless connectivity. Most devices do not have the capability built-in, but it is usually available as an option. For this reason, a PDA can be considered a MID and a possible target for the MIDP. Recognizing that PDAs are different from most cellular telephones and interactive

Figure 2.3 A personal digital assistant.

pagers, however, a second CLDC profile targeting PDAs is under development as this book is being written. The Personal Digital Assistant Profile (PDAP) will incorporate features of the MIDP but will included additional features to address the different (native) capabilities of a PDA. Check the book's Web site for more information about the PDAP.

Sun has released a MIDP implementation for Palm OS devices, known informally as MIDP4Palm, to satisfy the demand for a Sun-supported Java implementation on the largest family of PDAs while the PDAP was in development. If the PDAP is ready by the time you read this book, then you might want to consider using it for Palm development instead of the MIDP4Palm. If the PDAP is not ready, you will have to use the MIDP4Palm or else resort to third-party J2ME implementations, which expose Palm-specific classes. We discuss how to use MIDP4Palm in the next chapter.

Some PDAs have the capability to run a fuller version of Java. PersonalJava is available for high-end PDAs such as PocketPC devices, for example, as is Java 1.1.8 for Palm devices. If PersonalJava or J2SE is available on the devices you are targeting, you might be better off using them instead of CLDC-based profiles. Again, check the book's Web site for links to these alternatives.

MIDP Summary

Besides defining a MID, the MIDP specification also defines what a MIDP application is and what a MIDP application can do. This section summarizes what the MIDP specification describes and the classes it defines. We will cover these topics in more detail through the remainder of this book.

MIDlets and MIDlet Suites

One of the most important aspects of the MIDP specification is its definition of what constitutes an application and how one or more applications are packaged for delivery and installation onto a device.

A MIDP application is referred to as a *MIDlet* and in some ways resembles the J2SE concept of an applet. Like applets, MIDlets must extend a specific class (in this case, javax.microedition.midlet.MIDlet) and provide a public no-argument constructor, which enables the system software to create an instance of the MIDlet. The MIDlet class defines three abstract methods that the system software calls to start, pause, and destroy an application—startApp, pauseApp, and destroyApp—that are similar to the start, stop, and destroy methods of an applet (the init method is not found in the MIDlet model, and initialization is normally done in the MIDlet's constructor or in the first call to startApp). In the next chapter, we will discuss these methods and how they are called.

A collection of one or more MIDlets is packaged together into a JAR (Java archive) file to form what is called a *MIDlet suite*. The JAR file is important for a number of reasons:

- First, the JAR file contains *all* of the class files required by the MIDlets in the suite apart from those files already installed on the system (the CLDC and MIDP classes and any vendor-specific classes). The MIDP does not enable the sharing of class files between suites or the dynamic downloading and installation of new classes as an application runs.
- Second, the JAR manifest (a text file contained within the JAR file describing the JAR file's contents) defines important information about the MIDlets in the suite, such as the name, main class, and icon for each MIDlet as well as information about the vendor and the required profile and configuration versions.
- Third, the JAR contains any non-class resources—images, typically—used by the MIDlets in the suite. Only MIDlets within the suite can access these resources.
- Fourth, the JAR file is what the device installs or uninstalls; MIDlets in the same suite are installed or uninstalled as a unit.

The MIDP implementation on the device puts all the MIDlets in the same suite inside the same sandbox, allowing intra-suite interaction but not inter-suite interaction. In J2SE terms, this situation is as if the classes in the suite were loaded by using the same instance of a custom class loader.

A MIDlet suite is accompanied by an external file called an *application descriptor*.

What Is a Sandbox?

The *sandbox* metaphor is a way of describing the barriers that the Java run-time environment places in order to constrain and secure an application. In the J2SE applet model, the sandbox ensures that an untrusted applet cannot access the local file system and can only talk back to the host from which it was downloaded. In the MIDlet model, the sandbox ensures that a MIDlet can only load and use classes and resources from its MIDlet suite. The metaphor is derived from the act of placing a child in a sandbox in order to contain the child and to limit the child's activities.

This file is similar to the suite's manifest, and in fact, the two share some data in common. More importantly, however, the descriptor describes things about the suite so that a device can decide whether the suite can be downloaded or installed or run on the device. This information includes the size of the JAR file, the minimum amount of persistent memory required by the MIDlets in the suite, the version number of the suite, and so on. Placing this information in a separate file instead of in the JAR file manifest enables the device to quickly (and inexpensively) download the descriptor (from a Web site, for example) for analysis by the MIDP installation software. We will discuss the details of the application descriptor in the next chapter.

User Interface

As explained in the previous chapter, J2ME configurations do not define user interface classes. That task is left to the profiles and only to those profiles for which it is appropriate. The MIDP profile is one such profile. It defines a simple set of classes (defined in the `javax.microedition.lcdui` package and hence sometimes referred to as the LCDUI classes) for creating user interfaces for the small screens and limited input capabilities of mobile information devices.

The MIDP actually defines two levels of user interface, referred to as the *high-level* and *low-level* user interfaces (UIs). The high-level UI defines an application in abstract terms. Rather than controlling exactly what gets drawn on the screen and how button presses map to user input, the high-level UI defines generic classes that are portable across all MIDP devices, leaving it to each particular implementation to decide how to map those classes into an actual user interface. Direct access to the device's screen is not allowed, and raw key or pen events are not accessible when using the high-level UI classes.

The low-level UI classes, on the other hand, do provide direct access to the screen and to input events. The application can draw on the screen by using conventional two-dimensional (2-D) drawing primitives and is notified of raw key and pen events as they occur. None of the high-level classes are available when using the low-level application programming interface (API).

Note that an application *can* use both the high-level and the low-level UI classes, just not at the same time. The high-level UI is meant more for business applications and the low-level UI is more for games, but a business application can use the low-level UI to draw graphs and a game can use the high-level UI to display a list of high scores. We discuss the user interface classes in detail in Chapters 4 and 5.

Data Persistence

Many applications require the capability to store data for later retrieval. Ideally, this task is done with some kind of local data store. The alternative is to use the network to communicate with a remote data store. A remote data store might not always be accessible, however, due to network problems or because of the simple fact that the device itself might be disconnected from the network. For this reason, the MIDP specification requires devices to support some form of local data persistence. These local data stores are key to writing applications that work without network access.

The MIDP defines a set of classes and interfaces (in the `javax.microedition.rms` package) called the Record Management System, or RMS for short, for local data storage. Regardless of how the local data store is actually implemented, the RMS exposes it as a simple record-oriented database. In other words, each local data store—a *record store*—is a set of ordered records. The format of each record is unconstrained: Data is read and written as byte arrays of arbitrary size. Records are accessed by index, starting at 1, and each new record gets a unique index. The RMS also guarantees that writing a record is an atomic operation—either all the bytes are written to the record store or none are. Record stores are thus fairly robust, keeping their data consistent even when the application crashes.

Beyond the capability to read and write individual records, the RMS also provides a general-purpose enumeration capability that can filter and/or sort records based on application-defined criteria.

Chapter 7, "The Record Management System," discusses the RMS in detail.

Wireless Connectivity

Although the *Generic Connection Framework* (GCF) is defined in the CLDC, the configuration does not actually require support for any specific communication protocol, whether accessing the local file system, serial ports, or a network. A CLDC-based device might have none of these, after all. The MIDP, on the other hand, requires that a mobile information device support two-way wireless networking, and so it makes sense for it to support at least one two-way communication protocol.

The sole required protocol by the release of MIDP 1.0 is a subset of HTTP 1.1. This protocol is the same protocol used by a Web browser to fetch pages from a Web server, and it enables MIDP applications to communicate with any Web server on the Internet. Because HTTP is a request-response protocol, it can be used for two-way communication (albeit the client, in this case the mobile information device, must always initiate the conversation). The URL for an HTTP connection must start with "http:" and follow the usual rules for HTTP URLs.

To properly support HTTP, the MIDP defines a new `HttpConnection` interface that extends the GCF's `ContentConnection` interface. This new interface, part of the `javax.microedition.io` package, defines useful HTTP constants and provides methods for getting and setting header values and for controlling which request type (typically either GET or POST) is used. If headers are set by an application, the specification recommends that the `User-Agent` header be set to a string like `Profile/MIDP-1.0 Configuration/CLDC-1.0` and that the `Content-Language` header be set to the device locale, as in "`en-US`". Setting these values enables the Web server to identify the device as a J2ME-compliant device and to generate responses in the appropriate language.

Note that most MIDs are not directly connected to the Internet. HTTP support for these devices is provided by a gateway maintained by the network carrier. Unlike conventional HTTP proxy servers, such gateways are transparent to the MID.

What about other protocols? Most wireless devices have the capability to send and receive directed packets of information. These *datagrams* can often be used for point-to-point communication between two devices. The first version of the MIDP specification does not cover datagrams or any other protocol other than HTTP. This statement does not mean that the device will not support any other protocol; rather, it just means that HTTP is the only protocol that is guaranteed to be supported by all MIDP-compliant devices. Individual MIDP implementations are free to add their own support for additional communication protocols, ideally (but not necessarily) through the GCF. The next version of the MIDP specification might include support for additional protocols, but for now, applications that are interested in portability across devices must use HTTP.

Chapter 6, "Network Communication," will discuss wireless networking and the GCF in detail.

Additional J2SE Features

The MIDP adds three additional J2SE classes to those defined by the CLDC: `java.lang.IllegalStateException`, `java.util.Timer`, and `java.util.TimerTask`. These three classes are used by an application to create timers, which are background threads that execute code (tasks) at specified times. The behaviors are identical to those defined in J2SE 1.3.

Limitations and Exclusions

The MIDP specification does not attempt to cover every issue related to the installation or running of Java applications on mobile devices. The following issues are not covered by the specification:

System-level APIs. System-level APIs are classes that provide direct access to the features of a device, such as power management or telephony. The MIDP is only concerned with defining APIs for building user-oriented applications.

Application management. Beyond defining what a MIDlet's lifecycle is and how a MIDlet suite must be packaged, the MIDP does not address how MIDlet suites are installed on devices or how MIDlets are presented to and selected by the user. The implementation of the application management software (AMS, sometimes referred to as the Java Application Manager or JAM) is entirely up to the device vendor. The AMS might or might not be written in Java, for example, and might or might not support the installation of MIDlet suites by direct download from the Internet. Note, however, that the OTA specification does discuss the features and behaviors of the AMS, as we will see in the next section. For now, though, the OTA specification is just a series of recommendations.

Security. The MIDP does not add any additional features to augment the CLDC's security mechanisms or provide end-to-end communication security. In particular, note that while support for HTTP is required, there is no requirement to support HTTPS, the secure form of HTTP. Expect most devices to support it, however, because end-to-end security is a desirable feature (see Chapter 8, "Security," for more information about security).

Some of these exclusions might surprise you. You likely expect a MIDP-compliant cellular telephone to provide access to its address book and the capability to initiate calls. These issues are not covered by the specification. Remember, however, that the implementation might include vendor-supplied classes that provide access to these features and otherwise extend the basic functionality provided by the CLDC and the MIDP specifications. Using these classes makes your application non-portable, but that might not be as important as exposing and using the device's more advanced features.

OTA Provisioning Summary

Several months after the release of the MIDP 1.0 specification, the MIDP Expert Group released an addendum on the recommended way in which users of a wireless device could find, download, and install MIDlet suites. This process is referred to as *over-the-air provisioning* and is primarily meant as a guide for device vendors and network carriers. It does, however, define two new application descriptor attributes of interest to application developers. What follows is a short summary of the OTA specification.

Discovery

The primary goal of OTA provisioning is to make it possible and easy for the user of a wireless device to interact directly with Web sites on the Internet in order to find and download MIDlet suites. The process of finding a MIDlet suite is referred to as *discovery* of an application. The AMS must either use the built-in Web browsing capability of the device (most wireless devices now include some kind of microbrowser) or else provide its own equivalent capability. No matter how the task is done, the user must be able to connect to a particular Web site and follow a link to an application descriptor. The device can then download the application descriptor (a standard MIME type for the descriptor is defined by the MIDP specification, as we will see in the next chapter) and use it to start and guide the installation process.

Download and Installation

Once the application descriptor is downloaded, the device uses the information in the descriptor to download the JAR file containing the MIDlet suite. The device (and its network) must be capable of downloading JAR files of at least 30K in size. Downloading only occurs after reviewing the application descriptor to ensure that the minimum memory and version requirements of the suite are met and that the same or a higher version of the suite is not already installed on the device. When these conditions are met, the user is asked to confirm the download. The download process might require user authentication by using the standard HTTP authorization headers, in which case the AMS prompts the user for a userid and password in response to a challenge by the destination Web server (the provisioning server) or a proxy server along the way. After installation is complete, the device optionally sends an installation status report back to the Web server (an HTTP POST request) by using a URL defined in the application descriptor. Any cookie (a piece of data sent by the Web server in the headers along with a response) accompanying the download is sent back with the status report in order to identify the specific application download whose status is being reported. The cookie is discarded after installation is complete.

Activation and Removal

Once the application is installed, the user can activate it. How this activation is done is not defined by the OTA specification. The only recommendation is that if a MIDlet suite contains more than one MIDlet, the user should be asked which MIDlet is to run.

The user can remove an application at any point, and again the specification does not define how this procedure is done. The user must be asked to confirm the removal, however, and a message to that effect can be included in the application descriptor.

Development Tools

We conclude this chapter by briefly looking at the tools required to develop and test MIDP applications. This section is not exhaustive; rather, it merely presents some tools used in MIDP development and throughout this book—the ones that you are likely to encounter and use for your own development. Instructions for using the tools are found in the next chapter. Note that the vendors of MIDP-compliant platforms might also provide their own development tools to exploit the unique features of the platform or that are more convenient with which to program.

The Reference Implementation

Sun Microsystems makes a *reference implementation* of the MIDP available for downloading from its Web site. The reference implementation simulates a MIDP-compliant cell phone and enables you to install and test your MIDlets on a desktop computer before trying it on an actual device. The reference implementation is shown running in Figure 2.4. Several sample MIDlets are included with it.

Figure 2.4 The MIDP reference implementation.

Download the reference implementation by following the link from the main MIDP page on Sun Microsystems' Java Web site at `http://java.sun.com/products/midp`. The reference implementation is licensed under the *Sun Community Source License* (SCSL) and requires free registration with Sun's download center. Versions are available for Windows and Solaris. The most recent version of the reference implementation as this book is written is version 1.0.

The reference implementation is supplied as a ZIP file. To install it, simply extract the contents using WinZip or a similar unzip utility. The `jar` tool from the JDK can also unzip the contents. This book assumes that you have extracted the contents to the c:\midp-fcs directory.

Once you have installed the reference implementation, you can run the sample MIDlets by using this command sequence:

```
cd c:\midp-fcs\bin
midp -classpath ..\classes -descriptor ..\src\example\run.jad
```

Adjust the syntax accordingly for Solaris. Note that by default, the phone displays in black and white. You can set it to use color by defining an environment variable called `SCREEN_DEPTH`. Set it to 8 to show 256 colors, 4 for 16 colors, 2 for 4 colors, or 1 (the default if not set) for black and white:

```
set SCREEN_DEPTH=8
midp -classpath ..\classes -descriptor ..\src\example\run.jad
```

A complete source for the samples is found in the `src\example` directory. The procedures for building MIDlets and MIDlet suites using the reference implementation are described in the next chapter.

For further documentation on using the simulator, see the files in the `docs` directory.

The J2ME Wireless Toolkit

Not too long after the reference implementation was released, Sun also released a MIDP development toolkit for Windows called the J2ME Wireless Toolkit. The toolkit combines the MIDP reference implementation with tools to automate the building and test-

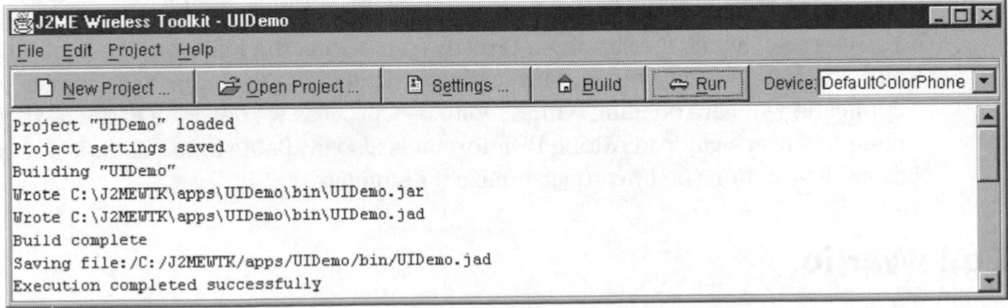

Figure 2.5 The J2ME Wireless Toolkit development environment.

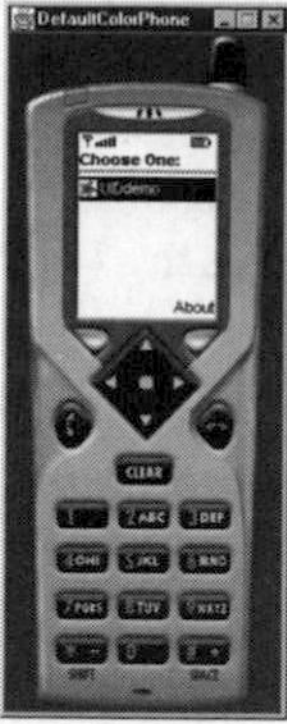

Figure 2.6 The J2ME Wireless Toolkit simulator.

ing of MIDlets and MIDlet suites. As you will see in the next chapter, building a MIDlet suite requires several steps, and the toolkit does most of it for you—all you will need is a text editor and an image editor. The toolkit's development environment, KToolbar, is shown running in Figure 2.5. The toolkit also integrates with Sun's Forte integrated development environment for Java. This environment includes the Community Edition of Forte for Java, available for free from Sun's Web site at www.sun.com/forte/index.html.

Download the toolkit by following the link from the J2ME Wireless Toolkit Web page at http://java.sun.com/products/j2mewtoolkit. You will need to have the J2SE 1.3 JDK installed first; links to the JDK are provided from the download page as well. The most recent version of the toolkit as this book is written is version 1.0.1 and is only available for the Windows platform. Version 1.0.3 was under development, and it or a higher version should be available by the time you read this text.

The toolkit is provided as a self-installing executable. It installs itself into the C:\J2MEWTK directory and adds itself to the Windows Start menu.

To run a MIDlet with the toolkit, open the J2ME Wireless Toolkit 1.0.1 program group on the Start menu and select Run MIDP Application . . . to launch the cellphone simulator. You will be prompted for an application descriptor (a JAD file). Navigate to the C:\J2MEWTK\apps\UIDemo\bin directory and select the `UIDemo.jad` file. The simulator shown in Figure 2.6 is displayed to let you run the UIDemo sample.

You can also launch the simulator directly from within the KToolbar application, which is also run from the Start menu. This method will, in fact, be your primary way of testing an application you are building with KToolbar—a process we describe in the next chapter. A complete user's guide in Adobe PDF format is also available in the Toolkit `doc` directory, as are instructions on how to customize the simulator.

CodeWarrior

Before it was acquired by Motorola, Metrowerks was a small niche player in the develop-

Is There a Need for Proprietary Tools?

With free tools readily available from Sun for MIDP development, you might wonder why there is a need for alternative and proprietary development tools from other vendors. There are a couple of reasons. The first is that there are already different Java development tools available on the market, and the vendors of those tools will enhance them with J2ME support. The second is that device vendors are free to extend the capabilities of their Java implementations with classes that are unique to their devices or platforms. If you need to write applications that use these classes—even if they will then be non-portable—you will need the vendor's tool or SDK. If you are just using the standard MIDP classes, however, you can use the tool with which you are most comfortable.

ment tool arena, producing a tool called CodeWarrior whose variants could develop C, C++, and Java programs for a variety of platforms, including Windows, Macintosh, and a number of handheld/embedded platforms (including Palm OS). CodeWarrior for Java is now the official development tool for J2ME-enabled devices from Motorola, including the iDEN i85s and Accompli 008 devices. Although Motorola formerly offered a separate J2ME software development kit (SDK) for its devices, the SDK is now part of CodeWarrior. CodeWarrior for Java can also be used to write Java applications for the J2SE and PersonalJava platforms.

CodeWarrior is not free, but you can download a free time-limited trial version of CodeWarrior for Java from Metrowerks' Web site at `www.metrowerks.com/desktop/java/trial`.

In the next chapter, we will present details on how to use CodeWarrior to build and run MIDlets.

The Next Generation

Although the MIDP specification and the reference implementation have not been out for that long, there is already work being done to develop the "next generation" of the profile. This work is being done through the Java Community Process as JSR-118, *Mobile Information Device Next Generation* (MIDP_NG) and is expected to be completed by the middle of 2002.

The next-generation MIDP specification, or MIDP-NG for short, is intended to extend the MIDP 1.0 specification with support for a number of more advanced features. Possible extensions include the following:

- HTTPS support for secure connectivity to a Web server
- Low-level datagram and socket network connectivity
- Exposing the push capabilities of a network at the application level
- Application signing and related security issues
- Sound support
- A basic Extensible Markup Language (XML) parser
- User interface extensions
- Formally folding the OTA provisioning recommendations into the MIDP specification
- Shared libraries and classes
- Billing extensions

Note that these are just possible extensions. The final list will not be known until the MIDP-NG specification is released in public draft form. As always, there will have to be some compromises made to support the variety of devices that are out there now, although it is true that as time passes, handheld devices become more powerful and make it possible to do things that are not feasible today. The MIDP will continue to evolve with the devices. It will take a while for MIDP-NG devices to make it onto the market, however, because it took almost a year after MIDP 1.0 was released for the first MIDP-enabled devices to appear.

Summary

We conclude our overview of the Mobile Information Device Profile. MIDP provides a small set of classes for building simple and portable interactive applications that can interact with Web servers but can also store and manipulate information locally. In the next chapter, we start to drill down into MIDP programming, understanding the MIDlet lifecycle and the creation and packaging of MIDlet suites.

CHAPTER 3

The MIDlet Lifecycle

The previous chapter introduced you to the Mobile Information Device Profile (MIDP). In this chapter, we look at how MIDP applications (MIDlets) are built and run. This description includes what defines a MIDlet, how to package one or more MIDlets into a MIDlet suite, and how to build the application descriptor for the suite. We also look at how MIDlets are activated and deactivated.

What Is a MIDlet?

As mentioned in the previous chapter, MIDlet is the term used to refer to a MIDP application. MIDlets must extend the `javax.microedition.midlet .MIDlet` class. A simple MIDlet looks like the following:

```
// A trivial MIDlet

package com.j2medeveloper.midpbook.ch03;

import javax.microedition.lcdui.*;
import javax.microedition.midlet.*;

public class MyMIDlet extends MIDlet
                      implements CommandListener {

    private Display display;
    private Command exitCommand = new Command( "Exit",
                                         Command.EXIT, 1 );
```

```
// Constructor

public MyMIDlet(){
    System.out.println( "MyMIDlet constructed" );
}

// Required by MIDlet class

protected void destroyApp( boolean unconditional )
                    throws MIDletStateChangeException {
    exitMIDlet();
}

protected void pauseApp(){
    System.out.println( "MyMIDlet paused" );
}

protected void startApp() throws MIDletStateChangeException {
    if( display == null ){ // first time called...
        initMIDlet();
    }

    System.out.println( "MyMIDlet started" );
}

// Event handling

public void commandAction( Command c, Displayable d ){
    if( c == exitCommand ){
        exitMIDlet();
    }
}

private void initMIDlet(){
    display = Display.getDisplay( this );
    display.setCurrent( new TrivialForm() );
}

public void exitMIDlet(){
    notifyDestroyed();
    System.out.println( "MyMIDlet destroyed" );
}

// A trivial UI screen

class TrivialForm extends Form {
    TrivialForm(){
        super( "MyMIDlet" );
        addCommand( exitCommand );
        setCommandListener( MyMIDlet.this );
    }
```

```
        }
    }
```

When run by using a simulator, this MIDlet displays a blank title screen and prints messages to the console window. A real MIDlet would not call `System.out.println`, of course, but would instead use the *user interface* (UI) classes described in the next chapter. Printing to the console is a simple way to trace and debug a MIDlet—more on this later.

From this example, we can derive the basic requirements of a MIDlet:

- The entry point is a public class that extends `javax.microedition.midlet.MIDlet`.
- The `MIDlet` subclass defines a public, no-argument constructor and implementations of the `destroyApp`, `pauseApp`, and `startApp` methods.
- When started, the MIDlet creates and displays some kind of user interface; MIDlets are interactive applications.
- The MIDlet classes are placed in Java packages (not really a requirement, but strongly recommended practice).

When a device wants to run a MIDlet, it creates an instance of the `MIDlet` subclass and calls its `startApp` method. Eventually, `destroyApp` will be called—usually by the MIDlet itself—to terminate the MIDlet, after which the device will release the instance to let the garbage collector reclaim it. We will discuss the MIDlet lifecycle in detail later in this chapter, but for now, let's look at the steps required to compile and prepare the MIDlet for installation on a device.

Building MIDlets

MIDlets and MIDlet suites can be created by hand by using the JDK and the MIDP reference implementation, by using a tool like KToolbar from the J2ME Wireless Toolkit, or by using a full-fledged *integrated development environment* (IDE) like CodeWarrior.

How MIDlets Are Built

Whether you are doing it manually or with a tool, MIDlet and MIDlet suites are built the same way. Doing it manually at least once is the best way to understand the process, although you will want to automate the procedure at least minimally by using scripts or batch files if you do not intend to use a tool. Make sure you have downloaded and installed the MIDP reference implementation and version 1.3 or higher of the JDK before attempting the following steps.

Compiling the MIDlet

The first step is to compile and preverify the code. Create a directory for your application, such as `c:\MyMIDlet` (all examples use Microsoft Windows syntax). Create three subdirectories: `src` to hold the MIDlet source, `tmpclasses` to hold the unverified class files, and `classes` to hold the preverified class files. (If you have resources, such as images or icons, you would create a fourth directory, `res`, and place them there.) Place the source file, `MyMIDlet.java`, in the `src` directory.

To compile the MIDlet, use the `javac` tool (in the root of your project directory) with the `-bootclasspath` option to override the standard J2SE classes (which are added to the classpath by default if you do not use the `-bootclasspath` option) with the MIDP classes:

```
javac -g:none -bootclasspath c:\midp\classes -d tmpclasses src\*.java
```

We assume that you have installed the MIDP reference implementation in `c:\midp`. A better syntax is to define and use the `MIDP_HOME` environment variable to refer to the MIDP installation directory:

```
set MIDP_HOME=c:\midp
javac -g:none -bootclasspath %MIDP_HOME%\classes -d tmpclasses
src\*.java
```

The `-d` option places the generated class files in the `tmpclasses` directory. These are the unverified class files. The MIDP reference implementation includes a `preverify` tool to convert the raw class files into preverified class files. On Windows, the syntax is as follows:

```
preverify -d classes -classpath %MIDP_HOME%\classes tmpclasses
```

The final, verified class files are placed in the `classes` directory. The `preverify` tool for Windows is found in the `build\win32\tools` directory; this syntax assumes that it is in the path, of course.

Organizing the Source Tree

You can organize the source to your MIDlet in two ways. The first way is to place all the source files directly into the `src` directory. The second way is to create subdirectories in the `src` directory that correspond to the package structure of the source and place the source files in the appropriate subdirectories. For example, instead of `src\MyMIDlet.java`, you would use the path `src\com\j2medeveloper\ midpbook\ch03\MyMIDlet.java` to mirror the source file's package structure. The first way is simpler—all the files are in a single directory for easy editing—but you will need to use the second way if you want to use the `javadoc` tool to generate reference documentation from the source.

The Icon

An icon—a small image—can (and should) be associated with a MIDlet. The icon is stored in PNG (Portable Network Graphics) format, a format that most paint programs can output. If not, you can find free utilities to convert an image from one of the more proprietary formats—GIF or Windows bitmap—to PNG format. Refer to the book's Web site for links.

Any icons used by your MIDlets must be included in the MIDlet suite along with any other non-code resources. Create a `res` subdirectory in your project directory. Create an `icons` subdirectory in the `res` directory (this action is not absolutely required, but it is useful to separate the different types of resources into different subdirectories). Then, create your icon as a 12-pixel-wide by 12-pixel-high color image and save it as `MyMIDlet.png` into the `icons` directory. You might find it easier to start with an existing icon from one of the samples that ships with the MIDP reference implementation.

The Manifest

Every MIDlet must be placed in a MIDlet suite. The MIDlet suite is a JAR file whose manifest includes a number of attributes that describe the MIDlets in the suite. Some of the attributes are optional, so here is a manifest for the MIDlet shown previously:

```
MIDlet-1: MyMIDlet, /icons/MyMIDlet.png,
com.j2medeveloper.midpbook.ch03.MyMIDlet
MIDlet-Name: MyMIDletSuite
MIDlet-Vendor: Ortiz-Giguere
MIDlet-Version: 1.0
MicroEdition-Configuration: CLDC-1.0
MicroEdition-Profile: MIDP-1.0
```

Each attribute is a name-value pair (one pair per line). The first attribute lists important properties about the MIDlet: its name, its icon, and its main class. The other attributes define information about the MIDlet suite, including its creator and version and the required configurations and profiles needed for installation. MIDlet attributes are described in detail later in this chapter.

Create a `bin` subdirectory in your project directory and place the manifest there, calling it `MANIFEST.MF`.

Building the Suite

With the manifest ready, you can now build the MIDlet suite by using the JDK's `jar` tool, still from the root of your project directory:

```
jar cfm bin\MyMIDlet.jar bin\manifest.mf -C res . -C classes .
```

The result is a MIDlet suite called `MyMIDlet.jar` in the project's `bin` directory that includes all the files in the `res` and `classes` directories as well as the manifest.

The Descriptor

Before running the MIDlet, you need to create an application descriptor for the MIDlet suite. The descriptor is like the manifest but with additional attributes:

```
MIDlet-1: MyMIDlet, /icons/MyMIDlet.png,
com.j2medeveloper.midpbook.ch03.MyMIDlet
MIDlet-Jar-Size: 1835
MIDlet-Jar-URL: MyMIDlet.jar
MIDlet-Name: MyMIDletSuite
MIDlet-Vendor: Ortiz-Giguere
MIDlet-Version: 1.0
MicroEdition-Configuration: CLDC-1.0
MicroEdition-Profile: MIDP-1.0
```

Place the descriptor in the `bin` directory, calling it `MyMIDlet.jad`. The `.jad` extension is defined by the MIDP specification as a way to identify a file as a Java application descriptor. The specification also defines a MIME (Multipurpose Internet Mail Extensions) type—`text/vnd.sun.j2me.app-descriptor`—to properly configure the downloading of descriptors from Web servers. The Web server must send this MIME type along with the descriptor contents whenever a Web client (such as the device's application installation software) asks for a descriptor.

Note the `MIDlet-Jar-Size` and `MIDlet-Jar-URL` attributes. The former is the size of the MIDlet suite's JAR file, and the latter is the path to the file. The path can be relative to the descriptor (as in this case, the two are found in the same directory), or it can be an absolute URL such as `http://www.somesite.com/jars/MyMIDlet.jar` if the suite is to be downloaded from a Web server.

Running the MIDlet

With the JAR and descriptor files built, you can now run the MIDlet by using the cell phone simulator included with the reference implementation. Ensure that the `midp` tool (found in the `bin` directory of your MIDP installation) is in the path, and use the following syntax to run your application:

```
midp -classpath bin\MyMIDlet.jar -descriptor bin\MyMIDlet.jad
```

A window like the one shown in Figure 3.1 pops up to simulate a MIDP-enabled cell phone. The cell phone screen lists the MIDlets in the suite. Start the MIDlet by pressing the button in the middle of the arrow buttons. The screen changes to the one shown in Figure 3.2, and you will see the following messages appear in your console window:

```
MyMIDlet constructed
MyMIDlet started
```

An instance of our MIDlet has been created, and its `startApp` method has been called.

To stop the MIDlet, you have two choices: either press the button directly below the "Exit" label on the left side of the cell phone screen or press the red telephone button to

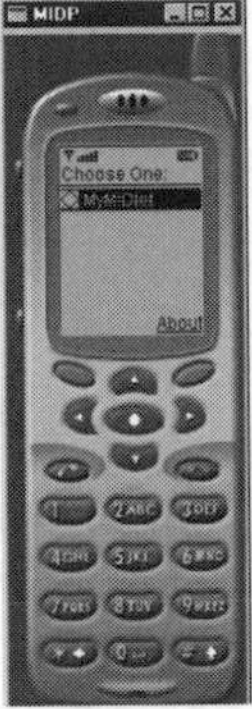

Figure 3.1 Running the MIDP simulator.

Figure 3.2 Running MyMIDlet.

the right of the down arrow button—the one where the telephone is completely horizontal. The MIDlet list reappears; and another line appears on the console:

```
MyMIDlet destroyed
```

The MIDlet's `destroyApp` method was called, and the MIDlet instance has been released for cleanup by the garbage collector. Congratulations, you have successfully created and run your first MIDlet. Close the cell phone simulator window in order to stop the `midp` tool. As the simulator shuts down, it prints a number of statistics about the application to the console.

Note that the simulator does support a number of options, which you can list by using the following command:

```
midp -help
```

An alternative way to run the MIDlet, for example, is to use the `-transient` option:

```
midp -transient file://bin/MyMIDlet.jad
```

Pass it an URL—starting with either "`file://`" or "`http://`"—to the application descriptor, which must have a valid `MIDlet-Jar-Size` attribute defined. An HTTP URL must include a valid host name and an absolute path, but a file URL can be a relative or an absolute path. The `-transient` option is used mostly to test the downloading of MIDlet suites from Web servers.

Building MIDlets with KToolbar

Although MIDlet building is not complicated, it does require several steps. The KToolbar application in the J2ME Wireless Toolkit can automate the process for you by creating the appropriate directories, maintaining the manifest and descriptor, compiling the source files, preverifying the class files, building the JAR file, and even running the simulator. KToolbar is not a complete integrated development environment—it has no built-in text editor—but it greatly simplifies the creation and management of MIDP projects. About the only thing that is missing from it is a way to automatically generate an Ant build file (Ant is a build tool for compiling and packaging Java applications) or a set of batch/shell scripts to non-interactively build a MIDlet suite.

Creating the Project

To create a new MIDlet suite, start the KToolbar application shown in Figure 3.3. (All KToolbar screen shots are from the 1.0.1 version.) Press the *New Project...* button to create a new MIDP project. The application prompts you for a project name and the name of the main class for the first MIDlet in the suite, as shown in Figure 3.4. Press the *Create Project* button on the dialog after filling in the appropriate information. KToolbar creates a subdirectory for the project in the `apps` directory of the J2ME Wireless Toolkit installation directory. (On Windows, this subdirectory is normally `c:\J2MEWTK\apps`.) It then creates `bin`, `classes`, `res`, `src`, and `tmpclasses` directories in the project directory, just as we did when creating a MIDP project by hand.

After creating the necessary directories, KToolbar prompts you for attribute values, as shown in Figure 3.5. These attribute values are used by KToolbar to automatically gen-

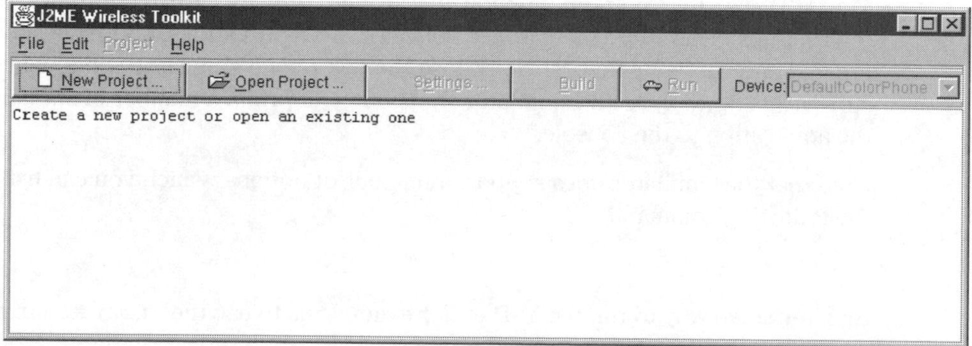

Figure 3.3 The KToolbar application.

New Project ...

Project Name: MyMIDlet

MIDlet Class Name: com.j2medeveloper.midpbook.ch03.MyMIDlet

Create Project | Cancel

Figure 3.4 Creating a new project.

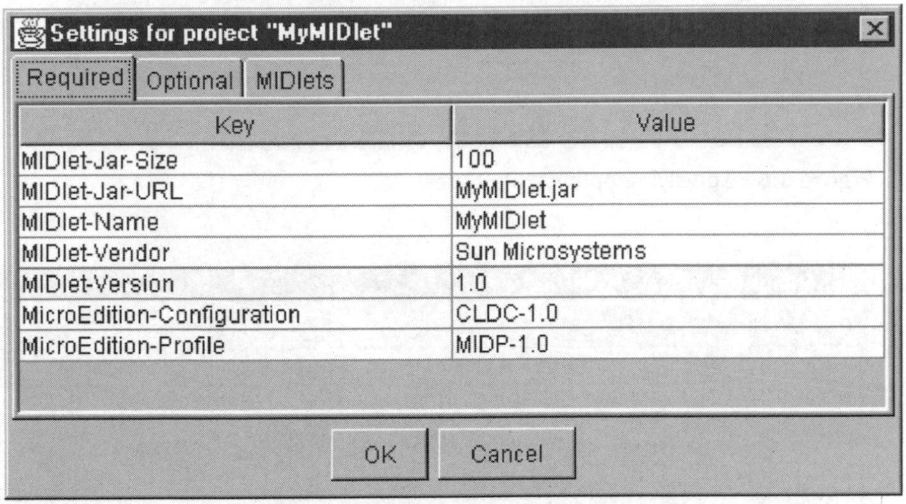

Settings for project "MyMIDlet"

Required | Optional | MIDlets

Key	Value
MIDlet-Jar-Size	100
MIDlet-Jar-URL	MyMIDlet.jar
MIDlet-Name	MyMIDlet
MIDlet-Vendor	Sun Microsystems
MIDlet-Version	1.0
MicroEdition-Configuration	CLDC-1.0
MicroEdition-Profile	MIDP-1.0

OK | Cancel

Figure 3.5 Specifying required attributes.

erate manifest and descriptor files. The first tab on the property sheet lists the required attributes of the project. Normally, the only one you change initially is `MIDlet-Vendor`, although for application deployment you will change the `MIDlet-Jar-URL` attribute. Note that `MIDlet-Jar-Size` does not need to be changed, because KToolbar will automatically change its value to reflect the true size of the JAR file whenever you build the project.

After setting the required attributes, change to the second tab to list the optional attributes (shown in Figure 3.6). These are all blank and can be left blank, but it is a good idea to describe the suite with the `MIDlet-Description` attribute. You can remove any of these attributes and even add new ones; when run, a MIDlet can initialize itself based on attributes you define here.

The final tab in the property sheet, shown in Figure 3.7, lists the MIDlets in the project and the three properties for each: the name, icon, and main class. If your suite has additional MIDlets, you would list them here. Change the icon of the first (and only) MIDlet to `/icons/MyMIDlet.png` by selecting the MIDlet and pressing the *Edit* button.

When you are done making attribute changes, press the *OK* button to dismiss the property sheet. The corresponding manifest and application descriptor files are then created

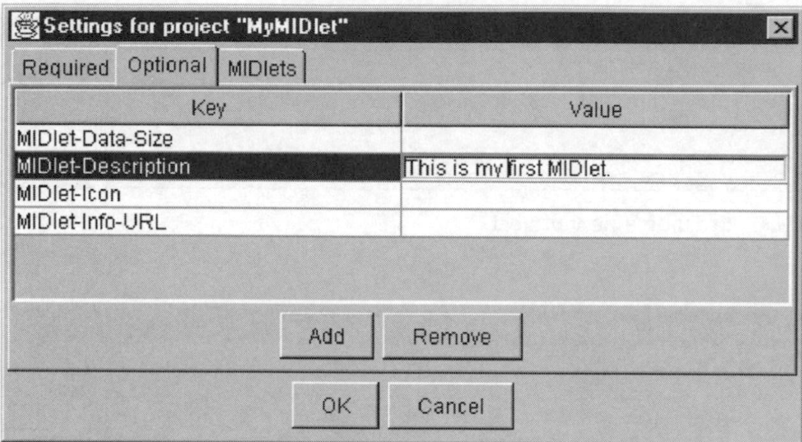

Figure 3.6 Specifying optional attributes.

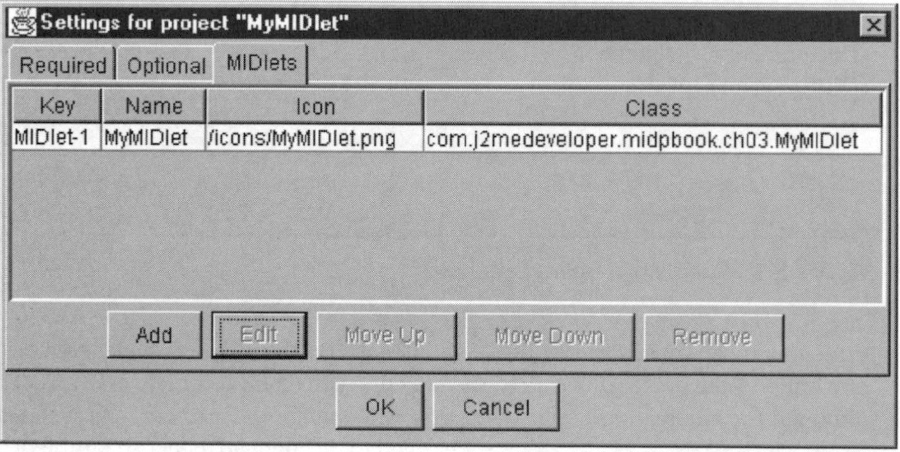

Figure 3.7 Specifying MIDlet properties.

in the `bin` directory. You can make further changes at any time by pressing the *Settings . . .* button in the toolbar. New manifest and descriptor files are created to reflect any changes you made.

At this point, you are ready to add the code and resources to the project. KToolbar does not provide any editing facilities; rather, you must use your favorite text and image editors to create these. Place your source files in the `src` directory and the images in the `res` directory, just as we did earlier in this section when building the MIDlet suite by hand. For convenience, the directory structure that we created mirrors that used by KToolbar.

Building the Project

Once you have defined the attributes, source, and icon for the project, you can compile the source, preverify the classes, and build the final JAR file in a single step by pressing the *Build* button. A progress bar enables you to track the individual steps. Any errors that occur are shown in the console window; correct the error and press the *Build* button again.

Running the Project

Once the project has been built, press the *Run* button to run the MIDlet suite by using an MIDP simulator, as shown in Figure 3.8. This simulator is much like the one in the reference implementation, but its look and behaviors are customizable (see the J2ME Wireless Toolkit documentation for details).

Building MIDlets with CodeWarrior

For even tighter integration of the edit-build-test development cycle, you can use a tool such as Metrowerks CodeWarrior for Java to build your MIDlets. CodeWarrior is a full-fledged *integrated development environment* (IDE) that can build and debug MIDP applications as well as other types of Java applications. The instructions here apply to version 6.4 of CodeWarrior for Java.

Creating the Project

To create a MIDlet suite with CodeWarrior, start the IDE and select the *New . . .* item from the *File* menu. Select *Java J2ME Stationery* in the resulting dialog and enter a name and directory for the new project, as shown in Figure 3.9, and press *OK*. In CodeWarrior terminology, project templates are referred to as stationery. A second dialog pops up from which you can select the specific type of J2ME project to create. Version

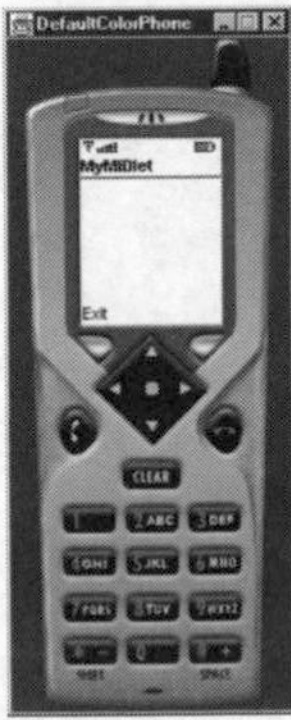

Figure 3.8 Running the KToolbar project.

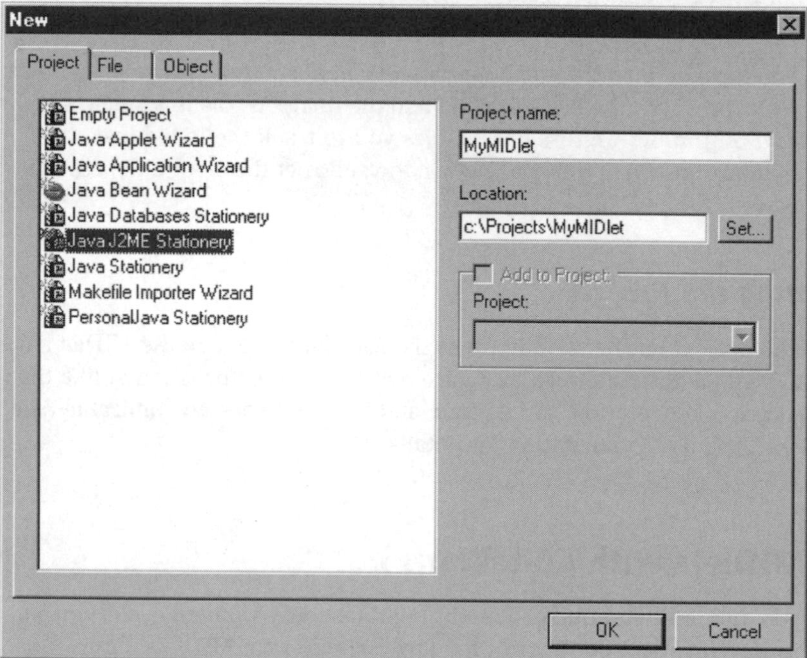

Figure 3.9 Selecting J2ME stationery in CodeWarrior.

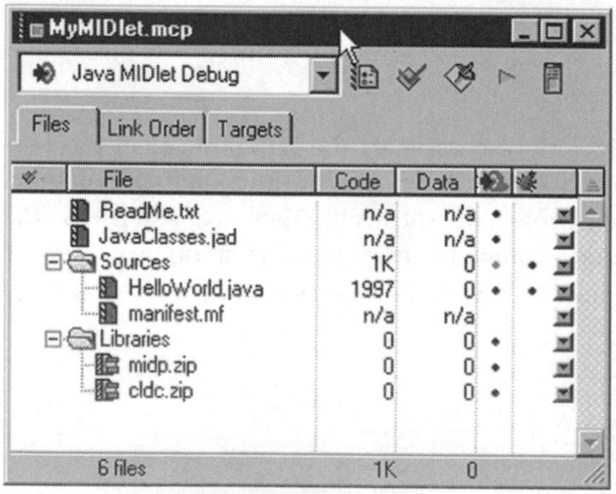

Figure 3.10 The CodeWarrior project window.

6.4 displays four choices: *J2ME MIDlet* (to build a standalone MIDlet), *J2ME MIDlet-Resource Support* (to build a MIDlet with resources), and *J2ME MIDlet Suite* (to build a complete MIDlet suite containing two or more MIDlets). Select *J2ME MIDlet Suite* and press *OK*.

CodeWarrior creates and initializes a simple MIDlet suite based on the MIDlet project stationery. The main project window is shown in Figure 3.10. This window lists the source files in the project and the class libraries used to compile the source. The initial project already includes a single Java source file for a basic MIDlet, `HelloWorld.java`. Right-click it and select *Delete* from the popup menu to remove it from the project.

Now, go back to the *File* menu and select the *New . . .* item again. This time, however, select the *File* tab in the resulting dialog—we will create a new file instead of a new project. Select *Text File* in the list of file types and enter `MyMIDlet.java` as the filename. Make sure the project directory is set correctly. Check the *Add to Project* checkbox and select the *MyMIDlet.mcp* project from the list of available projects. Then, check both the *Debug* and *Release* targets—a project can build different versions of the same code. The dialog should look like the one shown in Figure 3.11. Press *OK* to open a text editor for the new file.

The CodeWarrior text editor is a standard Windows-style text editor. Type the code for the `MyMIDlet` class, and close the editor. Now, select *Debug Settings . . .* from the *Edit* menu, or else press the leftmost icon in the project window toolbar to bring up the settings for the project. If not already selected, select *Java Target* from the list of target setting panels on the left-hand side of the dialog. Set the main class field to `com.j2medeveloper.midpbook.ch03.MyMIDlet`, as shown in Figure 3.12. While you're at it, select something other than `defaultdevice.props` for the simulator configuration file—the default is not a realistic depiction of a cell phone. Dismiss the dialog.

Back in the project window, select the *Make* icon (third from the left) or select *Make* from the *Project* menu. This selection builds the project. Now, enable debugging by selecting

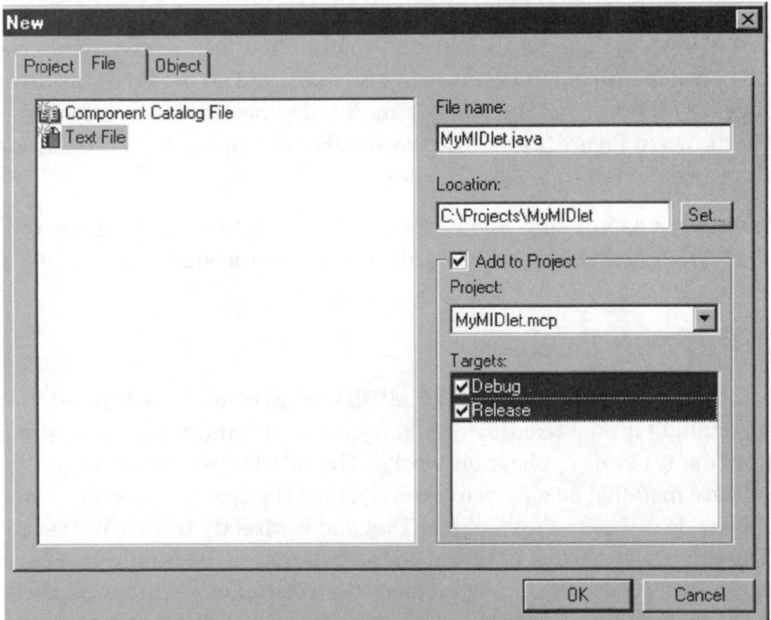

Figure 3.11 Adding a new file to the project.

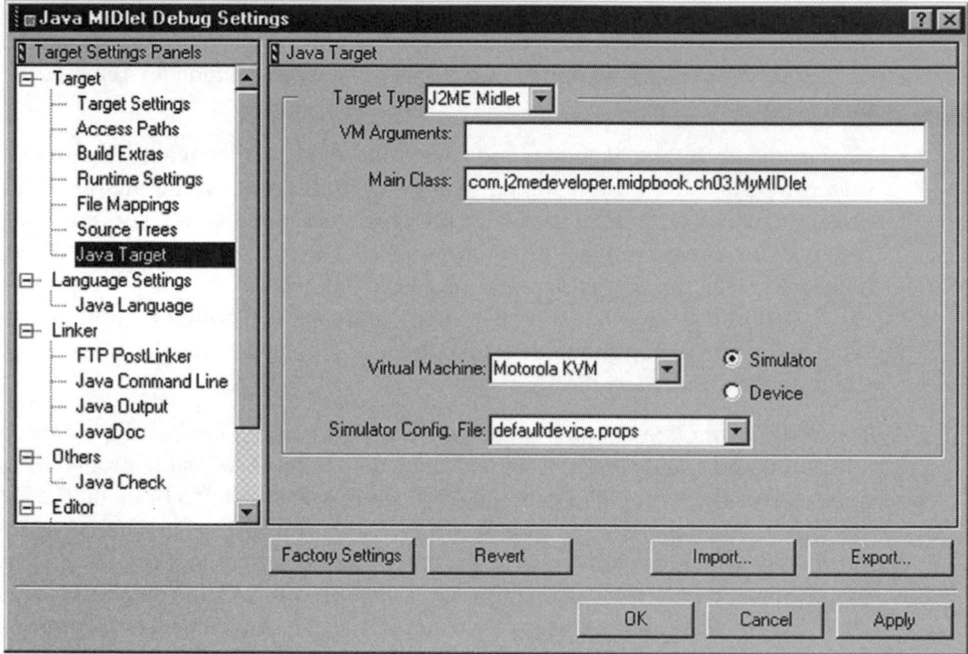

Figure 3.12 Setting the main class.

Enable Debugger from the *Project* menu and answering *Yes* to the resulting dialog. Then, select *Debug* from the *Project* menu to run the application. CodeWarrior opens a debugging window, shown in Figure 3.13, and stops on the first line of executable code in the MIDlet. You can step through the code, view variables, and so on. Press the arrow button in the debugging window to let the MIDlet run. A cell phone simulator is also opened, and the result is shown in Figure 3.14. Close the simulator or press the button labeled "Exit" to stop debugging and return to CodeWarrior.

For full instructions on using each type of J2ME stationery, be sure to read the `ReadMe.txt` file found in the projects you create with the stationery.

Installing MIDlets on Devices

Once you are satisfied with the way your MIDlet behaves when run in a simulator, you should try installing it on a real device and try running it there to fully appreciate how well (or how badly) your application works. The MIDP specification does not define how MIDlets are installed on a device, although the OTA specification does suggest that the device provide a way to download MIDlet suites directly from a Web server on the Internet. The other way to do it is via a desktop computer. The Motorola i85s, for example, currently uses a serial cable to connect the phone to a Windows-based desktop computer. An application (iDEN Update) is then run on the desktop computer to download MIDlet suites onto the phone. Different devices will have similar procedures, but

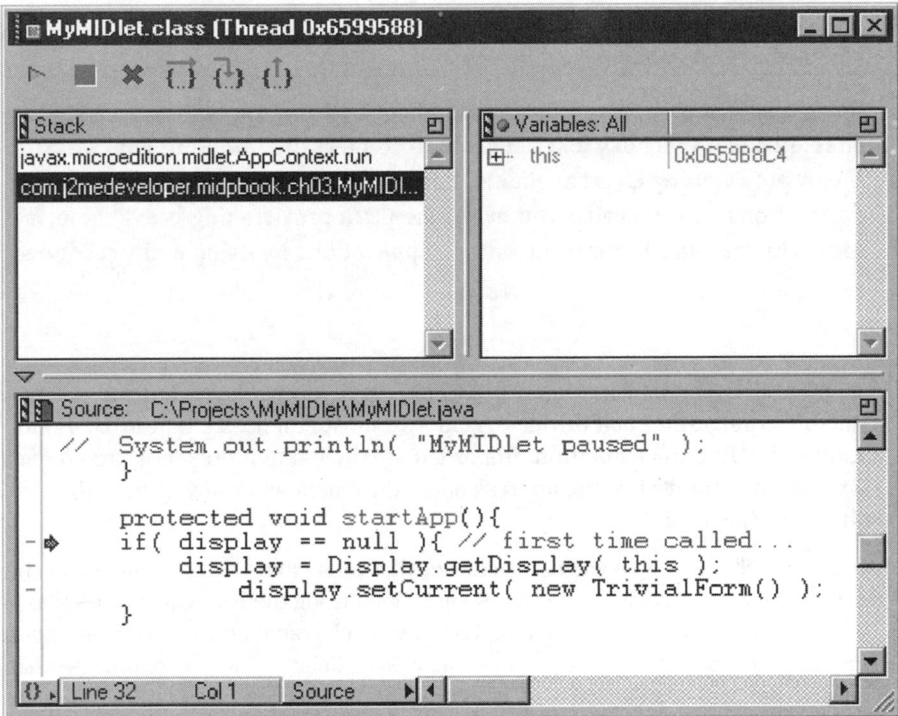

Figure 3.13 The CodeWarrior debugging window.

Figure 3.14 Running with the CodeWarrior simulator.

the specifics vary from manufacturer to manufacturer and even from device to device. Consult your device's documentation for details on how to install MIDlet suites.

Using MIDP4Palm

If you are interested in running your MIDP applications on Palm devices, a MIDP implementation is available for download from the Sun Web site, as mentioned in the previous

Invest in a Serial Cable

If you are serious about MIDP development and you are testing on a MIDP-enabled cell phone, buy a serial cable to connect the phone to your desktop PC. If OTA provisioning is not available, this method is the only way to get your applications on the device. But even when OTA provisioning is available, it is often cheaper and faster to download applications by using a direct connection.

chapter. This implementation, MIDP4Palm, lets you package and run MIDlet suites on suitably configured Palm devices. Again, we must emphasize that MIDP4Palm is simply another MIDP implementation. In particular, MIDP4Palm does not provide any support for accessing things like the address book, the calendar, or any of the other features you find on a typical PDA.

To use MIDP4Palm, you will need a device that runs Palm OS 3.5 or higher, or the Palm OS Emulator. Most development and testing is done using the Emulator, a desktop-based software emulation of a device running Palm OS. Unlike similar tools for other platforms, the Emulator accurately emulates—not simulates—a Palm OS device, enough so that the ROM image from an actual device is required in order to use the Emulator. The Emulator runs on Windows, Macintosh, or Unix/ Linux. You can find out more about the Emulator in the developer's area of the Palm OS Web site at www.palmos.com/dev/tech/ tools/emulator. Note that if you are using a Palm OS device manufactured by a vendor other than Palm, Inc., be sure to check that vendor's Web site for any updates to the Emulator specific to that device. As well, joining the vendor's developer program is recommended, as it gives you access to software development kits, debug ROM images, and other useful things. The rest of this section assumes that you have access to a Palm OS-based device (or to a properly configured Emulator) and that you know how to install and run applications on such a device.

After downloading MIDP4Palm, unzip it into an appropriate directory on your desktop computer. The first thing you need to do is install the MIDP.prc file—found in the `PRCfiles` subdirectory—onto your device. This file contains the complete MIDP runtime environment, including the interpreter and the MIDP 1.0 classes (including, of course, the classes defined by the Connected Limited Device Configuration), packaged as a standard Palm OS application. Although the file is rather hefty in size, close to 600K, only a single copy of it needs to reside on the device. After installing `MIDP.prc`, a new "Java HQ" icon appears in the device's application launcher. Tapping this icon displays a copyright screen with the familiar Java teacup logo and a Preferences button. Tapping the Preferences button displays a dialog that lets you control various features of the MIDP environment—more on this later.

Once the runtime environment is installed, it is time to run a few MIDlets. MIDP4Palm ships with a few sample MIDlets already converted into Palm applications, which you will also find in the PRCfiles subdirectory. A good place to start is with Games.prc, which contains four of the games that ship with the MIDP reference implementation. The games are packaged and installed as a single MIDlet suite, so tapping on the Games icon displays a list of the MIDlets that are available: Pong, Snake, StarCruiser, and Tiles. Tap any icon in the list to run the appropriate game.

At any point during an application's execution you can tap the device's menu button to display a menubar. From the menubar you can exit the application, beam the application (via infrared) to another device, and set application preferences. The application preferences control various aspects about the application: how many colors it requires, the drawing speed, button mappings, and so on. Many of these preferences can be set globally via the Java HQ application, but any preferences set from within an application override the global settings.

Of the available preferences, one of the most important is the networking option. Palm OS supports TCP/IP networking, but enabling it reduces the memory available to an application, so it should only be enabled for MIDlets that require network connectivity using the MIDP's `HttpConnection` class. Enabling networking at the Java level is not enough, however, since you must also ensure that the device itself is correctly configured for communication, whether through a PPP server when the device is in its cradle or via a wireless connection for devices equipped with wireless modems. Such configuration is beyond the scope of this book, but more information can be found in your device documentation. A recommended PPP server for Windows is mochaPPP, see `www.mochasoft.dk/palm.html#palmppp` for details. Emulator users have it easy —just check the "Redirect NetLib calls to host TCP/IP" in the Properties dialog.

To run your own MIDlets using MIDP4Palm, you first create a MIDlet suite and an accompanying application descriptor file. You then run the MIDP4Palm PRC Converter Tool, a J2SE 1.3 application that runs on your desktop. On Windows run the `converter.bat` file in the Converter subdirectory, making sure to set the `JAVA_PATH` environment variable to your JDK 1.3 installation directory. On other platforms, run the following command:

```
java -jar Converter.jar
```

Using the Converter Tool, browse to the appropriate directory on your system and select the descriptor for the MIDlet suite. The descriptor and the JAR file will be processed and converted into a PRC file, which you can then install and run on your device.

Note that because MIDP4Palm is still a beta product at the time of writing, some of the information presented here may have changed by the time you read this. Sun maintains a list of frequently asked questions about MIDP4Palm at `http://java.sun.com/products/midp/midp-palm-faq.html` which you should read for the most up-to-date information.

MIDlet Activation and Deactivation

Although the MIDP specification does not address *how* to activate a MIDlet installed on a device, it does state explicitly *what* the device must do to activate it. The specification describes the lifecycle of a MIDlet in detail, and it is important to understand that lifecycle in order to write properly behaved MIDlets.

MIDlet States

The application manager software (AMS)—the application management software that controls the activation and deactivation of MIDlets—maintains state information about each MIDlet. There are only three states possible:

- *active*—the application is running
- *paused*—the application has yet to run or is in an idle state
- *destroyed*—the application is terminated

A MIDlet enters the destroyed state only once and cannot change its state back to one of the other two states. At this point, the MIDlet is finished executing and is ready to be garbage collected. The MIDlet can move back and forth between the other two states, however, either at its own request or at the request of the application manager. Figure 3.15 shows the possible state changes.

More than one MIDlet can be in the active state at any given time, although only one MIDlet at a time has control of the display and access to user input. This application is known as the *foreground* application. How the user moves between active MIDlets or moves a MIDlet to a different state is not defined by the MIDP specification. It is possible, for example, that an incoming phone call would cause all active MIDlets to transition to the paused state to let the user answer the call. These details are left to the device manufacturer.

A MIDlet receives state change notifications through callback methods defined in the `javax.microedition.midlet.MIDlet` class: the `startApp`, `pauseApp`, and `destroyApp` methods previously mentioned. The `MIDlet` class also defines methods that the application invokes on itself to request a state change. Here are the members of the class:

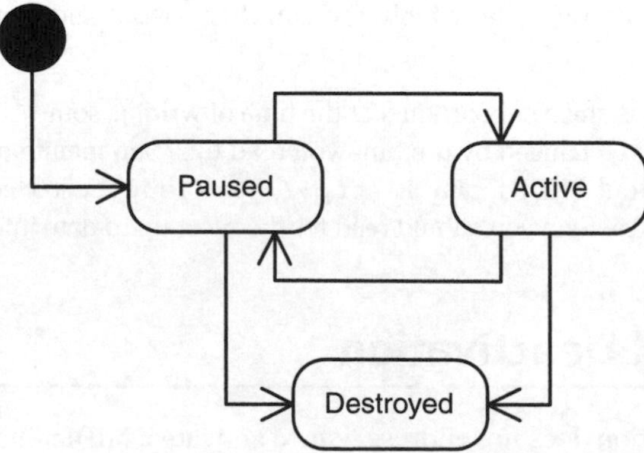

Figure 3.15 MIDlet state changes.

Keep a Reference to the MIDlet

The methods of the `MIDlet` class are the only way for an application to influence the application manager's behavior. Because they are instance (non-static) methods, you must pass a reference to the MIDlet instance to any class in your application that needs to call `notifyDestroyed`, `notifyPaused`, or `resumeRequest`. Alternatively, you can define those classes as nested (inner) classes contained by the main class in order to gain implicit access to those methods.

```
package javax.microedition.midlet;

public abstract class MIDlet {
    // Constructors
    protected MIDlet();

    // Methods
    protected abstract void destroyApp( boolean unconditional )
              throws MIDletStateChangeException;
    public final String getAppProperty( String key );
    public final void notifyDestroyed();
    public final void notifyPaused();
    protected abstract void pauseApp();
    public final void resumeRequest();
    protected abstract void startApp()
              throws MIDletStateChangeException;
}
```

Only the constructor and the `getAppProperty` method are not involved in managing the state of the MIDlet.

The MIDP also defines a new exception in the `javax.microedition.midlet` package called `MIDletStateChangeException`. A MIDlet can throw this exception to refuse a change to the active or (in limited cases) destroy states. A MIDlet cannot refuse a change to the paused state.

The Active State

The active state is the normal application state: the MIDlet is actively running and using system resources, although it is not necessarily the foreground application. A MIDlet enters the active state just before the application manager invokes the MIDlet's `startApp` method. This action normally occurs at least once after a new instance of a MIDlet is created and its constructor did not throw an exception. If the application does not want to enter the active state, it throws a `MIDletStateChangeException` from within the `startApp` method.

A paused application can transition to the active state at any time but never directly under its own control. Instead, it notifies the application manager that it is ready to return to the active state by invoking its `resumeRequest` method. The application manager chooses if and when to activate the MIDlet—immediate activation is not guaranteed. The MIDlet's `startApp` method will be called when it is activated.

The Paused State

The paused state is the idle state: the MIDlet is not actively using system resources and has in fact trimmed its resource usage to enable other applications to run or for the device to handle important events. A paused MIDlet is not suspended, however: any threads or timers it has started continue to run. The application's user interface is not displayed, and there is no interaction with the user. By continuing to run, though, the MIDlet can respond to timers and call `resumeRequest` to ask for reactivation.

An application transitions to the paused state for a number of reasons:

- Implicitly upon construction
- After the application manager calls an active MIDlet's `pauseApp` method and the latter returns without throwing an exception
- When an active MIDlet calls its `notifyPaused` method
- When the MIDlet throws a `MIDletStateChangeException` from its `startApp` method during a transition to the active state

If an exception occurs in a MIDlet's constructor, it immediately enters the destroyed state and is discarded. If an exception is thrown by `pauseApp`, the MIDlet also enters the destroyed state and a call to `destroyApp` is made to allow for cleanup.

Calling `notifyPaused` causes the MIDlet to immediately transition to the paused state. The `pauseApp` method is not called in this situation.

Ideally, a MIDlet entering the paused state should free up as much memory and other resources as possible, but it is not enforced in any way. Many MIDlets declare an empty `pauseApp` method and do not free anything.

The Destroyed State

The destroyed state indicates that a MIDlet has terminated and the resources associated with it can be freed by the system. Once in the destroyed state, the MIDlet cannot transition back to the other states.

A MIDlet transitions to the destroyed state for any of these reasons:

- An exception was thrown in the constructor.
- The application manager calls the `pauseApp` method and it throws an exception.

- The application manager calls the `destroyApp` method with the `unconditional` argument set to `true`.
- The application manager calls the `destroyApp` method with the `unconditional` argument set to `false` *and* the method does *not* throw a `MIDletStateChangeException`.
- The MIDlet calls its `notifyDestroyed` method.

Just as with `notifyPaused`, calling `notifyDestroyed` causes the MIDlet to immediately transition to the destroyed state. The `destroyApp` method is not called in this situation.

Note that a MIDlet is given the option to refuse a transition to the destroyed state if its `destroyApp` method is called with the `unconditional` argument set to `false`. To refuse the state change, it must then throw a `MIDletStateChange-Exception`; otherwise, the transition occurs and the MIDlet is deactivated.

Handling State Changes

There are two common errors to avoid when a MIDlet's state changes. The first error is to initialize the application each time `startApp` is called. It is common, for example, to see code like the following:

```
protected void startApp() throws MIDletStateChangeException {
    Form f = new Form( "MainForm" );
    .... // other init code here
    display.setCurrent( f );
}
```

The problem is that `startApp` can be called multiple times for the same MIDlet instance. Creating new user interface objects each time wastes memory (even if only temporarily) and is often incorrect because on transition back to the active state, the MIDlet should normally display the same user interface that was visible when it entered the paused state.

The solution is to do the initialization only once. In many cases, you can perform this task in the constructor or by explicitly initializing data members of the class. The `exitCommand` member of the `MyMIDlet` class is initialized in this way. Some things cannot—or should not—be done in the constructor, however. It is common to see this code in a MIDlet to obtain the `Display` object (used to control what is displayed on the screen—discussed in detail in the next chapter) associated with a MIDlet:

```
public class SomeMIDlet extends MIDlet {
    private Display display;

    public SomeMIDlet(){
        display = Display.getDisplay( this );
    }

    ...... // other code omitted
}
```

If you read the documentation for the Display.getDisplay method, however, you will see that the method is not guaranteed to work before the application manager calls startApp. Therefore, it is possible (but not likely) that this code will not work on some implementations. A better approach is to initialize the display member on the first call to startApp, which is easy to detect because its value will be null. This technique then becomes the perfect way to perform any once-only initialization required by the MIDlet:

```
public class BetterMIDlet extends MIDlet {
    private Display display;

    public BetterMIDlet(){
    }

    protected void startApp() throws MIDletStateChangeException {
        if( display == null ){
            initMIDlet();
        }
    }

    private void initMIDlet(){
        display = Display.getDisplay( this );
        ..... // other init code here
    }

    ..... // other code omitted
}
```

The other common error is to call notifyDestroyed without freeing any resources or saving the application's important data. Remember, finalizers do not exist in CLDC-based profiles, so the only way to free the resources used by an object is to do it explicitly. Instead of placing the cleanup code in the destroyApp method, place it in a separate exitMIDlet method that can be called from any location in the MIDlet:

```
public class BestMIDlet extends MIDlet {

    .... // startup code omitted

    public void exitMIDlet(){
        .... // add your cleanup code here
        notifyDestroyed();
    }

    protected void destroyApp( boolean unconditional )
                    throws MIDletStateChangeException {
        exitMIDlet();
    }

    public void commandAction( Command c, Displayable d ){
        if( c == exitCommand ){
```

```
                exitMIDlet();
            }
        }

        .... // other code omitted
    }
```

A separate method is not actually required if you make `destroyApp` public, but using a separate method avoids having to catch the `MIDletStateChange-Exception`. The call to `notifyDestroyed` ensures that the MIDlet enters the destroyed state no matter who calls `exitMIDlet`.

MIDlet Attributes

An important aspect of creating a MIDlet suite is defining the manifest in the JAR and the external application descriptor. The MIDP specification defines a number of attributes for each file, some of which are optional and some of which are shared between the two files. The values of shared attributes should be the same in both files, but if they are not the same, then the values in the application descriptor take precedence over the ones in the manifest. The exceptions are the `MIDlet-Name`, `MIDlet-Version`, and `MIDlet-Vendor` attributes, which must be identical in both. From a practical standpoint, the simplest way to build an application descriptor is to take the manifest and add the descriptor-specific attributes to it, which is essentially what the KToolbar tool does when it builds a MIDlet suite. In fact, some simulators or devices require you to perform this action in order to load and run the MIDlet suite.

Manifest Attributes

Manifest attributes pertain mostly to the internals of the MIDlet suite. They define the names, icons, and main classes of each MIDlet in the suite as well as other things that are shared with the application descriptor. Table 3.1 lists and describes the attributes defined by the MIDP specification.

Here is a sample manifest:

```
MIDlet-1: Solitaire, /icons/Solitaire.png, com.greatgames.Solitaire
MIDlet-2: Poker, /icons/Poker.png, com.greatgames.Poker
```

Creating Manifests and Descriptors

Manifests and application descriptors are just text files where each line contains the name of an attribute and a value for the attribute. A colon and some white space separate the attribute name from its value.

Table 3.1 Manifest Attributes

NAME	DESCRIPTION
MicroEdition-Profile	The name and version of the J2ME profile required to run the MIDlet suite; uses the same format as the `microedition.profiles` system property, as in MIDP-1.0. Required.
MicroEdition-Configuration	The name and version of the J2ME configuration required to run the MIDlet suite; uses the same format as the `microedition.configuration` system property, as in CLDC-1.0. Required.
MIDlet-<*n*>	The name, icon, and main class, separated by commas, of each MIDlet in the suite. If there are three MIDlets in the suite, for example, the manifest has these three attributes: MIDlet-1, MIDlet-2, and MIDlet-3. The name identifies the MIDlet to the user; the icon is the path to an image (in the portable PNG format) in the JAR file; and the class must extend the `javax.microedition.midlet.MIDlet` class. Required.
MIDlet-Data-Size	The minimum number of bytes of persistent storage that the MIDlet requires in order to run. Optional. If not specified, the default is zero.
MIDlet-Description	A description of the MIDlet suite. Optional.
MIDlet-Icon	The path of a PNG (a portable graphics format) file within the JAR file, used by the application management software to identify the MIDlet suite. Optional.
MIDlet-Info-URL	An URL describing the MIDlet suite in greater detail. Optional.
MIDlet-Name	The name of the MIDlet suite. Required.
MIDlet-Vendor	The vendor of the MIDlet suite. Required.
MIDlet-Version	The version number of the MIDlet suite. Must be in the format XX.YY or XX.YY.ZZ, where XX is the major revision number, YY is the minor revision, and ZZ is the optional micro revision number. If the micro revision number is omitted, it defaults to zero. Required.

```
MIDlet-3: Bridge, /icons/Bridge.png, com.greatgames.Bridge
MIDlet-Name: CardGames
MIDlet-Vendor: Great Games Inc.
MIDlet-Version: 1.0
MIDlet-Description: A fun set of card games.
MIDlet-Data-Size: 300
MIDlet-Icon: /icons/GreatGames.png
```

```
MicroEdition-Configuration: CLDC-1.0
MicroEdition-Profile: MIDP-1.0
```

Some things to note:

- Keep the MIDlet names as short as possible, because most MIDP devices have small screens.
- Start the paths to any icons with a slash character to indicate an absolute path within the JAR file.
- Define as many of the attributes as you can for completeness.

The manifest might also contain other attributes such as those generated by the `jar` tool. These are ignored by the application management software except that they are made available to the application via the `getAppProperty` method of the `MIDlet` class.

Application Descriptor Attributes

Descriptor attributes mostly describe the MIDlet suite itself, such as its size, version number, icon, and URL. Table 3.2 lists the attributes.

Table 3.2 Application Descriptor Attributes

NAME	DESCRIPTION
MIDlet-Data-Size	The minimum number of bytes of persistent storage that the MIDlet requires to run. Optional. If not specified, the default is zero.
MIDlet-Delete-Confirm	A text message to prompt the user when the application manager needs to confirm the deletion of the MIDlet suite. Defined by the OTA specification.
MIDlet-Description	A description of the MIDlet suite. Optional.
MIDlet-Info-URL	An URL that describes the MIDlet suite in greater detail. Optional.
MIDlet-Install-Notify	An URL to which the application manager sends an HTTP POST notification confirming the installation of the MIDlet suite. Defined by the OTA specification.
MIDlet-Jar-Size	The size of the MIDlet suite in bytes. Required.
MIDlet-Jar-URL	The URL from which to download the MIDlet suite. Required.
MIDlet-Name	The name of the MIDlet suite. Required.
MIDlet-Vendor	The vendor of the MIDlet suite. Required.
MIDlet-Version	The version number of the MIDlet suite. Must be in the format XX.YY or XX.YY.ZZ, where XX is the major revision number, YY is the minor revision, and ZZ is the optional micro revision number. If the micro revision number is omitted, it defaults to zero. Required.

Here is a sample descriptor:

```
MIDlet-Data-Size: 300
MIDlet-Description: A fun set of card games.
MIDlet-Jar-Size: 26879
MIDlet-Jar-URL: http://www.greatgames.com/downloads/cardgames.jar
MIDlet-Name: CardGames
MIDlet-Vendor: Great Games Inc.
MIDlet-Version: 1.0
MicroEdition-Configuration: CLDC-1.0
MicroEdition-Profile: MIDP-1.0
```

Remember that the application manager uses the descriptor to determine whether it is possible to download and install a given MIDlet suite onto the device, so define as many attribute values as possible (including those from the manifest).

Two of the attributes, `MIDlet-Delete-Confirm` and `MIDlet-Install-Notify`, are defined by the OTA specification and not by the MIDP specification. They are used in the wireless provisioning process.

Run-Time Attribute Access

Manifest and descriptor attributes are accessed by a MIDlet at runtime by using the `getAppProperty` method of the `MIDlet` class. Pass the name of the attribute as the argument and the attribute value is returned, or `null` is returned if the attribute is not defined. As mentioned, the attribute value in a descriptor takes precedence over the value of the same attribute in the manifest.

Do not forget that both the manifest and the application descriptor can contain programmer-defined attributes in addition to those defined by the MIDP specification. The application descriptor in particular is an easy way to customize the behavior of a set of MIDlets. For example, the descriptor could be generated dynamically on a Web server to include a unique key as an attribute value. This key could be read by the MIDlets in the suite and used in any communication back to the Web server to identify the device and/or the user.

Debugging MIDlets

Before we move on, a brief word about debugging MIDlets. The minimal capabilities of a Java VM for a MIDP device are defined in the CLDC specification. The CLDC does not require the VM to support the debugging of a Java application, unlike J2SE. Any debugging capabilities are strictly optional and can use proprietary interfaces for efficiency if necessary. Different tools provide different debugging capabilities. CodeWarrior, for example, lets you debug applications running in its cell phone simulator but only if preverification of the class files is disabled (the preverification scrambles the debugging information in the Java class files, which is why the Debug target of a CodeWarrior J2ME project disables preverification). The KToolbar in version 1.0.1 of the J2ME Wireless Toolkit, on the other hand, provides no debugging capabilities, though later versions do expose debugging information using the Java Debugging Wired Protocol (JDWP), allowing you to debug your applications using a tool like Forte for Java.

If no debugger is available, you can still use certain standard techniques to help you locate problem spots in your code. The simplest is to sprinkle `System.out.println` calls throughout your code for tracing purposes, which works well when the application is running in a simulator. Be sure to remove or disable the calls before releasing the MIDlet outside your development group. An easy way to perform this task is to define a simple `Debug` class whose sole purpose is to define a single `static final boolean` data member. Build two versions of the class: one that looks like the following:

```
public class Debug {
    public static final boolean on = true;
}
```

and a second that is identical except for the data member value:

```
public class Debug {
    public static final boolean on = false;
}
```

Place the source files in separate directories because they are in the same package, and share the same class name. You then include one or the other file when compiling your project and prefix your calls to `println` as follows:

```
if( Debug.on ) System.out.println( "in startApp" );
```

This action enables the Java compiler to completely remove the `println` calls when `Debug.on` is `false`.

Alternatively, define one or more tracing levels where the output is controlled by the value of an attribute in the descriptor. Consider the following fragment from a MIDlet as an example:

```
public class AnotherMIDlet extends MIDlet {
    public static int debugLevel = 0;

    public AnotherMIDlet(){
        try {
            String level = getAppProperty( "Debug-Level" );
            if( level != null ){
                try {
                    debugLevel = Integer.parseInt( level );
                }
                catch( NumberFormatException e ){
                }
            }
        }
        catch( Exception e ){
        }
    }
```

```
    ..... // other code omitted
}
```

The value of debugLevel is set according to the value of the Debug-Level attribute in the descriptor. Different trace levels output different amounts of information.

Console messages via System.out.println are not the only way to trace your application's behavior. You can also sprinkle the code with alerts, which are simple user interface components that display text messages to the user. We discuss alerts in the next chapter. The nice thing about alerts is that they will always work, even on a real device. They do disrupt the user's experience, however. A better and more ambitious approach is to log messages to an internal buffer and provide a way for the user to examine that buffer at various points throughout the application's execution. The truly ambitious person can use the MIDP's HTTP support to forward log messages to a servlet or JSP on a Web server for storage and analysis.

Last, but not least, *always* test your MIDlets on a real device. It is important to note that even though all MIDP-compliant implementations follow the official specifications, each vendor has its own implementation with possibly different bugs that are not reproducible on an emulator. Also, emulators do not always faithfully represent the actual behavior of your MIDlet on the device. Fortunately, device vendors usually provide for ways to debug your application when running on the device. On the Motorola i85s, for example, all your System.out.println messages can be seen on your desktop by using your serial cable in conjunction with some kind of communications package like HyperTerminal. Use the following steps to debug applications on your i85s:

- Start HyperTerminal, which comes as part of your Windows installation.
- Create a new connection: call it i85s.
- Select the appropriate COM port your serial cable is plugged into.
- In the properties dialog, configure as follows: Data bits to "8", Parity to "non", Stop bits to "1", and Flow control to "hardware".
- Save the newly created i85s profile.

To enable Java debugging, type the following command sequence in the HyperTerminal window: AT+WS46=252;+WS45=0;+IAPPL=2;D Restart your MIDlet; you should now see all the debugging information in the HyperTerminal window. You can save all the output into files for later use.

For other devices, refer to the manufacturer's documentation on how to do device-specific debugging.

Summary

In this chapter, we have learned how to define and build basic MIDlets and how MIDlets transition between different running states. The next chapter discusses how to create basic user interfaces for MIDP applications.

CHAPTER 4

User Interface Basics

MIDlets are interactive applications, and even the most minimal MIDlet requires some kind of user interface. The Expert Group that defined the Mobile Information Device Profile (MIDP) decided not to use any of the existing Java 2 Standard Edition (J2SE) user interface classes—the Abstract Windowing Toolkit (AWT) and the Swing extensions to AWT—because of space limitations and because the AWT model was too dependent on the capabilities of a conventional desktop computer. Mobile devices have smaller screens and different input methods than desktop computers. They often do not have the horsepower required to draw multilayered windowed interfaces. If Swing is sometimes slow on a desktop computer, imagine what it would be like on a mobile device. For these and other reasons, the MIDP defines its own set of user interface (UI) classes. They are not as sophisticated or as numerous as what AWT provides, but they are flexible enough to work on any device. Because the application's user interface is so important, we spend two chapters discussing the MIDP user interface classes. This chapter introduces and explains each class individually, while the next chapter shows you how to combine the classes in order to create compelling user interfaces. Definitions for all the classes described here are also found in Appendix A.

The MIDP User Interface Model

Conventional desktop computer user interfaces are very mouse-oriented and window-oriented. The user uses a mouse or other pointing device to initiate actions, using the keyboard primarily as a text-entry device. Windows or other user interface components can be layered, moved, and resized on a relatively large screen area. This kind of user interface works well for most people, but it does pose problems for those who have visual or physical impairments. It also does not scale well to small devices, which might offer a keyboard or keypad as the only input device and do not have a large enough display for moveable windows.

The MIDP uses a different approach. Instead of dividing the display into multiple windows, the MIDP user interface model considers the display to consist of a single, fixed-size window whose contents are controlled by one application (or the system) at any time. The window displays one of a set of virtual *displayables*, which are user interface components that are the same height and width as the window. As the application runs, it changes the displayable that the window shows. The application is like a deck of cards—only the topmost card in the deck is visible at any given time. Displaying a different card means shuffling the deck to make another card the topmost card. This method is exactly how the MIDP user interface classes work, but with displayables instead of cards—in J2SE terms, like using AWT's `CardLayout` layout manager.

What kind of user interface components does the MIDP define? The MIDP user interface classes are grouped into three sets, all in the `javax.microedition.lcdui` package. The first set, the *high-level user interface API*, defines components for displaying text and images, getting text input, alerting the user, and so on, as shown in Table 4.1. The application cannot control how these components look or behave, instead letting the MIDP implementation decide how to display and interact with the components. Code that uses the high-level user interface application programming interface (API) is portable across all MIDP-enabled devices. The second set, the *low-level user interface API*, defines components for drawing directly onto the display and trapping and interpreting raw device input. The classes are listed in Table 4.2. Code that uses the low-level user interface API might not be portable if it depends on specific features of a device, such as the screen resolution or the presence of a pointing device or touch-sensitive screen, or if it uses any proprietary extensions. You can use the low-level API in a portable fashion, though, if you program defensively and do not assume anything about device characteristics. The final set, the *common user interface API*, consists of the classes that do not fit in the other two sets, and they are listed in Table 4.3.

As discussed in Chapter 2, "The Mobile Information Device Profile," the high-level and low-level APIs target different kinds of applications. The high-level API is designed for business applications while the low-level API is designed for game applications. Business applications require more complex user interface components while games require direct access to the display and the stream of raw input events. It *is* possible to use the two APIs

Cards and Markup Languages

The MIDP is not the only environment to use a deck of cards as the basis for its user interface model. The markup languages used in cellphone-based microbrowsers–*Wireless Markup Language* (WML) and HDML–are also card based.

Table 4.1 High-Level User Interface API

CLASS/INTERFACE	DESCRIPTION
Alert	Displays a message for the user; a top-level window
AlertType	Defines the types of predefined alerts and their accompanying sounds
Choice	Defines the methods common to the ChoiceGroup and List components
ChoiceGroup	Displays a list of selectable items; for use on a Form
DateField	Displays an editable date or time field; for use on a Form
Form	Displays a series of user interface components on one screen; a top-level window
Gauge	Displays a value within a range of values
ImageItem	Displays an image; for use on a Form
Item	Base class for components that are placed on Form components
ItemStateListener	Listener interface for state changes to Item components
List	Displays a list of selectable items; a top-level window
Screen	Base class for top-level windows in the high-level UI API
StringItem	Displays a read-only string; for use on a Form
TextBox	Displays an editable string; a top-level window
TextField	Displays an editable string; for use on a Form
Ticker	Displays a scrolling marquee; used with Screen objects

Table 4.2 Low-Level User Interface API

CLASS	DESCRIPTION
Canvas	Displays an application-defined top-level window
Font	Provides information about the fonts available on the device
Graphics	Provides methods for drawing onto a Canvas or onto an offscreen image buffer

in the same application, however. A business application might use the low-level APIs to draw graphs and other charts, and a game might use the high-level APIs to display the list of high scores. The only restriction is that you cannot use high-level and low-level classes on the same displayable. But it is certainly acceptable to switch from a low-level displayable to a high-level displayable or vice-versa.

Table 4.3 Common User Interface API

CLASS/INTERFACE	DESCRIPTION
Command	Defines the semantic information of an action; can be associated with any top-level window
CommandListener	Receives commands
Display	Provides the basic interface to the display
Displayable	The base class for all top-level windows in the high-level and low-level UI APIs
Image	Defines a bitmapped image

The Common User Interface API

We start by looking at the capabilities that are independent of the high-level and the low-level APIs, as defined by the classes and interfaces of the common user interface API.

Accessing the Display

The device's display is accessed by using the `Display` class, whose definition is as follows:

```
package javax.microedition.lcdui;

public class Display {
    // Methods
    public void callSerially( Runnable r );
    public Displayable getCurrent();
    public static Display getDisplay(
            javax.microedition.midlet.MIDlet c );
    public boolean isColor();
    public int numColors();
    public void setCurrent( Displayable next );
    public void setCurrent( Alert alert,
            Displayable nextDisplayable );
}
```

To use the `Display` class, the MIDlet must first obtain an instance of the class by using the static `getDisplay` method, as we saw in this code fragment from Chapter 3:

```
public class MyMIDlet extends MIDlet {
    Display display;

    protected void startApp() throws MIDletStateChangeException {
        if( display == null ){
            initMIDlet();
```

```
        }
    }

    private void initMIDlet(){
        display = Display.getDisplay( this );
        display.setCurrent( ..... ); // set the initial displayable
    }

    ..... // etc. etc.
}
```

The getDisplay method takes a MIDlet instance as its only parameter and returns the unique Display object associated with the MIDlet. The system maintains distinct Display objects for each MIDlet to ensure that the MIDlets do not interfere with each other.

It is common practice for the MIDlet to store a reference to its Display object upon startup. Often, you will see it coded in the MIDlet's constructor as follows:

```
public class SomeMIDlet extends MIDlet {
    Display display;

    public SomeMIDlet(){
        display = Display.getDisplay( this );
    }

    ..... // etc. etc.
}
```

As mentioned in the previous chapter, this method is not guaranteed to work in all implementations. The correct approach is to obtain the reference on the first call to startApp, as shown in the initMIDlet method earlier.

Note that the other classes in your MIDlet require access to the Display object. A simple way to do this is to pass the MIDlet instance to each class that needs the Display object. The other classes can access the MIDlet's display member (assuming that it is declared with public or package access) or call Display.getDisplay to obtain the Display object. Making your classes nested inner classes of the main MIDlet class makes things even simpler, because the classes have implicit access to the containing class' data members and methods.

Setting the Current Displayable

The MIDlet's Display object is used to set the *current displayable*. The current displayable is the topmost "card" in the "deck" of displayables that make up the application—the user interface component shown by the application on the display. You set the current displayable by calling the setCurrent method, which takes as its only argument a reference to a Displayable object:

```
Display     display = ....;
Displayable next = new Form( "Demo" );

display.setCurrent( next ); // make form the current displayable
```

The `Displayable` class is the root class for all top-level windows defined by the MIDP in both the high-level and low-level APIs, including the `Form` class shown in this example. An alternate version of `setCurrent` takes two arguments: an `Alert` and a `Displayable`. But we will defer discussion of it to later in this chapter.

After calling `setCurrent`, the system will—at some point soon after, but not necessarily right away—make the new `Displayable` current, hiding the `Displayable` that was previously shown (if any). You can obtain the current displayable at any point in the program's execution by calling `getCurrent`.

Using Commands

One of the features of a top-level window (a subclass of `Displayable`) is the capability of the application to register *commands* with the window. Commands define the semantic information for an action—the name of the action, the type of action, and a relative priority for the action. The system uses this information to assign individual actions to one or more of the buttons on the device, grouping them into menus as necessary if there are more actions than buttons. The user triggers an action by pressing the appropriate button or sequence of buttons. The application reacts by performing the desired action.

Defining Commands

Commands are defined by creating instances of the `Command` class:

```
package javax.microedition.lcdui;

public class Command {
    // Constructors
    public Command( String label, int commandType, int priority );

    // Methods
    public int getCommandType();
    public String getLabel();
    public int getPriority();

    // Fields
    public static final int BACK = 2;
    public static final int CANCEL = 3;
    public static final int EXIT = 7;
    public static final int HELP = 5;
    public static final int ITEM = 8;
    public static final int OK = 4;
```

```
    public static final int SCREEN = 1;
    public static final int STOP = 6;
}
```

For example, an "exit" command (to quit an application) and a "back" command (to return to the previous application screen) might be defined as follows:

```
Command exitCommand = new Command( "Exit", Command.EXIT, 1 );
Command backCommand = new Command( "Back", Command.BACK, 1 );
```

The arguments to the Command constructor are easy to explain:

- The first argument, label, is a user-friendly label for the action. This label is normally a short but descriptive verb (the shorter the better). Note that the device might display an alternate label based on the action type.
- The second argument, commandType, describes the action type. There are eight possible action types defined in the Command class. They are listed and explained in Table 4.4.
- The third argument, priority, defines the priority of the action relative to other actions. This value is a positive value starting at 1. A lower value indicates a higher priority. More than one action can use the same priority value.

Once commands are associated with a window, the MIDP implementation assigns each command to a different button. The assignments are device-dependent. For example, if a device has a button that is customarily used as a "back" button, the highest-priority command of type BACK is ideally—but not necessarily—assigned to that button. If there are more commands than buttons available, the implementation must provide a way to access all the commands through some kind of menu (itself accessible via one of the buttons).

Consider the exitCommand and backCommand variables defined earlier. When registered on the same window, the result might be the display shown in Figure 4.1. The device has two programmable buttons, so each command is assigned to a different button. Now, define a third command as follows:

```
Command helpCommand = new Command( "Help", Command.HELP, 5 );
```

Table 4.4 Command Types

TYPE	MEANING
BACK	Navigate back to the previous screen.
CANCEL	Cancel the current screen and move to a previous screen.
EXIT	Exit the application.
HELP	Display online help.
ITEM	Apply the action to the currently selected item on the screen.
OK	Confirm the current screen and move to the next screen.
SCREEN	Apply the action to the entire screen.
STOP	Stop the operation in progress.

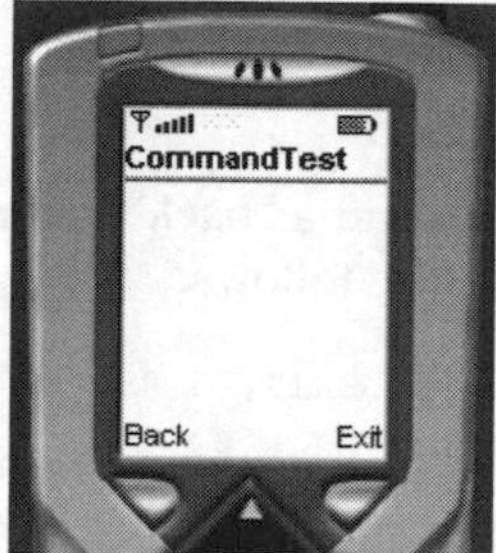

Figure 4.1 Registering two commands on a two-button device.

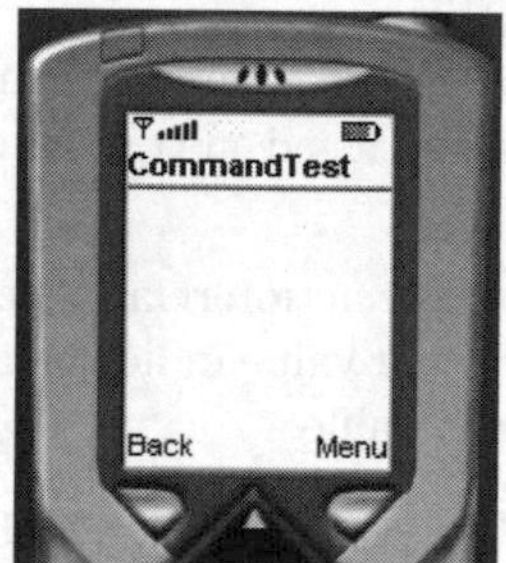

Figure 4.2 Registering three commands on a two-button device.

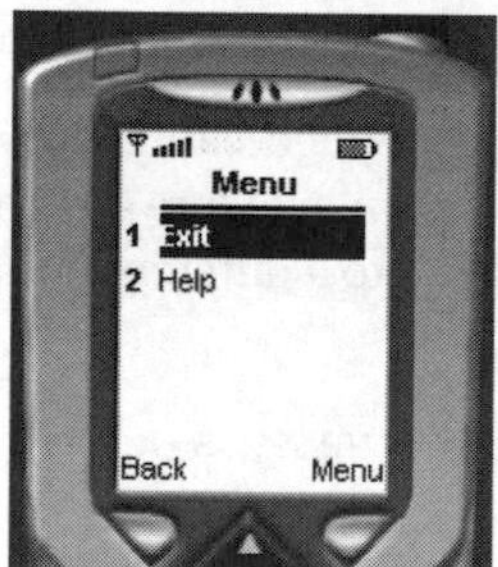

Figure 4.3 Selecting a command from the menu.

When registered on the same window as the other two, the display changes to the one shown in Figure 4.2. Because the device only has two programmable buttons, it assigns two of the commands to the same button and labels that button as "Menu." Pressing the button displays the menu shown in Figure 4.3, from which the user selects the desired command. Remember that these are just sample assignments. Two different devices might display the same set of commands differently.

`Command` objects are immutable and can be created at any point in the application's execution, even before the `startApp` method is called. For this reason, you will often see them declared as members of the main MIDlet class.

Registering Commands

To register a command with a top-level window, use the window's addCommand method. For example:

```
Form form = new Form( "Demo" );
form.addCommand( exitCommand );
form.addCommand( backCommand );
```

When the window becomes the current displayable, it runs through its list of registered commands and assigns buttons appropriately.

You can deregister a command at any time by using the removeCommand method:

```
form.removeCommand( exitCommand );
```

This can be useful when using the same window instance in different contexts.

Changing a command's label is desirable at times. Because commands are immutable, however, the Command class does not provide a method to change the label. Instead, this is done by replacing the command with a new command, as in the following example:

```
// Initialize
int pending = 0;
String nextCmdLabel = "Next";
List list = new List( "Pending Items", List.EXCLUSIVE );
Command nextCmd = new Command( nextCmdLabel, Command.OK, 1 );
list.addCommand( nextCmd );

..... // other code, where the content of pending is updated

// Time to update nextCmd w/ actual number of 'pending items'.
// There is no method to rename a command, so remove/add cmd
list.removeCommand( nextCmd );
nextCmdLabel = "Next";
if (pending > 0) nextCmdLabel += "(" + pending + ")";
nextCmd = new Command( nextCmdLabel, Command.SCREEN, 1 );
list.addCommand( nextCmd );
```

The previous code creates a list with a command whose label accurately indicates how many items are pending.

Responding to Commands

When the user triggers a command, nothing happens automatically in response to the command. The triggering generates an event for the application to trap. The application then performs the appropriate action.

To receive command events, the application implements the CommandListener interface, consisting of a single commandAction method:

```
public interface CommandListener {
    void commandAction( Command c, Displayable d );
}
```

The listener is registered by invoking a window's `setCommandListener` method, passing it the appropriate reference:

```
CommandListener l = ....; // get listener
form.setCommandListener( l );
```

Note that only one listener at a time can be registered with a window. Whenever a command is triggered, the listener's `commandAction` method is invoked. To make it possible to share the same listener across different windows, a reference to the window is passed to the listener along with a reference to the triggered command. The listener uses this information to perform the appropriate action.

The main MIDlet class is often a command listener:

```
public class MyMIDlet extends MIDlet
                      implements CommandListener {
    private Display display;
    private exitCommand = new Command( "Exit", Command.EXIT, 1 );
    private helpCommand = new Command( "Help", Command.HELP, 2 );

    .... // code omitted

    private void initMIDlet(){
        display = Display.getDisplay( this );
        Form f = new Form( "Demo" );
        f.addCommand( exitCommand );
        f.addCommand( helpCommand );
        f.setCommandListener( this );
        display.setCurrent( f );
    }

    public void commandAction( Command c, Displayable d ){
        if( c == exitCommand ){
```

Which Command Was Triggered?

There are two ways to determine which command was triggered. The first way is to use the `Command` object's `getLabel` method to obtain the command label. The second is to compare the `Command` object itself with the `Command` instances created by the application. The second way is generally better because it does not require changes to the code if the command labels change, such as when an application is localized.

```
                exitMIDlet();
            } else if( c == helpCommand ){
                displayHelp();
            }
        }
    }
```

An alternative is to use an anonymous inner class:

```
public class MyMIDlet extends MIDlet {
    private Display display;
    private exitCommand = new Command( "Exit", Command.EXIT, 1 );
    private helpCommand = new Command( "Help", Command.HELP, 2 );

    .... // code omitted

    private void initMIDlet(){
        display = Display.getDisplay( this );
        Form f = new Form( "Demo" );
        f.addCommand( exitCommand );
        f.addCommand( helpCommand );
        f.setCommandListener( new CommandListener() {
            public void commandAction( Command c, Displayable d ){
                if( c == exitCommand ){
                    exitMIDlet();
                } else if( c == helpCommand ){
                    displayHelp();
                }
            }
        } );
        display.setCurrent( f );
    }
}
```

The choice is yours, but remember that each inner class you create adds to the size and complexity of your MIDlet.

Using Images

Bitmapped graphics are an important part of many applications, so the MIDP defines an `Image` class to create and manage bitmaps:

```
package javax.microedition.lcdui;

public class Image {
  // Methods
    public static Image createImage( Image image );
    public static Image createImage( String name )
            throws java.io.IOException;
    public static Image createImage( int width, int height );
    public static Image createImage( byte[] imagedata,
```

```
                int imageoffset, int imagelength );
        public Graphics getGraphics();
        public int getHeight();
        public int getWidth();
        public boolean isMutable();
    }
```

To create an image, you must use one of the static `createImage` methods. To load an image stored in the MIDlet suite's JAR file, use this syntax:

```
// Load PNG from JAR file
try {
    Image img = Image.createImage( "/images/cubes.png" );
}
catch( java.io.IOException e ){
}
```

The argument is the absolute path to the image in the JAR file. The image must be stored in Portable Network Graphics (PNG) format. The return value is an immutable (read-only) `Image` object. Alternatively, you can create a mutable (read-write) `Image` object by specifying a width and height for the image:

```
// Create offscreen buffer
Image img = Image.createImage( 100, 100 );
```

You can then draw directly into this image by calling its `getGraphics` method to obtain a `Graphics` object for the image. We will talk more about the `Graphics` class later in this chapter. The image is in effect an offscreen buffer that you can use for double buffering purposes.

To create an immutable copy of a mutable image, use this syntax:

```
// Make immutable copy
Image img1 = ....; // original
Image img2 = Image.createImage( img1 );
```

Only immutable images can be used with the high-level API. The `isMutable` method enables you to check the mutability of an image. Creating a mutable copy of an immutable image requires a bit more work:

What Is Double Buffering?

Double buffering is a common graphics technique where individual drawing operations are performed on an offscreen image buffer. After completing the operations, the entire image then is copied onto the screen in a single operation. This action can greatly reduce the amount of flicker the user sees, especially when running animations.

```
// Make mutable copy
Image img1 = ....; // original
Image img2 = Image.createImage( img1.getWidth(), img1.getHeight() );
Graphics g = img2.getGraphics();
g.drawImage( img1, 0, 0, Graphics.TOP | Graphics.LEFT );
```

Use the fourth and final version of `createImage` to create an immutable image from a raw byte array:

```
// Create from byte image
byte[] data = ....; // image data, perhaps from network
Image img = Image.createImage( data, 0, data.length );
```

The image must be in PNG format. For more information about the PNG format, see the World Wide Web Consortium (W3C) Web site at `www.w3.org/Graphics/PNG/`. Any good image editing software should be able to save images in PNG format.

The Low-Level User Interface API

With some basic features defined by the common user interface API, we can now explore the low-level and high-level APIs. We start first with the low-level API, which has fewer classes than the high-level API.

The Canvas Class

The heart of the low-level API is the `Canvas` class a subclass of `Displayable`. It is one of the larger classes defined by the MIDP:

```
package javax.microedition.lcdui;

public abstract class Canvas
    extends Displayable {
    // Constructors
    protected Canvas();

    // Methods
    public int getGameAction( int keyCode );
    public int getHeight();
    public int getKeyCode( int gameAction );
    public String getKeyName( int keyCode );
    public int getWidth();
    public boolean hasPointerEvents();
    public boolean hasPointerMotionEvents();
    public boolean hasRepeatEvents();
    protected void hideNotify();
    public boolean isDoubleBuffered();
    protected void keyPressed( int keyCode );
```

```
    protected void keyReleased( int keyCode );
    protected void keyRepeated( int keyCode );
    protected abstract void paint( Graphics g );
    protected void pointerDragged( int x, int y );
    protected void pointerPressed( int x, int y );
    protected void pointerReleased( int x, int y );
    public final void repaint();
    public final void repaint( int x, int y, int width, int height );
    public final void serviceRepaints();
    protected void showNotify();

    // Fields
    public static final int DOWN = 6;
    public static final int FIRE = 8;
    public static final int GAME_A = 9;
    public static final int GAME_B = 10;
    public static final int GAME_C = 11;
    public static final int GAME_D = 12;
    public static final int KEY_NUM0 = 48;
    public static final int KEY_NUM1 = 49;
    public static final int KEY_NUM2 = 50;
    public static final int KEY_NUM3 = 51;
    public static final int KEY_NUM4 = 52;
    public static final int KEY_NUM5 = 53;
    public static final int KEY_NUM6 = 54;
    public static final int KEY_NUM7 = 55;
    public static final int KEY_NUM8 = 56;
    public static final int KEY_NUM9 = 57;
    public static final int KEY_POUND = 35;
    public static final int KEY_STAR = 42;
    public static final int LEFT = 2;
    public static final int RIGHT = 5;
    public static final int UP = 1;
}
```

The only top-level window defined by the low-level API, the `Canvas` class, has direct access to the display and to the device's input events. This flexibility comes at a price, however, because the application is entirely responsible for drawing the contents of a canvas and for responding to the user's input.

`Canvas` is an abstract class, so to create a canvas you must define your own class that extends `Canvas` and that implements the `paint` method. A minimal canvas looks like the following:

```
import javax.microedition.lcdui.*;

public class MinimalCanvas extends Canvas {
    MinimalCanvas(){
    }
```

```
    protected void paint( Graphics g ){
        // canvas paints itself here
    }
}
```

To make the canvas visible, call Display.setCurrent:

```
Display display = ....;
Canvas c = new MinimalCanvas();
display.setCurrent( c );
```

Also, because Canvas extends Displayable, you can register Command objects with a canvas and set the canvas's command listener appropriately. Note that any commands you do register take precedence over any input handling the canvas does. In other words, if a command is assigned to a particular button, the canvas will never directly receive input events for that button.

The system calls the canvas's paint method whenever the canvas needs repainting, such as after displaying a system-drawn menu. An application can initiate a repaint by using the repaint method, which schedules a repaint at the next convenient moment. You can force a repaint to occur immediately, however, by calling serviceRepaints immediately after calling repaint. The serviceRepaints method blocks until all pending repaint requests have finished.

The getWidth and getHeight methods return the width and height of the canvas, which is the total area available for drawing. For flicker-free graphics, check the isDoubleBuffered method to determine whether double buffering is automatically performed by the system (in other words, the Graphics object passed to the paint method is for an offscreen image buffer and not the actual display) or if it is something your application must do itself.

To know when a canvas is shown and hidden, have it override the showNotify and hideNotify methods, as in the following code:

```
public class MyCanvas extends Canvas {
    ..... // code omitted

    protected void showNotify(){
        // canvas is shown, start background threads
        // and other expensive operations
    }

    protected void hideNotify(){
        // canvas is hidden, free up resources
    }
}
```

These methods are useful for starting and stopping timers and other tasks that only need to be active when the canvas is actually active onscreen.

Drawing Primitives

The Graphics class, passed to a canvas whenever it needs to be repainted, defines the methods that a canvas can use to draw on the display:

```
package javax.microedition.lcdui;

public class Graphics {
    // Methods
    public void clipRect( int x, int y, int width, int height );
    public void drawArc( int x, int y, int width, int height,
            int startAngle, int arcAngle );
    public void drawChar( char character, int x, int y, int anchor );
    public void drawChars( char[] data, int offset, int length,
            int x, int y, int anchor );
    public void drawImage( Image img, int x, int y, int anchor );
    public void drawLine( int x1, int y1, int x2, int y2 );
    public void drawRect( int x, int y, int width, int height );
    public void drawRoundRect( int x, int y, int width, int height,
            int arcWidth, int arcHeight );
    public void drawString( String str, int x, int y, int anchor );
    public void drawSubstring( String str, int offset, int len,
            int x, int y, int anchor );
    public void fillArc( int x, int y, int width, int height,
            int startAngle, int arcAngle );
    public void fillRect( int x, int y, int width, int height );
    public void fillRoundRect( int x, int y, int width, int height,
            int arcWidth, int arcHeight );
    public int getBlueComponent();
    public int getClipHeight();
    public int getClipWidth();
    public int getClipX();
    public int getClipY();
    public int getColor();
    public Font getFont();
    public int getGrayScale();
    public int getGreenComponent();
    public int getRedComponent();
    public int getStrokeStyle();
    public int getTranslateX();
    public int getTranslateY();
    public void setClip( int x, int y, int width, int height );
    public void setColor( int RGB );
    public void setColor( int red, int green, int blue );
    public void setFont( Font font );
    public void setGrayScale( int value );
    public void setStrokeStyle( int style );
    public void translate( int x, int y );
    // Fields
    public static final int BASELINE = 64;
    public static final int BOTTOM = 32;
```

```
    public static final int DOTTED = 1;
    public static final int HCENTER = 1;
    public static final int LEFT = 4;
    public static final int RIGHT = 8;
    public static final int SOLID = 0;
    public static final int TOP = 16;
    public static final int VCENTER = 2;
}
```

Note that a `Graphics` object can also be used to draw onto an offscreen image buffer.

The methods of the `Graphics` class define a small, two-dimensional drawing API. The basic line drawing methods are `drawArc`, `drawLine`, `drawRect`, and `drawRoundRect`. The methods are mostly self-explanatory. For example, to draw a line from the top left corner of a canvas to its bottom right corner, use this code:

```
protected void paint( Graphics g ){
    g.drawLine( 0, 0, getWidth(), getHeight() );
}
```

To draw a circle or oval, use the `drawRoundRect` method and set the `arcWidth` and `arcHeight` arguments equal to the `width` and `height` arguments:

```
protected void paint( Graphics g ){
    int rw = getWidth();
    int rh = getHeight();
    // Draw a circle/oval
    g.drawRoundRect( 0, 0, rw, rh, rw, rh );
}
```

You can also draw filled versions of arcs and rectangles by using `fillArc`, `fillRect`, and `fillRoundRect`.

You perform all drawing by using the current color, which is a 24-bit RGB (red, green, and blue) value that is transformed appropriately by the implementation to match the device's capabilities. You set the current color by calling `setColor`:

```
protected void paint( Graphics g ){
    g.setColor( 0, 0, 0 );
    g.drawLine( 0, 0, getWidth(), 0 );
    g.setColor( 255, 0, 0 );
    g.drawLine( getWidth(), 0, getWidth(), getHeight() );
}
```

There is no method to clear the canvas. To clear it, set the color to white and draw a rectangle the width and height of the canvas:

```
protected void paint( Graphics ){
    g.setColor( 255, 255, 255 );
    g.fillRect( 0, 0, getWidth(), getHeight() );
}
```

You draw images by using `drawImage`; its last argument specifies the anchor point of the image:

```
Image img = ....; // get image
g.drawImage( img, 0, 0, g.TOP | g.LEFT );
```

The anchor point defines which pixel in the image is relative to the x and y arguments. Possible values for the anchor point are `BOTTOM`, `VCENTER`, and `TOP` for the vertical component and `LEFT`, `HCENTER`, and `RIGHT` for the horizontal components.

The `Graphics` class also defines methods for setting the clipping rectangle, translating the coordinate origin, and drawing dotted lines instead of solid lines.

Drawing Text

The `Font` class is used in conjunction with the `Graphics` class to draw text. Its definition is as follows:

```
package javax.microedition.lcdui;

public final class Font {
    // Methods
    public int charWidth( char ch );
    public int charsWidth( char[] ch, int offset, int length );
    public int getBaselinePosition();
    public static Font getDefaultFont();
    public int getFace();
    public static Font getFont( int face, int style, int size );
    public int getHeight();
    public int getSize();
    public int getStyle();
    public boolean isBold();
    public boolean isItalic();
    public boolean isPlain();
    public boolean isUnderlined();
    public int stringWidth( String str );
    public int substringWidth( String str, int offset, int len );
    // Fields
    public static final int FACE_MONOSPACE = 32;
    public static final int FACE_PROPORTIONAL = 64;
    public static final int FACE_SYSTEM = 0;
    public static final int SIZE_LARGE = 16;
    public static final int SIZE_MEDIUM = 0;
    public static final int SIZE_SMALL = 8;
    public static final int STYLE_BOLD = 1;
    public static final int STYLE_ITALIC = 2;
    public static final int STYLE_PLAIN = 0;
    public static final int STYLE_UNDERLINED = 4;
}
```

Although there is no facility in the MIDP for an application to create its own fonts, it can use the `Font` class to obtain information about the fonts that are available. Three font faces are potentially available: `FACE_MONOSPACE`, `FACE_PROPOR-TIONAL`, and `FACE_SYSTEM`. Three sizes are potentially available: `SIZE_SMALL`, `SIZE_MEDIUM`, and `SIZE_LARGE`. Four styles are potentially available: `STYLE_PLAIN`, `STYLE_BOLD`, `STYLE_ITALIC`, and `STYLE_UNDERLINED`. A `Font` instance is obtained by invoking the static `Font.getFont` method with the appropriate values for face, size, and style:

```
Font f = Font.getFont( Font.FACE_MONOSPACE, Font.SIZE_MEDIUM,
                       Font.STYLE_BOLD | Font.STYLE_UNDERLINED );
```

The system attempts to find the closest font that matches the desired characteristics. It will always return a valid `Font` object, even if that `Font` object does not actually match what was requested. Call `Font.getDefaultFont` to obtain information about the default font used by the implementation.

The `Font` class defines the following methods for obtaining information about the size of a character or a string: `charWidth`, `charsWidth`, `getBaselinePosition`, `getH-eight`, `stringWidth`, and `substringWidth`. Use these methods to perform the calculations necessary for word wrapping or other similar text display chores.

To draw text, call `Graphics.setFont` to set the appropriate font and then call one of these methods: `drawChar`, `drawChars`, `drawString`, or `draw-Substring`. As with images, each method takes an anchor point. The anchor point defines which pixel in the drawn text is relative to the x and y coordinates. `VCENTER` is not a legal value for the vertical component of the anchor point when drawing text. Use `BASELINE`—referring to the baseline of the font—instead.

Handling Keyboard Input

A canvas receives key events whenever the canvas is the current displayable (and the MIDlet is in the foreground state) and the user presses a button. To handle the events, the canvas must override the `keyPressed`, `keyReleased`, and/or `keyRepeated` methods:

```
public class MyCanvas extends Canvas {
    ..... // code omitted

    protected void keyPressed( int keyCode ){
        // key was pressed
    }

    protected void keyReleased( int keyCode ){
        // key was released
    }

    protected void keyRepeated( int keyCode ){
        // key is repeating
```

```
    }
}
```

A single keyCode argument is passed to all three methods, identifying the key that was pressed or released by its key code. Wherever possible, a key code maps directly to the Unicode value for that key. As well, the Canvas class defines a number of key codes corresponding to the keys on a standard telephone keypad: KEY_NUM0 to KEY_NUM9 plus KEY_POUND and KEY_STAR. Testing for a specific character other than those is just a matter of casting a positive key code to a char:

```
protected void keyPressed( int keyCode ){
    if( keyCode > 0 ){
        char ch = (char) keyCode;
        if( ch == 'a' || ch == 'A' ){
            // do something....
        }
    }
}
```

Negative values are used for system-specific keys that have no obvious Unicode mapping. Cursor keys are an example. Instead of requiring the application to avoid these non-Unicode keys, the MIDP specification defines a way to map both standard and non-standard keys into *game actions*. A game action is a gaming-related event from the following list of supported events: UP, DOWN, LEFT, RIGHT, FIRE, GAME_A, GAME_B, GAME_C, and GAME_D. At a minimum, a device must support UP, DOWN, LEFT, RIGHT, and FIRE actions, mapping at least one key on the device to each action. Ideally, the device should also support the four generic actions GAME_A to GAME_D, but there might not be enough keys to support this function. At runtime, an application can easily determine whether a key code corresponds to a game action by calling the getGameAction method:

```
protected void keyPressed( int keyCode ){
    int action = getGameAction( keyCode );
    switch( action ){
        case UP:
            // move up
            break;
        case DOWN:
            // move down
            break;
    }
    ..... // etc. etc.
}
```

Use game actions in your keyboard processing wherever possible in order to be maximally portable.

Note that keyRepeat events only occur when a canvas' hasRepeatEvents returns true.

Handling Pointer Input

A canvas can also receive pointer events. A pointer event is an event generated by an input device such as a mouse or a touch-sensitive screen. Not every MIDP-enabled device supports pointers, so trapping pointer events is strictly optional and is done by overriding the `pointerDragged`, `pointerPressed`, and `pointerReleased` methods:

```
public class MyCanvas extends Canvas {
    ..... // code omitted

    protected void pointerPressed( int x, int y ){
        // pointer was pressed
    }

    protected void pointerReleased( int x, int y ){
        // pointer was released
    }

    protected void pointerDragged( int x, int y ){
        // pointer is dragging
    }
}
```

The x and y arguments are the position of the pointing device when the event occurred. A canvas can determine whether the device supports pointer events by calling the `hasPointerEvents` and `hasPointerMotionEvents` methods.

Playing Sounds

There is no direct sound support in the low-level API. In fact, the only sounds available to a MIDP application are those played when an alert is shown. A canvas can use predefined `AlertType` objects to activate those sounds:

```
Display display = ....;

// Play a sound
AlertType.ERROR.playSound( display );
```

See the section on alerts for more details on how to use `AlertType`. Note that there is no guarantee as to what kind of sound is actually produced; you might want to let the user configure the application's use of those sounds.

Serializing Code

Unlike Swing, the MIDP user interface classes are thread-safe. The user interface can be accessed and modified from any thread in the application. In particular, events delivered to a canvas are sent one at a time by a single system thread with the next event handler called only after the previous event handler returns; in other words, the events are delivered *serially*. Generally, an application has no control over the order in which events are delivered. Paint events are the exception, however, because there are times when you want to run code only after any pending paint requests have been processed. When animating, for example, you do not want to draw a new image until the previous image has finished drawing.

There are two ways to ensure that your code runs when there are no more paint requests to process. The first is to call the canvas' `serviceRepaints` method to immediately process any pending paint requests. If paint events are pending, this action causes an immediate call to the canvas' `paint` method from the current thread or from another thread; `serviceRepaints` does not return until `paint` does, and you have no control over which thread is used to do the painting. This situation is a potential danger. If your code locks an object required by the `paint` method and calls `serviceRepaints`, the system might call `paint` on another thread, and the two threads will deadlock.

The second way is to call the `Display` object's `callSerially` method, passing it an object that implements the familiar `java.lang.Runnable` interface. This action places the `Runnable` in the system event queue after any pending paint requests. The system event thread serially invokes the object's `run` method after the paint requests are processed. For example, say you want to play a sound whenever you redraw a canvas. Define the following class:

```
public class PlaySound implements Runnable {
    private Display   display;

    public PlaySound( Display display ){
        this.display = display;
    }

    public void run(){
        AlertType.CONFIRMATION.playSound( display );
    }
}
```

Invoke `callSerially` each time you call the canvas' `repaint` method:

```
Display display = ...;
Canvas canvas = ...; //
canvas.repaint();
display.callSerially( new PlaySound( display ) );
```

The `PlaySound` object's `run` method will be invoked after the canvas' `paint` method is called.

The High-Level User Interface API

The high-level API has the richest set of classes and the most functionality. It is possible to build sophisticated applications by using only classes from the common and the high-

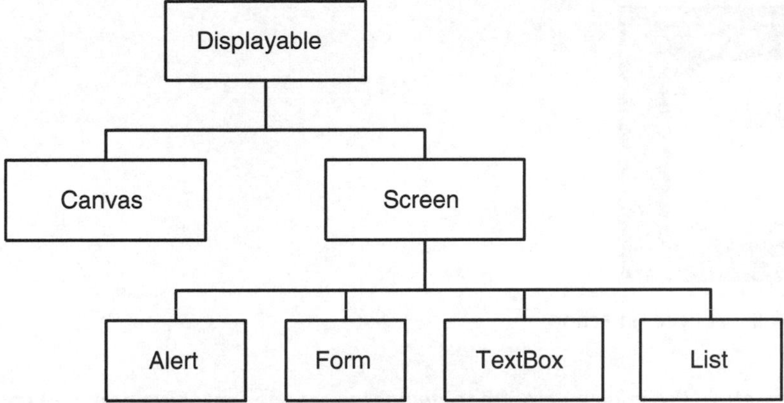

Figure 4.4 The MIDP top-level window hierarchy.

level APIs, avoiding the low-level APIs altogether. In this section, we look at the user interface components defined by the high-level APIs.

Screens and Tickers

Top-level windows in the high-level API are referred to as *screens* because they extend the `Screen` class. The `Screen` class in turn extends the `Displayable` class. The complete set of top-level windows defined by the MIDP is shown in Figure 4.4. There are four subclasses of `Screen`. The `Canvas` class, part of the low-level API, is the only class that does not extend `Screen`.

The `Screen` class extends `Displayable` with four new methods:

```
package javax.microedition.lcdui;

public abstract class Screen
    extends Displayable {
    // Methods
    public Ticker getTicker();
    public String getTitle();
    public void setTicker( Ticker ticker );
    public void setTitle( String s );
}
```

Two of the methods, `setTitle` and `getTitle`, set and get a screen's title. A title is optional, but you should specify one whenever possible to help the user navigate through the application. Keep the title as short as possible. All of `Screen`'s subclasses let you specify a title in their constructors, so you will rarely call `setTitle` directly.

The other two methods are `setTicker` and `getTicker`, which get and set the screen's *ticker*. A ticker is an object of class `Ticker` that automatically displays and scrolls a string in an area at the top or bottom of the screen. The exact location of the ticker on the

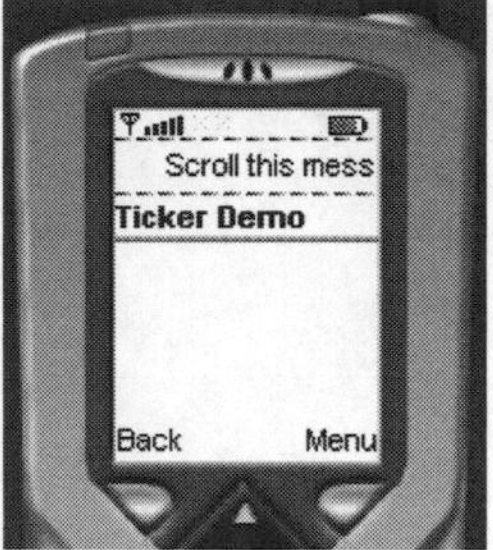

Figure 4.5 A ticker in action.

screen is left to the implementation to decide, as are the font, direction, and speed of the text. The following code shows how to create and use a ticker:

```
Display display = ....;
Screen  screen = new Form( "Ticker Demo" );
Ticker  ticker = new Ticker( "Scroll this message, please." );

screen.setTicker( ticker );
display.setCurrent( screen );
```

Figure 4.5 shows the ticker in action. You can change a ticker's message at any time by calling its `setString` method. The definition for `Ticker` is as follows:

```
package javax.microedition.lcdui;

public class Ticker {
    // Constructors
    public Ticker( String str );

    // Methods
    public String getString();
    public void setString( String str );
}
```

You can also set the same ticker on different `Screen` objects, and as you move from screen to screen the device attempts to keep the ticker in the same location on the display. To remove a ticker from a screen, pass `null` to `setTicker`.

Alerts

To notify the user of an error, warning, or other condition, use an *alert*. An alert is an instance of the `Alert` class, whose definition is as follows:

```
package javax.microedition.lcdui;

public class Alert
    extends Screen {
```

```
    // Constructors
    public Alert( String title );
    public Alert( String title, String alertText, Image alertImage,
            AlertType alertType );

    // Methods
    public void addCommand( Command cmd );
    public int getDefaultTimeout();
    public Image getImage();
    public String getString();
    public int getTimeout();
    public AlertType getType();
    public void setCommandListener( CommandListener l );
    public void setImage( Image img );
    public void setString( String str );
    public void setTimeout( int time );
    public void setType( AlertType type );

    // Fields
    public static final int FOREVER = -2;
}
```

Alerts are displayed for short periods of time or until the user dismisses them, after which another displayable is shown. Besides being used for errors and warnings, alerts are often used to confirm the successful completion of an operation and may only be shown for a couple of seconds.

An alert has five property settings—a title, a message, an image, a type, and a timeout. The first four values can be set in the constructor or individually by calling the appropriate methods. A title and a message should always be specified, but the image and type can be `null`.

Like all high-level UI components, the exact layout of an alert is beyond the application's control. If an image is supplied and the device supports images, it will be shown next to or above the message. The message can be of arbitrary length—the implementation will scroll it if necessary—but it should be as short as possible.

The alert type determines the sound that the device plays when it displays the alert. There are five possible types: `ALARM`, `CONFIRMATION`, `ERROR`, `INFO`, and `WARNING`. These types are all defined as static final members of the `AlertType` class. `AlertType` defines a single method, `playSound`, to play the sound associated with an alert type. The device selects the most appropriate sound for the alert type, although different alert types can use the same sound. Of course, if the device does not support sound or the alert type is set to `null`, no sound is played when the alert is displayed.

The timeout value is the number of milliseconds that the alert is to be displayed before it is automatically dismissed by the system. If you do not specify a value, a default timeout of two or three seconds is used—the `getDefaultTimeout` method returns the exact value used by the system. The special value `FOREVER` is used to keep the alert onscreen until explicitly dismissed by the user. Such an alert is called a *modal* alert.

Figure 4.6 A simple alert.

To display an alert, use the two-argument version of `Display.setCurrent`, passing the alert as the first argument and a non-alert displayable as the second argument. For example:

```
Display display = .....;
Alert   alert = new Alert( "Error", "You goofed!", null, null );
Form    form = new Form( "Try again" );

display.setCurrent( alert, form );
```

The alert is displayed for a few seconds, as shown in Figure 4.6, before being dismissed—and a new displayable shown in its place.

A more complicated alert can be created and displayed by using this code:

```
Display display = .....;
Alert   alert = new Alert( "Success" );
Form    form = new Form( "Demo Form" );

alert.setString( "It worked" );
alert.setTimeout( Alert.FOREVER );
alert.setType( AlertType.CONFIRMATION );

try {
    alert.setImage( Image.createImage( "/images/thumbsup.png" ) );
}
catch( java.io.IOException e ){
}

display.setCurrent( alert, form );
```

This alert, shown in Figure 4.7, plays a confirmation sound and displays an image from the MIDlet suite's JAR file.

Note that unlike other top-level windows, you cannot attach commands to the `Alert` class. It enforces this rule by overriding the `addCommand` and `setCom-mandListener` methods to throw `IllegalStateException` whenever they are invoked.

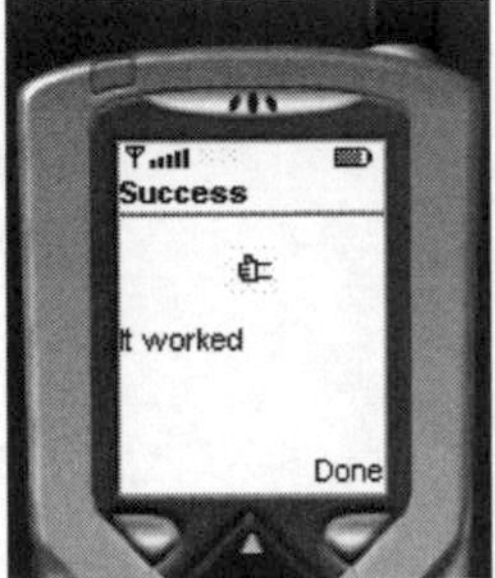

Figure 4.7 A more complex alert.

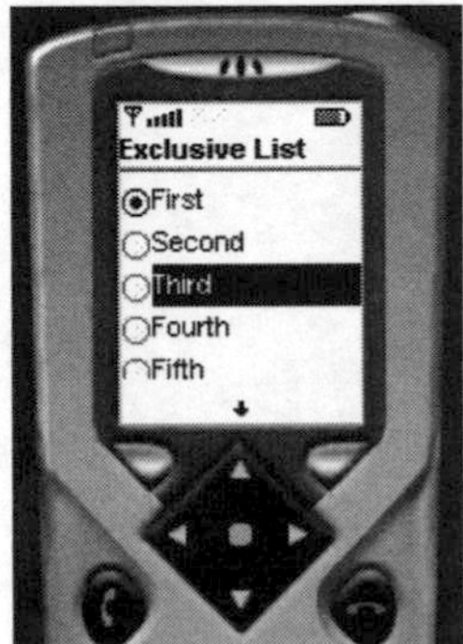

Figure 4.8 An EXCLUSIVE mode list.

Lists

The `List` class is a screen that displays a list of strings. An image can also be associated with each string. The user can navigate through the list and select one or more of the strings. When done selecting items, the user triggers a command that then uses the selected item(s) to perform an appropriate action.

A list has three selection modes. In the `EXCLUSIVE` mode, only one item at a time can be selected, and selecting a new item automatically deselects any existing selected item. You select by moving a cursor to the desired item and pressing a button, and which button is pressed depends entirely on the implementation. Figure 4.8 shows an `EXCLUSIVE` mode list. In the `MULTIPLE` mode, however, several or all items in the list can be selected at the same time. Selecting is done the same way as in the `EXCLUSIVE` mode except that there is also a way to deselect items, usually by moving the cursor to a selected item and toggling its state with the selection button. Figure 4.9 shows a `MULTIPLE` mode list. The final mode, the `IMPLICIT` mode, is like the `EXCLUSIVE` mode except that the item under the cursor is implicitly selected each time the cursor moves. And unlike the other two modes, which do not trigger any events when the user presses a button to select or

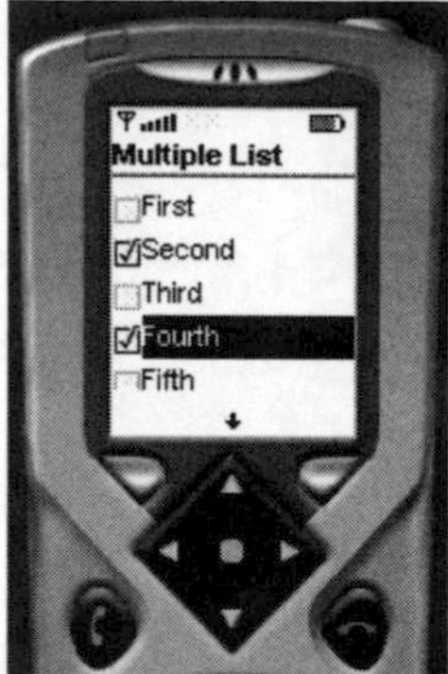

Figure 4.9 A `MULTIPLE` mode list.

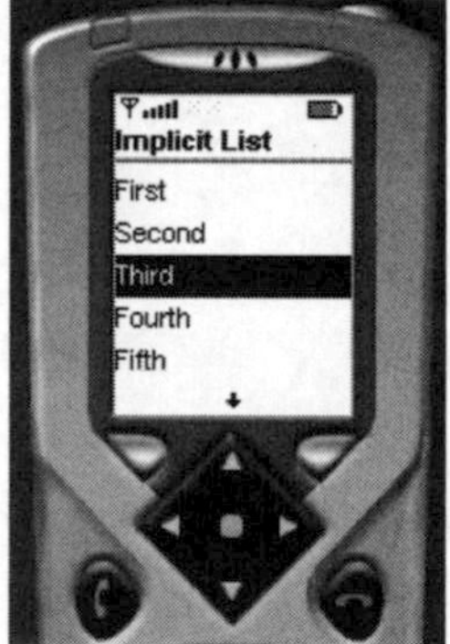

Figure 4.10 An `IMPLICIT` mode list.

deselect an item, the `IMPLICIT` mode does trigger a command when the user selects a new item. Figure 4.10 shows an `IMPLICIT` mode list.

A list's selection mode is set when the `List` object is constructed, as in the following example:

```
List list = new List( "Sample List", List.EXCLUSIVE );
```

The `List` class declares methods for adding list items and setting and getting the state of those items. Most of the methods are implementations of the `Choice` interface, which is shared with the `ChoiceGroup` class (as we will see later). The `List` class is defined as follows:

```
package javax.microedition.lcdui;

public class List
    extends Screen
```

```
    implements Choice {
    // Constructors
    public List( String title, int listType );
    public List( String title, int listType,
            String[] stringElements, Image[] imageElements );

    // Methods
    public int append( String stringElement, Image imageElement );
    public void delete( int index );
    public Image getImage( int index );
    public int getSelectedFlags( boolean[] selectedArray_return );
    public int getSelectedIndex();
    public String getString( int index );
    public void insert( int index, String stringElement,
            Image imageElement );
    public boolean isSelected( int index );
    public void set( int index, String stringElement,
            Image imageElement );
    public void setSelectedFlags( boolean[] selectedArray );
    public void setSelectedIndex( int index, boolean selected );
    public int size();

    // Fields
    public static final Command SELECT_COMMAND;
}
```

Note that `EXCLUSIVE`, `IMPLICIT`, and `MULTIPLE` are constants defined by the `Choice` interface and therefore do not appear in the definition of the `List` class.

To add items to a list, call the append method:

```
list.append( "First", null );
list.append( "Second", null );
```

The second argument to append is an image to display with the string. The image is optional and might not be supported by all devices. If you do use an image, keep it small and make sure that all the images used in the list are of the same width and height.

The append, `delete`, `insert`, and `set` methods can be called at any time to modify the list. For example, this code deletes all items in a list:

```
public void deleteAll( List list ){
    int n = list.size();
    while( n > 0 ){
        list.delete( --n );
    }
}
```

Note that item indices start at 0, and the `size` method returns the number of items currently in the list. To obtain the index of the selected item in an `EXCLUSIVE` or `IMPLICIT` list, call `getSelectedIndex`. For `MULTIPLE` mode, call `getSelectedFlags` instead, passing in an array of boolean values. The application can set the selected states of items by using the setSelected-Index and setSelectedFlags methods.

To do anything useful with a List, you must set its command listener and register one or more Command objects. An IMPLICIT list triggers a predefined SELECT_COMMAND object when the user selects an item, but the other two modes do not trigger any events at all. Consider the following MIDlet fragment:

```
public class ListMIDlet extends MIDlet {
    ..... // code from before omitted

    class EditMenu extends List implements CommandListener {
        EditMenu(){
            super( "Select one:", IMPLICIT );
        }

        void init(){
            append( "Set userID", null );
            append( "Set password", null );
            addCommand( exitCommand );
            setCommandListener( this );
        }

        public void commandAction( Command c, Displayable d ){
            if( c == exitCommand ){
                exitMIDlet();
            } else if( c == List.SELECT_COMMAND ){
                int which = getSelectedIndex();
                switch( which ){
                    case 0:
                        editUserID();
                        break;
                    case 1:
                        editPassword();
                        break;
                }
            }
        }

        ..... // editUserID, editPassword methods omitted
    }
}
```

The EditMenu inner class extends the List class to implement a simple menu. The MIDlet displays the menu by creating an instance of EditMenu, initializing that instance and calling Display.setCurrent to make the list the current displayable:

```
public void showEditMenu(){
    EditMenu menu = new EditMenu();
    menu.init();
    display.setCurrent( menu );
```

the user selects an item (triggering a SELECT_ COMMAND) or

een that displays editable text. Its definition is as follows:

```
ition.lcdui;

:ring title, String text, int maxSize,
raints );

e( int offset, int length );
etPosition();
rs( char[] data );
straints();
Size();
String();
t( String src, int position );
t( char[] data, int offset, int length,
ion );
ars( char[] data, int offset, int length );
nstraints( int constraints );
Size( int maxSize );
ring( String text );
;
```

ring up to a given number of characters, with or without con-
acters that are acceptable. The class has a single constructor, used as follows:

```
TextBox tb = new TextBox( "Enter Name:", "joe", 50, TextField.ANY );
display.setCurrent( tb );
```

The result is the text box shown in Figure 4.11. The first argument is the screen title; the second argument is the initial text to display (which can be `null` if there is no initial value); the third argument is the maximum size in characters of the text box; and the fourth argument defines the constraints on the input values. Note that constraint values are actually defined by the `TextField` class, not by the `TextBox` class. `TextField` is discussed in the next section. `TextBox` and `TextField` share many methods in common, but oddly enough there is no common interface defined.

The possible constraint values for a text box are as follows:

- `TextField.ANY`—The user can enter any string
- `TextField.EMAILADDR`—The user can only enter an e-mail address

Avoid Password Masking

Password masking makes sense when you are using a regular keyboard, but it is an obstacle when using a keypad. Remember, multiple characters are assigned to the same key, so entering even the simplest of strings can involve pressing the same key several times in a row. With password masking enabled, the user has no idea if he or she has selected the correct character except by remembering which character is mapped to which key and carefully counting the number of key presses.

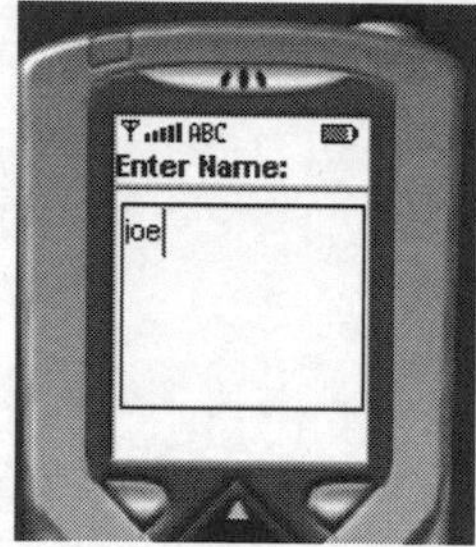

Figure 4.11 A text box.

- `TextField.NUMERIC`—The user can only enter an integer
- `TextField.PHONENUMBER`—The user can only enter a phone number
- `TextField.URL`—The user can only enter a URL

In addition, any of these values can be combined with the `TextField.PASSWORD` constraint to mask the values displayed by the text box. The `PASSWORD` constraint only makes sense with the `ANY` and `NUMERIC` constraints, though.

The application can retrieve the string in the text box at any point by calling its `getString` method. This action is normally done in response to the triggering of a command. The text box does expose methods such as `insert` and `delete` for directly manipulating its contents, but it is rare to have a need for these.

Remember that text entry on some small devices, particularly cell phones, can be a slow and painful process for the user. If you can, explore alternatives to entering text, such as letting the user select an item in a list instead.

Forms and Items

The final screen type defined by the high-level API is the `Form` class. A `Form` object is a container for user interface components that extend the `Item` class. Apart from its title, a `Form` displays no content of its own. Its basic responsibility is to arrange the `Item` objects it contains and to enable the user to navigate between them. Forms can be used to display information and to interact with the user in a free-form manner that is not available with the other screen types.

Using Forms

The Form class is defined as follows:

```
package javax.microedition.lcdui;

public class Form
    extends Screen {
    // Constructors
    public Form( String title );
    public Form( String title, Item[] items );

    // Methods
    public int append( Image image );
    public int append( Item item );
    public int append( String str );
    public void delete( int index );
    public Item get( int index );
    public void insert( int index, Item item );
    public void set( int index, Item item );
    public void setItemStateListener( ItemStateListener iListener );
    public int size();
}
```

To use a form, create a Form object and add the desired items to the form by using the form's append method:

```
Item item1 = ....;
Item item2 = ....;

Form f = new Form( "Demo Form" );
f.append( item1 );
f.append( item2 );
```

For most forms, this task is all that you need to do, except of course for registering commands and setting the form's command listener. The Form class does define a number of methods such as delete, insert, and size for dealing with the individual items on a form, but they are rarely invoked unless you are doing something advanced like building forms dynamically from resource definitions.

Note that the append method is overloaded to accept String and Image objects as well as Item objects. These alternate versions are convenience methods that create new StringItem and ImageItem objects, respectively, before appending them to the form.

Using Items

User interface objects contained by a form must extend the abstract `Item` class:

```
package javax.microedition.lcdui;

public abstract class Item {
    // Methods
    public String getLabel();
    public void setLabel( String label );
}
```

The `Item` class defines two methods, `getLabel` and `setLabel`, for getting and setting a label associated with the item. If the label is non-`null`, the form draws it with the item, keeping the two as close together as possible.

Some form items are editable, like the `TextField` item. These items trigger events whenever the user changes their values. The application can trap these events by registering an `ItemStateListener` with a form by using the form's `setItemStateListener` method. The `ItemStateListener` interface defines a single `itemStateChanged` method as follows:

```
public interface ItemStateListener {
    void itemStateChanged( Item item );
}
```

When the user modifies a `ChoiceGroup`, `Gauge`, `DateField`, or `TextField` item, it triggers a call to the listener's `itemStateChanged` method, passing a reference to the changed item as the only argument.

The remainder of this section describes the individual item types available for use on a form.

ChoiceGroup Items

The `ChoiceGroup` class enables the user to select one or more strings from a list of strings. Its definition is as follows:

```
package javax.microedition.lcdui;

public class ChoiceGroup
    extends Item
    implements Choice {
    // Constructors
    public ChoiceGroup( String label, int choiceType );
    public ChoiceGroup( String label, int choiceType,
            String[] stringElements, Image[] imageElements );

    // Methods
    public int append( String stringElement, Image imageElement );
```

```
    public void delete( int index );
    public Image getImage( int i );
    public int getSelectedFlags( boolean[] selectedArray_return );
    public int getSelectedIndex();
    public String getString( int i );
    public void insert( int index, String stringElement,
            Image imageElement );
    public boolean isSelected( int index );
    public void set( int index, String stringElement,
            Image imageElement );
    public void setSelectedFlags( boolean[] selectedArray );
    public void setSelectedIndex( int index, boolean selected );
    public int size();
}
```

Like the List class, it implements the Choice interface. A ChoiceGroup item can only be used in EXCLUSIVE mode or MULTIPLE mode, however. In EXCLUSIVE mode, it behaves like—and might look like—a set of radio buttons, while in MULTIPLE mode it behaves like a set of checkboxes. Consider the following code:

```
public class CGForm extends Form implements ItemStateListener {

    public static void showForm( Display display ){
        CGForm f = new CGForm();
        f.init();
        display.setCurrent( f );
    }

    CGForm(){
        super( "First" );
        setItemStateListener( this );
    }

    void init(){
        ChoiceGroup cg = new ChoiceGroup( "Select:",
                                          ChoiceGroup.EXCLUSIVE );
        cg.append( "First", null );
        cg.append( "Second", null );
        cg.append( "Third", null );
        append( cg );
    }

    // For EXCLUSIVE mode, update the title whenever
    // a new item is selected

    public void itemStateChanged( Item item ){
        ChoiceGroup cg = (ChoiceGroup) item;
        setTitle( cg.getString( cg.getSelectedIndex() ) );
    }
}
```

Figure 4.12 A choice group in exclusive mode.

Calling the showForm method creates a form with a single choice group that registers itself as the item state change listener. When the user selects one of the choices, the form updates its title to reflect the new choice, as shown in Figure 4.12. Change the choice group to MULTIPLE mode, and you will need to change the itemStateChanged method because the choice group's get-SelectedIndex method will always return -1:

```
// For MULTIPLE mode, update the title whenever
// an item is toggled on or off

public void itemStateChanged( Item item ){
    ChoiceGroup cg = (ChoiceGroup) item;
    StringBuffer buf = new StringBuffer();
    boolean[] arr = new boolean[ cg.size() ];

    cg.getSelectedFlags( arr );
    for( int i = 0; i < arr.length; ++i ){
        if( arr[i] ){
            if( buf.length() > 0 ) buf.append( '+' );
            buf.append( cg.getString( i ) );
        }
    }

    if( buf.length() == 0 ) buf.append( "<none>" );
    setTitle( buf.toString() );
}
```

The choice group is shown in Figure 4.13.

As with a list, an image can be associated with each string in a choice group.

DateField Items

The DateField class enables the user to edit a date or time. Its definition is as follows:

```
package javax.microedition.lcdui;

public class DateField
```

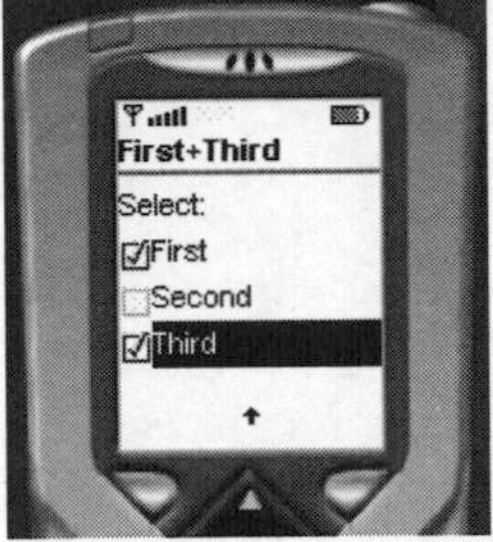

Figure 4.13 A choice group in multiple mode.

```
    extends Item {
    // Constructors
    public DateField( String label, int mode );
    public DateField( String label, int mode,
            java.util.TimeZone timeZone );

    // Methods
    public java.util.Date getDate();
    public int getInputMode();
    public void setDate( java.util.Date date );
    public void setInputMode( int mode );
    public String toString();

    // Fields
    public static final int DATE = 1;
    public static final int DATE_TIME = 3;
    public static final int TIME = 2;
}
```

A `DateField` has three possible modes: `DATE` to edit only a date, `TIME` to edit only a time, or `DATE_TIME` to edit both a date and a time. You set the mode in the constructor. A second form of the constructor lets you specify a time zone to use if the device's default zone is not appropriate.

A newly created date field does not have an initial time or date set. Consider the following example, a form with a single, uninitialized date field in `DATE` mode:

```
Form f = new Form( "Empty DateField" );
DateField df = new DateField( "Date:", DateField.DATE );
f.append( df );
```

The form is shown in Figure 4.14. When the user selects the date field, the MIDP implementation displays a date editor. One possible implementation is shown in Figure 4.15. The MIDP specification does not describe how the date editor works, so other implementations are possible. After selecting a date, the form is updated with the new date information as shown in Figure 4.16. A date field in `TIME` or `DATE_TIME` mode would behave similarly but with different editors. Note that the three-argument date field constructor enables you to specify a time zone that the field should use for its calculations—the two-argument constructor uses the default time zone for the device.

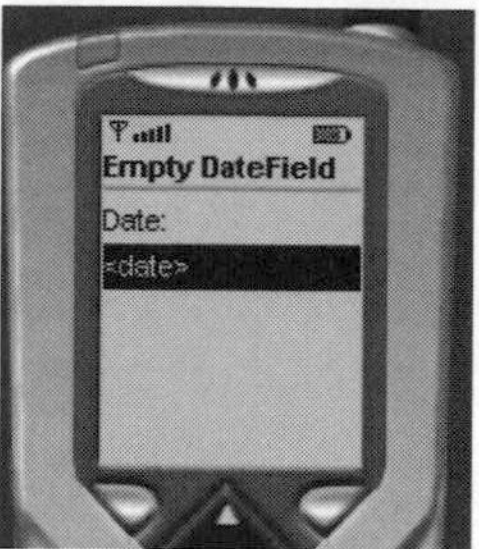

Figure 4.14 An uninitialized date field.

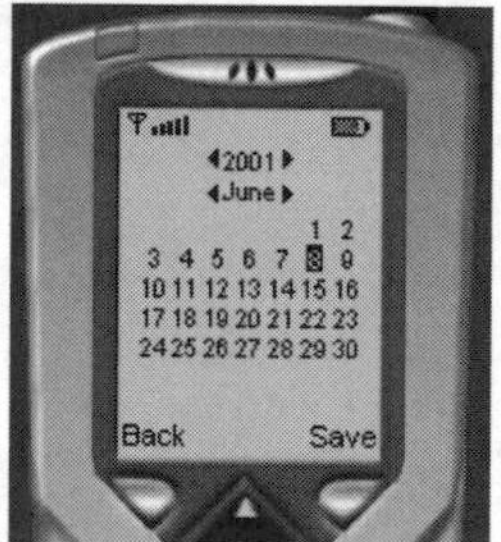

Figure 4.15 A date editor.

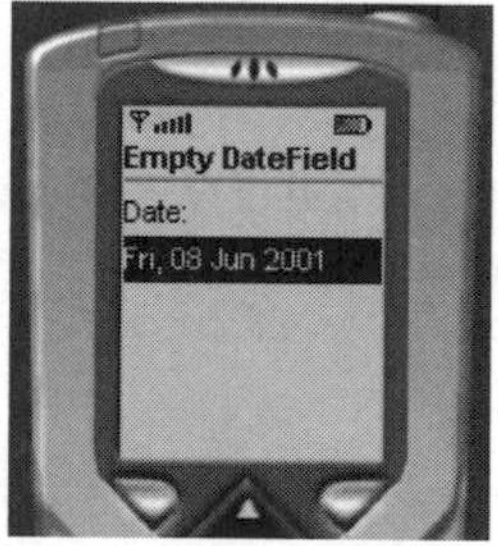

Figure 4.16 The date field after selecting a date with the date editor.

To set a specific date and/or time, call the `setDate` method, passing a `java.util.Date` object as an argument. A `Date` represents a moment in time as an offset (in milliseconds) from January 1, 1970 at 00:00:00 GMT. This is where the `java.util.Calendar` class comes into play, because it enables you to operate on dates and times by using more natural values. Here is how to initialize a date field to a specific date and time:

```
DateField df = new DateField( "A date and time:", DateField.DATE_TIME );
Calendar c = Calendar.getInstance();
c.set( Calendar.MONTH, Calendar.AUGUST );
c.set( Calendar.DATE, 12 );
```

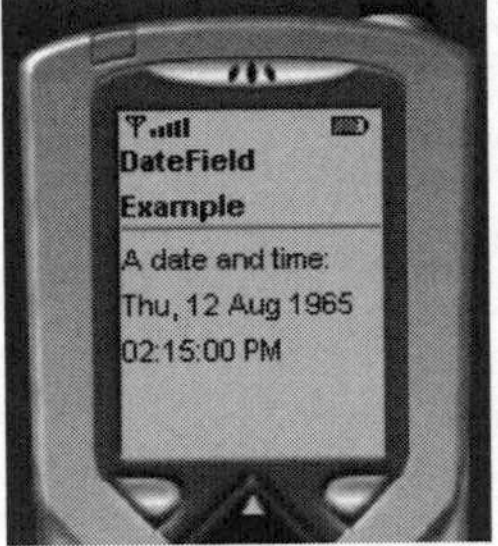

Figure 4.17 A date field initialized to a specific time and date.

```
c.set( Calendar.YEAR, 1965 );
c.set( Calendar.HOUR_OF_DAY, 14 );
c.set( Calendar.MINUTE, 15 );
c.set( Calendar.SECOND, 45 );
c.set( Calendar.MILLISECOND, 0 );
df.setDate( c.getTime() );
```

The initialized date field is shown in Figure 4.17. Call `getDate` at any time to obtain the current date or time stored by the date field. Again, the `Calendar` class can be used to convert the raw `Date` value returned by `getDate` into normal dates and times.

Gauge Items

The `Gauge` class uses a bar graph to display a value within a range. Its definition is as follows:

```
package javax.microedition.lcdui;

public class Gauge
     extends Item {
     // Constructors
     public Gauge( String label, boolean interactive, int maxValue,
             int initialValue );

     // Methods
     public int getMaxValue();
     public int getValue();
     public boolean isInteractive();
     public void setMaxValue( int maxValue );
     public void setValue( int value );
}
```

A gauge has a minimum value of 0 and a maximum value as defined by the application. The current value of the gauge is always between the minimum and maximum values. Gauges can be interactive or non-interactive; only interactive gauges can have their values changed by the user. Here is an example of a non-interactive gauge that displays the value 5 in the range 0 to 10:

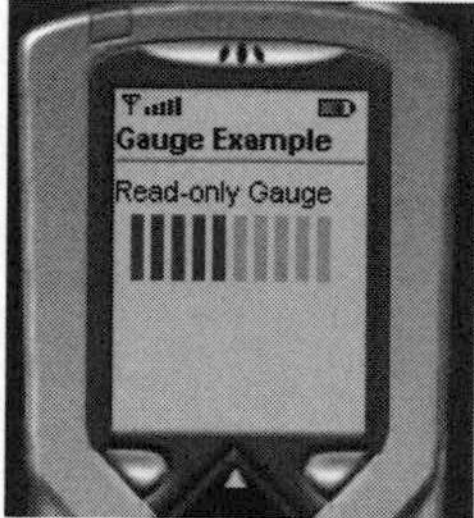

Figure 4.18 A non-interactive gauge.

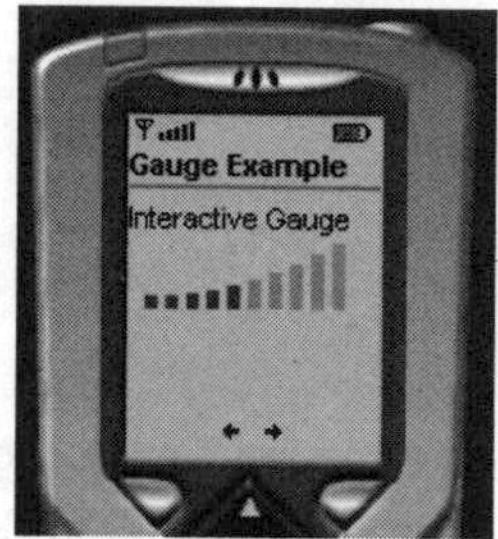

Figure 4.19 An interactive gauge.

```
Form f = new Form( "Gauge Example" );
Gauge g = new Gauge( "Read-only Gauge", false, 10, 5 );
f.append( g );
```

This gauge is shown in Figure 4.18. Changing the constructor's second parameter to `true` makes the gauge interactive, as shown in Figure 4.19, enabling the user to adjust the range by using buttons on the keypad. The `getValue` and `setValue` methods get and set the gauge's current value, adjusting the bar graph accordingly.

ImageItem Items

The `ImageItem` class displays an image. Its definition is as follows:

```
package javax.microedition.lcdui;

public class ImageItem
    extends Item {
    // Constructors
    public ImageItem( String label, Image img, int layout,
            String altText );

    // Methods
    public String getAltText();
    public Image getImage();
    public int getLayout();
```

```
    public void setAltText( String altText );
    public void setImage( Image img );
    public void setLayout( int layout );

    // Fields
    public static final int LAYOUT_CENTER = 3;
    public static final int LAYOUT_DEFAULT = 0;
    public static final int LAYOUT_LEFT = 1;
    public static final int LAYOUT_NEWLINE_AFTER = 512;
    public static final int LAYOUT_NEWLINE_BEFORE = 256;
    public static final int LAYOUT_RIGHT = 2;
}
```

The layout of an image item can be controlled to a limited degree. The item can be placed on the left or right side of the form or centered on the form. Here is a simple example:

```
Image image = ...;
ImageItem item = new ImageItem( null, image,
                                ImageItem.LAYOUT_LEFT, "!" );
Form f = new Form( "Start" );
f.append( "Press " );
f.append( item );
f.append( " to start" );
```

The resulting form is shown in Figure 4.20. You can also specify whether the image item should be placed on a separate line and whether any items that follow should also be on a separate line. Modify this example by changing the layout value:

```
ImageItem item = new ImageItem( null, image,
                                ImageItem.LAYOUT_CENTER |
                                ImageItem.LAYOUT_NEWLINE_BEFORE |
                                ImageItem.LAYOUT_NEWLINE_AFTER,
                                "!" );
```

The result is shown in Figure 4.21. Notice how the image is now centered on a separate line. In general, you can OR either or both of LAYOUT_NEWLINE_AFTER and LAYOUT_NEWLINE_BEFORE with one of LAYOUT_LEFT, LAY-OUT_RIGHT, or LAYOUT_CENTER. A default layout, LAYOUT_DEFAULT, cannot be combined with any other value. Note

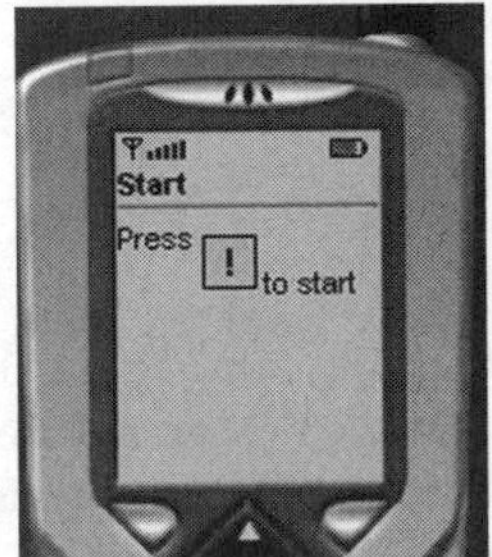

Figure 4.20 An image item.

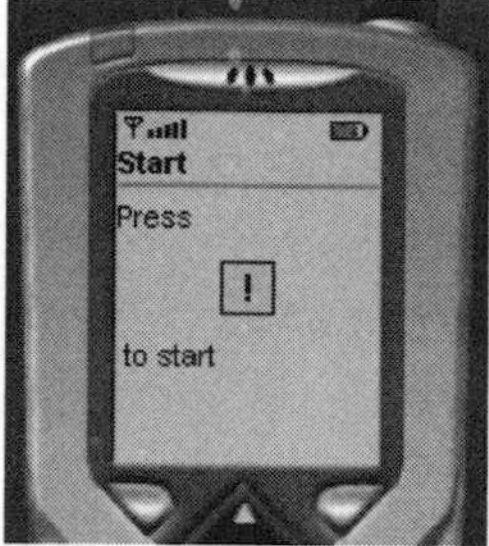

Figure 4.21 A centered image item.

that any layout you specify is merely a hint to the form; it is not obliged to follow any specific layout.

Not all devices support images, so for those that do not, you can specify some alternate text to display in place of the image.

StringItem Items

The `StringItem` class displays a string of text. Its definition is as follows:

```
package javax.microedition.lcdui;

public class StringItem
    extends Item {
    // Constructors
    public StringItem( String label, String text );

    // Methods
    public String getText();
    public void setText( String text );
}
```

A string item is the simplest of form items. The form is responsible for wrapping the text and respecting any embedded newlines in the string. If the string is too large to display on the form, the system must provide a way to scroll the form's contents or otherwise display the entire string. Here is a form with several string items on it:

```
Form f = new Form( "Strings" );
f.append( "This is an implicit string item. " );
f.append( "Some more text.\n" );
f.append( new StringItem( null, "Text on another line." ) );
```

Note that the `Form` class provides two methods for appending a `StringItem`. One of the methods takes as an argument an `Item` (or `StringItem`) while the second method is a helper method that takes as an argument a `String` from which a `StringItem` is created before the actual `append` operation takes place.

The form is shown in Figure 4.22.

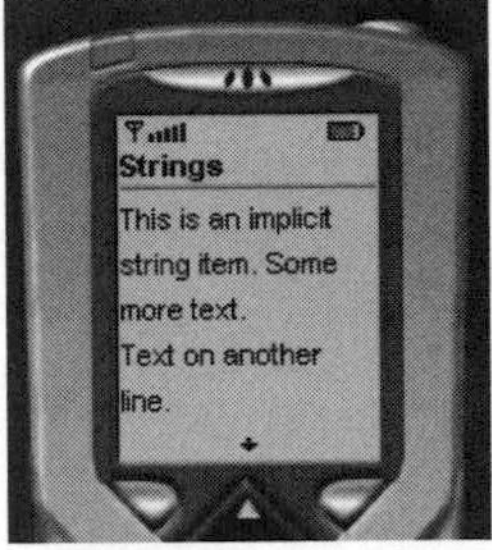

Figure 4.22 A form with string items.

TextField Items

The final item class, `TextField`, displays editable text. Its definition mirrors that of `TextBox`:

```
package javax.microedition.lcdui;

public class TextField
    extends Item {
    // Constructors
    public TextField( String label, String text, int maxSize,
            int constraints );

    // Methods
    public void delete( int offset, int length );
    public int getCaretPosition();
    public int getChars( char[] data );
    public int getConstraints();
    public int getMaxSize();
    public String getString();
    public void insert( String src, int position );
    public void insert( char[] data, int offset, int length,
            int position );
    public void setChars( char[] data, int offset, int length );
    public void setConstraints( int constraints );
    public int setMaxSize( int maxSize );
    public void setString( String text );
    public int size();

    // Fields
    public static final int ANY = 0;
    public static final int CONSTRAINT_MASK = 65535;
    public static final int EMAILADDR = 1;
    public static final int NUMERIC = 2;
    public static final int PASSWORD = 65536;
    public static final int PHONENUMBER = 3;
```

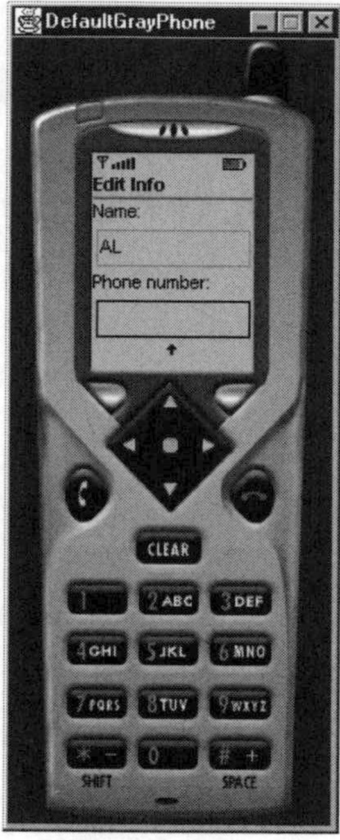

Figure 4.23 A form with two text fields.

```
    public static final int URL = 4;
}
```

In fact, its behavior is identical to that of `TextBox`, except of course that the editable text is a field on a form instead of an entire screen. To prompt the user for a name and phone number, for example, you can use two text fields on the same form:

```
TextField name = new TextField( "Name:", "AL", 30, TextField.ANY );
TextField phone = new TextField( "Phone Number:", null, 30,
                                  TextField.PHONENUMBER );
Form f = new Form( "Enter Info" );
f.append( name );
f.append( phone );
```

The result is shown in Figure 4.23. The application can retrieve the current value of a text field at any time by calling its `getString` method.

Summary

We have covered a lot of material in this chapter, but we are not done with the user interface classes yet. The next chapter continues our exploration of the MIDP UI classes but from a more practical standpoint: We will combine the classes to build complete user interface examples.

CHAPTER 5

User Interface Examples

In the previous chapter, we introduced the Mobile Information Device Profile (MIDP) user interface (UI) classes. In this chapter, we will build concrete examples that use those classes. Most of our time is spent building the user interface for a business application. The application is an email client and uses most of the high-level application programming interfaces (APIs). We also present a simple game to demonstrate the use of the low-level API. We end with an example that combines the high-level and low-level APIs to display multiple, simultaneous alerts—something that the MIDP does not directly support.

A Simple Email Client

Our first example is an email client—an application that enables the user of a device to read, create, and send email messages. This kind of application is easy to understand, but its user interface is complex enough to exercise most of the components shown in Figure 5.1. The email client is fairly basic, but it enables a user to log in, access the inbox, read a specific message, and send new messages.

The email client is one piece of a client-server solution. The server piece is a servlet or JSP running in a Web server. The client communicates with the Web server by using the Hypertext Transfer Protocol (HTTP), exchanging information as Extensible Markup Language (XML) documents. Although some of the communication code is presented here, we also discuss it in other chapters. See Chapter 6, "Network Communication," for information on wireless networking and Chapter 9, "Using XML in MIDP Applications," for information about XML. The code for the servlet is available online from the book's Web site. Note that this email client could be improved in several ways; for

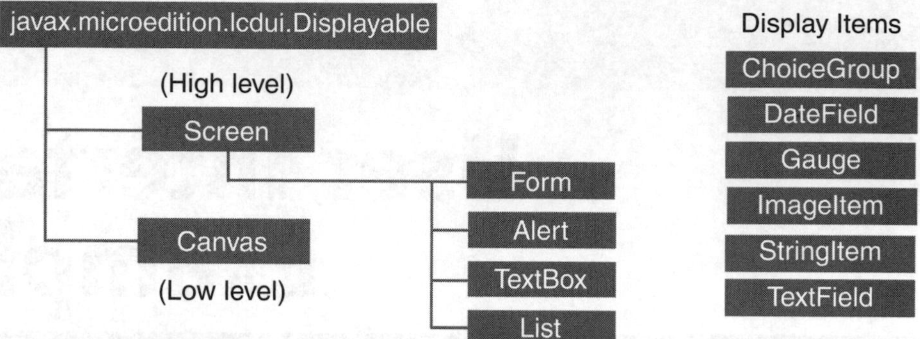

Figure 5.1 The core MIDP user-interface components.

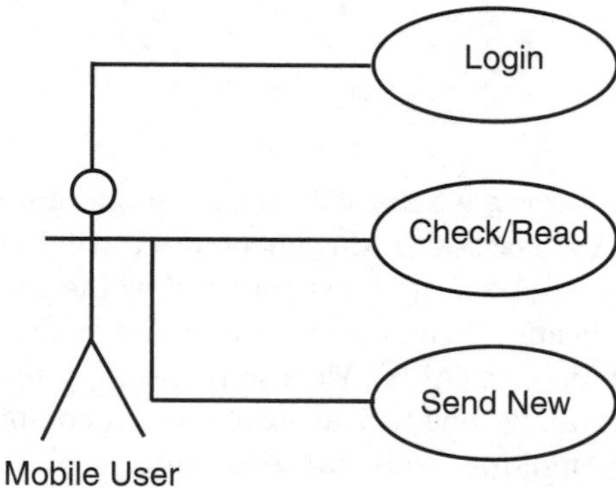

Figure 5.2 UML use-case diagram for a sample email MIDlet.

example, by modifying it to store messages locally on the device. But its main purpose is to demonstrate how to build a moderately complex user interface.

Our sample email client has a very simple UML use-case diagram, as shown in Figure 5.2. This email client has seven basic user-interface elements:

- A welcome screen
- An authentication or login screen
- An options/actions screen
- An inbox screen
- A details screen
- A composition screen
- An activity indicator screen

The rest of this section describes the screens and the code behind them.

The Welcome Screen

The first screen of our sample application is the welcome screen. This alert screen displays an image plus some text, welcoming the user to our application. Here are the required steps:

- Load the image from the JAR file by using `Image.createImage`.
- Construct the `Alert` instance.
- Display the alert by using the two-argument form of `Display.setCurrent`.

The screen is shown in Figure 5.3 and is coded as follows:

```
// Display the welcome screen

Alert welcomeAlert;
try {
    Image img = Image.createImage("/og.png");

    welcomeAlert = new Alert("Welcome",
                         "Ortiz-Giguere-Wiley",
                         img,
                         null);
}
catch(Exception e) {
    System.out.println("Error w/ displaying welcome
                    screen" + e);
}

// Make welcomeAlert the current displayable, upon
// its dismissal, display the loginForm

display.setCurrent( welcomeAlert, loginForm );
```

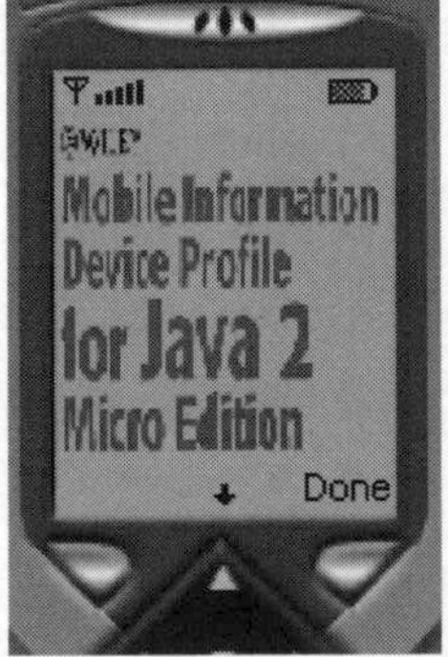

Figure 5.3 The welcome screen.

The alert uses the default timeout value. Insert the following line after constructing the alert to make it modal:

```
welcomeAlert.setTimeout( Alert.FOREVER );
```

Use modal alerts if it is critical that the user reads the alert. Note that if the message is too long and/or the image is too big for the display, the system might make the alert modal and provide the user with a way to view the hidden parts of the alert.

The other screens follow a similar pattern: first you create a screen, then you add commands and items to it, and then you set and write the event handlers. Typical steps when creating a high-level API screen are as follows:

- Create Command objects.
- Create a `Screen` subclass (`List`, `Form`, and so on).
- Add (append) the defined commands to the screen.
- Set up the command and/or item listener event handler.
- Write the command and/or item listener event handler.

The Login Screen

The login screen prompts the user for a username and a password, as shown in Figure 5.4. Once the user enters the information and presses the OK button, the user is authenticated.

This screen is a form with two text fields: one for the username and one for the password, and the other for a command. First, we create the command object:

```
private static final Command okCmd =
           new Command("OK", Command.OK, 1 );
```

Remember what the arguments represent: the first argument is the label, the second is the type, and the third is the command priority. The `Command.OK` type is used because it most closely matches the purpose of the command. The type and priority are just

Figure 5.4 The login screen.

hints to the display manager. How a command is actually displayed is entirely up to the implementation.

Next, define data members to hold the username and password:

```
private String username  = null;
private String password  = null;
```

Similarly, define two text fields, one for each value:

```
private static TextField userField = new
               TextField("User Name:",
                         null,
                         30,
                         TextField.ANY);

private static TextField pwdField = new
               TextField("Password:",
               null,
               30,
               TextField.PASSWORD);
```

Note that the password field's constraint is set to `TextField.PASSWORD` in order to demonstrate how a password field works. As we discussed in the last chapter, however, you might not want to use the `PASSWORD` constraint because it complicates user input.

Next, create the login form and append the text fields to it:

```
loginForm = new Form("Welcome");
loginForm.append(userField);
loginForm.append(pwdField);
```

Another way is to create an array of `Item` objects and pass it into the form's constructor:

```
// Alternative implementation
private static Item[] loginTextFieldArray =
                           { userField, pwdField };


.....

loginForm = new Form( "Welcome", loginTextFieldArray );
```

Now, add the command to the form and assign a command listener:

```
loginForm.addCommand(okCmd);
loginForm.setCommandListener(this);
```

The assumption here is that the containing class implements the `CommandListener` interface and defines a `commandAction` method:

```
public class Email extends MIDlet
                   implements CommandListener {

    public void commandAction(Command c,
                              Displayable d) {
        if( d == loginForm ){
            boolean rc;

            if (c == okCmd) {
                username = userField.getString();
                password = pwdField.getString();

                // authenticate the user
                rc = authenticate(username, password);

                if (rc == false )
                    display.setCurrent(authFailedAlert,
                                      emailChoices);
                else
                    display.setCurrent(emailChoices);
            }
        } else {
            ..... // handle other displayables here
        }
    }

    ..... // other code omitted
}
```

The `commandAction` method is called whenever the user presses the OK button on the login form. The method acts differently based on which displayable initiated the command. For the login form, it gets the username and password from the text fields and calls an authentication routine (not shown here) to validate the input and to login the user. If the authentication fails, an alert (not shown here) is displayed; otherwise, the choices screen is displayed.

As a side note, recall that an application can also be notified of changes to interactive items as they occur. Implement the `ItemListener` interface and register the listener by calling the form's `setItemStateListener` method. For example, the `Email` class could implement `itemListener` as follows:

First, indicate that the class implements `ItemStateListener`:

```
public class Email extends MIDlet implements CommandListener,
ItemStateListener.
```

Next, define the `itemStateChanged` method, which will be invoked by the display manager as `Item` events occur:

```
public void itemStateChanged(Item i) {
    if(i == userField) {
```

```
            System.out.println("itemStateChanged / userField");
        }
        else
        if( i == pwdField ){
            System.out.println("itemStateChanged / pwdField");
        }
    }
```

The Options Screen

The options screen gives the user the choice of reading or composing email, as shown in Figure 5.5. Selecting Read initiates the wireless retrieval of email messages from the server by using HTTP and XML. Selecting Compose enables the user to enter a new email message that is wirelessly delivered to the server over HTTP. Please refer to Chapter 6 on how to use HTTP for networking. Please refer to Chapter 9 on how to leverage XML.

Creating the Screen

This screen is a `List` with two `Commands`. As with the login screen, first we create the command objects for the OK and Back commands. Note that commands can be re-used across screens, in other words, the following commands can be the same as the ones we created for the login screen:

```
private static final Command okCmd =
          new Command("OK", Command.OK, 1);
private static final Command backCmd =
          new Command("Back", Command.BACK, 1);
```

Next, create the list of email choices. To minimize the number of keystrokes when a selection is made, an implicit list is used. Recall that in an implicit list, a selection causes immediate notification if a `CommandListener` is registered:

Figure 5.5 The email options screen.

```
emailChoices = new List(
                  "Choose",
                   List.IMPLICIT);
emailChoices.append("Read", null);
emailChoices.append("New", null);
```

An alternative way to create the list is to create an array of strings with the choices to display and to pass it to the list's constructor:

```
private static String[] choiceStrings = { "Read","New" };
emailChoices = new List(
                  "Choose",
                  List.IMPLICIT,
                  choiceStrings,
                  null);
```

Yet another way to accomplish the same results is to use a `ChoiceGroup` within a `Form`. `ChoiceGroup` and `List` behave similarly, but you would use a form when you need to display multiple items on the same screen, such as multiple lists of choices or a combination of lists and input fields. Because in our example we have only one set of choices to display, it is simpler to use the `List` class.

Now, add the commands to the list and assign a command listener:

```
emailChoices.addCommand(backCmd);
emailChoices.addCommand(okCmd);
emailChoices.setCommandListener(this);
```

Note that you could create a helper method that allows you to quickly append fields and add commands and set the command listener for you. Bytecode saving techniques such as this are important on resource-constrained devices. Let's take a look at what a helper method for adding commands would look like:

```
private void setCommands(Displayable displayable,
                         Command commands[],
                         CommandListener listener) {

    for(int i=0;i<commands.length;i++) {
      displayable.addCommand(commands[i]);
    }

    displayable.setCommandListener(listener);
  }
```

Then, instead of adding individual commands as we did above, creating a list is done like this:

```
static String[] emailChoiceStrings = { "Read","New" };
static Command[] emailOptionsCmds = {backCmd, okCmd};
emailChoices = new List(
                  "Choose",
```

```
                        List.IMPLICIT,
                        emailChoiceStrings,
                        null);
UIHelper.setCommands(emailChoices, emailOptionsCmds, this);
```

Similar techniques can be used for other repetitive tasks such as appending items to forms.

To process the commands, implement the `CommandListener` interface and the `commandAction` method:

```
public void commandAction(Command c,
                          Displayable d) {

  ..... // other Displayable code here

  /*
   * Handle Commands for emailChoices List Screen
   */
    if (d == emailChoices) {

      if (c == backCmd)
          display.setCurrent(loginForm); // go back
      else
      if (c == okCmd) {

         // get user selection Index
         int i = emailChoices.getSelectedIndex();
         switch (i) {

         case READ:

            /*
             * Retrieving email over the network is a long
             * task. EmailRetrievalTask is a Runnable that
             * fetches email in the background and displays
             * them when done.
             */
            EmailRetrievalTask ert = new EmailRetrievalTask();
            ert.go();    // start thread
            break;

            case COMPOSE:

            display.setCurrent(composeForm);
            break;
         }

      } // okCmd
  } // emailChoices Displayable

  ..... // other Displayable code here

}
```

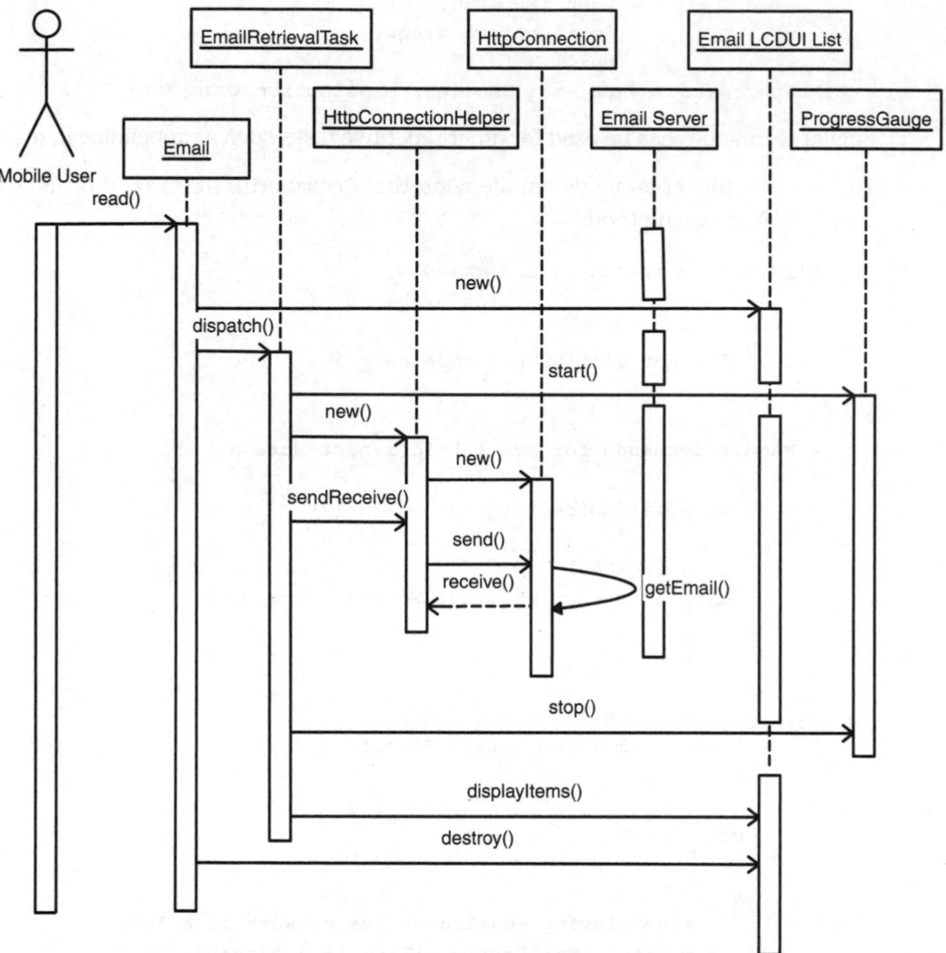

Figure 5.6 The UML sequence diagram for retrieving email.

Pressing OK or Back results in `commandAction` being invoked where the source of the command (a `Displayable` object) and the command in question are identified. If the command is Back, the user is taken to the previous screen, which is the `loginScreen` form. If the command is OK, then the user's selection is determined: for Read, a thread of execution (`EmailRetrievalTask`) to retrieve email is started because reading from the network is a slow task; and for "New email," the user is directly taken to the compose email screen.

The UML sequence diagram shown in Figure 5.6 depicts the sequence of steps that take place when retrieving email in response to the user's Read request.

The EmailRetrievalTask Class

Let's look at the `EmailRetrievalTask`, the background task/thread that is responsible for retrieving email messages and presenting the results to the user.

Perform Network I/O on a Separate Thread

Any methods called from within `commandAction` must return quickly to ensure that the user interface remains responsive. Perform long operations on a separate thread. Network I/O is a good example of the kind of processing that should be dispatched in a thread. Not only does it ensure a friendly, non-blocking user interface, but it also makes it possible for you to display and update the operation's progress.

```
/**
 * This Runnable/TimerTask retrieves email headers and
 * bodies from server using the HttpConnectionHelper class.
 * This runnable can run on the foreground or run in
 * the background while retrieving then coming to the
 * foreground to present results.
 * For HTTP I/O use the HttpConnectionHelper class.
 */
class EmailRetrievalTask extends TimerTask {

    private Thread  th;
    private HttpConnectionHelper hch;
    private boolean visible = true;

    /**
     * Constructor
     */
    EmailRetrievalTask() {
        th = new Thread(this);
    }

    /**
     * Start the email retrieval task
     */
    public void go() {
        th.start();
    }

    /**
     * Sets the visible (vs. background) property
     */
    public void setVisible(boolean v) {
        visible = v;
    }

    /**
```

```
     * This Runnable's run method
     */
    public void run() {

        String response   = null; // http response
        ProgressGauge pg = null; // progress indicator
        Hashtable params = null; // URL parameters
        emailVector      = null; // vector of emessages

        // dispatch progress indicator, if this thread
        // has been dispatched in foreground/visible mode
        if ( visible == true)
            pg = new ProgressGauge("Retrieving email",
                                   display);

        // Build get message query string
        params = new Hashtable();
        params.put("username", username);
        params.put("password", password);
        params.put("action",   "get_messages");

        // Clean up existing UI list of email messages.
        // Send HTTP request and wait for response.
        // Then parse the response and re-build UI list.
        try {
            int i, sz;

            // clean up the emailMsgs List
            sz = emailMsgs.size();
            for (i=0; i<sz; i++) {
                emailMsgs.delete(0);
            }

            // Set/compose targetURL and send HTTP request,
            // wait for response.
            String targetURL =
                "http://"+serverURL+":"+serverPort;
            hch = new HttpConnectionHelper(targetURL,
                       EMAIL_CONTROLLER,
                       params);
            response = hch.sendReceive();

            // parse the response.
            // we have 2 implementations, one for NanoXML
            // and one for kXML... try the one you want
            // Results (EmailMessages) are put Into a
            // Vector for consumption.
            emailVector =
              EmailParser_NanoXML.parse(response.trim());
            // uncomment to parse using kXML
```

```
//                 emailVector =
//                   EmailParser_kXML.parse(response.trim());

                   // re-build UI list of email subjects
                   for (i = 0; i < emailVector.size(); i++) {
                      EmailMessage em = (EmailMessage)
                                        emailVector.elementAt(i);
                      emailMsgs.append(em.getSubject(), null);
                   }

                   lastEmailRetrieval =
                      System.currentTimeMillis();
               }
               catch (Exception e) {
                   ErrorAlert ea = new ErrorAlert(
                           "Error processing Email",
                           "An error was encountered while
                              retrieving email",
                           e,
                           null,
                           display);
               }
               finally {
                   params = null;
                   try {
                     hch.close();
                   }
                   catch( IOException ioe ) {
                   }
                   if( visible == true) {
                       pg.stop(); // notify to stop
                       display.setCurrent(emailMsgs); // display
                   }
               }
           } // run()
       } //  EmailRetrievalTask()
```

Note that EmailRetrievalTask extends TimerTask, which in turn implements Runnable. This function enables us to schedule EmailRetrieval-Task as a cyclic background task. The following code fragment shows how to schedule EmailRetrievalTask as a task:

```
private static long REFRESH_TIME = 1000*60*3; // 3 min.
private Timer backgroundEmailRetrievalTimer;
EmailRetrievalTask backgroundEmailRetrievalTask;
backgroundEmailRetrievalTask = new
            EmailRetrievalTask();
backgroundEmailRetrievalTimer = new Timer();
backgroundEmailRetrievalTimer.schedule(
                backgroundEmailRetrievalTask,
            0,
            REFRESH_TIME);
```

First, define a variable that holds the repeat every time in milliseconds. Next, define a `Timer` object that enables us to schedule threads and an `Email-RetrievalTask` object, which is the actual thread that will retrieve the email. Next, create the `Email-RetrievalTask` and `Timer` objects and schedule `backgroundEmailRetrieval-Task` to run every `REFRESH_TIME` milliseconds.

The Inbox Screen

The Inbox screen displays the email messages that are in the inbox, as shown in Figure 5.7. The user can choose which email to view in more detail.

This screen is a `List` with two `Commands` similar to the email options screen. In fact, they are almost identical except for the screen title and the list's content.

First, we create the command objects for the OK and the Back command just as we did before, ideally reusing the same `Command` objects. Next, create the list of email messages. In this case, we use the two-argument constructor because we do not know the contents of the list until the messages are read. An exclusive list is used instead of an implicit list because only one email message can be selected at a time, but exclusive mode provides better visual separation between the individual list elements:

```
emailMsgs = new List("InBox", List.EXCLUSIVE);
```

Next, add the OK and Back commands:

```
emailMsgs.addCommand(backCmd);
emailMsgs.addCommand(okCmd);
```

As previously covered, set the command listener for the screen:

```
emailMsgs.setCommandListener(this);
```

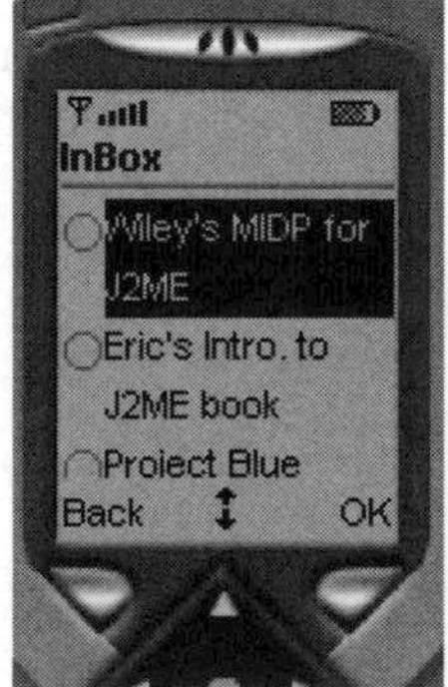

Figure 5.7 The inbox screen.

And, as with previous screens, implement the `CommandListener` interface and define the `commandAction` method. If the Back command was selected, return to the previous screen (the options screen). If the selected command is OK, display the message details for the selected email:

```
public void commandAction(Command c,
                          Displayable d) {

   ..... // other Displayable code here

   // Handle event screen w/ email messages
   if (d == emailMsgs) {
      if (c == backCmd) {
          display.setCurrent(emailChoices);
      }
      else if (c == okCmd) {
         int sz = detailsForm.size();

         // clean form
         for (int i = 0; i<sz; i++) {
             detailsForm.delete(0);
         }

         // Determine user selection.
         int i = emailMsgs.getSelectedIndex();

         if ( i >= 0 ) {
           EmailMessage em =
               (EmailMessage)emailVector.elementAt(i);

           // get details for selected EMAIL from vector
           detailsForm.setTitle(em.getSubject());
           detailsForm.append("DATE:"+em.getDate().trim() );
           detailsForm.append("\n");
           detailsForm.append("FROM: "+em.getFrom().trim());
           detailsForm.append("\n");
           detailsForm.append("MESSAGE:"+ em.getBody().trim());
         }
      }
      display.setCurrent(detailsForm);
   } // emailMsgs Displayable
}
```

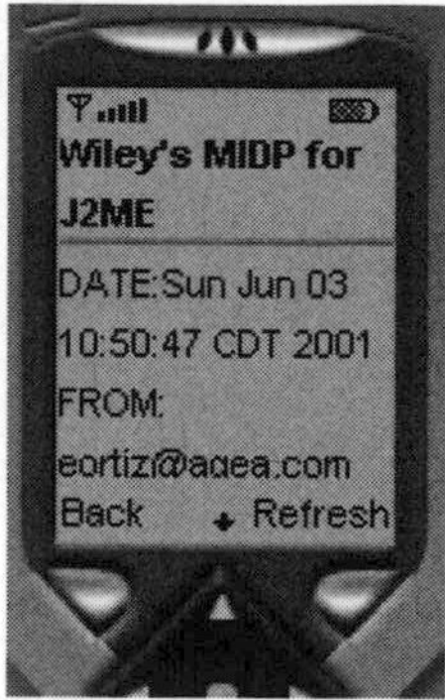

Figure 5.8 The email details screen.

The Email Details Screen

The email details screen gives the user the details or content of a given email message, as shown in Figure 5.8. Recall that the previous screen provided a list of email messages (the inbox) from which the user could select to view in more detail.

This screen is made of a form that contains three string items: the date, the sender's email address, and the message body field. This form also has two commands: Back and Refresh. The Back command takes the user back to the previous screen, `emailChoices`. The Refresh command re-fetches email messages and redisplays them. As with previous screens, first create the Back and Refresh commands:

```
private static final Command backCmd = new
            Command("Back",
            Command.BACK,
            1);
private static final Command refreshCmd = new
            Command("Refresh",
            Command.SCREEN,
            1);
```

Note that the type of refresh command is `Command.SCREEN`. Use `Command.SCREEN` to indicate an application-defined command. Next, create the form, add the commands, and set the command listener:

```
detailsForm = new Form("Message");
detailsForm.addCommand(backCmd);
detailsForm.addCommand(refreshCmd);
detailsForm.setCommandListener(this);
```

Next, implement the command listener and define `commandAction`. Note that only one command listener is implemented per class. The following code fragment is part of `commandAction`:

```
public void commandAction(Command c,
                          Displayable d) {
   ..... // other Displayable code here

   if (d == detailsForm) {
      if (c == backCmd) {
         display.setCurrent(emailMsgs);
      } else if (c == refreshCmd) {
         EmailRetrievalTask ert = new EmailRetrievalTask();
         ert.go();
      }
   } // Email Details Displayable

   ..... // other Displayable code here
}
```

The command handling for this screen is very simple. If the Back command is selected, go back to the previous screen, which is the `emailMsgs` list of email messages. Otherwise, dispatch the `EmailRetrievalTask` to refresh the inbox list. We covered `EmailRetrievalTask` earlier in this chapter.

The Compose Screen

The compose email screen enables the user to create a new email message, as shown in Figure 5.9.

Creating the Screen

This screen is made up of a form, three text fields—for the "to," "subject," and "message-body" parts of the message—and two commands, Back and OK. If the Back command is selected, the user is taken to the previous screen, the email options screen. If OK is selected, a thread is dispatched to perform the actual network I/O. Recall that any methods called by `commandAction` must return quickly, and if not, you should dispatch a thread.

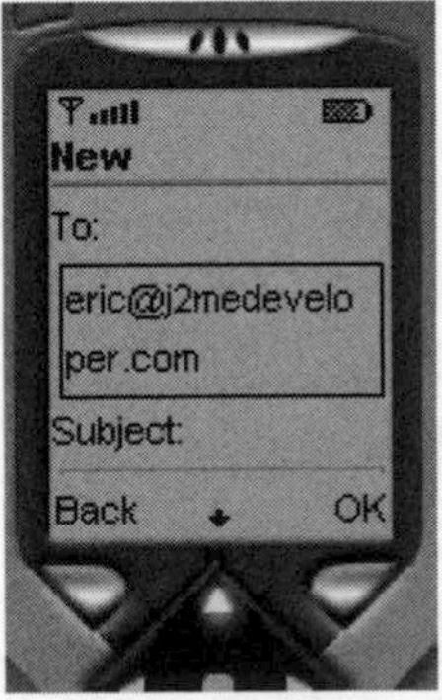

Figure 5.9 The compose email screen.

Create the text fields first (one for each part of the message). All of these text fields accept ANY type of character sequence, except the "to" field, which has an input constraint of EMAILADDR. Recall that input constraints are used to limit the type of input data:

```
private static TextField toField = new
          TextField("To:",
                   null,
                   30,
                   TextField.EMAILADDR);
private static TextField subjectField = new
           TextField("Subject:",
                     null,
                     30,
                     TextField.ANY);
private static TextField bodyField = new
           TextField("Message:",
                     null,
                     100,
                     TextField.ANY);
```

Next, create the command objects:

```
private static final Command okCmd = new
           Command("OK",
                  Command.OK,
                  1);
private static final Command backCmd = new
           Command("Back",
                  Command.BACK,
                  1);
```

Next create the form, append the text fields, and add the commands. Finally, set the command listener:

```
composeForm = new Form("New");
composeForm.append(toField);
composeForm.append(subjectField);
composeForm.append(bodyField);
composeForm.addCommand(backCmd);
composeForm.addCommand(okCmd);
composeForm.setCommandListener(this);
```

An alternative way of creating the form is using the two-argument constructor that enables us to create the form and append the text fields all in one call:

```
private static Item[] composeTextFieldArray =
                     {toField, subjectField, bodyField};
loginForm = new Form("New",
                     composeTextFieldArray);
```

```
composeForm.addCommand(backCmd);
loginForm.addCommand(okCmd);
loginForm.setCommandListener(this);
```

Next, add the following code fragment to the `commandAction` method. If Back is selected, take the user to the previous screen (the choices screen). If OK is selected, dispatch a thread to send the email:

```
if (d == composeForm) {

   if (c == backCmd) {
      display.setCurrent(emailChoices);
   }
   else
   if (c == okCmd) {
      EmailComposerTask ect = new EmailComposerTask();
      ect.go();
   }

} // Compose Email Displayable
```

Sometimes it is useful to store configuration data in property files, which enables your MIDlets to be easily configurable without having to rebuild them. You can store configuration data (name-value pairs) in the MIDlet suite's application descriptor. Our email example retrieves the user's email address from the descriptor by using the following code fragment:

```
// get "from" property. Configure this value as
// appropriate
String from = midlet.getAppProperty("UserEmail");
```

Let's look at the descriptor. Note the sequence of name/value pairs. Our email example uses `UserEmail` for the `from` field email address when sending email:

```
MIDlet-1: Email,, com.j2medeveloper.email.Email
MIDlet-Jar-Size: 34435
MIDlet-Jar-URL: midp-pdg.jar
MIDlet-Name: Email
MIDlet-Vendor: Ortiz-Giguere
MIDlet-Version: 1.0
ServerPort: 80
ServerURL: j2megw.j2medeveloper.com
UserEmail: eortiz@j2medeveloper.com
UserName: eortiz
UserPassword: de*43kfd
```

The EmailComposerTask Class

Let's look at `EmailComposerTask`, the class that is responsible for submitting the new email information over the wireless network to the server. This class uses a separate thread to send email:

```
/**
 * This task / thread of execution submits a new email
 *  to the email controller.
 */
class EmailComposerTask implements Runnable {

   Thread  th;

   /**
    * EmailComposerTask constructor
    */
   EmailComposerTask() {
      th = new Thread(this);
   }

   /**
    * EmailComposerTask go/start method
    */
    public void go() {
       th.start();
    }

    /*
     * run method for this Runnable
     */
    public void run() {
       HttpConnectionHelper hch;
       String response = null;

       // Dispatch ProgressGauge thread (activity Indicator)
       ProgressGauge pg = new ProgressGauge("Sending
                                    Email", display);

       // get "from" property. Configure this value as
       // appropriate
       String from = midlet.getAppProperty("UserEmail");

       // Build XML request.  Enclose message body within
       // a CDATA section (i.e. Ignore/don't parse)
       StringBuffer xmlReq = new StringBuffer();
       xmlReq.append("<?xml version=\"1.0\" ?>");
       xmlReq.append("<emailmessages count=\"1\">");
       xmlReq.append("<emailmessage>");
       xmlReq.append("<to>");
       xmlReq.append(toField.getString());
       xmlReq.append("</to>");
       xmlReq.append("<from>");
       xmlReq.append(from);
       xmlReq.append("</from>"); // from "property" file
       xmlReq.append("<subject>");
       xmlReq.append(subjectField.getString());
```

```
xmlReq.append("</subject>");
xmlReq.append("<body><![CDATA]");
xmlReq.append(bodyField.getString());
xmlReq.append("[]></body>");
xmlReq.append("</emailmessage>");
xmlReq.append("</emailmessages>");

// Build request parameters (name/value pairs)
Hashtable params = new Hashtable();
params.put("username", username);
params.put("password", password);
params.put("action",   "send_message");

/*
 * try to send the email
 */
try {

   // set/compose targetURL and send HTTP request,
   // wait for response.
   String targetURL =
         "http://"+serverURL+":"+serverPort;
   hch = new HttpConnectionHelper(
                                 targetURL,
                                 EMAIL_CONTROLLER,
                                 params);
   hch.setMessageBody(xmlReq); // use POST
   response = hch.sendReceive();

}
catch (Exception e) {

   ErrorAlert ea = new ErrorAlert(
     "Error processing email",
     "An error was encountered while sending new email",
     e,
     null,
     display);
}
finally {
   xmlReq = null;
   try {
      hch.close();
   }
   catch( IOException ioe ) {
    ..... // handle the exception
   }
   pg.stop();  // notify progress gauge to quit
   display.setCurrent(emailChoices);
}
```

```
        } // run()
    } // EmailComposerTask()
```

The `EmailComposerTask` that we just covered provides a way of sending email by using our own XML API. An alternative approach is covered in Chapter 9, "Using XML in MIDP Applications," where we show how to send email by using the *Simple Object Access Protocol* (SOAP).

The Activity Indicator Screen

The activity indicator provides visual feedback to the user that processing is actually occurring, as shown in Figure 5.10. This screen is usually displayed when performing lengthy network tasks, such as reading or sending email over the wireless network.

The activity indicator screen is a form with a gauge that is used to provide the user with a visual indication of network activity. First, define a class that extends `Form` and that implements `Runnable`:

```
public class ProgressGauge extends Form implements Runnable
```

In the constructor, create the thread of execution and assign to it the lowest priority possible. The activity indicator is a non-critical task, and as such we want to ensure that its execution has minimal impact on other threads. Create the gauge item and append it to the form. Start the thread, catching any exception:

```
/**
 * Constructor
 * @param title The title to display
 * @param disp The display
 */
public ProgressGauge(String title, Display d) {
    super("Please wait...");
    try {
        display = d;
        th = new Thread(this);
        th.setPriority(Thread.MIN_PRIORITY);
```

Figure 5.10 The activity screen.

```
            g = new Gauge(title, false, 1000, 0);
            append(g);
            start();

        }
        catch (Exception e) {
          ..... // exception code
        }
    }
```

Next, define start and stop public methods so that the creator of the activity indicator can start and stop the thread. Only start the thread if it is not already active, of course:

```
/**
 *  Start thread of execution.
 */
public void start() {
   // only start the thread if not alive
   if(th.isAlive() == false)
     th.start();
}

/**
 *  Stop this thread of execution
 */
public void stop() {
   bye = true;
}
```

Next, we have the actual thread body. This thread loops until notified to stop. Its logic is simple: increment the gauge value until its maximum value is reached, reset the gauge back to 0, and repeat the cycle. The effect is a gauge that moves from left to right, indicating network activity. The thread can be stopped gracefully by calling the stop method. The thread yields and sleeps to minimize its impact on other more important threads:

```
/**
 * This Runnable's run method
 */
public void run() {

   int i;
   display.setCurrent(this);

   // do until notified to stop/quit
   while (bye == false) {

  for(i=0; i < g.getMaxValue(); i++) {
     g.setValue(i);
```

```
          th.yield();
        }
        g.setValue(0);
        try {
          th.sleep(500); // for half a millisecond
        }
            catch(InterruptedException e) {
              .....
            }
        }
        g = null;
    } // run
```

This section completes the sample email application. The complete source code can be found on the book's Web site at `www.wiley.com/compbooks/ortiz`.

A Simple Game

The next example demonstrates how to use the low-level user interface API to build a game by drawing directly onto the display and responding to raw input events. The game is *very* simple: you move a spaceship around the display to avoid falling stars. The game screen is shown in Figure 5.11. Although very simple, the game does illustrate a few important points:

- How to serialize events with `Display.callSerially`
- How to do double-buffering if the system does not support it
- How to use timers
- How to perform general drawing and event handling

The game uses a single screen to display everything. Again, it is not a complicated game, so do not expect much out of it. The remainder of this section describes the three classes that make up the game.

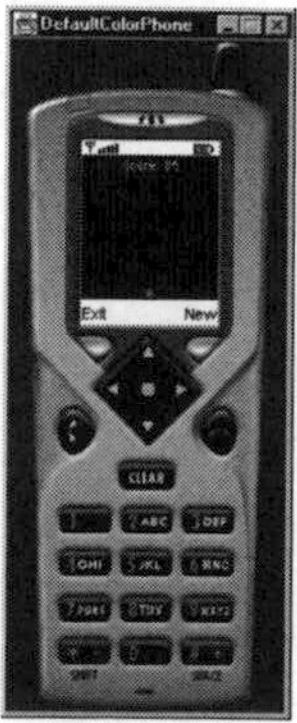

Figure 5.11 The game screen.

The SimpleGame Class

We start by defining the MIDlet class, `SimpleGame`. Most of the game logic is actually in the `GameScreen` inner class, which we will look at later. The MIDlet class starts as follows:

```
public class SimpleGame extends MIDlet
                        implements CommandListener {

    Display     display; // MIDlet's display
    GameScreen  gameScreen; // the game canvas

    // Common commands

    Command     exitCommand = new Command( "Exit",
                                           Command.EXIT,
                                           1 );
    Command     newGameCommand = new Command( "New",
                                              Command.SCREEN,
                                              1 );

    ..... // other code here
}
```

Again, because most of the logic is in another class, the MIDlet class defines just a few data members: a reference to the `Display`, a reference to the canvas used to display the game, and a couple of commands. Because the game is simple, we only have two commands to worry about: an Exit command to quit the MIDlet and a New command to start a new game. The logic for the commands is of course handled in the `commandAction` method, which immediately follows the empty constructor:

```
public SimpleGame() {
    // all initialization done in initMIDlet
}

public void commandAction( Command c, Displayable d ){
    if( c == exitCommand ){
        exitMIDlet();
    } else if( c == newGameCommand ){
        gameScreen.newGame();
    }
}
```

Obviously, the command handling would be more complex if the game had several screens.

After the constructor (which is empty because we defer all initialization to the `initMIDlet` method, as explained in Chapter 3) and the `commandAction` method are defined,we are left with the methods to start, stop, and pause the MIDlet. Let's start with `destroyApp`:

```
protected void destroyApp( boolean unconditional )
                   throws MIDletStateChangeException {
    if( !unconditional && gameScreen != null &&
        gameScreen.isActive() ){
        throw new MIDletStateChangeException();
    }

    exitMIDlet();
}
```

What is interesting here is that if `destroyApp` is called with its `unconditional` argument set to `false`, we abort the MIDlet destruction as long as a game is active. You abort by throwing a `MIDletStateChangeException`. If no game is active or the abort request is unconditional, we call `exitMIDlet` to clean things up:

```
private void exitMIDlet(){
    if( gameScreen != null ){
        gameScreen.endGame();
    }

    notifyDestroyed();
}
```

MIDlet initialization is done in the `startApp` method, of course, and we use the technique described in Chapter 3 to ensure that initialization is only done once by moving the initialization into a separate `initMIDlet` method:

```
private void initMIDlet(){
    display = Display.getDisplay( this );
    gameScreen = new GameScreen();
    display.setCurrent( gameScreen );
    gameScreen.newGame();
}

protected void startApp()
                  throws MIDletStateChangeException {
    if( display == null ){
        initMIDlet();
    }

    if( gameScreen.isPaused() ){
        gameScreen.resume();
    }
}
```

Notice the call to `gameScreen.isPaused`. Whenever possible, write your applications so that they can be paused by the system when the `pauseApp` method is called:

```
protected void pauseApp() {
    gameScreen.pause();
}
```

Pausing the game causes the game to stop the timer that it has started, as we will see shortly. Stopping the thread means that the game will not repaint the screen or let the stars continue to fall. Resuming the game restarts the timer.

The Scroller Class

The game uses a timer to scroll the stars, so we need to define a subclass `java.util.TimerTask` in order to do the scrolling:

```
class Scroller extends TimerTask {
    public void run(){
        display.callSerially( gameScreen );
    }
}
```

As you can see, this class is quite trivial. All it does is serialize a call to the game canvas, which implements the `java.lang.Runnable` interface. When the canvas is then called through its `run` method, it will scroll itself. Serializing the call ensures that the scrolling occurs after any pending repaint requests have been processed. By making `Scroller` an inner class of `SimpleGame`, it has implicit access to the `display` and `gameScreen` data members of the latter.

The timer is started whenever a new game is started or a paused game is resumed by using this code:

```
timer = new Timer();
timer.schedule( new Scroller(), 100, 100 );
```

A repeating timer is used to scroll the display every 100 milliseconds or so.

The GameScreen Class

Now we come to the heart of our game. The `GameScreen` class is where all the game logic resides. Like the `Scroller` class, `GameScreen` is defined as an inner class of `SimpleGame` so that it has implicit access to the latter's data members and methods:

```
class GameScreen extends Canvas implements Runnable {
    Random   generator = new Random();
    int      height;  // display area height
    int      width;  // display area width
    int[]    stars;  // array to hold star positions
    Image    offscreen; // for double buffering
    int      shipX, shipY; // ship position
    boolean  isColor; // if display is color
    int      score;  // current score
    Font     smallFont;  // for displaying score
    Font     bigFont;  // for displaying end game message
    boolean  paused;  // whether game is paused or not
    Timer    timer;  // for scrolling stars
```

```
    ..... // other code here
}
```

Unlike SimpleGame, GameScreen defines a number of data members to track the state of the game and to store information about the display. Most of these are initialized in the constructor:

```
public GameScreen(){
    height      = getHeight();
    width       = getWidth();
    stars       = new int[ height ];
    isColor     = display.isColor();

    // If the canvas isn't automatically double buffered,
    // create an offscreen image to do our own
    // double buffering.

    if( !isDoubleBuffered() ){
        offscreen = Image.createImage( width, height );
    }

    // Store the fonts we need.  Remember, the system
    // may substitute its own fonts.

    smallFont = Font.getFont( Font.FACE_PROPORTIONAL,
                              Font.STYLE_PLAIN,
                              Font.SIZE_SMALL );

    bigFont = Font.getFont( Font.FACE_PROPORTIONAL,
                            Font.STYLE_UNDERLINED |
                            Font.STYLE_BOLD,
                            Font.SIZE_LARGE );

    // Setup the two commands we respond to.

    addCommand( exitCommand );
    addCommand( newGameCommand );
    setCommandListener( SimpleGame.this );
}
```

The height and width members store the height and width of the display area, and the isColor member stores whether or not the display can show different colors. We will need that information to decide which colors to use when drawing. The stars array holds the star positions: each element of the array holds the horizontal position of a single star, with the element index storing the vertical position. In other words, there can be at most one star defined per row of pixels. The smallFont and bigFont members store the fonts that we will use to draw the score and the end game message. And of course, the constructor also adds the two command objects to the canvas and sets the canvas' command listener.

Perhaps the most interesting aspect of the initialization is the support for double buffering. As explained in Chapter 4, double buffering is a technique used to perform flicker-free animation. The constructor checks to see whether the device supports automatic double buffering. If it does not, it allocates an offscreen buffer equal to the height and width of the display. The `paint` method will then use this buffer to do its drawing, as we will see shortly.

The `newGame` method is called whenever a new game is to be started. This action happens when the MIDlet starts or when the user triggers the New command. The code for `newGame` is as follows:

```
public void newGame(){
    score  = 0;
    shipX  = width / 2 - 3;
    shipY  = height - 2;
    paused = false;

    for( int i = 0; i < height; ++i ){
        stars[i] = -1;
    }

    timer = new Timer();
    timer.schedule( new Scroller(), 100, 100 );
}
```

The score is reset to 0, the ship's initial position is set, the stars are initialized (no stars are initially defined), and the timer is started to get the game going. The counterpart to `newGame` is the `endGame` method, which ends the current game:

```
public void endGame(){
    paused = false;

    if( timer != null ){
        timer.cancel();
        timer = null;
    }
}
```

Ending the game is fairly simple. All we really do is shut down the timer. Notice the use of the `paused` data member in both `newGame` and `endGame`. It is also used in the `isPaused`, `pause`, and `resume` methods:

```
public boolean isPaused(){
    return paused;
}

public void pause(){
    if( isActive() ){
        if( timer != null ){
            timer.cancel();
```

```
                timer = null;
            }

            paused = true;
        }
    }

    public void resume(){
        if( paused ){
            timer = new Timer();
            timer.schedule( new Scroller(), 100, 100 );
            paused = false;
        }
    }
```

These methods enable the MIDlet to pause the game by canceling the timer and resume it later by starting a new timer. When the timer is active, of course, an instance of the `Scroller` class is notified whenever it is time to update the display, and it in turn serializes a call to the `GameScreen` class's run method:

```
public void run(){
    if( isActive() ){
        scroll();
    }
}

public boolean isActive(){
    return( timer != null );
}

public void scroll() {
    for( int i = height-1; i > 0; --i ){
        stars[i] = stars[i-1];
    }

    stars[0] = ( generator.nextInt() % ( 3 * width ) );
    if( stars[0] >= width ){
        stars[0] = -1;
    }

    repaint();
}
```

If the game is active—a timer is active—then the existing stars all scroll down and a new star in a random horizontal position is generated at the top of the screen. The call to `repaint` then ensures that the display is repainted by queuing a call to the canvas's `paint` method:

```
protected void paint( Graphics g ){
    Graphics saved = g;
```

```
        if( offscreen != null ){
            g = offscreen.getGraphics();
        }

        drawStars( g );
        drawScore( g, ++score );
        drawShip( g, shipX, shipY );

        if( hasHit( shipX, shipY ) ){
            if( isActive() ){
                AlertType.ERROR.playSound( display );
                endGame();
            }

            drawGameOver( g );
        }

        if( g != saved ){
            saved.drawImage( offscreen, 0, 0,
                             Graphics.LEFT | Graphics.TOP );
        }
    }
```

Notice how the `paint` method supports double buffering. If double buffering is not implemented on the device, the constructor will have defined an offscreen buffer. If the offscreen buffer is defined, the paint method uses the buffer's `Graphics` object to perform its drawing. After the drawing is complete, it then copies the contents of the offscreen buffer onto the display by using a single call to `drawImage` on the original `Graphics` object.

The drawing is delegated to several separate routines:

```
    private void drawGameOver( Graphics g ){
        if( isColor ){
            g.setColor( 0, 0, 255 );
        } else {
            g.setColor( 255, 255, 255 );
        }

        g.setFont( bigFont );
        g.drawString( "GAME OVER", width / 2, height / 2,
                      g.HCENTER | g.BASELINE );
    }

    private void drawScore( Graphics g, int val ){
        if( isColor ){
            g.setColor( 0, 255, 0 );
        } else {
            g.setColor( 255, 255, 255 );
```

```
        }

        g.setFont( smallFont );
        g.drawString( "Score: " + val, width / 2, 0,
                      g.HCENTER | g.TOP );
    }

    private void drawStars( Graphics g ){
        g.setColor( 0, 0, 0 );
        g.fillRect( 0, 0, width, height );

        g.setColor( 255, 255, 255 );

        for( int y = 0; y < height; ++y ){
            int x = stars[y];
            if( x == -1 ) continue;

            g.drawLine( x, y, x, y );
        }
    }

    private void drawShip( Graphics g, int x, int y ){
        if( isColor ){
            g.setColor( 255, 0, 0 );
        } else {
            g.setColor( 255, 255, 255 );
        }

        g.drawLine( x, y-1, x+5, y-1 );
        g.drawLine( x, y-2, x+5, y-2 );
        g.drawLine( x+1, y-3, x+4, y-3 );
        g.drawLine( x+1, y-4, x+4, y-4 );
        g.drawLine( x+2, y-5, x+3, y-5 );
    }
```

Notice how most of the drawing routines set the drawing color differently if the device supports color. This feature is not strictly necessary, however, because the device maps colors automatically to the number of colors supported by the device. On monochrome devices, however, it is sometimes better to do your own color mapping or even to draw things differently.

The ship is drawn as a series of lines, not from a bitmapped image. The drawing is done in this manner because the MIDP 1.0 specification does not require the device to support transparent images. Because the ship is of irregular shape and the background is important (you want to see stars pass close by the ship), the ship is drawn explicitly. Of course, there is also a method defined to determine whether the ship has hit any star:

```
    private boolean hasHit( int x, int y ){
        int pos = stars[y-1];
        if( pos >= x && pos <= x+5 ) return true;
```

```
        pos = stars[y-2];
        if( pos >= x && pos <= x+5 ) return true;
        pos = stars[y-3];
        if( pos >=x+1 && pos <=x+4 ) return true;
        pos = stars[y-4];
        if( pos >=x+1 && pos <=x+4 ) return true;
        pos = stars[y-5];
        if( pos >=x+2 && pos <=x+3 ) return true;
        return false;
    }
```

If the ship has hit a star, the `paint` method draws the "game over" message shown in Figure 5.12 and ends the current game.

The only thing left now is for the game to respond to the user's keypad events:

```
    protected void keyPressed( int keyCode ){
        moveShip( keyCode );
    }

    protected void keyRepeated( int keyCode ){
        moveShip( keyCode );
    }

    private void moveShip( int keyCode ){
        if( !isActive() ) return;

        boolean redraw = false;

        int action = getGameAction( keyCode );
        if( action == UP ){
            if( shipY > 10 ){
                --shipY;
                redraw = true;
            }
        } else if( action == DOWN ){
```

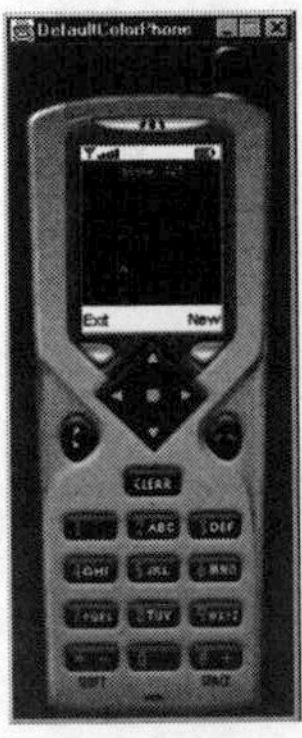

Figure 5.12 The game is over.

```
                if( shipY < height - 2 ){
                    ++shipY;
                    redraw = true;
                }
            } else if( action == LEFT ){
                if( shipX + 4 >= 0 ){
                    --shipX;
                    redraw = true;
                }
            } else if( action == RIGHT ){
                if( shipX < width - 2 ){
                    ++shipX;
                    redraw = true;
                }
            }

            if( redraw ){
                repaint();
            }
        }
```

If the game is active, the ship is moved whenever the user presses the UP, DOWN, LEFT, or RIGHT buttons. The game ensures that the ship stays on the screen, only repainting the screen when the ship actually moves.

This section completes our examination of the code behind a simple game.

Triggering Multiple Alerts

Our final example shows how to combine the high-level and low-level user interface APIs in a single application. We perform this task by writing a class that can be used to properly display multiple alerts that are triggered almost simultaneously.

The code presented here was originally developed by one of the authors for publication as a J2ME Tech Tip on Sun's Java Developer Connection Web site and is reprinted here by kind permission of Sun Microsystems.

The Problem

If your application triggers two or more alerts simultaneously from different threads, you will not get the behavior that you would expect. The problem is with the call that displays the alert:

```
Alert   alert = ....;
Display display = ....;

display.setCurrent( alert, display.getCurrent() );
```

There are two problems here. The first is that `setCurrent` will immediately show the alert, replacing any alert that might be onscreen at the time and that the user might not have finished reading. The second is that `getCurrent` might return null or a reference to another alert. Alerts should never be the final destination of a `setCurrent` call.

What you really want to do is queue the calls that display the alerts so that the alerts are shown one at a time, proceeding to the next alert only when the user dismisses the current alert. The problem is that no event is triggered when an alert is dismissed. This situation is not a problem with non-modal alerts—you could start a timer and just show the next alert after the current alert's timeout expires—but there is no way to know when a modal alert is dismissed (at least, not directly).

The AlertRouter Class

As it happens, there is an *indirect* way to tell when a modal alert is dismissed: make the alert destination—the displayable that is shown when the alert is dimissed—a `Canvas` and override the latter's `showNotify` and `hideNotify` methods. When the canvas is displayed, look for the next alert in the queue and display it. This code is the basic behavior of the `AlertRouter` class:

```
package com.j2medeveloper.util;

import java.util.*;
import javax.microedition.lcdui.*;

public class AlertRouter extends Canvas {
    private Display     display;
    private Vector      pending = new Vector();
    private Displayable destination;
    private Alert       current;

    public AlertRouter( Display display ){
        this.display = display;
    }

    protected void paint( Graphics g ){
        // no painting
    }

    protected synchronized void showNotify() {
        if( pending.size() > 0 ){
            current = (Alert) pending.elementAt( 0 );
            pending.removeElementAt( 0 );
            display.setCurrent( current, this );
        } else {
            current = null;
            display.setCurrent( destination );
        }
    }
```

```
    public void showAlert( Alert alert ) {
        showAlert( alert, null );
    }

    public synchronized void showAlert( Alert alert,
                                        Displayable next ){
        if( next != null ){
            destination = next;
        } else if( destination == null ){
            destination = display.getCurrent();
            if( destination == null ){
                destination = this;
            }
        }

        pending.addElement( alert );

        if( current == null ){
            display.setCurrent( this );
        }
    }
}
```

As you can see, AlertRouter is a canvas that does no painting. It uses a vector to maintain a queue of pending alerts and to display them in turn until there are no more to display.

The MultiAlert Example

A simple example shows how to use the AlertRouter class. The following MIDlet, MultiAlert, triggers alerts at random times from different threads, sometimes simultaneously:

```
import javax.microedition.midlet.*;
import javax.microedition.lcdui.*;
import java.util.*;
import com.j2medeveloper.util.*;

public class MultiAlert extends MIDlet {
    Display      display;
    Command      exitCommand = new Command( "Exit",
                                       Command.EXIT, 1 );
    Timer        timer1 = new Timer();
    Timer        timer2 = new Timer();
    Timer        timer3 = new Timer();
    MainForm     form = new MainForm();
    AlertRouter  router;

    public MultiAlert() {
    }
```

```
    private void initMIDlet(){
        display = Display.getDisplay( this );
        router = new AlertRouter( display );

        timer1.schedule( new AlertTrigger( "Alert 1",
                         "This is alert #1" ), 5000, 10000 );
        timer2.schedule( new AlertTrigger( "Alert 2",
                         "This is alert #2" ), 5000, 7000 );
        timer3.schedule( new AlertTrigger( "Alert 3",
                         "This is alert #3" ), 5000, 9000 );
    }

    protected void destroyApp( boolean unconditional ) {
        timer1.cancel();
        timer2.cancel();
        timer3.cancel();
    }

    protected void startApp() {
        if( display == null ){
            initMIDlet();
            display.setCurrent( form );
        }
    }

    protected void pauseApp() {
    }

    public void exitMIDlet(){
        destroyApp( true );
        notifyDestroyed();
    }

    class AlertTrigger extends TimerTask {
        public AlertTrigger( String title, String message ){
            this.title = title;
            this.message = message;
        }

        public void run(){
            Alert alert = new Alert( title, message,
                                     null, null );
            alert.setTimeout( Alert.FOREVER );
            router.showAlert( alert );
        }

        private String title;
        private String message;
    }
```

```
        class MainForm extends Form implements CommandListener {
            public MainForm(){
                super( "MultiAlert Demo" );
                addCommand( exitCommand );
                setCommandListener( this );
            }

            public void commandAction( Command c, Displayable d ){
                exitMIDlet();
            }
        }
    }
```

To use the alert router, create an instance of the `AlertRouter` class, passing it a reference to the MIDlet's `Display` object. Then, each time you want to display an alert, use the alert router's `showAlert` method, which has two forms that are analogous to the two forms of `Display.setCurrent`.

Summary

In this chapter, we have looked at some simple but fairly comprehensive examples of building user interfaces by using both the high-level and low-level APIs defined by the MIDP. The user interface is obviously an important part of any application, but there are also other aspects that we need to cover. We now leave our exploration of user interfaces and move on to an important topic: how to communicate with the external world via wireless networking.

CHAPTER 

Network Communication

In Chapter 1, "Java 2 Micro Edition Basics," we briefly covered the Connected Limited Device Configuration (CLDC) and the classes and interfaces that are collectively known as the *Generic Connection Framework* (GCF). The GCF abstracts the concepts of files, networking, and other input/output mechanisms into a *single*, generic application programming interface (API). As a CLDC-based profile, the Mobile Information Device Profile (MIDP) leverages and extends the GCF by providing the low-level protocol implementations that enable MIDP developers to create network-aware applications. MIDP implementations are required to support Hypertext Transfer Protocol (HTTP) connectivity at a minimum, although individual implementations are also free to add further support. In this chapter, we will discuss how to perform network communication in your MIDP applications. We start with a look at the GCF and then focus on the HTTP support defined by the MIDP specification.

The Generic Connection Framework

As a profile built on top of the CLDC, the MIDP leverages the GCF for its network APIs and semantics. As we explained earlier, the main motivation behind the creation of a new connection framework is to reduce memory footprint, because MIDP devices (mainly cell phones and interactive pagers) do not necessarily have a lot of available memory. Recall that memory requirements for MIDP devices are at least 128K of non-volatile (persistent, like flash or ROM) memory for the MIDP software, 8K of non-volatile memory for application-defined storage, and 32K of volatile (RAM) memory for the Java run-time heap. Because of the large memory footprint and unnecessary functionality in the J2SE

Table 6.1 CLDC java.io Classes

PACKAGE	Class
java.io	ByteArrayInputStream
	ByteArrayOutputStream
	DataInput
	DataInputStream
	DataOutput
	DataOutputStream
	InputStream
	InputStreamReader
	OutputStream
	OutputStreamWriter
	PrintStream
	Reader
	Writer

`java.io` and `java.net` packages, the decision was made to offer similar and more generic functionality by using the GCF.

The java.io and java.net Packages

Because MIDP devices are resource and memory constrained, every byte counts. The J2SE `java.io` and the related `java.net` packages total (in JDK 1.3) 16 interfaces, 71 classes, and 24 exceptions for a total compiled size of about 316K. For this reason, the CLDC defines a reduced version of `java.io` and leaves out the `java.net` package entirely, replacing the omitted classes with a new package: the `javax.microedition.io`. Together, the `java.io` and `javax.microedition.io` packages total 11 interfaces, 12 classes, and six exceptions for a total of size of about 28K.

The CLDC subset of the `java.io` package contains only the most useful or necessary classes and methods. The classes are shown in Table 6.1.

Let's look at one of the changes in the class hierarchy of the CLDC `java.io` package when compared to its J2SE equivalent. In J2SE, `DataInputStream` extends `FilterInputStream`:

```
java.lang.Object
  |
  +--java.io.InputStream
        |
        +--java.io.FilterInputStream
```

```
            |
            +--java.io.DataInputStream
```

The CLDC `DataInputStream` directly extends `InputStream`:

```
java.lang.Object
  |
  +--java.io.InputStream
        |
        +--java.io.DataInputStream
```

A few reorganizations such as this one keep the `java.io` package small and yet quite familiar.

The CLDC does *not* include any classes or interfaces from the `java.net` package. Everything is now defined as part of the GCF.

GCF Classes

The CLDC does not mandate support for any specific network protocols. Such decisions and implementations are left to the profiles, such as the MIDP, which mandates support for a subset of HTTP 1.1. What the CLDC defines is the GCF, a set of classes for performing a variety of communication tasks. The set of classes that make up the GCF are shown in Figure 6.1.

As you can see, the GCF provides support for datagrams, serial input, serial output, two-way input/output streams (such as the Transmission Control Protocol, or TCP), and

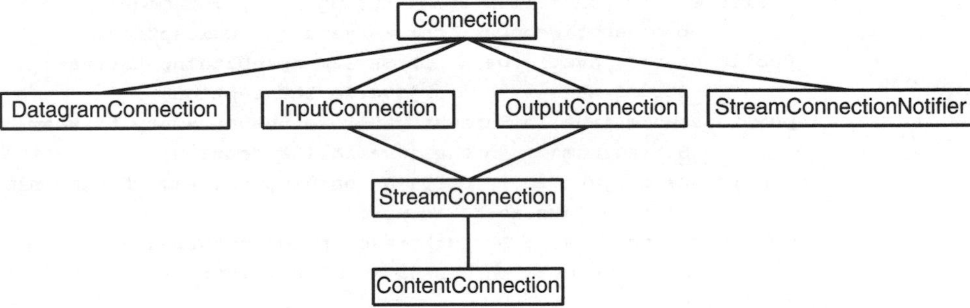

Figure 6.1 The Generic Connection Framework classes and interfaces.

java.io and the Generic Connection Framework

The GCF uses the classes and interfaces in the `java.io` package for input and output streams. Specifically, the GCF depends on the `DataInput` and `DataOutput` interfaces and the `InputStream`, `OutputStream`, `DataInputStream`, and `DataOutputStream` classes.

simple Web content—plus a way to be notified of waiting client connections (to implement servers). Note that as we move down the interface hierarchy, the `Connection` interfaces not only inherit behavior and functionality, but also become more functional. The remainder of this section covers the classes and interfaces of the GCF in detail.

The Connector Class

The only non-exception class (as opposed to an interface) in the `javax.microedition.io` package, the `Connector` class defines the factory methods to obtain connections by using the GCF. A Universal Resource Identifier (URI) describing the connection, whose syntax we will explain shortly, is passed to one of the methods which then attempts to create the appropriate type of connection. A `ConnectionNotFoundException` is thrown if the connection could not be created because the profile does not support it.

Class Description

The methods within the `Connector` class can be summarized as follows: three methods to create or open new `Connection` objects and four convenience methods to directly open stream connections. The `Connector` class definition is as follows:

```
public class Connector {
    // Methods
    public static Connection open( String name )
             throws java.io.IOException;
    public static Connection open( String name, int mode )
             throws java.io.IOException;
    public static Connection open( String name, int mode,
            boolean timeouts ) throws java.io.IOException;
    public static java.io.DataInputStream openDataInputStream(
            String name ) throws java.io.IOException;
    public static java.io.DataOutputStream openDataOutputStream(
            String name ) throws java.io.IOException;
    public static java.io.InputStream openInputStream( String name )
             throws java.io.IOException;
    public static java.io.OutputStream openOutputStream(
            String name ) throws java.io.IOException;
    // Fields
    public static final int READ = 1;
    public static final int READ_WRITE = 3;
    public static final int WRITE = 2;
}
```

The arguments to the `Connector.open` method are as follows:

- `name` is the URI to which we will connect.
- `mode` is the connection mode for connection types that support the concepts of read-only, write-only, and read-write connections.
- `timeouts` indicates whether the application wants an exception thrown if the connection times out.

Table 6.2 Connection Interfaces Defined by the CLDC

INTERFACE	DESCRIPTION
Connection	Base interface for all connection types defined by the GCF
InputConnection	Defines an input stream connection
OutputConnection	Defines an output stream connection
StreamConnection	Defines a two-way stream with input and output capabilities
StreamConnectionNotifier	Waits for incoming stream connections
ContentConnection	Defines a two-way stream connection that returns information about the content of its input stream
DatagramConnection	Defines a connection that is capable of sending or receiving datagrams

The last two arguments are optional. If `mode` is not specified, it defaults to `READ_WRITE`. The default `timeouts` value is `false`. If an argument does not make sense for a particular protocol, its value is ignored.

The `Connector` class throws the following exceptions:

1. `IllegalArgumentException` if the URI was not valid
2. `ConnectionNotFoundException` if the specified protocol is not supported
3. `IOException` for any other kind of error

The result of a call to `Connector.open` is an object that implements the `Con-nection` interface or one of its subinterfaces. Table 6.2 lists the valid `Connection` objects that can be returned. Profiles are free to add to this list by defining new interfaces that extend `Connection` or one of its subinterfaces as in the case of MIDP which defines `HttpConnection`.

Uniform Resource Identifiers

A URI is a standard way of identifying resources on the *World Wide Web* (WWW). The syntax is documented in a specification referred to as RFC 2396. The format of a URI is as follows:

```
<scheme>:<scheme-specific-part>
```

As you can see, the format is quite general. Here are some sample URIs:

1. `protocol://user@host:port/resource`
2. `http://www.j2medeloper.com:80/controller.jsp?method=get&usr=eric`
3. `datagram://www.j2medeveloper.com:7001`

Not All Protocols Are Supported

We cannot emphasize this fact enough: the set of protocols implemented by a particular CLDC-based device is entirely up to the profile or profiles on the device and to any additional support provided by the device vendor. If in doubt, read the profile specification and the device documentation. In particular, note that the MIDP 1.0 specification only mandates support for HTTP. Support for any other protocol, whether it be HTTPS, datagrams, or sockets, is entirely optional.

The **<scheme>** part of a URI specifies the protocol to use. The list of supported protocols is up to the profile and to the device vendor. The `Connection.open` method uses the scheme to determine what type of connection to create, usually by mapping the name of the scheme to an internal factory class that it then uses to do the actual work of creating the connection.

After the protocol comes the **<scheme-specific-part>**, the format of which depends entirely on the protocol being used. As you can see, URIs can be very general. An HTTP URL is a specific kind of URI, and sometimes you will hear the terms URL and URI used interchangeably.

Making a Connection

Here is a simple example of how to make a connection with the GCF:

```
public void openConnection(String url) throws IOException {
    HttpConnection c = null;

    try {

        // open an HTTP connection
        c = (HttpConnection)
             Connector.open("http://www.j2medeveloper.com:8080");
        ..... // open Input stream, send request, read response, parse
    }
    catch (Exception e) {
       ..... // handle exception
    }
    ..... // other code
}
```

Note that `Connector.open` returns a `Connection` object that you must then cast to the correct subinterface. The subinterface to use is determined by the type of connection; you must consult the profile specification or vendor documentation to know which interface to use, although you can usually guess based on the characteristics of the connection.

The Connection Interface

The Connection interface is the base interface for all connection types defined by the GCF. It is also the most basic type of connection you can create. The Connection interface consists of a single method to close the active connection:

```
public interface Connection {
    void close() throws java.io.IOException;
}
```

Close a connection as soon as you are done with it, as in this example:

```
public void openConnection(String url) throws IOException {
    Connection c = null;
    try {
        // open a connection
        c = (Connection)Connector.open(url);

        // Connection Is the most basic type of connection.  Not much
        // we can do with a simple connection, but close It.  See
        // HttpConnection.
    }
    catch (IOException ioe) {
        .... // handle the exception
    }
    finally {
        if (c != null){
            c.close();
        }
    }
}
```

In particular, be sure to close the connection as part of any exception handling that your application performs. It is good practice to close your connections within a finally block.

The InputConnection Interface

The InputConnection interface defines an input stream connection. This interface defines two methods for the creation of input streams. The first is a raw input stream of type java.io.InputStream, and the second is a java.io.DataInputStream. The interface definition is as follows:

```
public interface InputConnection extends Connection {
    java.io.DataInputStream openDataInputStream()
            throws java.io.IOException;
    java.io.InputStream openInputStream()
            throws java.io.IOException;
}
```

Any kind of connection that can return a stream of data will implement the InputConnection interface or one of its subinterfaces. Here is how to use InputConnection:

```
public void openInputConnection(String url) throws IOException {
    InputConnection c = null;
    InputStream is = null;
    int ch=0;

    try {
       c = (InputConnection)Connector.open(url);
       is = c.openInputStream();

       // read until EOF (-1)
       while ( ch != -1 ) {
       ch = is.read();
      ..... // process received data
       }
    }
    catch (IOException ioe) {
       .... // handle the exception
    }

    // clean up
    finally {
        if (is!= null)
          is.close();
        if (c!= null)
          c.close();
    }
}
```

Note the call to close the input stream as well as the `InputConnection` object itself. Closing the connection object will also close any streams obtained from it, but it is good practice to close the individual streams separately. In fact, you should close a stream as soon as possible in order to free up any system resources it might be using.

The OutputConnection Interface

The `OutputConnection` interface defines an output stream connection. This interface is very similar to `InputConnection`, except of course it is for opening *output* streams. This interface defines two methods for the creation of output streams of type `java.io.OutputStream` and `java.io.DataOutputStream`. Its definition is as follows:

```
public interface OutputConnection extends Connection {
    java.io.DataOutputStream openDataOutputStream()
             throws java.io.IOException;
    java.io.OutputStream openOutputStream()
             throws java.io.IOException;
}
```

Use `OutputConnection` to create/open new output stream connections. To close the connection, invoke the connection's close method. `IOException` is thrown if some kind of I/O error is encountered. The following code fragment opens an `OutputConnection` and writes a string to the stream as a set of bytes:

```
public void openOutputConnection(String url,
                                  String outchars) throws IOException {

    OutputConnection c = null;
OutputStream os = null;
int ch=0;

// open an output connection,an output stream. close.
try {
    c = (OutputConnection)Connector.open(url);
    os = c.openOutputStream();
    os.write(outchars.getBytes());
    os.flush(); // force buffered bytes to be written out
}
catch (IOException ioe) {
      .... // handle the exception
}

// clean up state
finally {
    if (os!= null)
        os.close();
    if (c!= null)
        c.close();
}
}
```

Note that writing a string this way is efficient, but it assumes a specific character set encoding. If you want to write a string and read it from the server (the ultimate endpoint of the output stream), you are better off using a `DataOutputStream` and calling the latter's `writeUTF` method to encode the string in UTF-8 format to ensure that its contents are transferred correctly.

The StreamConnection Interface

The `StreamConnection` interface is for protocols that are capable of two-way stream communication. This interface defines no methods itself and extends both `InputConnection` and `OutputConnection`:

```
public interface StreamConnection extends InputConnection,
                                          OutputConnection {
    // no methods added
}
```

The following code fragment demonstrates the use of `StreamConnection`:

```
public void openStreamConnection(String url ) throws IOException {
    StreamConnection c = null;
```

```
        InputStream is = null;
        OutputStream os = null;
        int ch=0;

        // open a stream connection, and an input and output streams.
        try {
            c = (StreamConnection)Connector.open(url);
            is = c.openInputStream();
            os = c.openOutputStream();
           .... // read, process, send, etc.
        }
        // trap any I/O errors/exceptions
        catch (IOException ioe) {
           .... // handle the exception
        }
        // clean up state
        finally {
            if (is!= null)
                is.close();
            if (os!= null)
                os.close();
            if (c!= null)
                c.close();
             }
        }
}
```

Again, it is just a combination of the input stream and output stream connection types.

The StreamConnectionNotifier Interface

The `StreamConnection` interface defines a server connection—a connection type that enables the application to wait for incoming stream connections. It defines a single method that blocks the current thread until an incoming connection arrives:

```
public interface StreamConnectionNotifier extends Connection {
    StreamConnection acceptAndOpen() throws java.io.IOException;
}
```

The new connection is returned when the `acceptAndOpen` method unblocks. On devices that support server sockets, for example, you would use this interface to wait for incoming socket connections. The relevant code fragment is as follows:

```
public void waitForNewConnections(String url) throws IOException {

    StreamConnectionNotifier c = null;
    StreamConnection sc = null;
    InputStream is = null;
    OutputStream os = null;
```

```
// open a stream connection notifier and block for new
// connections, open an input and an output stream. close.
try {
    c = (StreamConnectionNotifier)Connector.open(url);
    sc = c.acceptAndOpen(); // block
    is = sc.openInputStream();
    os = sc.openOutputStream();
         .... // once the connection is accepted, read, send, etc.
}
       catch (IOException ioe) {
       .... // handle the exception
}
// clean up state
finally {
    if (is!= null)
        is.close();
    if (os!= null)
        os.close();
    if (sc!= null)
        sc.close();
    if (c!= null)
        c.close();
    }
}
```

Server functionality is something that you will rarely find on a CLDC-based device, though, so it is unlikely that you will be using this interface.

The ContentConnection Interface

The `ContentConnection` interface extends `StreamConnection` by adding methods that return information about the contents of an input stream:

```
public interface ContentConnection extends StreamConnection {
    String getEncoding();
    long getLength();
    String getType();
}
```

For example, you can use `getLength()` to retrieve the length of the data to be read (if it is known). If the stream is an HTTP response, you can use the methods to retrieve the values of different HTTP headers as follows:

1. Use `getType()` to retrieve the value of the `Content-Type` HTTP header.
2. Use `getEncoding()` to retrieve the value of the `Content-Encoding` HTTP header.
3. Use `getLength()` to retrieve the value of the `Content-Length` HTTP header.

Note that these methods throw no exceptions, but they might not return any information. The following code fragment shows how to use ContentConnection:

```
public void openContentConnection(String url) throws IOException {
    ContentConnection c = null;
    InputStream is = null;
    int len=0;
    int ch=0;

    // open a content connection, an input stream. get length. close.
    try {
        c = (ContentConnection)Connector.open(url);
        is = c.openInputStream();
        len = (int)c.getLength();
        .... // read content, process, send, receive, etc.
    }
    catch (IOException ioe) {
      .... // handle the exception
    }
    // clean up state
    finally {
      if(is!= null)
         is.close();
      if(c!= null)
         c.close();
    }
}
```

Note that the MIDP supports HTTP and defines its own extension of Content-Connection that defines many more methods for dealing with the content of the HTTP response stream. We will discuss HTTP connectivity later in this chapter.

The DatagramConnection and Datagram Interfaces

The DatagramConnection interface defines a connection that is capable of sending or receiving datagrams, which are raw packets of data. The Datagram interface defines the methods for dealing with data packets sent or received by using DatagramConnection. The definition of DatagramConnection is as follows:

```
public interface DatagramConnection extends Connection {
    int getMaximumLength() throws java.io.IOException;
    int getNominalLength() throws java.io.IOException;
    Datagram newDatagram( int size ) throws java.io.IOException;
    Datagram newDatagram( byte[] buf, int size )
            throws java.io.IOException;
    Datagram newDatagram( int size, String addr )
            throws java.io.IOException;
    Datagram newDatagram( byte[] buf, int size, String addr )
```

```
                throws java.io.IOException;
        void receive( Datagram dgram ) throws java.io.IOException;
        void send( Datagram dgram ) throws java.io.IOException;
}
```

Use one of the `newDatagram` methods to create new datagrams. All access to the data held by a datagram is done by using the `Datagram` interface:

```
public interface Datagram extends java.io.DataInput,
                                  java.io.DataOutput {
        String getAddress();
        byte[] getData();
        int getLength();
        int getOffset();
        void reset();
        void setAddress( String addr ) throws java.io.IOException;
        void setAddress( Datagram reference );
        void setData( byte[] buf, int offset, int len );
        void setLength( int len );
}
```

In general, a datagram connection is a lightweight packet-delivery mechanism that does not guarantee the delivery of messages. Use datagrams if your application sends short messages and the lack of message reliability is not an issue, if your application is sensitive to communications latency, if HTTP is not available, or if you want to implement your own network protocol. Keep in mind that if reliable message delivery is important to your application, you might be required to implement a message structure (maybe containing message sequence numbers and flags) and extra logic to handle the lack of reliability. Alternatively, use a stream connection.

The `Datagram` interface is very similar to its J2SE counterpart, `java.net.DatagramPacket`. The main differences between both mainly revolve around the datagram *addressing* scheme. The GCF specifies endpoint addresses via the URI provided when creating a connection via `Connector.open(URI)` or via the `setAddress` methods shown earlier. Datagram addressing in J2SE is IP-based and is accomplished via the `InetAddress` class. The `Datagram` methods are used as follows:

- Use `Datagram.setAddress( String addr )` to overwrite the address (URI) specified when the `DatagramConnection` was originally created.
- Use `Datagram.setAddress( Datagram reference )` to make the address of the datagram equal to the address of the datagram passed as the argument. Use this method to overwrite the address specified when creating the `DatagramConnection`.
- Use `Datagram.setData()` to set the datagram's data from a byte array.
- Use `Datagram.setLength()` to set the length of the datagram.

The following helper class creates, opens, sends, and receives datagrams. You can use this helper class to write your own chat application, or any other application that sends and receives small packets of data:

```
package com.j2medeveloper.net;

import javax.microedition.io.*;
import java.io.*;

public class DatagramConnectionHelper {

    DatagramConnectionHelper() {
    }

    /**
     * Send a datagram
     */
    public void sendDatagram (String addr, byte[] message) {

        DatagramConnection dc = null;
        Datagram datagram = null;

        try {

            // open DatagramConnection
            dc = (DatagramConnection)Connector.open(addr);

            // Create and send datagram packet, then close.
            datagram = dc.newDatagram(message,
                                      message.length,
                                      addr);
            dc.send(datagram);
            dc.close();
        }
        catch (Exception e) {
            .... // handle the exception
        }
        finally {
            if (dc != null) {
                dc.close();
        }
    } // sendDatagram

    /**
     * Receive a datagram
     */
    public byte[] receiveDatagram (String addr) {

        DatagramConnection dc = null;
        Datagram datagram = null;
        byte[] message = null;

        try {

            // open DatagramConnection
```

```
                dc = (DatagramConnection)Connector.open(addr);

                // Wait for Datagram to arrive
                dc.receive(datagram);

                // Datagram received extract buffer and return It
                message = datagram.getData();
                dc.close();
            }
            catch (Exception e) {
              .... // handle the exception
        }
            finally {
                if (dc != null) {
                    dc.close();
                }
            }
            return message;

        } // receive datagram
    }
```

Let's look at a code fragment that uses `DatagramConnectionHelper` to send a datagram:

```
// create a DatagramConnectionHelper
DatagramConnectionHelper dch = new DatagramConnectionHelper();
try {
   String url = "datagram://chat.j2medeveloper.com:8030";
   byte[] msg = "Hello there!".getBytes();
   dch.sendDatagram( url, msg ); // send datagram
}
catch(Exception e) {
   .... // handle exception
}
```

Similarly, here is how to use `DatagramConnectionHelper` to read a datagram:

```
// create a DatagramConnectionHelper
DatagramConnectionHelper dch = new DatagramConnectionHelper();
try {
   String url = "datagram://chat.j2medeveloper.com:8030";
   byte[] msg = dch.receiveDatagram(url); // read datagram
}
catch(Exception e) {
   .... // handle exception
}
```

To reiterate, however, be aware that a MIDP-enabled device will not necessarily expose a datagram protocol even if it is using a wireless packet-switched network. The MIDP 1.0 specification only requires support for HTTP.

The ConnectionNotFoundException Class

The final piece of the GCF is the `ConnectionNotFoundException` class. The `Connector` class throws this exception when the requested connection protocol is not supported by the implementation. Its definition is as follows:

```
public class ConnectionNotFoundException extends java.io.IOException {
    public ConnectionNotFoundException();
    public ConnectionNotFoundException( String s );
}
```

You can use the exception to try alternate protocols. For example, say that you want to use HTTPS on a device if it is supported and fallback to HTTP if it is not supported. The code to do that is quite simple:

```
HttpConnection conn = null;
String path = "//www.j2medeveloper.com/index.html";

try {
    conn = (HttpConnection) Connector.open( "https:" + path );
}
catch( ConnectionNotFoundException cne ){
    try {
        conn = (HttpConnection) Connector.open( "http:" + path );
    }
    catch( IOException e ){
    }
}
catch( IOException ioe ){
}
```

If you cannot fall back to another protocol, be sure to inform the user about it instead of just reporting an I/O exception. And always notify the user before automatically switching from an expected secured connection to an unsecured one.

Wireless Networking with the MIDP

The MIDP 1.0 specification addresses networking requirements by supporting a subset of HTTP 1.1. The MIDP specification defines a new connection type, the `javax.microedition.io.HttpConnection` interface, which exposes all the features of the HTTP protocol. As it stands, HTTP is the only guaranteed communication mechanism that a MIDP 1.0 application can use to communicate with the external world. Luckily, HTTP is easily used as a tunneling protocol for exchanging all kinds of information, not just for fetching pages of HTML or other visual markup. In fact, more and more applications are using HTTP to exchange XML documents—something that we leveraged in the e-mail client example in the previous chapter and that we will discuss in more detail in Chapter 9, "Using XML in MIDP Applications."

Hypertext Transfer Protocol

The Hypertext Transfer Protocol (HTTP) is an Internet standard application-level protocol that has been the foundation of the World Wide Web since 1990 when Tim Berners-Lee created it. The latest HTTP standard, HTTP 1.1, is documented as RFC 2616 on the World Wide Web Consortium's Web site. HTTP is a good choice as a protocol to support because it can make its way through most corporate firewalls. By installing custom servlets, JSP pages, or other Web server extensions, a MIDP client can use HTTP to gain access to corporate information.

HTTP Overview

HTTP is a text-based request and response protocol with the capability to exchange binary data. HTTP communication usually takes place over TCP/IP (with a default port of 80), but nothing precludes HTTP from being implemented on top of other protocols and/or ports. The only requirement or assumption is that HTTP is implemented on top of a transport protocol that provides connection reliability (a virtual circuit).

A typical HTTP operation is one where a client (referred to as a *user agent*) sends a request to an origin server (typically a Web server) and the server responds with a status and possibly with content. The HTTP specification of the typical operation is as follows:

> A client sends a request to the server in the form of a request method, URI, and protocol version, followed by a MIME-like message containing request modifiers, client information, and possible body content over a connection with a server. The server responds with a status line, including the message's protocol version and a success or error code, followed by a MIME-like message containing server information, entity metainformation, and possible entity-body content.

See Figure 6.2 for an example of a typical HTTP operation.

Other more complicated HTTP operations are supported as well, where intermediary agents such as proxies, gateways, and/or tunnels exist between the client and the server. From our perspective (the client's), all that matters is that the client makes a request to an origin server for a particular resource/service and that the server responds with appropriate results packaged in an HTTP response. Please refer to the HTTP specification for more information on proxies, gateways, and tunnels with respect to HTTP.

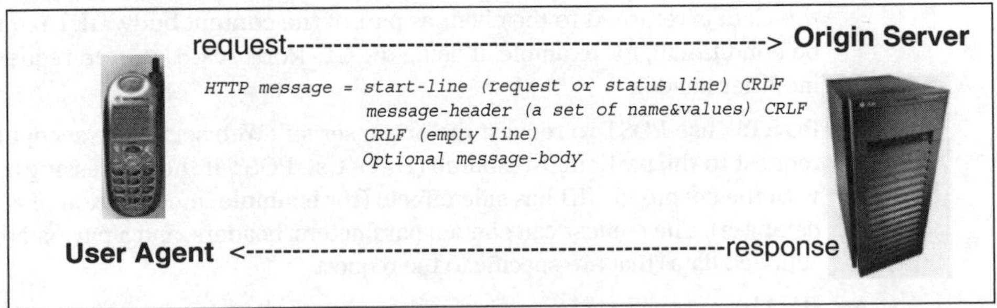

Figure 6.2 Typical operation of HTTP and message format.

The HTTP Request/Response Cycle

HTTP is a request/response protocol with a message format that follows the generic message format as specified by RFC 822 (standard for the format of ARPA Internet Text Messages, 1982). HTTP messages (entities) have *three* basic sections, each of which are separated by a *carriage return and line feed* (CRLF):

```
(1) <Message Type> CRLF
(2) <Message Header(s)> CRLF - optional
    CRLF
(3) <Message/Content Body> - optional
```

Let us look in more detail at each of the sections that makes an HTTP message:

1. **Message type:** The first line of a request/response which follows the following format:

```
Request line format:
<Method> <Request-URI> <HTTP-Version> CRLF

Response/status line format:
<HTTP-Version> <Status-Code> <Reason-Phrase> CRLF
```

Let us look at some examples:

```
Request line example:
GET /emailController.jsp?action=get HTTP/1.1

Response/status line example:
HTTP/1.1 200 OK
```

As mentioned before, MIDP 1.0 only implements a subset of HTTP/1.1, with GET, POST and HEAD as the only supported request methods (i.e. OPTIONS, PUT, DELETE, TRACE and CONNECT are not supported). Let us look in more detail at the request methods that are available to us:

- **GET:** the default request operation. Use GET to retrieve the information (or access a resource) specified by the URI. Use GET if the request is considered idempotent (in other words, it has no lasting observable effect on the state of what you are accessing). If the resource specified by the URI produces data, this data is returned to the client as part of the content body. GET requests can be conditional, for example, if using the `If-Modified-Since` request modifier header.
- **POST:** use POST to request the origin server (Web server) to accept the request to the particular resource (URI). Use POST if the processing associated with the specified URI has side effects (for example, modification of a database). The request can contain parameters, headers, and a payload (client-supplied data) that are specific to the request.
- **HEAD:** use HEAD for testing purposes or to determine whether a given URI will produce different content. With HEAD, you can retrieve information

specified by the URI but without receiving content back in the response (just headers).

2. **Message headers:** Optional. Also known as meta-information, message headers are a set of name-value pairs defined by the particular request or response. For example:

```
Accept: text/xml
Host: www.host.com:80
Connection: Keep-Alive
Set-Cookie: AppServerSession=293kcl030c;path=/
User-Agent: Profile/MIDP-1.0 Configuration/CLDC-1.0
```

   The MIDP 1.0 specification recommends that if the application defines *any* headers, it should set the `User-Agent` header to a string like `Profile/MIDP-1.0 Configuration/CLDC-1.0` and the `Content-Language` header to the device locale, as in "`en-US`". Setting these values enables the Web server to identify the device as a J2ME-compliant device and to generate responses in the appropriate language.

3. **Content body:** Optional. The content body "carries" the actual payload (the entity body) for the particular request/response, if any.

Let us look at a simple HTTP request and a possible response. The request has one argument, `action`, which in this example is equal to "`emailmessages`." The response is an XML document that comes as part of the response content body:

HOW AN HTTP REQUEST LOOKS:

```
GET /emailController.jsp?action=get_emailmessages HTTP/1.1
User-Agent:Profile/MIDP-1.0 Configuration/CLDC-1.0
Accept:text/xml
Host:www.myhost.com:80
Content-Length:0
Content-Language:en-US

<Content Body goes here, if any>
```

HOW AN HTTP RESPONSE LOOKS:

```
HTTP/1.1 200 OK
Server:.WebLogic 5 1 0 Service.Pack.6.09/20/2000.21:03:19#84511
Content-Length:209
Content-Type:text/xml
Connection:Keep-Alive
SetCookie:WebLogicSession=
OwDXzTM56Eqd7uI3S0mAkcGXBNh3nANzvYC0s23qCsTYRR;path=/

<?xml.version="1.0" encoding ="UTF-8"?><emailmessages
count="1"><emailmessage>
<from>eric@giguere.com</from><date>Fri.Mar09.11:49:10.CST
2001</date><subject>Code Review</subject><msgid>3</msgid><body>I need
some documents for the code review
tomorrow</body></emailmessage></emailmessages>
```

The first line of the response defines a status code that the client can use to determine whether the requested operation succeeded or not. The response carries additional information in the response's headers and in the content of the response.

Full treatment of the ins and outs of HTTP is beyond the scope of this book. There are many good books and online documents available that discuss HTTP in detail. As well, we do not cover what it takes to build the server code that actually receives the HTTP request from the client and generates the appropriate response. You will likely perform this task by writing a servlet or a JSP page, but the techniques vary depending on what kind of data you are sending back and forth and what server-side platform or technology you are using.

The HttpConnection Interface

Because the MIDP 1.0 specification requires MIDP implementations to support HTTP-based communication, it also defines a new interface to deal specifically with the various parts of the HTTP request/response cycle. This new interface, `HttpConnection`, is defined in terms of the *Generic Connection Framework* (GCF).

Class Definition

The `HttpConnection` interface is part of the `javax.microedition.io` package, and its definition is as follows:

```
public interface HttpConnection extends ContentConnection {
    // Methods
    long getDate() throws java.io.IOException;
    long getExpiration() throws java.io.IOException;
    String getFile();
    String getHeaderField( int n ) throws java.io.IOException;
    String getHeaderField( String name ) throws java.io.IOException;
    long getHeaderFieldDate( String name, long def )
            throws java.io.IOException;
    int getHeaderFieldInt( String name, int def )
            throws java.io.IOException;
    String getHeaderFieldKey( int n ) throws java.io.IOException;
    String getHost();
    long getLastModified() throws java.io.IOException;
    int getPort();
    String getProtocol();
    String getQuery();
    String getRef();
    String getRequestMethod();
    String getRequestProperty( String key );
    int getResponseCode() throws java.io.IOException;
    String getResponseMessage() throws java.io.IOException;
```

```
    String getURL();
    void setRequestMethod( String method )
            throws java.io.IOException;
    void setRequestProperty( String key, String value )
            throws java.io.IOException;
    // Fields
    String GET = "GET";
    String HEAD = "HEAD";
    int HTTP_ACCEPTED = 202;
    int HTTP_BAD_GATEWAY = 502;
    int HTTP_BAD_METHOD = 405;
    int HTTP_BAD_REQUEST = 400;
    int HTTP_CLIENT_TIMEOUT = 408;
    int HTTP_CONFLICT = 409;
    int HTTP_CREATED = 201;
    int HTTP_ENTITY_TOO_LARGE = 413;
    int HTTP_EXPECT_FAILED = 417;
    int HTTP_FORBIDDEN = 403;
    int HTTP_GATEWAY_TIMEOUT = 504;
    int HTTP_GONE = 410;
    int HTTP_INTERNAL_ERROR = 500;
    int HTTP_LENGTH_REQUIRED = 411;
    int HTTP_MOVED_PERM = 301;
    int HTTP_MOVED_TEMP = 302;
    int HTTP_MULT_CHOICE = 300;
    int HTTP_NOT_ACCEPTABLE = 406;
    int HTTP_NOT_AUTHORITATIVE = 203;
    int HTTP_NOT_FOUND = 404;
    int HTTP_NOT_IMPLEMENTED = 501;
    int HTTP_NOT_MODIFIED = 304;
    int HTTP_NO_CONTENT = 204;
    int HTTP_OK = 200;
    int HTTP_PARTIAL = 206;
    int HTTP_PAYMENT_REQUIRED = 402;
    int HTTP_PRECON_FAILED = 412;
    int HTTP_PROXY_AUTH = 407;
    int HTTP_REQ_TOO_LONG = 414;
    int HTTP_RESET = 205;
    int HTTP_SEE_OTHER = 303;
    int HTTP_TEMP_REDIRECT = 307;
    int HTTP_UNAUTHORIZED = 401;
    int HTTP_UNAVAILABLE = 503;
    int HTTP_UNSUPPORTED_RANGE = 416;
    int HTTP_UNSUPPORTED_TYPE = 415;
    int HTTP_USE_PROXY = 305;
    int HTTP_VERSION = 505;
    String POST = "POST";
}
```

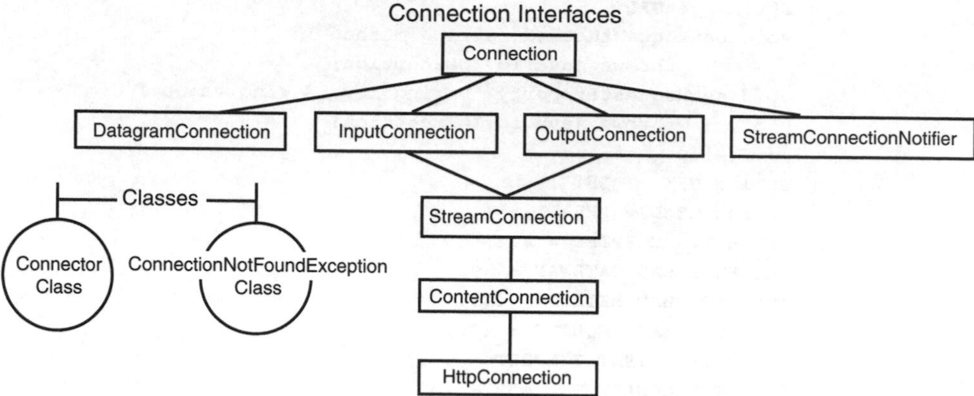

Figure 6.3 The GCF including HttpConnection.

If we revisit the GCF interface hierarchy shown at the beginning of this chapter, you will find the `HttpConnection` at the bottom of the hierarchy as shown in Figure 6.3.

In addition to exposing new methods for dealing with HTTP requests and responses, the `HttpConnection` interface also defines many constant values. Most of the constants define the HTTP status codes that are sent back as part of an HTTP response.

The `HttpConnection` interface defines many methods to handle HTTP connectivity. It offers similar functionality to the `java.net.HttpURLConnection` (and its superclass `java.net.URLConnection)` class defined in J2SE but within the context of the GCF. Most of the methods actually deal with the response, not with the HTTP request. A few, such as `setRequestMethod` (to set the HTTP method to use when sending the request) or `setRequestProperty` (to set an HTTP header in the request), deal specifically with the request.

HTTP Connection States

HTTP connections as defined by the `HttpConnection` interface can be in one of three states: setup, connected, and closed. The states are shown in Figure 6.4 and are defined as follows:

- The connection is in the *setup state* when the connection to the server has not yet been made. The client has the opportunity to set the request method and to set any request headers.
- The connection then transitions to the *connected state*, where it sends the request to the Web server and waits for the response. The connection is active at this point. The transition occurs whenever a call is made to one of the "get" methods defined by `HttpConnection` or if the application asks for an input stream to read any response data.
- Finally, the connection moves to the *closed state*. No methods can be invoked in the closed state; doing otherwise results in an IOException.

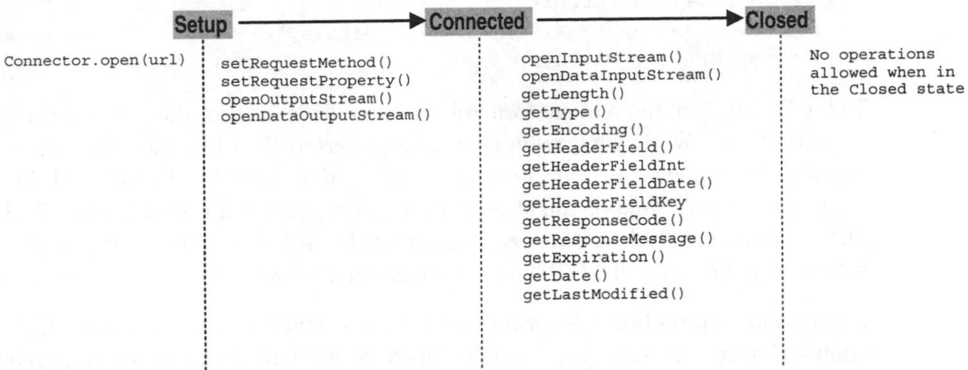

Figure 6.4 HTTP connection states

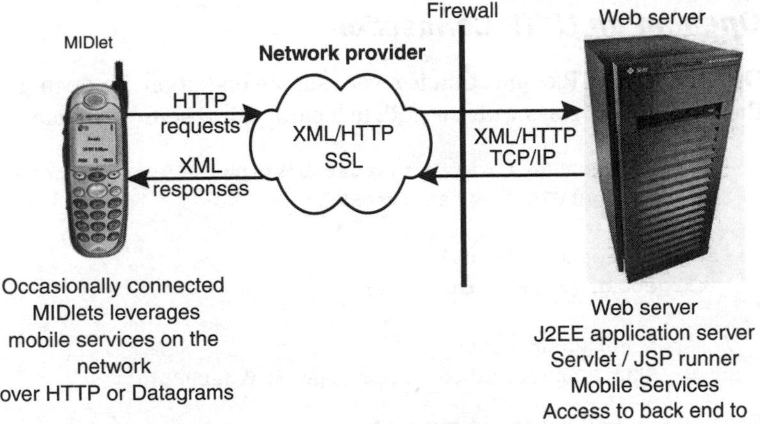

Figure 6.5 Typical operation of a network-aware MIDlet.

Communicating with the External World by Using HTTP

A typical network-aware MIDP application leverages HTTP for network connectivity with corporate servers. These servers usually run some kind of mobile application gateway built on top of a Java 2 Enterprise Edition (J2EE) application server. The trend is to leverage HTTP and XML for data exchange and integration, as illustrated in Figure 6.5.

Note that the device rarely makes the HTTP connection itself. The current typical configuration is where the device communicates wirelessly with a gateway that is run by the network carrier and the gateway is connected to the Internet and makes the ultimate connection to the Web server. Note that in the future, most wireless networks (and handsets) will support IP natively, allowing for point-to-point networking without the need for a gateway in the middle.

```
        Wireless network                              Internet     |(Firewall)
  [MIDP]<----------------->[Wireless Gateway]<-------------->[Web server]
 [device] GPRS, CDMA, etc.                          HTTP/TCP/IP    |
```

To the Web server, the request from the wireless device is just like any other request from a conventional Web client, such as a desktop-based Web browser. The gateway might impose limitations on the amount of data that can be transferred in a single request/response cycle or might only allow access to certain well-known TCP/IP ports. These kinds of details are not addressed by the MIDP specification. Apart from such restrictions, however, the HTTP communication must appear to be seamless and direct.

In the following sections, we will explore how to build a network-aware MIDlet: how to open an `HttpConnection`, set HTTP headers and URL parameters, send requests and receive responses, perform some session management, and parse an XML response. We will put all those pieces together into the `HttpConnectionHelper` class, which is a convenience class for handling HTTP connections.

Opening an HTTP Connection

Opening an HTTP connection is a very simple operation. To open a connection, we use the `Connector` class with the URL to a particular resource/service:

```
// set targetURL to effectiveURL(host+port) + parameters,
String targetURL = effectiveURL;

if(URLparameters != null)
  targetURL += URLparameters;

// open HttpConnection
hc = (HttpConnection)Connector.open(targetURL);
```

Recall that a URI has the following form:

```
<scheme>:<scheme-specific-part>
```

The URI format for the "http" scheme, known as a URL, has the following form (the parts in brackets "[]" are optional):

```
HTTPURL = "http:" "//" host [ ":" port ] [ resource_path [ "?" query ]]
```

If a port is not specified, port 80 is assumed. It is assumed that the identified resource is located at the specified server that is listening for connections on the specified port, that the requested resource is found on the specified path, and that the resources accept the parameters specified by a query string. For example:

```
http://myhost.com/emailController.jsp?username=sarylda&password=sarylda&
action=get_email
```

The individual details vary with the URL, of course. Note that in the example above, credential information (username and password) is being passed as part of the URL query string. This technique is not the recommended practice as URLs are usually logged on the

Web server's HTTP logs. All sensitive information should be sent within the message body and properly protected using encryption techniques.

Setting and Getting HTTP Headers

Before making the actual request, HTTP message headers are set. HTTP message headers are name-value pairs that provide the server or the client with information such as the type of connection, the type of connecting user agent, cookie information, and so on. Here are some sample headers, for example:

```
Host: www.host.com:80
Connection: Keep-Alive
Set-Cookie: AppServerSession=293kcl030c;path=/
User-Agent: Profile/MIDP-1.0 Configuration/CLDC-1.0
```

Note that application parameters are usually passed by using the query string part of the URL. Although message headers can be used to pass application information (parameters), this method is not considered good practice. HTTP headers are traditionally used for non-application, specific request/response information such as "HTTP protocol extensions" (for example, cookies and SOAP). In general, send application-specific information within the HTTP message body. In the MIDP, HTTP headers sent with a request are referred to as request properties. To set these, use the `HttpConnection.setRequestProperty` method.

The following code fragment—part of the `HttpConnectionHelper` class—sets the HTTP request headers:

```
// Set up the user defined message headers hashtable
messageHeaders = new Hashtable();
messageHeaders.put("username","damian");
messageHeaders.put("password","dje34ie");
setRequestHeaders(messageHeaders); // set the headers
```

The `setRequestHeaders` method is defined as follows:

```
private void setRequestHeaders(Hashtable messageHeaders)
    throws IOException {
    try {
          // set HTTP headers:
          //  User-Agent to MIDP/CLDC client
          //  Accept to XML
          //  Content-Language to en-US
          //  Connection to close(as we do not leverage keepalive)
          hc.setRequestProperty("User-Agent",
                    "Profile/MIDP-1.0 Configuration/CLDC-1.0" );

          // Content-Language must/should be a config value
          hc.setRequestProperty("Content-Language", "en-US");
          hc.setRequestProperty("Accept", "text/xml");
```

```
            hc.setRequestProperty("Connection", "close");

            //  set cookie, if one exists for this session
            if (cookie != null) {
                 hc.setRequestProperty("Cookie", cookie);
            }

            // Set any user defined headers
            if (messageHeaders != null) {
                  Enumeration enum = messageHeaders.keys();

                  while (enum.hasMoreElements()) {
                    String key   = (String)enum.nextElement();
                    String value = (String)messageHeaders.get(key);
                    hc.setRequestProperty(key, value);
                  }

            }
        }
        catch (IOException ioe) {
          . . . // handle exception
        }
}
```

Note the calls to set the `User-Agent` and `Content-Language` headers. As mentioned, the MIDP specification recommends that these headers be set to appropriate values in order to properly identify the client to the server.

To read the HTTP headers returned with responses, use one of the `HttpConection.getHeader` methods such as `getHeaderField`:

```
// extract received Cookie, if any
cookie = hc.getHeaderField( "Set-Cookie" );
```

Response headers can only be read after the connection has transitioned to the connected state, of course.

Passing Parameters to the Server

Application parameters are passed to the server usually via the query string part of the URL, as shown in bold:

```
HTTPURL = "http:" "//" host [ ":" port ] [ resource_path [ "?" query ]]
```

Query strings start with a "?" followed by name/value pairs separated by "&." For example:

```
?username=damian&password=diana&action=get_email
```

You must pay attention to the argument values within the query part of the URL. Certain characters are reserved for use to delineate parts of the URL and the HTTP header and must be replaced (URL encode) with special encodings. The following code fragment builds a query string from a set of parameters stored in a hash table:

```
// Build Hashtable of parameters
params = new Hashtable();
params.put("username", "damian");
params.put("password", "diana");
params.put("action",   "get_email");
setURLparameters(params);
```

The `setURLparameters` method is defined as follows:

```
public void setURLparameters(Hashtable params) {
    String name, value, param;

    if (params != null) {
        URLparameters = "?";

        // for each parameter
        Enumeration enum = params.keys();
        while (enum.hasMoreElements()) {
            name  = (String)enum.nextElement(); // key param. name
            value = (String)params.get(name); // get its value
            param = name+"="+encodeURL(value); //encode & concat.

            if(enum.hasMoreElements())
                param += "&"; // next param.

            URLparameters += param;
        }
    }
}
```

The World Wide Web Consortium describes the process of URL encoding as "space characters are replaced by '+', and then reserved characters are replaced by '%HH', a percent sign and two hexadecimal digits representing the ASCII code of the character. Line breaks, as in multi-line text field values, are represented as CR LF pairs, i.e. '%0D%0A'." The following method is a very simple implementation of such URL encoding rules:

```
private String encodeURL(String url) {
   StringBuffer s = new StringBuffer();
   int len = url.length();
   for(int i = 0; i < len; i++) {

      char ch = url.charAt(i);

      // no need to encode digits
      if (ch >= '0' && ch <= '9')
         s.append(ch);
      else
      // no need to encode letters
```

```
         if (ch >= 'a' && ch <= 'z' || ch >= 'A' && ch <= 'Z')
            s.append(ch);
         else
         // encode whitespace
         if (ch == ' ')
            s.append('+');
         else {
            // encode anything else as a reserved character
            s.append('%');
            s.append(Hex((ch & 0xF0) >> 4));
            s.append(Hex(ch & 0x0F));
         }
      }
      return s.toString();
   }

   private char Hex(int c) {
      if (c < 10)
         return (char)('0' + c);
      else
         return (char)(c - 10 + 'A');
   }
```

Sending Content with a Request

We can also send content—a byte stream—to the Web server as part of the HTTP request. If there is content to send, set the request method to POST instead of the default GET. You must also set the `Content-Type` and `Content-Length` request headers appropriately. The `Content-Type` tells the server the *Multipurpose Internet Mail Extensions* (MIME) type of the byte stream. A common value to use is `application/x-www-form-urlencoded`, which is the type used to submit HTML form data.

Write the data to the output stream as follows:

```
// Set prev. defined user HTTP request headers
setRequestHeaders();

// send (POST) body / content, if any
if (contentBody != null) {
     // Set HTTP request method to POST.
    hc.setRequestMethod(HttpConnection.POST);
     // set Content-Type as encoded URL.
    hc.setRequestProperty(
           "Content-Type",
           "application/x-www-form-urlencoded");
     // set Content-Length.
    hc.setRequestProperty
           ("Content-Length", ""+contentBody.length() );
     // Send Content body.
    os = hc.openOutputStream();
```

Always Set the Content Length

The `Content-Length` header should always be set by the application when sending data with a request. If you do not perform this task, the `HttpConnection` class will set it for you but it might be off by a byte or two due to a bug.

```
        os.write(contentBody.getBytes());
        os.close();
    }
    else {
        // Set HTTP request method to GET.
        hc.setRequestMethod(HttpConnection.GET);
    }
```

Note that when exchanging XML documents, you can set the MIME type of the data to `text/xml` and not do any encoding. The Web server can then retrieve the XML document directly from the request data without having to decode it.

Waiting for the Response

As soon as you have set the request method and the request headers and written the data (if any) that accompanies the request to the connection's output stream, call one of the "get" methods to transition to the connected state. The `HttpConnection` class will format and send the HTTP request to the Web server and wait for the latter's response, blocking until a response arrives or until the request times out.

Processing the Response

Recall that the format of an HTTP response begins with a status line, optionally followed by headers, which in turn are optionally followed by a message body. As we saw earlier, a typical HTTP response looks as follows:

```
(1)   HTTP/1.1 200 OK
(2)   Server:.WebLogic 5 1 0 Service.Pack.6.09/20/2000.21:03:19#84511
(3)   Content-Length:209
(4)   Content-Type:text/xml
(5)   Connection:Keep-Alive
(6)   <?xml.version="1.0" encoding ="UTF-8"?><emailmessages
count="1"><emailmessage>
<from>eric@giguere.com</from><date>Fri.Mar09.11:49:10.CST
2001</date><subject>Code Review</subject><msgid>3</msgid><body>I need
some documents for the code review
tomorrow</body></emailmessage></emailmessages>
```

The status code, part of the status line (line 1 above) and obtained by calling `getResponseCode`, is of particular interest because it indicates whether or not the request was successful. A status code of `HttpConnection.HTTP_OK` (the integer value 200) is normally what you want to see. You should, however, be prepared to handle redirection requests (`HTTP_MOVED_PERM`, `HTTP_MOVED_TEMP`, and `HTTP_TEMP_REDIRECT`) in case files or resources on the Web server have moved. Other response headers (for example, lines 2 to 5 above) are read by using the various "getHeader" methods.

An HTTP response often includes a stream of data (for example, line 6 above) in addition to the response headers. The `Content-Type` response header indicates the MIME type of the data. As well, the `Content-Length` response header is ideally set to a non-negative value in order to indicate the number of bytes in the data stream. You cannot always count on this situation, however, and if the length is equal to -1, then you must read the data in small pieces until an end-of-data indication is reached. Here is an example of how to process an HTTP response:

```
HttpConnection hc = ....;

// remember received Cookie, if any
cookie = hc.getHeaderField( "Set-Cookie" );

// open Input stream and get content length
is  = hc.openInputStream(); // open stream & get response HTTP headers
len = (int) hc.getLength();

// right here add processing associated with
// response message headers

// now read the response
StringBuffer receivebuffer = new StringBuffer();

// get content body, if any
if( len != -1) {
   int ch;
   // Read exactly Content-Length bytes
   for(int i = 0; i < len; i++) {
       if((ch = is.read()) != -1) {
           receivebuffer.append((char) ch);
       }
   }
} else {
   //Read until the connection is closed.
   while ((ch = is.read()) != -1) {
   len = is.available() ;
   receivebuffer.append((char)ch);
   }
}is.close();
response = receivebuffer.toString();
..... // process response, for example parse and display
```

The code above reads `Content-Length` bytes or until the connection is closed, and it assumes that the byte stream sent by the server is a string of ASCII characters. Certainly, some error checking should be added to ensure that the data is not too large to fit into the available memory.

HTTP Sessions

HTTP is a stateless protocol, and as such, keeping state is the responsibility of the application. There are two main techniques used on the Web to maintain HTTP session state: *cookies* and *URL rewriting.*

URL rewriting is a technique where extra information is encoded within the URL itself. This technique is useful when a client (or a gateway used by the client) does not support cookies and the server (or developer) has control over the URLs sent back to the client as part of a response. As long as the client uses the URLs sent to it by the server to communicate with the server, the session can be tracked.

Cookies (HTTP state management mechanism: RFC 2109/2965 and 2964) are pieces of state information that the server sends to the client via a response message header; specifically, the `Set-Cookie` header. The client stores this state information. When making a subsequent request, the client returns the appropriate cookie to the appropriate server based on the server's domain and path. Cookies are the preferred method of exchanging state information in HTTP, but note that the MIDP does not have native support for cookies. Cookie support is implemented by the application.

The syntax of the `Set-Cookie` response header is as follows:

```
Set-Cookie: NAME=VALUE;expires=DATE;path=PATH;domain=DOMAIN_NAME; secure
```

The parts of the `Set-Cookie` header have the following meanings:

1. *NAME=VALUE*: The only required attribute for `Set-Cookie`, it indicates the name of the cookie and its value.
2. *expires:* Indicates the lifetime of the cookie
3. *path:* the subset of URLs in a domain for which the cookie is valid.
4. *domain:* Indicates the domain for which the cookie is valid. When searching for valid cookies, the cookie domain is compared to the Internet domain name of the host from which the URL will be fetched. If there is a domain match, then a path match is attempted to determine whether the cookie should be sent.
5. *secure:* Indicates to only transfer this cookie over secure connections (HTTPS)

Once the server sends a cookie to the client, the client should include the cookie as a request header in every subsequent request to that server until the cookie expires. The format of the `Cookie` request header is as follow:

```
Cookie: NAME1=VALUE1;NAME2=VALUE2..., where VALUE Is a String
```

Here is a simple example of how to process cookies, taken from the `HttpConnection-Helper` class we will define shortly. Note that in this example cookies are not persisted and only remain valid while the application is running, and no checking is done to ensure that the cookies are sent only with HTTP requests that match the specific domain and path sent with the cookie. First of all, the cookie is remembered by checking for the `Set-Cookie` response header when processing the response:

```
cookie = hc.getHeaderField( "Set-Cookie" );
```

Whenever a request is sent, the cookie is sent as part of the request:

```
if (cookie != null) {
    hc.setRequestProperty("Cookie", cookie);
}
```

Note that the previous example assumes that there is only a single `Set-Cookie` response header. Multiple cookies can in fact be sent back with an HTTP response, in which case the code should be adjusted to work with that case. It is common, however, for a Web server to set only a single cookie—one cookie is all that is needed to maintain the session information on the server.

Chapter 7, "The Record Management System," covers a reference implementation for `CookieJar` and `Cookie` classes that we can adapt to our `HttpCo-nectionHelper` class, enabling us to support long-lived HTTP sessions—sessions that persist even when the application terminates and restarts.

Cookie Restrictions

There are some limitations with respect to cookies. Note that the cookie limitations imposed on standard Web clients (Web browsers) are different from the ones imposed on MIDP clients. The following list describes the limitations on Web browsers:

- 300 total cookies
- 4 kilobytes per cookie
- 20 cookies per server or domain

As mentioned earlier, there is no native support for cookies in the MIDP HttpConnection implementation. The OTA recommendation specification, however, does allow cookies to be used as part of the provisioning process. It calls for a maximum cookie size of 256 bytes. No limitations on cookies are defined in the MIDP specification, but the number and size of cookies used should be kept as small as possible. You can find more information about cookies at `http://home.netscape.com/newsref/std/cookie_spec.html`.

Security

The first version of the MIDP lacks native support for network security. This situation is a problem, because security is very important in mobile applications where sensitive information is transmitted across wireless networks and the Internet. The good news is that this limitation is being addressed by the MIDP Expert Group, which is currently working on extending the MIDP to natively support HTTPS—the secure form of HTTP. Handset manufacturers have also recognized this limitation and are including HTTPS support on their devices. From a MIDP application development perspective, with only a few client changes, combined with proper server-side digital certificate configuration, your MIDP application can communicate with a server on the Internet by using end-to-end security. Please refer to Chapter 8, "Security," for more information about security.

The HttpConnectionHelper Class

The `HttpConnectionHelper` class is a convenience class that provides added functionality to the `HttpConnection` interface. With only a few statements, we can create and open an `HttpConnection`, send requests, and wait for HTTP responses. This class provides minimal support for cookies as well as minimal support for URL redirection.

A typical use of the `HttpConnectionHelper` class follows. The constructor for the `HttpConnectionHelper` class takes three arguments: URL (host and port information), resource, and parameters:

```
// Use HttpConnectionHelper to connect to targetURL, send request and
// receive response.

HTTPConnectionHelper hc;
String response;

// Set params. for URI query string
params = new Hashtable();
params.put("username", username);
params.put("password", password);
params.put("action", "get_messages");

try {
   // Compose targetURL and create a HttpConnectionHelper to send HTTP
   // request and wait for the XML response.

   String targetURL = "http://"+gatewayURL+":"+gatewayPort;
   hch = new HttpConnectionHelper(targetURL,
                                  EMAIL_CONTROLLER,
                                  params);
   response = hch.sendReceive();
   ..... // do something with the response
}
catch( Exception e ){
}
```

Do not forget that network operations can be quite slow, so whenever possible use a separate thread to make HTTP connections.

Here is the complete code for the `HttpConnectionHelper` class:

```
package com.j2medeveloper.net;

import java.io.*;
import java.util.*;
import javax.microedition.io.*;
/**
 * Helper class to connect over HTTP to origin servers, automatically
 * handling any redirections that may occur and only returning a
 * connection to the final URL and and some cookie management
 */
public class HttpConnectionHelper {

    private boolean          debug          = true;
    private HttpConnection   hc             = null;
    private String           originalURL    = null;
    private String           effectiveURL   = null;
    private Hashtable        messageHeaders = null;
    private String           contentBody    = null;
    private String           URLparameters  = null;
    private String           URLresource    = null;
    private String           requestMethod  = null;
    private static String    cookie         = null;

    /**
     * Creates a HttpConnectionHelper.
     * This version of the constructor attempts to resolve
     * URL redirection.
     * @param url The target URL
     * @param resource The URL resource
     * @param params The URL parameters (for query string)
     * @throws IOException If a connection error occurs.
     */
    public HttpConnectionHelper(String url,
                                String resource,
                                Hashtable params)
        throws    IOException {

        originalURL = url;
        setURLresource(resource);
        setURLparameters(params);

        // Handle any redirections.
        effectiveURL = determineEffectiveURL(url, resource);
    }
```

```
/**
 * Close the HTTP Connection
 */
public void close() throws IOException {
  hc.close();
}

/**
 * Sets the URL resource.
 * @param URL resource
 */
 public void setURLresource(String resource) {

     URLresource = resource;
 }

/**
 * Sets the URL parameters.
 * @param params a Hashtable containing parameters
 */
 public void setURLparameters(Hashtable params) {

    String name, value, param;

    if (params != null) {
        URLparameters = "?";

        Enumeration enum = params.keys();

        while (enum.hasMoreElements()) {

            name  = (String)enum.nextElement();
            value = (String)params.get(name);
            param = name + "=" + encodeURL(value);
            if(enum.hasMoreElements())
              param += "&";

            URLparameters += param;

        }
    }
 }

/**
 * Sets the content body that we want to POST
 * @param The content body
 */
public void setContentBody(String body) {
    contentBody = body;
}
```

```
    /**
     * Sets the headers for HTTP request
     * @param The request headers
     */
    public void setMessageHeaders(Hashtable headers) {
        messageHeaders = headers;
    }

    /**
     * Sets the requestMethod property.
     * @param The request method
     */
    public void setRequestMethod(String method) {
        requestMethod = method;
    }

     /**
      * Send HTTP request, and receive the HTTP response
      * @throws IOException if a connection error occurs.
      * @return Response
      */
     public String sendReceive()
            throws IOException {

        InputStream    is       = null;
        OutputStream   os       = null;
        String         response = null;
        int            ch       = 0;
        int            len      = 0;
        String         cookie   = null;

        try {
            //
            // --------
            //  SETUP phase
            // --------
            //

            // set targetURL (effectiveURL=url+resource) + parameters,
            // open HttpConnection
            String targetURL = effectiveURL;
            if(URLparameters != null)
               effectiveURL += URLparameters;
            hc = (HttpConnection)Connector.open(targetURL);

            // --------
            //  CONNECTED phase
            // --------

            // Set HTTP request headers
             setRequestHeaders();
```

```
// send (POST) content body, if any
if (contentBody != null) {

     // Set HTTP request method to POST,
     // set Content-Type and Content-Length and send body.
    hc.setRequestMethod(HttpConnection.POST);
    hc.setRequestProperty(
            "Content-Type",
            "application/x-www-form-urlencoded");
    hc.setRequestProperty
           ("Content-Length", ""+contentBody.length() );
    os = hc.openOutputStream();
    os.write(contentBody.getBytes());
    os.flush();
}
else {

    // Set HTTP request method to GET
    hc.setRequestMethod(HttpConnection.GET);
}

// remember received Cookie, if any
cookie = hc.getHeaderField( "Set-Cookie" );

// open stream (gets HTTP response headers),
// get Content-Length
is  = hc.openInputStream();
len = (int) hc.getLength();

//
// right here add processing associated with
//  YOUR response message headers
//

// now read the response(get content body), if any
StringBuffer receivebuffer = new StringBuffer();
if( len != -1) {

    // Read exactly Content-Length bytes, In bulk
    byte[] data = new byte[len];
    int actual = is.read(data,0,len);
    receivebuffer.append(new String(data,0,actual));
}
else {

    // Read until the connection is closed.
    while ((ch = is.read()) != -1) {
      len = is.available() ;
      receivebuffer.append((char)ch);
    }
}
```

```
            response = receivebuffer.toString();
        }
        catch (Exception e) {
          throw new IOException(
              "HTTPConnector error: " + e.getMessage());
        }

        // Clean up.
        finally {
            try {
                if (is != null)
                  is.close();

                if (os != null)
                  os.close();

                if (hc != null)
                  hc.close();
            }
            catch (IOException ioe) {
             .... // handle the exception
            }
        } // finally

        //
        //  CLOSE phase
        //

        return response;

    } // sendReceive

    /**
     * Determines effective URL. Handles HTTP redirections until target
     * URL Is found
     * @param  URL
     * @throws IOException if a connection error occurs.
     * @return Effective URL
     */
    private String determineEffectiveURL(String url, String resource)
        throws IOException
    {
        int    rc;
        String eURL = null;
        String rURL = url+resource;

        // do while we have not found the effective/ultimate URL
        while( rURL != null ) {

            eURL = rURL;
```

```
        // open HTTP connection; set request headers, get
        // response and remember received cookie, if any
        hc = (HttpConnection)Connector.open(rURL);
        setRequestHeaders(); // set request headers
        rc = hc.getResponseCode(); // get HTTP status
        cookie = hc.getHeaderField( "Set-Cookie" );

        switch( rc ) {

            // handle redirection codes
            case HttpConnection.HTTP_MOVED_PERM:
            case HttpConnection.HTTP_MOVED_TEMP:
            case HttpConnection.HTTP_SEE_OTHER:
            case HttpConnection.HTTP_TEMP_REDIRECT:

                rURL = hc.getHeaderField( "Location" );

                // handle improper syntax

                if( rURL != null && rURL .startsWith( "/" ) ) {

                    StringBuffer b = new StringBuffer();
                    b.append( "http://" );
                    b.append( hc.getHost() );
                    b.append( ':' );
                    b.append( hc.getPort() );
                    b.append( rURL );
                    rURL = b.toString();
                }
                else {

                    //  some sites do not respond correctly
                    if( rURL != null && rURL .startsWith( "ttp:" ) ) {
                        rURL = "h" + rURL ;
                    }
                }

                hc.close();
                break;

            default:
                rURL = null;
                break;

        } // switch

    } // while( effectiveURL != null )

    return eURL;

}   // setEffectiveURL
```

```
/**
 * Set HTTP request headers
 * @throws IOException if a connection error occurs.
 */
private void setRequestHeaders()
    throws IOException {

    try {

        /**
         * set MIDP headers:
         *   User-Agent to MIDP/CLDC
         *   Accept to XML
         *   Content-Language to en-US
         *   Connection as close, as we are not leveraging Keepalive
         */
        hc.setRequestProperty("User-Agent",
            "Profile/MIDP-1.0 Configuration/CLDC-1.0" );
        hc.setRequestProperty("Content-Language", "en-US");
        hc.setRequestProperty("Accept", "text/xml");
        hc.setRequestProperty ("Connection", "close");

        //  set cookie, if one exists for this session
        if (cookie != null) {
           hc.setRequestProperty("Cookie", cookie);
        }

        // set headers passed by caller
        if (messageHeaders != null) {

            Enumeration enum = messageHeaders.keys();

            while (enum.hasMoreElements()) {

              String key   = (String)enum.nextElement();
              String value = (String)messageHeaders.get(key);
              hc.setRequestProperty(key, value);
            }

        } // if (headers != null)
    }
    catch (IOException ioe) {
     ..... // handle exception
    }
} // setRequestHeaders()

/**
 * Encodes a URL
 * @param str URL to encode
 * @returns encoded URL String
 */
```

```
    private String encodeURL(String url) {

        StringBuffer s = new StringBuffer();
        int len = url.length();
        for(int i = 0; i < len; i++) {

            char ch = url.charAt(i);

            // no need to encode digits
            if (ch >= '0' && ch <= '9')
                s.append(ch);
            else
            // no need to encode letters
            if (ch >= 'a' && ch <= 'z' || ch >= 'A' && ch <= 'Z')
                s.append(ch);
            else
            // encode whitespace
            if (ch >= ' ')
                s.append('+');
            else {
               // encode anything else as a reserved character
                s.append('%');
                s.append(Hex((ch & 0xF0) >> 4));
                s.append(Hex(ch & 0x0F));
            }
        }
        return s.toString();
    }

    /**
     * Returns the HEX value of a character
     */
    private char Hex(int c) {
        if (c < 10)
            return (char)('0' + c);
        else
            return (char)(c - 10 + 'A');
    }
}
```

Summary

In this chapter, we have covered the GCF and MIDP's HTTP support. Before continuing, be sure to study Figure 6.6, which shows the GCF connection hierarchy in detail.

We will now proceed to discuss how data is persisted using the MIDP's Record Management System.

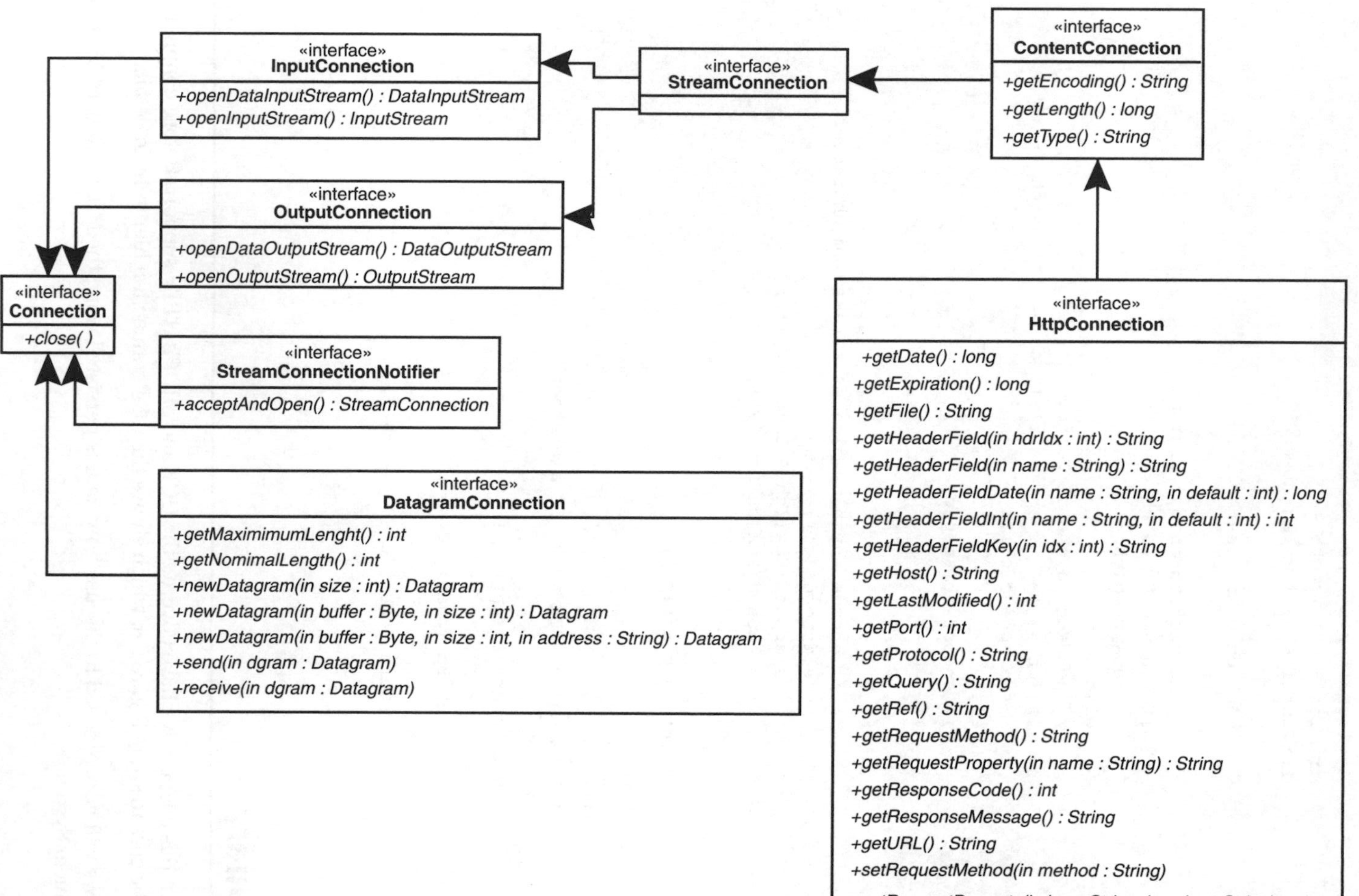

Figure 6.6 Details of the GCF connection interface hierarchy.

CHAPTER 7

The Record Management System

An important feature for many applications is the capability to store information persistently so that the data is available the next time the application runs. Even simple applications use this capability—if only to store user preferences. Data-driven applications, like those involved in sales force automation, obviously depend on data persistence even more. Without persistence, the alternative is to store and retrieve data by using the network, which means that the application will not work if the device is out of network coverage. Current wireless networks are also very slow, which would affect the application's overall performance.

As we saw in Chapter 2, "The Mobile Information Device Profile," the MIDP provides a data persistence mechanism called the Record Management System (RMS). In this chapter, we will explore the RMS classes and interfaces in detail in order to understand how to store and manage persistent data. Along the way, we will build some utilities that can help you in your own programming.

Overview

In RMS terminology, a persistent datastore is called a *record store*. A record store manages a set of *records*, which are variable-size byte arrays. All access to the records is done through the record store. The MIDP specification does not define any restrictions on the size of individual records or on the number of records in a record store, but individual MIDP implementations can define their own limits. On a Palm device, for example, each record can be no more than 64K in length because of restrictions imposed by the Palm operating system. Obviously, the amount of persistent storage available on a device places an absolute limit on the size of a record store. Because the devices you will be dealing with can be quite restricted, try to keep the amount of data stored in record stores to a minimum.

The MIDP specification does not specify how record stores are implemented. On devices with file systems, for example, the record store might be a file. This is how the simulator in the MIDP reference implementation or the J2ME Wireless Toolkit stores its data—as database files on the desktop computer's hard disk. On most devices, though, data is stored in non-volatile memory.

A record store is *not* a relational database. In fact, the record store knows nothing about the internal layout of its records; there are no fields or columns defined. It is up to the application(s) using the database to decide how data is stored in a record and what each record represents. The record store only tracks the following information:

- The name of the record store, up to 32 Unicode characters long. The name must be unique within the MIDlet suite.
- The number of records in the record store
- A record identifier (record ID) for each record. The ID starts at 1 and increments each time a record is added to the record store.
- A timestamp (the time of the last modification to the record store). A modification occurs whenever a record is updated, added, or deleted.
- The size of each record
- The total size of the record store
- The remaining storage space available to grow the record store
- A version number to track changes. The version number increments each time the record store is modified. The initial value of the version number is not specified, except that it must be a positive integer.

No Access to Native Databases

A common question asked by novice MIDP programmers is whether it is possible to access the device's native databases by using the RMS. For example, on a Palm device all persistent storage is done by using databases that are in effect a superset of what is available with the RMS. Each record store is in fact a native database. The RMS does not expose, however, any of the special features of a Palm database, nor does it provide direct access to all of the data in the database that underlies a record store (data that the RMS uses to manage the records in the record store). Remember that the RMS is meant to provide a *portable* way to store data persistently, presenting a common and abstract API that shields the application from the underlying implementation. To do anything more requires special, non-portable classes provided by the implementation.

Record stores are uniquely identified by name within a MIDlet suite. In other words, MIDlets in the same MIDlet suite can share record stores. MIDlets in different suites can reuse those names to create their own record stores, but there is no way to share a record store across two or more suites. In fact, the MIDP specification does not allow direct communication of any kind between MIDlets in different suites. The only way to send data from one MIDlet to another is to use implementation-specific classes (if any) or a third-party intermediary, such as a Web server.

Record stores are thread-safe, allowing different threads—even in different MIDlets—to access a record store simultaneously without data corruption. The RMS synchronizes all read and write operations and guarantees that record reading and writing are atomic operations. A record store does not do any record locking, however, leaving it up to the MIDlets that are using the record store to agree on a scheme to avoid overwriting each other's data. MIDlets in the same suite can use shared classes to synchronize access to individual records.

The records in a record store can be enumerated, sorted, and filtered in application-defined ways.

No automatic facilities are provided to backup a record store, to store it off the device, or to exchange data with external databases. The implementation might choose to provide these or other additional features, but only as non-portable extensions.

Basic Operations

Record stores support all the operations expected of a persistent store: The capability to create new record stores and delete old ones; the capability to create, delete, and update records; and the capability to enumerate and sort records. A single class, `RecordStore`, and a small set of interfaces and exceptions provide all the aforementioned capabilities. All RMS classes and interfaces are defined in the `javax.microedition.rms` package.

The RecordStore Class

The `RecordStore` class is the heart of the RMS. Each record store is represented by an instance of `RecordStore`, whose definition is as follows:

```
package javax.microedition.rms;

public class RecordStore {
    // Methods
    public int addRecord( byte[] data, int offset, int numBytes )
              throws RecordStoreNotOpenException,
                     RecordStoreException,
                     RecordStoreFullException;
```

```
public void addRecordListener( RecordListener listener );
public void closeRecordStore()
          throws RecordStoreNotOpenException,
                 RecordStoreException;
public void deleteRecord( int recordId )
          throws RecordStoreNotOpenException,
                 InvalidRecordIDException,
                 RecordStoreException;
public static void deleteRecordStore( String recordStoreName )
          throws RecordStoreException,
                 RecordStoreNotFoundException;
public RecordEnumeration enumerateRecords( RecordFilter filter,
        RecordComparator comparator, boolean keepUpdated )
          throws RecordStoreNotOpenException;
public long getLastModified()
          throws RecordStoreNotOpenException;
public String getName() throws RecordStoreNotOpenException;
public int getNextRecordID() throws RecordStoreNotOpenException,
                 RecordStoreException;
public int getNumRecords() throws RecordStoreNotOpenException;
public byte[] getRecord( int recordId )
          throws RecordStoreNotOpenException,
                 InvalidRecordIDException,
                 RecordStoreException;
public int getRecord( int recordId, byte[] buffer, int offset )
          throws RecordStoreNotOpenException,
                 InvalidRecordIDException,
                 RecordStoreException;
public int getRecordSize( int recordId )
          throws RecordStoreNotOpenException,
                 InvalidRecordIDException,
                 RecordStoreException;
public int getSize() throws RecordStoreNotOpenException;
public int getSizeAvailable()
          throws RecordStoreNotOpenException;
public int getVersion() throws RecordStoreNotOpenException;
public static String[] listRecordStores();
public static RecordStore openRecordStore(
        String recordStoreName, boolean createIfNecessary )
          throws RecordStoreException,
                 RecordStoreFullException,
                 RecordStoreNotFoundException;
public void removeRecordListener( RecordListener listener );
public void setRecord( int recordId, byte[] newData, int offset,
        int numBytes ) throws RecordStoreNotOpenException,
                 InvalidRecordIDException,
                 RecordStoreException,
                 RecordStoreFullException;

}
```

A summary of RecordStore's methods is shown in Table 7.1. If the class definition looks complicated, it is because most methods throw one or more exceptions. The RMS defines five exception classes:

- InvalidRecordID is thrown when an operation is attempted on a non-existent record.
- RecordStoreException is the base class for all record store exceptions and is thrown when none of the other exceptions are appropriate.

Table 7.1 RecordStore Method Descriptions

METHOD	DESCRIPTION
addRecord	Adds a new record to the record store, specifying its initial content. Returns the ID of the new record.
addRecordListener	Registers a listener with the record store. Listeners are notified whenever the record store is modified.
closeRecordStore	Closes an open record store.
deleteRecord	Deletes a record from the record store. The record IDs of the records that follow are *not* adjusted.
deleteRecordStore	Deletes a record store from the device's persistent storage.
enumerateRecords	Enumerates the records in the record store. The records can be filtered and sorted according to application-supplied rules. The enumeration also can track changes to the record store as they occur and adjust itself accordingly.
getLastModified	Returns the record store timestamp.
getName	Returns the record store name.
getNextRecordID	Returns the next record ID to be assigned to a new record.
getNumRecords	Returns the number of records in the record store.
getRecord	Returns the contents of a specific record.
getRecordSize	Returns the size of a record.
getSize	Returns the total size of the record store, including any overhead used to manage the records.
getSizeAvailable	Returns the amount of memory available to grow the record store.
getVersion	Returns the record store version.
listRecordStores	Lists the record stores in the MIDlet suite.
openRecordStore	Opens a record store, optionally creating it if not found.
removeRecordListener	Deregisters a record listener.
setRecord	Updates a record with new content. The entire record is updated.

- RecordStoreFullException is thrown when the record store is full.
- RecordStoreNotFoundExeption is thrown when an operation is attempted on a non-existent record store.
- RecordStoreNotOpenException is thrown when an operation is attempted on an unopened record store.

Full definitions for each exception can be found in Appendix A, but they are all nearly identical. Each exception class inherits directly or indirectly from java .lang.Exception (not RuntimeException) and defines two constructors— one that takes no arguments and one that takes a single string as an argument. Unless you are building utility classes, it is unlikely that you will have to instantiate and throw any of these exceptions yourself.

The exceptions, of course, are indications that something has gone wrong with a record store operation. You must catch and deal with any of these exceptions, either individually or by catching the base class, RecordStoreException. The general pattern is fairly simple:

```
RecordStore rs = ....; // a record store instance

try {
    // do something here with the record store
}
catch( RecordStoreException e ){
    // an error has occurred
}
```

In the examples that follow, the exception handling will sometimes be omitted for clarity, but be sure to include appropriate error handling in your own code.

Note that the RMS also defines four interfaces for use by the RecordStore class. Three of these interfaces—RecordComparator, RecordEnumeration, and RecordFilter—are used in the record enumeration process, which we will discuss later. The fourth interface, RecordListener, is a listener interface for tracking changes to a record store.

Opening and Closing a Record Store

Except for deleting and listing record stores, all other record store operations require an open RecordStore instance with which to work. You open a record store by calling the static openRecordStore method:

```
try {
    RecordStore rs = RecordStore.openRecordStore( "MyData", false );
    .....
    rs.closeRecordStore();
}
catch( RecordStoreException e ){
}
```

This is the only way to obtain a RecordStore instance, because the class does not define any public constructors. A record store remains open until you call closeRecordStore, after which any operation you attempt on the record store will throw RecordStoreNotOpenException. As such, you should immediately discard any reference to a record store after you have closed it.

You can open a record store multiple times, either in the same MIDlet or in other MIDlets in the suite, in which case the same instance of RecordStore is returned by openRecordStore. The RMS tracks the number of times a record store has been opened and will not actually close it until the closeRecord-Store method is invoked the same number of times. Therefore, it is perfectly safe to call openRecordStore if you are unsure that a record store is open as long as you balance it with a call to closeRecordStore.

The first argument to openRecordStore is the name of the record store, up to 32 characters long. The second argument tells the RMS what to do if the record store does not exist. If true, the RMS will create a new record store with that name; otherwise it will throw RecordStoreNotFoundException. If you need to initialize a record store when it is created, you can use the following code:

```
RecordStore rs = null;

try {
    rs = RecordStore.openRecordStore( "MyData", false );
}
catch( RecordStoreNotFoundException e ){
    try {
        rs = RecordStore.openRecordStore( "MyData", true );
        ..... // initialize record store here
    }
    catch( RecordStoreException e ){
        // could not create it....
    }
}
catch( RecordStoreException e ){
    // some other error...
}
```

A simpler approach, however, is to always pass true to openRecordStore and call getNumRecords:

```
RecordStore rs = null;

try {
    rs = RecordStore.openRecordStore( "MyData", true );
    if( rs.getNumRecords() == 0 ){
        ..... // initialize record store here
    }
}
catch( RecordStoreException e ){
```

```
        // some other error....
    }
```

This situation assumes, of course, that an empty record store is an error. If it is not, open the record store with `true` as the second argument and do not bother catching `Record-StoreNotFound` or calling `getNumRecords`. Always catch `RecordStoreException`, however, because it might not be possible to open the record store if the device has run out of memory or due to some other internal error. Your application should likely exit at this point unless the application can continue to work without the record store.

If a record store cannot be created because not enough memory is available, `Record-StoreFullException` is thrown. Your application can catch this exception and ask the user to free up some memory in order for the application to run.

Listing and Deleting Record Stores

The `RecordStore` class defines two other static methods: `listRecordStores` to obtain the list of record stores created by the MIDlets in the MIDlet suite and `deleteRe-cordStore` to delete a record store from persistent storage. The `listRecordStores` method returns an array of strings where each string is the name of a record store. Here is an example of populating a `List` user interface object with the list of record stores:

```
import javax.microedition.lcdui.*;
import javax.microedition.rms.*;

.....

void populateList( List list ){
    String[] stores = RecordStore.listRecordStores();
    if( stores != null ){
        for( int i = 0; i < stores.length; ++i ){
            list.append( stores[i], null );
        }
    } else {
        list.append( "[no record stores]", null );
    }
}
```

Note that `listRecordStores` returns `null` if there are no record stores in the MIDlet suite. It also is one of only three methods that do not throw any exceptions.

Although the record stores in a MIDlet suite are deleted automatically by the application management software whenever the suite is removed from a device, an application can explicitly delete a record store by calling `deleteRecord-Store` and passing it the name of the record store to delete:

```
try {
    RecordStore.deleteRecordStore( "MyData" );
}
catch( RecordStoreException e ){
}
```

Only unopened record stores can be deleted. If the record store is open and in use by a MIDlet, the delete operation fails and throws `RecordStoreException`.

Creating and Deleting Records

Records are created and deleted by using the `addRecord` and `deleteRecord` methods on an open record store. The arguments to `addRecord` are a byte array, an offset into the byte array, and the number of bytes to read out of the byte array. For example:

```
RecordStore rs = ....;
byte[]      data = new byte[]{ 0, 1 };
int         id = 0;

try {
    id = rs.addRecord( data, 0, data.length );
}
catch( RecordStoreFullException e ){
    // oops, we're full!
}
catch( RecordStoreException e ){
    // some other error
}
```

This coding creates a new record and initializes it with two bytes of data. It is legal to create an empty, or zero-length, record:

```
id = rs.addRecord( null, 0, 0 ); // create empty record
```

The return value is the ID of the newly created record, which will always be an integer greater than zero. The first record created in a record store has an ID of 1. The ID is used with other methods to specify the record on which to perform other operations. If a record could not be created because there was not enough room in the record store, `RecordStoreFullException` is thrown. If the creation failed for another reason, `RecordStoreException` is thrown.

A record can be deleted at any time by calling `deleteRecord` and passing in the ID of the record to delete:

```
RecordStore rs = ....;
int         id = ....;

try {
    rs.deleteRecord( id );
}
catch( InvalidRecordIDException e ){
}
catch( RecordStoreException e ){
}
```

If the record does not exist, `InvalidRecordIDException` is thrown. If the record could not be deleted for some other reason, `RecordStoreException` is thrown.

Deleting a record does not change the ID of any other record in the record store. In other words, record IDs within a record store are unique as long as the record store itself is not deleted. The record ID can therefore be used as a key. The ID to be assigned to the next record that is created can be obtained by calling `getNextRecordID`; the ID remains valid until the next successful call to `addRecord`. This technique can be useful when creating records in different record stores that reference each other. If different threads (possibly in different MIDlets) can modify a record store simultaneously, however, you should use some kind of synchronization to ensure that the value returned by `get-NextRecordID` remains valid for the current thread until it calls `addRecord`. For example, you could use the `synchronized` statement to obtain locks on the `RecordStore` instances involved:

```
byte[] setRecordID( byte[] data, int id ){
    // add code here to insert the id into
    // the record data and return the modified data
    .....
}

void createMutualReferences( RecordStore rs1, RecordStore rs2,
                             byte[] data1, byte[] data2 )
                         throws RecordStoreException {
    byte[] tmp;

    synchronized( rs1 ){
        synchronized( rs2 ){
            int n1 = rs1.getNextRecordID();
            int n2 = rs2.getNextRecordID();

            data1 = setRecordID( data1, n2 );
            data2 = setRecordID( data2, n1 );

            rs1.addRecord( data1, 0, data1.length );
            rs2.addRecord( data2, 0, data2.length );
        }
    }
}
```

When synchronizing in this manner, however, be careful to avoid deadlock, which can happen when different threads lock the record store instances in different orders.

Reading and Writing Records

Data is read from or written to a record by using the `getRecord` and `set-Record` methods. There are two versions of `getRecord`. The simplest version returns the record contents as a byte array:

```
byte[] data = rs.getRecord( id );
```

If the record is empty, `null` is returned; otherwise, the method returns an array containing the record contents. The second version copies the record contents into an existing byte array starting at the given offset:

```
byte[] data = new byte[100];
int    len;

len = rs.getRecord( id, data, 0 );
```

The application must ensure that the byte array is large enough to contain the record contents; otherwise, the method throws ArrayIndexOutOfBounds-Exception. The method returns the number of bytes. The second version of getRecord is more general than the first version. In fact, the most likely implementation of the first getRecord is as follows:

```
public byte[] getRecord( int id ) throws
                                    RecordStoreNotOpenException,
                                    InvalidRecordIDException,
                                    RecordStoreException {
    byte[] data = null;
    int    size = getRecordSize( id );

    if( size > 0 ){
        data = new byte[size];
        getRecord( id, data, 0 );
    }

    return data;
}
```

The implementation is free to do otherwise, of course, but this situation would certainly imply that it is more efficient to use the second version of get-Record (more on this subject later). Note the call to getRecordSize to obtain the size of the record in bytes. This size is the size of the record contents, not the size of the record itself; there might be additional overhead associated with each record that you cannot directly determine except by calling getSize to obtain the size of the entire record store.

The getRecord methods throw InvalidRecordIDException if the record does not exist, RecordStoreNotOpenException if the record store is not open, or RecordStoreException if an internal error occurs.

To update an existing record, call setRecord:

```
int         id = ....;
RecordStore rs = ....;
byte[]      data = ....;

rs.setRecord( id, data, 0, data.length );
```

The first argument is the record ID, and the last three arguments are the same arguments that you pass to addRecord: The byte array to store, the offset into the byte array, and the number of bytes to store. The method throws Record-StoreFullException in addition to those thrown by getRecord.

Note that there is no way to read or write *part* of a record. You must always read or write the entire record. Changing a record usually means reading it into a byte array, making the change in memory, and then writing the byte array back to the record store.

What the application stores in a record is entirely up to you. As mentioned before, the record store deals with raw byte arrays. Byte arrays are rarely convenient for the application to deal with, however, so later in this chapter we will discuss how to read and write records with more conventional input and output streams.

Whenever possible, minimize the number of times you read or write records. In particular, avoid writing records until absolutely necessary, because on some platforms writing to persistent storage is much more expensive than reading persistent data.

Tracking Changes to a Record Store

There are times when an application needs to know when a record store was last modified. The `getLastModified` method returns the time of the last modification in milliseconds, the same format returned by `System.current-TimeMillis`. For example, to check whether a record store has been modified within the last hour, use the following code:

```
long time = System.currentTimeMills() - ( 1000 * 60 * 60 );
if( rs.getLastModified() >= time ){
    // do something...
}
```

Alternatively, if you just want to know whether the record store has been modified since you last checked it, call `getVersion` to get the current version number:

```
int oldVersion = ....; // store the old version somewhere

if( rs.getVersion() > oldVersion ){
    // do something....
}
```

The version increments each time the record store is modified and is guaranteed to be greater than zero. A quick comparison against a previously stored value is all you need to know if the record store has been modified.

The application also can register a listener with the record store to be immediately notified whenever the record store is modified. The listener interface defines three methods:

```
package javax.microedition.rms;

public interface RecordListener {
    void recordAdded( RecordStore recordStore, int recordId );
    void recordChanged( RecordStore recordStore, int recordId );
    void recordDeleted( RecordStore recordStore, int recordId );
}
```

The `recordAdded` method is called in response to `addRecord`, `record-Changed` in response to `setRecord`, and `recordDeleted` in response to `deleteRecord`. The record store reference and the ID of the modified record are passed to the methods so that the same listener can be used to track changes to different record stores. Note that the methods are always called *after* the record store has been modified.

Use addRecordListener to register a listener with an open record store. Unlike the setCommandListener method of javax.microedition.lcdui .Displayable, addRecordListener lets you register multiple listeners with a record store. To deregister the listener, call removeRecordListener. Note that when a record store is closed, all registered listeners are automatically deregistered.

Advanced Operations

A few record store operations are more advanced than the ones we just covered. Enumerating the list of records in a record store can be quite complex if filtering and sorting is involved, for example. Also, reading and writing data efficiently and conveniently is non-trivial.

Enumerating Records

The RMS tracks the number of records in a record store, but the record IDs do not follow a specific pattern because any number of deleted record IDs can lie between each active record ID. A way is needed to enumerate the valid records—or their IDs—in order to perform common operations such as searching or sorting.

The Brute Force Approach

One way to enumerate the records is to use the brute force approach and to call getRecordSize for each possible record ID, starting with record 1 and continuing up to (but not including) the value returned by getNextRecordID. Simply catch and ignore any InvalidRecordIDException that is thrown. For example, here is a way to build a vector of valid record IDs by using the brute force approach:

```
import java.util.Vector;
import javax.microedition.rms.*;

// The brute force approach - not recommended!

public Vector enumerateBruteForce( RecordStore rs ){
    Vector v = new Vector();
    try {
        int lastID = rs.getNextRecordID();
        for( int id = 1; id < lastID; ++id ){
            try {
                rs.getRecordSize( id );
                v.addElement( new Integer( id ) );
            }
            catch( InvalidRecordIDException e ){ // ignore it
            }
        }
```

```
        }
        catch( RecordStoreException e ){
            return null;
        }

        return v;
    }
```

There is a much better way to perform this action, however, and it involves a new enumeration interface: RecordEnumeration.

The RecordEnumeration Interface

The RecordEnumeration interface is defined as follows:

```
package javax.microedition.rms;

public interface RecordEnumeration {
    void destroy();
    boolean hasNextElement();
    boolean hasPreviousElement();
    boolean isKeptUpdated();
    void keepUpdated( boolean keepUpdated );
    byte[] nextRecord() throws InvalidRecordIDException,
                        RecordStoreNotOpenException,
                        RecordStoreException;
    int nextRecordId() throws InvalidRecordIDException;
    int numRecords();
    byte[] previousRecord() throws InvalidRecordIDException,
                        RecordStoreNotOpenException,
                        RecordStoreException;
    int previousRecordId() throws InvalidRecordIDException;
    void rebuild();
    void reset();
}
```

The interface is similar in purpose to the java.util.Enumeration with which you are already familiar but with more features. It defines a bidirectional enumeration of the records in a record store that can optionally adjust itself as the record store is modified.

Using RecordEnumeration

To obtain a RecordEnumeration, call an open record store's enumerate-Records method. The method takes three arguments—the first is a reference to a filter interface, the second is a reference to a sorting interface, and the third is a boolean indicating whether the enumerator updates itself as the record store is modified. We will look at filtering and sorting shortly, so we will ignore the arguments for now and concentrate on using the enumeration for general-purpose record store traversal.

To iterate through all the records in a record store, use the following code:

```
RecordEnumeration enum = rs.enumerateRecords( null, null, false );
while( enum.hasNextElement() ){
    int id = enum.nextRecordId();
    // do something here with the ID
}
enum.destroy();
```

The order of the records is undefined, and no tracking of record store modifications is performed. This method is the recommended way to do a general traversal of a record store. Note that the enumeration is bidirectional, so you can call `hasPreviousElement` and `previousRecordId` to go backwards from the current position in the enumeration. Do not forget to catch `Invalid-RecordIDException`; if the enumeration is not tracking modifications to the record store, it is entirely possible that it will return the ID of a record that another thread has deleted after the current thread obtained the enumeration.

For convenience, `RecordEnumeration` also defines a `nextRecord` method that can replace a call to `getRecord`. For example, consider this code:

```
RecordEnumeration enum = rs.enumerateRecords( null, null, false );
while( enum.hasNextElement() ){
    byte[] data = rs.getRecord( enum.nextRecordId() );
    // do something here with the data
}
enum.destroy();
```

You can simplify this code as follows:

```
RecordEnumeration enum = rs.enumerateRecords( null, null, false );
while( enum.hasNextElement() ){
    byte[] data = enum.nextRecord();
    // do something with the data
}
enum.destroy();
```

A `previousRecord` method is also defined. The methods throw the same exceptions as `getRecord`. Note that it might be more efficient to explicitly call `getRecord` instead of using these convenience methods (more on that topic a bit later).

The `numRecords` method returns the number of record IDs in the enumeration. For a simple enumeration like the ones mentioned previously, `num-Records` will equal the number of records in the record store at some point in time. The exact number can vary because a simple enumeration can traverse the record store incrementally instead of doing an entire traversal when it is first created.

You can reset an enumeration to its initial state at any time by calling `reset`. You can also force it to update itself to reflect the current state of the record store by calling `rebuild`. When you are done with an enumeration, call its `destroy` method.

Tracking Changes

An enumeration can track changes made to the record store and adjust itself accordingly so that it never returns the IDs of deleted records and never misses newly created records. You create such an enumeration by passing `true` as the third argument to `enumerateRecords`:

```
// Create a tracking enumeration
RecordEnumeration enum = rs.enumerateRecords( null, null, true );
```

You can also enable or disable an enumeration's tracking of a record store at any time by calling its `keepUpdated` method. The `isKeptUpdated` method returns the enumeration's current tracking status.

Note that tracking changes to a record store can have serious performance implications and should be avoided in most cases.

Filtering Records

A `RecordEnumeration` can return a *subset* of the records in a record store by filtering out records that do not match specific criteria. The filtering is done by an object that implements the `RecordFilter` interface, defined as follows:

```
package javax.microedition.rms;

public interface RecordFilter {
    boolean matches( byte[] candidate );
}
```

A reference to the filter is passed as the first argument to `enumerateRecords`. The enumeration calls the filter's `matches` method to determine whether a given record is to be included in the enumeration or not. The filter examines the record data and returns `true` if the record is to be included in the enumeration and returns `false` if not. Consider the following filter:

```
// Filter out empty records

public class FilterEmpties implements RecordFilter {
    public boolean matches( byte[] candidate ){
        return( candidate.length > 0 );
    }
}
```

This filter removes empty records from an enumeration. The enumeration is created as follows:

```
RecordEnumeration enum = rs.enumerateRecords( new FilterEmpties(),
                                              null, false );
```

Only one filter can be used with an enumeration, but it is easy to combine filters by using these two helper classes:

```
public class FilterOR implements RecordFilter {
    private RecordFilter f1;
    private RecordFilter f2;

    public FilterOR( RecordFilter f1, RecordFilter f2 ){
        this.f1 = f1;
        this.f2 = f2;
    }

    public boolean matches( byte[] candidate ){
        return f1.matches( candidate ) || f2.matches( candidate );
    }
}

public class FilterAND implements RecordFilter {
    private RecordFilter f1;
    private RecordFilter f2;

    public FilterAND( RecordFilter f1, RecordFilter f2 ){
        this.f1 = f1;
        this.f2 = f2;
    }

    public boolean matches( byte[] candidate ){
        return f1.matches( candidate ) && f2.matches( candidate );
    }
}
```

These classes can be used to build conditional filters that check several different criteria. For example, say that you need to search for all records that refer to a specific employee and a specific date. If you defined `FilterEmployee` and `FilterDate` classes, you could create a combined filter like the following:

```
String       employee = ....;
Date         date = ....;
RecordFilter filter = new FilterAND( new FilterEmployee( employee ),
                                     new FilterDate( date ) );
```

Note that a filter only ever gets access to the record data, not to the record ID. In other words, you cannot do any filtering based on the record ID; the filtering is based exclusively on the record contents, the meaning of which is only known to the application.

Filters can be used by themselves or in conjunction with a comparator, which we will describe in the next section.

Sorting Records

A `RecordEnumeration` can also *sort* the records by comparing them to each other to obtain their relative orders. The sorting is done by an object that implements the `RecordComparator` interface, defined as follows:

```
package javax.microedition.rms;

public interface RecordComparator {
    int compare( byte[] rec1, byte[] rec2 );

    int EQUIVALENT = 0;
    int FOLLOWS = 1;
    int PRECEDES = -1;
}
```

A reference to the comparator is passed as the second argument to `enumerateRecords`. The enumeration calls the comparator's `compare` method to determine the relative order of two records. The method returns `PRECEDES` if the first record precedes the second record in the sort order, `FOLLOWS` if the first record follows the second record, and `EQUIVALENT` if the two records are equivalent. Here is a simple comparator that sorts records by using the first byte of data:

```
public class FirstByteComparator implements RecordComparator {
    public int compare( byte[] rec1, byte[] rec2 ){
        byte val1 = ( rec1.length > 0 ? rec1[0] : 0 );
        byte val2 = ( rec2.length > 0 ? rec2[0] : 0 );

        if( val1 < val2 ){
            return PRECEDES;
        } else if( val1 > val2 ){
            return FOLLOWS;
        } else {
            return EQUIVALENT;
        }
    }
}
```

Again, only the data for the records is passed to the comparator, not the record IDs. Sorting records is useful in many situations, but it also affects the performance of the enumeration (especially when combined with a filter).

Using Streams to Read and Write Records

A record store's `getRecord` and `setRecord` methods are simple but not particularly convenient. An application rarely stores its data as a set of byte arrays. Instead, the data is likely stored as strings, integers, or even objects. The application must map the data into byte arrays and back in order to persist the data by using the RMS. Input and output streams defined in the `java.io` package make it easy to transform the data appropriately.

Use `ByteArrayInputStream` to convert a byte array to an input stream. Bytes read by using the input stream are read directly from the byte array. Pass the byte array to the stream's constructor. Similarly, use `ByteArrayOutput-Stream` to define an output stream that writes to an in-memory buffer. The buffer contents can be obtained as a byte array at any time by calling the output stream's `toByteArray` method.

Byte array input and output streams are most often combined with other stream classes in order to conveniently read and write different kinds of data. The `DataInputStream` and `DataOutputStream` classes are often used because they define methods for reading and writing strings and primitive data types. For example, here is how to write a record consisting of a boolean, an integer, and a string:

```
try {
    ByteArrayOutputStream bout = new ByteArrayOutputStream();
    DataOutputStream      dout = new DataOutputStream( bout );

    dout.writeBoolean( true );
    dout.writeInt( 20 );
    dout.writeUTF( "A string" );
    dout.flush();

    byte[] data = bout.toByteArray();
    rs.addRecord( data, 0, data.length );

    bout.reset();
}
catch( IOException e ){
}
catch( RecordStoreException e ){
}
```

Note how the underlying byte array output stream is reset after the record is added, which enables you to make further calls to the data output stream in order to create another new record without having to construct new instances of `ByteArrayOutputStream` or `DataOutputStream`.

The code to read the record back is as follows:

```
try {
    byte[]               data = rs.getRecord( id );
    ByteArrayInputStream bin = new ByteArrayInputStream( data );
    DataInputStream      din = new DataInputStream( bin );

    boolean first = din.readBoolean();
    int     second = din.readInt();
    String  third = din.readUTF();
}
catch( IOException e ){
}
catch( RecordStoreException e ){
}
```

Reusing the `ByteArrayInputStream` and `DataInputStream` instances is also possible, as shown in the next section.

Efficiently Reading Records

One of the things to avoid when programming MIDP-enabled devices is *object churning*. Churning refers to the creation and abandonment of many objects in a short period of time. Churning can overwhelm the garbage collector and cause the application to temporarily use more memory than it needs and also slows it down as the garbage collector works hard to find and discard the unused objects.

It is easy to create many new objects when enumerating the records in a record store. Calling `getRecord` creates and returns a new byte array. You can avoid this situation, however, by using the version of `getRecord` that uses an existing byte array and by making sure that the byte array is always large enough to read the next record. For example:

```
try {
    RecordEnumeration    enum = rs.enumerateRecords( null, null, false );
    byte[]               data = null;
    ByteArrayInputStream bin;
    DataInputStream      din;

    while( e.hasNextElement() ){
        int id = e.nextRecordId();
        int size = rs.getRecordSize( id );
        if( size == 0 ) continue;

        if( data == null || data.length < size ){
            data = new byte[ size + 20 ]; // growth factor
            bin  = new ByteArrayInputStream( data );
            din  = new DataInputStream( bin );
        }

        rs.getRecord( id, data, 0 );
        din.reset();

        boolean first = din.readBoolean();
        int     second = din.readInt();
        String  third = din.readUTF();

        doSomething( first, second, third ); // process data
    }
}
catch( IOException e ){
}
catch( RecordStoreException e ){
}
```

This example checks the size of each record and automatically grows the byte array that is used to read the record contents. The data input stream's `reset` method is called after each record is read, which also resets the byte array input stream. The input stream objects are reused for reading each record and are discarded only when the byte array has grown to accommodate a bigger record size. If you know that the records in a record store are all of fixed size or are less than a predetermined maximum size, you can make the reading even simpler by omitting the code to grow the array.

Mapping Objects to Records

CLDC-based profiles, including the MIDP, do not support object serialization. In other words, there is no automatic way to convert an object to a byte stream and vice-versa. If the capability was supported, it would be trivial to store serialized objects in a record store. But serialization is not supported, so we need an alternate way to persist an object into a record store.

You can easily add serialization support to a class by defining `serialize` and `deserialize` methods that write and read objects into and out of byte arrays. Take, for example, a `User` class that holds two strings—a name and a password:

```
public class User {
    private String password;
    private String name;

    public User(){
        this( null, null );
    }

    public User( String name, String password ){
        this.name = name;
        this.password = password;
    }

    public String getName() { return name; }
    public String getPassword() { return password; }
}
```

Define the following methods, either in the class itself (the preferred approach) or in a separate helper class:

```
public synchronized byte[] serialize(){
    try {
        ByteArrayOutputStream bout = new ByteArrayOutputStream();
        DataOutputStream      dout = new DataOutputStream( bout );

        dout.writeUTF( name != null ? name : "" );
        dout.writeUTF( password != null ? password : "" );
        dout.flush();

        return bout.toByteArray();
    }
    catch( Exception e ){
        return null;
    }
}
```

```
public synchronized boolean deserialize( byte[] data ){
    try {
        ByteArrayInputStream bin = new ByteArrayInputStream( data );
        DataInputStream      din = new DataInputStream( bin );

        name = din.readUTF();
        password = din.readUTF();
        return true;
    }
    catch( Exeption e ){
        return false;
    }
}
```

These methods are not as efficient as they could be. They should really share and reuse the input and output streams as discussed in the previous sections. It should be obvious how `serialize` and `deserialize` work, though. Storing an object is simple:

```
User   u = new User( "john", "1ij32" );
byte[] data = u.serialize();

if( data != null ){
    rs.addRecord( data, 0, data.length );
}
```

Also, reading the object is just as simple:

```
User   u = new User();
byte[] data = rs.getRecord( id );

u.deserialize( data );
```

Note how the serialization methods deal with byte arrays and not directly with records. This function insulates the objects from having to know where they are stored. You can even use this simple serialization format to move objects across the network.

Using External Databases

Chances are good that at least some of the data that an application needs is stored externally in a relational database or in some other repository. Getting the data out of the external database and onto the device and vice-versa then becomes a matter of great importance. One possible scenario is that the application uses HTTP to communicate with a servlet running in a Web server. The servlet acts as the intermediary between the application and the external database, transforming the data in both directions. This section describes, at a high level, how to implement this scenario.

Communicating with the Servlet

The client application—the MIDlet—uses HTTP (or HTTPS if the device supports it; refer to the next chapter) as a transport mechanism for the data. In other words, communication between the application and the servlet is *tunneled* over HTTP. For MIDlet-to-server communication, this method is really the preferred choice because no other protocols are required by the MIDP specification, but it is also a common use for HTTP in other similar scenarios. Even IIOP, a protocol used in CORBA-based distributed computing, can be tunneled over HTTP. HTTP tunneling is often the only way to get data past a corporation's firewalls. This is an important feature, because the device on which the MIDlet runs is not on the corporate intranet—at least, not without special arrangements with the network operators who run the gateways that link the device to the Internet.

Outline and Sample Code

Because the HTTP protocol and its use by a MIDlet was covered in detail in the previous chapter, let's outline how the MIDlet-servlet communication occurs:

- The servlet is installed on a host, say `acme.com`, as `/servlet/sync`. The application connects to the servlet by using URLs that start with "`http://acme.com/servlet/sync/`."
- The servlet extends `javax.servlet.http.HttpServlet` and overrides the `doPost` method. We use the HTTP POST method to transfer data.
- The servlet's `doPost` method uses the remainder of the request path (the part after `/servlet/sync`, as returned by `HttpServletRequest.getPathInfo`) to determine which specific action the application wishes to perform. If the servlet only supports a single action (the target of the data exchange does not change), then this action might not be necessary.
- The application prepares the data to be tunneled over HTTP and ideally determines its length in bytes.
- The application uses the `HttpConnection` interface introduced in the last chapter to establish a connection between the device and the servlet. The application sets the `User-Agent`, `Content-Language`, `Accept`, `Connection`, and `Content-Length` headers appropriately before obtaining an output stream for the HTTP connection and writing the data to that output stream.
- After the output stream is closed, the application waits for a response from the server. The servlet, meanwhile, receives the application's request and uses the path information to determine the correct course of action. The servlet then calls `HttpServletRequest.getInputStream` to obtain an input stream for the data sent by the application.
- The servlet reads the data and uses it to communicate with the external database. This communication can be direct, by using a JDBC database connection, or indirect, by using Enterprise JavaBeans or some other intermediate objects and/or

servers. The servlet can communicate with a data synchronization server instead of a database, for example, and let the server take care of getting data in and out of databases and handling data conflicts and other errors.

- The servlet uses the `HttpServletResponse` object to set a status code, to set the MIME type for the response, and to obtain an output stream for the response. It must also set the `Content-Length` header appropriately. It writes its response to the output stream and exits the `doPost` method.
- The application unblocks and checks the response code. If the response code is as expected, it obtains an input stream and starts reading and processing the response.

Some code samples show how all of these tasks can be accomplished. The application connects to and sends its data by using code similar to the following:

```
public byte[] sendAndReceive( byte[] toServer ){
    HttpConnection conn = null;
    InputStream    in = null;
    OutputStream   out = null;
    byte[]         fromServer = null;

    try {
        conn = (HttpConnection)
                    Connector.open( "http://acme.com/servlet/sync/" );

        conn.setRequestMethod( HttpConnection.POST );
        conn.setRequestProperty( "User-Agent",
                    "Profile/MIDP-1.0 Configuration/CLDC-1.0" );
        conn.setRequestProperty( "Content-Language", "en-US" );
        conn.setRequestProperty( "Accept", "application/octet-stream" );
        conn.setRequestProperty( "Connection", "close" );
        conn.setRequestProperty( "Content-Length",
                    Integer.toString( toServer.length ) );

        out = conn.openOutputStream();
        out.write( toServer );
        out.close();
        out = null;

        int rc = conn.getResponseCode();

        if( rc == HttpConnection.HTTP_OK ){
            ByteArrayOutputStream bout = new ByteArrayOutputStream();

            in = conn.getInputStream();
            int len = conn.getLength();
            if( len != -1 ){
                for( int count = 0; count < len; ++count ){
                    bout.write( in.read() );
                }
            } else {
```

```
                int val;
                while( ( val = in.read() ) != -1 ){
                    bout.write( val );
                }
            }

            fromServer = bout.toByteArray();
        } else {
            // bad status code - do something here
        }
    }
    catch( Exception e ){
        // error - do something here
    }

    if( out != null ){
        try { out.close(); } catch( Exception e ){}
    }

    if( in != null ){
        try { in.close(); } catch( Exception e ){}
    }

    if( conn != null ){
        try { conn.close(); } catch( Exception e ){}
    }

    return fromServer;
}
```

You can, of course, use the `HttpConnectionHelper` class introduced in the last chapter to make the connection to the Web server. You will have to modify it to send binary data instead of string data.

The servlet code is fairly simple:

```
protected void doPost( HttpServletRequest req, HttpServletResponse res )
        throws ServletException, IOException {
    InputStream in = req.getInputStream();
    int         len = req.getContentLength();

    ..... // process the data

    // Now prepare the response....

    res.setStatus( HttpServletResponse.SC_OK );
    res.setContentLength( .... ); // set appropriately

    OutputStream out = res.getOutputStream();
    ..... // write out the response
}
```

The hard part is processing the data from the client and generating the appropriate response, which of course we cannot go into here because it is very specific to a particular installation.

Formatting the Data

The sample code assumes that the client and the servlet are exchanging raw binary data; in other words, sending byte arrays back and forth. The contents of those arrays can be almost anything. They could be the raw records from a record store or serialized forms of objects.

An alternative to sending binary data is to exchange XML documents. XML is covered in detail in Chapter 9. Using XML has advantages and disadvantages. XML documents are easy to create and parse and can be validated against known formats. They are character-based, however, and fairly verbose, so exchanging XML documents wirelessly can take longer than exchanging the equivalent binary data.

RMS Utility Classes

We end this chapter with a few utility classes that demonstrate the use of the RMS. All of the classes defined here are in the `com.j2medeveloper.util` package. The code for each class is presented in full but with minimal comments, followed by a simple example of how it is used. Study the code to gain some further insight into the RMS classes. Be sure to check the book's Web site for more detailed descriptions and updates to the code.

HashtableHelper: Saving and Restoring Hashtables

The `HashtableHelper` class defines serialization methods for saving and restoring `Hashtable` objects. The objects stored in the hashtable are converted to strings when stored, and when restored they will be restored as string values:

```
package com.j2medeveloper.util;

import java.io.*;
import java.util.*;

/**
 * Defines routines to serialize/deserialize a Hashtable.
 * The hashtable is assumed to contain non-empty string keys
 * and string values.
 */

public class HashtableHelper {
```

```
// Save hashtable as a byte array

public static byte[] serialize( Hashtable h ){
    Enumeration enum = h.keys();

    try {
        ByteArrayOutputStream bout = new ByteArrayOutputStream();
        DataOutputStream      dout = new DataOutputStream( bout );

        while( enum.hasMoreElements() ){
            String key = (String) enum.nextElement();
            if( key.length() > 0 ){
                dout.writeUTF( key );
                dout.writeUTF( h.get( key ).toString() );
            }
        }

        dout.writeUTF( "" );
        dout.flush();

        return bout.toByteArray();
    }
    catch( Exception e ){
        return new byte[0];
    }
}

// Restore hashtable from a byte array

public static boolean deserialize( Hashtable h, byte[] data ){
    h.clear();

    if( data == null || data.length == 0 ) return true;

    try {
        ByteArrayInputStream bin = new ByteArrayInputStream( data );
        DataInputStream      din = new DataInputStream( bin );
        String               key;
        String               value;

        while( true ){
            key = din.readUTF();
            if( key.length() == 0 ) break;

            value = din.readUTF();
            h.put( key, value );
        }

        return true;
    }
    catch( Exception e ){
```

```
                    return false;
                }
            }
        }
```

Here is some code that demonstrates how to save a hashtable as a single record in a record store:

```
import java.util.*;
import com.j2medeveloper.*;

.....

RecordStore rs = ....;
Hashtable   h = new Hashtable();

h.put( "firstname", "Eric" );
h.put( "lastname", "Giguere" );
h.put( "email", "eric@j2medeveloper.com" );

byte[] data = HashtableHelper.serialize( h );
int id = rs.addRecord( data, 0, data.length );
```

This code restores the hashtable:

```
data = rs.getRecord( id ); // get back the data
HashtableHelper.deserialize( h, data );
```

One use for this class is to save user preferences, as demonstrated in the next utility class.

UserPreferences: Saving and Restoring User Preferences

The `UserPreferences` class manages a set of user preferences, a set of persistent name-value pairs. The persistence is done by storing the name-value pairs in a record store called "UserPreferences". The class only exposes static methods in order to control access to the underlying hashtable. The preferences are shared by all the MIDlets in a MIDlet suite because the hashtable is a singleton object. The class is defined as follows:

```
package com.j2medeveloper.util;

import java.io.*;
import java.util.*;
import javax.microedition.rms.*;

/**
 * Manage a set of user preferences.  The preferences are stored
 * as strings in a hash table.
 */
```

```
public class UserPreferences {
    private static Hashtable _dirty = false;
    private static Hashtable _prefs = null;

    // Convenience method

    private static void closeRecordStore( RecordStore rs ){
        try {
            rs.closeRecordStore();
        }
        catch( Exception e ){
        }
    }

    // Return preference as a boolean value

    public static boolean getBoolean( String key, boolean defaultValue ){
        String val = getString( key, null );
        if( val != null ){
            if( val.equals( "true" ) || val.equals( "1" ) ) return true;
            if( val.equals( "false" ) || val.equals( "0" ) ) return false;
        }

        return defaultValue;
    }

    // Return preference as an integer value

    public static int getInt( String key, int defaultValue ){
        String val = getString( key, null );
        if( val != null ){
            try {
                return Integer.parseInt( val );
            }
            catch( NumberFormatException e ){
            }
        }

        return defaultValue;
    }

    // Gets the hashtable, creating and loading it if necessary

    private static Hashtable getPrefs(){
        if( _prefs == null ){
            _prefs = new Hashtable();
            _dirty = false;
            load();
        }
```

```
        return _prefs;
    }

    // Return preference as a string value

    public static synchronized String getString( String key,
                                                 String defaultValue ){
        Hashtable h = getPrefs();
        Object val = h.get( key );

        if( val instanceof String ){
            return (String) val;
        } else if( val != null ){
            return val.toString();
        }

        return defaultValue;
    }

    // Load preferences hash table from the database

    private static void load(){
        RecordStore rs = null;

        try {
            rs = RecordStore.openRecordStore( "UserPreferences", false );
            byte[] data = rs.getRecord( 1 );
            HashtableHelper.deserialize( _prefs, data );
        }
        catch( InvalidRecordIDException e ){
            closeRecordStore( rs );
            rs = null;
            try {
                RecordStore.deleteRecordStore( "UserPreferences" );
            }
            catch( RecordStoreException e1 ){}
        }
        catch( Exception e ){
        }

        if( rs != null ) closeRecordStore( rs );
    }

    // Release hashtable to free up memory

    public static synchronized void release(){
        if( _prefs != null ){
            if( _dirty ){
                save();
            }
```

```
            _prefs.clear();
            _prefs = null;
        }
    }

    // Store preferences hashtable in the database

    public static synchronized void save(){
        if( _prefs == null ) return;

        RecordStore rs = null;

        try {
            rs = RecordStore.openRecordStore( "UserPreferences", true );
            if( rs.getNumRecords() == 0 ){
                rs.addRecord( null, 0, 0 );
            }
            byte[] data = HashtableHelper.serialize( _prefs );
            rs.setRecord( 1, data, 0, data.length );
            _dirty = false;
        }
        catch( Exception e ){
        }

        if( rs != null ) closeRecordStore( rs );
    }

    // Set preference value as boolean

    public static void setBoolean( String key, boolean val ){
        setString( key, val ? "true" : "false" );
    }

    // Set preference value as integer

    public static void setInt( String key, int val ){
        setString( key, Integer.toString( val ) );
    }

    // Set preference value as string

    public static synchronized void setString( String key, String val ){
        if( key != null ){
            Hashtable h = getPrefs();
            if( val != null ){
                h.put( key, val );
            } else {
                h.remove( key );
            }
            _dirty = true;
        }
```

```
        }
    }
```

You can obtain a user preference at any time by calling the getBoolean, getInt, or getString methods, as in the following example:

```
String  name = UserPreferences.getString( "user.name", null );
boolean debug = UserPreferences.getBoolean( "debug", false );
int     lastScore = UserPreferences.getInt( "score", 0 );
```

The first argument is the name of the preference, and the second argument is the default value to return if the preference is not found. Preferences are set by using setBoolean, setInt, or setString:

```
UserPreferences.setString( "user.name", "Eric" );
UserPreferences.setBoolean( "debug", true );
UserPreferences.setInt( "score", 1298 );
UserPreferences.save();
```

Preferences are only saved to a record store when you call the save method. The HashtableHelper class is used to save the hashtable into a record. When the application pauses or exits, it should call UserPreferences.release in order to discard the hashtable. The next call to getInt, getBoolean, or getString will automatically reload the hashtable from the record store.

RecordReader: Reading Records Conveniently

The RecordReader class makes it simple to read data from a class by automatically creating and managing the required ByteArrayInputStream and DataInputStream objects. RecordReader implements the DataInput interface and so exposes most of the same methods that DataInputStream does. Its definition is as follows:

```
package com.j2medeveloper.util;

import java.io.*;
import javax.microedition.rms.*;

/**
 * Manage the efficient reading of primitive data types and
 * strings from a record store.
 */

public class RecordReader implements DataInput {

    private RecordStore     _rs = null;
    private byte[]          _data = null;
    private int             _length = -1;
    private int             _id = 0;
    private DataInputStream _din = null;
```

```
    private int                _minSize;

    public RecordReader( RecordStore rs ){
        this( rs, 100 );
    }

    public RecordReader( RecordStore rs, int minSize ){
        _rs      = rs;
        _minSize = minSize;
    }

    public byte[] getByteArray() { return _data; }

    public int getLength() { return _length; }

    public byte[] moveTo( int id )
                      throws RecordStoreNotOpenException,
                             InvalidRecordIDException,
                             RecordStoreException,
                             IOException
    {
        _length = _rs.getRecordSize( id );

        if( _data == null || _length > _data.length ){
            _data = new byte[ Math.max( _length, _minSize ) ];
            _din  = new DataInputStream(
                          new ByteArrayInputStream( _data ) );
        }

        _rs.getRecord( id, _data, 0 );
        _id = id;
        _din.reset();

        return _data;
    }

    public void readFully(byte b[]) throws IOException {
        _din.readFully( b );
    }

    public void readFully(byte b[], int off, int len)
                                   throws IOException {
        _din.readFully( b, off, len );
    }

    public int skipBytes(int n) throws IOException {
        return _din.skipBytes( n );
    }

    public boolean readBoolean() throws IOException {
        return _din.readBoolean();
    }
```

```
    public byte readByte() throws IOException {
        return _din.readByte();
    }

    public int readUnsignedByte() throws IOException {
        return _din.readUnsignedByte();
    }

    public short readShort() throws IOException {
        return _din.readShort();
    }

    public int readUnsignedShort() throws IOException {
        return _din.readUnsignedShort();
    }

    public char readChar() throws IOException {
        return _din.readChar();
    }

    public int readInt() throws IOException {
        return _din.readInt();
    }

    public long readLong() throws IOException {
        return _din.readLong();
    }

    public String readUTF() throws IOException {
        return _din.readUTF();
    }
}
```

To quickly and easily read records, create an instance of RecordReader—passing it a reference to an open record store. Call the moveTo method to move to a particular record ID and then call the appropriate DataInput methods to read the data from the record. For example:

```
RecordStore       rs = ...;
RecordReader      reader = new RecordReader( rs );
RecordEnumeration enum = rs.enumerateRecords( null, null, false );

while( enum.hasNextElement() ){
    reader.moveTo( enum.nextRecordId() );

    int    emp_id = reader.readInt();
    String emp_fname = reader.readUTF();
    String emp_lname = reader.readUTF();
    ..... // etc. etc.
}
```

Note: The `RecordReader` class shown here is taken from a J2ME Tech Tip written by one of this book's authors and is reprinted here with the kind permission of Sun Microsystems.

CookieJar: Storing HTTP Cookies

The `CookieJar` class stores HTTP cookies in one or more record stores. An application can use `CookieJar` to track the cookies sent to it by various Web sites in response to HTTP requests. To perform this action, it also needs to use the `Cookie` class to represent the individual cookies.

The Cookie Class

The `Cookie` class stores the various fields of an HTTP cookie. It defines `serialize` and `deserialize` methods for saving and restoring the cookie as well as other useful methods. The class is defined as follows:

```
package com.j2medeveloper.util;

import java.io.*;
import java.util.*;

/**
 * Stores the fields of an HTTP cookie.
 */

public class Cookie {

     // Required fields

     public String  name;
     public String  value;
     public String  domain;

     // Optional fields

     public String  comment = null;
     public int     maxAge = -1;
     public String  path = null;
     public boolean secure = false;
     public int     version = 0;

     // Constructs an empty cookie

     public Cookie(){
     }
```

```
// Constructs a cookie from its serialized form

public Cookie( byte[] data ){
    if( !deserialize( data ) ){
        clear();
    }
}

// Clears the cookie contents

public void clear(){
    name = null;
    value = null;
    domain = null;
    comment = null;
    maxAge = -1;
    path = null;
    secure = false;
    version = 0;
}

// Whether a path is empty or not

public boolean isEmptyPath(){
    return( path == null || path.length() == 0 );
}

// Compares two cookies

public boolean isMatch( Cookie c ){
    if( name == null || c.name == null ) return false;
    if( value == null || c.value == null ) return false;
    if( domain == null || c.domain == null ) return false;

    if( name.equals( c.name ) && domain.equals( c.domain ) ){
        if( isEmptyPath() && c.isEmptyPath() ){
            return true;
        } else if( path != null && c.path != null ){
            return path.equals( c.path );
        }
    }

    return false;
}

// Compares the cookie to the given host and path

public boolean isMatch( String destHost, String destPath ){
    if( domain == null ) return false;
    if( !domain.equals( destHost ) &&
        !destHost.endsWith( domain ) ) return false;
```

```
        if( path == null ) return true;
        return destPath.startsWith( path );
    }

    // Sets the cookie by parsing a Set-Cookie header value

    public boolean setFromHeader( String headerValue,
                                  String defaultDomain,
                                  String defaultPath ){

        clear();

        domain = defaultDomain;
        ...tPath;

        ...Value.indexOf( '=' );
        ...turn false;

        ...ue.substring( 0, pos );
        ...eaderValue.substring( pos+1 );

        ...ue.indexOf( ';' );

        ...derValue;
        ...se; // no domain!

        ...Value.substring( 0, pos );
        ...headerValue.substring( pos+1 );

        ...Value.length() > 0 ){
        ...eld;

        ...derValue.indexOf( ';' );
        ... 0 ){
        ...d = headerValue;
        ...erValue = "";

        ...d = headerValue.substring( 0, pos );
        ...lerValue = headerValue.substring( pos+1 );

        ...fieldName = null;
        ...fieldValue = null;

        ...field.indexOf( '=' );
        ...s < 0 ){
        ...eldName = field.toLowerCase();
            } else {
                fieldName = field.substring( 0,
                                   pos ).toLowerCase();
```

```
                fieldValue = field.substring( pos + 1 );
            }

            if( fieldName.equals( "domain" ) ){
                domain = fieldValue;
            } else if( fieldName.equals( "comment" ) ){
                comment = fieldValue;
            } else if( fieldName.equals( "path" ) ){
                path = fieldValue;
            } else if( fieldName.equals( "secure" ) ){
                secure = true;
            } else if( fieldName.equals( "version" ) ){
                version = Integer.parseInt( fieldValue );
            } else if( fieldName.equals( "max-age" ) ){
                maxAge = Integer.parseInt( fieldValue );
            }
        }

        return true;
    }
    catch( Exception e ){
        return false;
    }
}

// Save the cookie as a byte array

public byte[] serialize(){
    if( name == null || value == null || domain == null )
        return null;

    try {
        ByteArrayOutputStream bout = new ByteArrayOutputStream();
        DataOutputStream      dout = new DataOutputStream( bout );

        dout.writeUTF( name );
        dout.writeUTF( value );
        dout.writeUTF( domain );
        dout.writeUTF( path != null ? path : "" );
        dout.writeInt( version );
        dout.writeBoolean( secure );
        dout.writeInt( maxAge );
        dout.writeUTF( comment != null ? comment : "" );
        dout.flush();

        return bout.toByteArray();
    }
    catch( Exception e ){
        return null;
    }
}
```

```
    // Restore the cookie from a byte array

    public boolean deserialize( byte[] data ){
        clear();

        if( data == null || data.length == 0 ) return false;

        try {
            ByteArrayInputStream bin = new
                    ByteArrayInputStream( data );
            DataInputStream      din = new DataInputStream( bin );

            name = din.readUTF();
            value = din.readUTF();
            domain = din.readUTF();
            path = din.readUTF();
            version = din.readInt();
            secure = din.readBoolean();
            maxAge = din.readInt();
            comment = din.readUTF();

            return true;
        }
        catch( Exception e ){
            return false;
        }
    }
}
```

The CookieJar Class

The `CookieJar` class manages the cookies held by an application. Its definition is as follows:

```
package com.j2medeveloper.util;

import java.io.*;
import java.util.*;
import javax.microedition.rms.*;

/**
 * Manages a set of cookies by persisting them to a record
 * store.
 */

public class CookieJar {

    private String _name; // record store name
```

```
// Constructs a cookie jar using the given record store name

public CookieJar( String name ){
    _name = name;
}

// Adds a cookie to the record store

public boolean addCookie( Cookie cookie ){
    return addOrRemoveCookie( cookie, true );
}

// This method does the actual adding or deleting.

private boolean addOrRemoveCookie( Cookie cookie, boolean add ){
    boolean     ok = false;
    RecordStore rs = open( _name );
    byte[] cookieData = cookie.serialize();

    if( rs != null && cookieData != null ){
        try {
            RecordFilter f = new MatchExact( cookie );
            RecordEnumeration enum =
                           rs.enumerateRecords( f, null, false );
            if( enum.hasNextElement() ){
                int id = enum.nextRecordId();
                if( add ){
                    rs.setRecord( id, cookieData,
                                  0, cookieData.length );
                } else {
                    rs.deleteRecord( id );
                }
            } else if( add ){
                rs.addRecord( cookieData, 0, cookieData.length );
            }

            enum.destroy();
            ok = true;
        }
        catch( Exception e ){
        }

        close( rs );
    }

    return ok;
}

// Closes a record store.

private void close( RecordStore rs ){
    try {
```

```
            rs.closeRecordStore();
        }
        catch( Exception e ){
        }
    }

    // Returns the set of cookies that match the given URL.

    public Cookie[] listCookies( String url ){
        Vector v = new Vector();
        RecordStore rs = open( _name );

        if( rs != null ){
            try {
                RecordFilter f = new MatchURL( url, v );
                RecordEnumeration enum =
                            rs.enumerateRecords( f, null, false );
                while( enum.hasNextElement() ){
                    enum.nextRecordId();
                }
                enum.destroy();
            }
            catch( Exception e ){
            }

            close( rs );
        }

        Cookie[] list = new Cookie[ v.size() ];
        v.copyInto( list );
        return list;
    }

    // Opens a record store

    private RecordStore open( String name ){
        try {
            return RecordStore.openRecordStore( name, true );
        }
        catch( Exception e ){
            return null;
        }
    }

    // Removes a cookie from the record store

    public boolean removeCookie( Cookie cookie ){
        return addOrRemoveCookie( cookie, false );
    }

    // Inner class that filters cookies based on whether
    // they match the given URL
```

```
class MatchURL implements RecordFilter {
    private boolean _useHTTPS = false;
    private String  _host;
    private String  _path;
    private Vector  _list;

    MatchURL( String url, Vector v ){
        if( url.startsWith( "http://" ) ){
            url = url.substring( 7 );
        } else if( url.startsWith( "https://" ) ){
            url = url.substring( 8 );
            _useHTTPS = true;
        }

        int pos = url.indexOf( '/' );
        if( pos < 0 ){
            _host = url;
            _path = "/";
        } else {
            _host = url.substring( 0, pos );
            _path = url.substring( pos );
        }

        _list = v;
    }

    public boolean matches( byte[] data ){
        Cookie c = new Cookie( data );
        if( !c.secure || _useHTTPS ){
            if( c.isMatch( _host, _path ) ){
                _list.addElement( c );
            }
        }
        return false; // always return false
    }
}

// Inner class that filters cookies based on
// whether they match a specific cookie

class MatchExact implements RecordFilter {
    private Cookie _compareTo;

    MatchExact( Cookie c ){
        _compareTo = c;
    }

    public boolean matches( byte[] data ){
        Cookie c = new Cookie( data );
        return _compareTo.isMatch( c );
```

```
            }
        }
    }
```

Using Cookie and CookieJar Together

An application that is interested in persisting cookie information creates an instance of `CookieJar`. The name passed to the constructor is used to create the underlying record store:

```
CookieJar cjar = new CookieJar( "MyCookies" );
```

Cookies are stored by calling the cookie jar's `addCookie` method:

```
Cookie c = new Cookie();
c.setFromHeader( "abcd=hello", "acme.com", "/" );
cjar.addCookie( c );
c = new Cookie();
c.setFromHeader( "xyz=boo;max-age=-1", "acme.com", "/test" );
cjar.addCookie( c );
```

Normally, new cookies would be created from the value of any `Set-Cookie` headers returned by an HTTP response, not from string constants. The header format was discussed in Chapter 6. The last two arguments to `setFrom-Header` define the default domain and path for the cookie in case the header value does not define `DOMAIN` and `PATH` fields.

At any time, you can ask the cookie jar to give you the list of cookies to send along with an HTTP request to a specific URL. For example:

```
Cookie[] list = cjar.listCookies(
                    "http://www.acme.com/index.html" );
```

Only the cookies whose domain and path values match those of the URL are returned.

To remove a cookie, call the cookie jar's `removeCookie` method.

Summary

This chapter covered the MIDP Record Management System in quite some detail. We are now ready to move beyond the MIDP APIs and explore more abstract topics, such as security and XML and how they relate to the MIDP.

CHAPTER 8

Security

Security is an important requirement for wireless business applications. The Mobile Information Device Profile (MIDP) provides application security by using a sandbox to keep MIDlet suites from interacting with each other, but it does not really define any security mechanism for MIDlets to use when communicating with the external world. There are things you can do, however, to enhance the security of your MIDlet's communications, and we will explore those mechanisms in this chapter. We start with a short primer on security and then see what can be done with today's MIDP implementations.

Security Basics

The same security measures that apply to the wired Internet also apply to wireless networks and applications. There are different levels of security that an application can implement with different costs and complexities. Most security solutions provide three things—user authentication, access control, and data encryption. Not every application needs security, because not every application exchanges confidential or otherwise sensitive information with external servers. Remember, though, that the wireless Internet is just as insecure, if not more so, than the wired Internet.

Concepts and Terminology

The following terms and concepts are commonly used when discussing security:

- *Authentication* is the process of identifying a given user—of ensuring that a person is who they claim to be. Authentication can be accomplished by challenging the user to enter a username and password or by exchanging digital certificates and signatures.

- *Authorization*, also referred to as *access control*, determines whether a particular user has permission to perform certain actions. Authorization depends on authentication.
- *Confidentiality* is an important aspect of security. Confidentiality prevents other parties from intercepting and viewing sensitive information. Confidentiality is achieved by encrypting the data. *Encryption* is the process of encoding information so that only the intended parties or recipients can decode it. The parties use *keys* to decrypt the data. Without the key, the information is useless.
- *Data integrity* ensures that data is not tampered with as it moves from the sender to the receiver. If tampering does occur, the receiver can detect it and reject the data. A common technique to maintain data integrity is to combine encryption with a *message digest*—a hash value computed from the message itself. The digest is combined with a secret key to form a *message authentication code* (MAC) or cryptographic checksum. The recipient computes the MAC and compares it with the original MAC encoded in the message to ensure that no one has tampered with the message.
- *Non-repudiation* identifies the parties involved in a given transaction so that the involved parties cannot deny their involvement in the transaction. As with authorization, non-repudiation depends on authentication.
- *End-to-end security* is the capability to have a robust and secure session or channel from a client device to another device or server without having to decode the data at any point along the communication path. The concern with end-to-end security in the wireless world was sparked by the initial implementation of security by WAP 1.1, where data packets from the wireless device are decrypted and then re-encrypted by the *Wireless Access Protocol* (WAP) gateway on the network operator's premises. This decryption/encryption, known informally as the "gap in WAP," is necessary because of the different security protocols used by the wireless and wired sides of WAP communication (WTLS versus TLS/SSL). WAP 1.2 alleviates this deficiency by enabling a second WAP gateway to be installed in the actual premises of the enterprise or content provider. WAP 1.3 fixes this deficiency by using WTLS tunneling techniques that enables true end-to-end security.

Perhaps the most important concept, though, is that of a *security policy*. A security policy details the procedures and measures that applications must follow in order to deal with confidential information. Security is more than just encrypting data, and a formal policy helps ensure that security considerations are always taken into consideration—something that is extremely important when building wireless applications. A good book to read on security policy is *Secrets and Lies: Digital Security in a Networked World* by Bruce Schneier (John Wiley & Sons, 2000).

Typical Security Risks

You must always assume that sensitive data is at risk while in transit on the network between a client and a server. You need to be aware of a number of common security risks:

- *Spoofing* is a technique used to gain unauthorized access to computers by pretending to be someone else and creating fake responses. Use authentication and data encryption to minimize the risk of unauthorized access to sensitive data and/or resources.
- *Sniffing* is the monitoring of network traffic. Sniffing can be very dangerous because sniffing tools are readily available and easy to use while being almost impossible to detect. Data encryption can minimize the risk of low-level packet sniffing, but there are other sniffing scenarios of which you should be aware. For example, Web servers typically store HTTP GET/POST request *Uniform Resource Locators* (URLs) for monitoring purposes. These logs can be in clear text, so any data that you pass as part of the request URL is information that is available to people who have access to these logs. For this reason, it is usually better to send sensitive data (encrypted or not) in the body of an HTTP POST request.
- *Data tampering* is the interception and modification of data. Note that data integrity can be compromised while in transit on the network and when it is stored on the server as well. Use authentication, authorization, and data encryption to minimize data tampering.

These are just a few of the most common risks. Of course, it also is important to understand that not all risks can be avoided, and in fact, not all security countermeasures are worth implementing. Again, see the *Secrets and Lies* book for a good discussion of security risks.

Security Measures and Solutions

There are different security measures and solutions available to help you write secure applications.

Firewalls

Firewalls are a widely used mechanism to control and monitor network traffic, and to protect a private network that is connected to the Internet. A firewall physically sits between the private network and the Internet. Network administrators can configure the firewall by defining filters to allow or prevent certain types of network traffic through the firewall. For example, many corporations do not allow Telnet traffic to be initiated from outside their network. Typical firewalls can be configured to allow or deny access based on the following criteria:

- The target resource (URL) including UDP and TCP port numbers
- The host or network IP address of the host that is requesting the service
- The user who is requesting the service (uses authentication)
- The time of day and day of week of the request
- The current number of connections for the service

In addition, firewalls can perform packet filtering, double-reverse *Dynamic Name Service* (DNS) name resolution checks to ensure that the requesting host is who it claims to be, route checking, and other checks. Also, all network traffic through the firewall can be logged in detail, which can help in a post-mortem analysis of security breaches and failures.

HTTP Password Authentication

RFC 2617, one of the documents produced by the World Wide Web Consortium (W3C), defines two types of authentication for HTTP request/response cycles: HTTP basic access authentication and HTTP digest access authentication. The goal of HTTP authentication is only to identify and authenticate the user while protecting the user's credentials during transit on the network. The actual HTTP content is not protected or encrypted in any way. With basic authentication, usernames and passwords are sent in clear text (or optionally encoded by using BASE 64) over the network, meaning that they are vulnerable to sniffing tools. With digest authentication, a message digest or hash function (MD5, a 128-bit encoded sequence) of the password and a random challenge are used. To use HTTP basic/digest authentication, the Web servers and firewalls have to be properly configured.

The HTTP authentication is based on the challenge-response paradigm. If the server requires the client to authenticate, the server sends an "unauthorized" status code in response to the original request. The response includes a `WWW-Authenticate` header. The client must then challenge the user by asking for the credential information. The client resubmits its request with an `Authorization` header set to the encoded credentials. Let's look at the flow/operation of a client and server that use basic authentication:

1. The client requests a page/resource/service:

```
GET /.../xyz/index.html HTTP/1.1
     etc...
```

2. The server (HTTP) responds:

```
HTTP/1.1 401 Unauthorized
WWW-Authenticate: Basic realm="My Realm"
-OR-
WWW-Authenticate: Digest realm="My Realm"
     etc...
```

3. The client challenges the user and collects credential:

```
GET /.../xyz/index.html HTTP/1.1
Authorization: Basic JD9033d5LFKD03KDJ DJFK4DKFS22 (using Base 64
encoding for Basic authentication and 128 bit MD5 encoding for Digest
authentication)
     etc...
```

Digest authentication is similar to the basic authentication shown earlier, except for two things. First, the server response in Step 2 indicates `Digest` instead of `Basic`. The client challenges the user and collects credential information, but this time the credentials (the username and password) are encrypted by computing an MD5 function (MD5 is the default algorithm, but others can be used) from a value provided by the server in combination with the username, the password, the HTTP method, and the requested URI. The result is a 128-bit checksum that represents the encoded credentials. The `HttpConnectionHelper` class in Chapter 6, "Network Communication," can easily be changed to support either form of HTTP authentication.

Data Encryption and Public Key Cryptography

Data encryption is a mathematical transformation process that converts data into an unreadable form. Encryption ensures confidentiality and privacy by making your sensitive data unreadable even if unintended recipients gain access to it. Decryption is the reverse process, where encrypted data is transformed back into its original readable form. Encryption and decryption require a secret piece of information known as the secret key. Encryption can be either symmetric or asymmetric.

Symmetric encryption uses a single key to encrypt and decrypt all messages. Symmetric algorithms or ciphers are faster and simpler than asymmetric ciphers but require a secure way to share the secret key. The problem, of course, is how to securely share a secret key *before* a secure channel is created, because the creation of the channel requires the secret key. The most well-known symmetric encryption system is the *Data Encryption Standard* (DES), but other symmetric algorithms include IDEA, 3DES, and the Rivest family of ciphers (RC2, RC4, and RC5).

Asymmetric or public key encryption, invented by Whitfield Diffie and Martin Hellman in 1976, avoids the key sharing required by symmetric encryption by using *two* keys: A public key that can be distributed in a non-secure fashion and that is used to encrypt messages, and a private key that is never transmitted and that is used to decrypt messages. Public and private keys are related to each other in a way that makes it almost impossible to calculate the private key when given the public key. A public key system works as follows: If Eric wants to send a secure message to Enrique, Eric uses Enrique's public key to encrypt the message. Eric gains access to Enrique's public key usually from Enrique's *digital certificate* (see the next section). After receiving the message from Eric, Enrique can decode or decrypt the message by using his private key (to which only he has access). Well-known asymmetric algorithms include RSA (Rivest, Shamir, and Adelman), *Elliptic Curve Cryptography* (ECC), and *Diffie-Hellman* (DH). The most predominant algorithm is RSA, but the least expensive in terms of processing power and key size is ECC, which has the attributes to become an industry standard for mobile devices.

In practice, asymmetric algorithms are more complicated and slower—sometimes up to 1,000 times slower—than symmetric algorithms and are vulnerable to attacks known as chosen-plaintext attacks. However, while symmetric algorithms are faster, they have the logistic problem of how to securely distribute the secret key. The best practical solution is to combine both asymmetric and symmetric encryption into what is known as a public key crypto system. Here, a public key algorithm is used to encrypt and securely distribute a randomly computed session key that is later used by a symmetric algorithm to encrypt/decrypt all of the messages for that particular session. This method is how public key cryptography works today. The *Secure Socket Layer* (SSL), which we cover later, uses this combined solution. With SSL, for example, Eric gets Enrique's public key from Enrique (Enrique actually sends his digital certificate that contains his public key), and Eric generates a random key (the session key) and encrypts it by using Enrique's public key. Eric then sends Enrique the encrypted message with the session key to Enrique, who decrypts the message by using his private key. This session key becomes the symmetric key to be used to encrypt/decrypt all subsequent messages between them for the active session. We will talk more about this topic later in this chapter.

Digital Certificates and Public Key Infrastructure

To minimize attacks, public key encryption introduced the concept of digital certificates. A digital certificate is an electronic document or passport that a user buys from a *certificate authority* (CA). The certificate identifies the user and includes the user's public key. Digital certificates can verify the sender's identity (if you trust the certificate authority that issued the certificate) and provide a way for others to send encrypted messages to the user by using the public key embedded in the certificate. Digital certificates are signed by the certificate authority to ensure that no one has tampered with them.

One way to describe digital certificates is to use X.509, an industry standard for user authentication. X.509 certificates also are known as public key certificates. Information within an X.509 digital certificate includes the certificate version, serial number, algorithm used to sign the certificate, the name of the certificate authority that issued the certificate, the certificate's period of validity, the unique name of the user, the user's public key, information about the algorithm used to create the user's public key, and the signature (fingerprint) and algorithm used for the signature of the CA that issued the certificate. The name of the CA and user are stored in the X.500 *Distinguished Name* (DN) format so that it will be unique across the Internet. Distinguished names have the form "`CN=`*`common-name`*, `OU=`*`organizational-unit`*, `O=`*`organization`*, `L=`*`locality-name`*, `S=`*`state-name`*, `C=`*`country`*," for example, "`CN=SUNM, OU=Java Software Division, O=Sun Microsystems Inc, S=CA, L=Palo Alto, C=US`."

A simpler version of the X.509 digital certificate is the WAP WTLS digital certificate, which was created because X.509 certificates are too big. WTLS certificates share some of the same information as the X.509 certificate, such as the version of the certificate, the algorithm used to sign the certificate, the name of the CA that issued the certificate, the period of validity, the unique name of the user, the user's public key, and the signature (fingerprint) and algorithm used for the signature of the CA.

Because enterprises or organizations can themselves become CAs and because of the notion that a certified user can sign other users' certificates, digital certificates can be chained to form a tree of trust. To validate a chained certificate, an application must walk through the chain to find the root certificate authority. If the root CA is not recognized, the certificate is not valid.

To make asymmetric cryptography more effective, a network of certification authorities, registration servers, directory services, and databases storing certificates is required. This complex organization of systems and rules is called *public key infrastructure* (PKI), where the "public key" reflects the notion that PKI is based on asymmetric encryption. PKI is a combination of encryption technologies, software, and services. PKI defines a single security solution by combining digital certificates, public key cryptography, and certificate authorities. PKI is still considered young, and its adoption has been slow. In a PKI scenario, if Eric wants to send a message to Enrique, he first obtains Enrique's digital certificate. Eric can verify the validity of the certificate by validating it with a certificate authority that he trusts. If it is valid, he uses the public key embedded in the certificate to send Enrique a message.

There are two ways to get certificates: you can create one yourself by using tools such as the J2SE `keytool` or by asking a certificate authority to issue you one. You can create and sign your own certificate, but many places do not accept self-signed certificates.

Message Digests and Digital Signatures

Next, we look at message digests and signatures, which are used for data integrity and authentication.

Message Digests

A message digest is a quasi-unique number or checksum computed by using a one-way hash function. The input to the hash function is a message of arbitrary length, and its output is a fixed-length checksum or value known as the *message digest*:

```
messageDigest = new MD5Digest(msg); // compute MD5 digest
```

The value is quasi-unique because its uniqueness depends on the algorithm that is used to generate the hash value. A good hash function is one that has low or zero collisions; in other words, computing the hash value of two different values should not produce the same hash value. You usually create message digests by using a one-way hash function, such as MD5 (Message Digest from RSA) or SHA-1 (Secure Hash Algorithm). SHA-1 is the current algorithm of choice because it appears to be stronger than MD5, but both are good hash functions.

Because a message digest faithfully represents a given message, we can use it to validate the integrity of the message. By computing the hash value of a message or a document, we can validate it by re-computing the hash value and comparing it with the original hash value. If they are not the same, the message has been changed.

Cryptography is a fascinating area and fortunately there are a number of free/ open implementations available to us to explore. Let's take a look at an implementation of an MD5 one-way hash function as described in Bruce Schneier's book, *Applied Cryptography* (John Wiley & Sons), and as implemented by the Legion of the Bouncy Castle, an open source project that has created Java classes for cryptography:

```
//
// Copyright (c) 2000 The Legion Of The Bouncy Castle
```

```
//   (http://www.bouncycastle.org)
//
package org.bouncycastle.crypto.digests;

import org.bouncycastle.crypto.Digest;

/**
 * implementation of MD5 as outlined in "Handbook of Applied
 *  Cryptography", pages 436-437.
 */
public class MD5Digest extends GeneralDigest
{
    private static final int    DIGEST_LENGTH = 16;

    private int     H1, H2, H3, H4;         // IV's

    private int[]   X = new int[16];
    private int     xOff;

     /**
      * Standard constructor
      */
    public MD5Digest()
    {
        reset();
    }

     /**
      * Copy constructor.  This will copy the state of the provided
      * message digest.
      */
     public MD5Digest(MD5Digest t)
     {
          super(t);

          H1 = t.H1;
          H2 = t.H2;
          H3 = t.H3;
          H4 = t.H4;

          System.arraycopy(t.X, 0, X, 0, t.X.length);
          xOff = t.xOff;
     }

    public String getAlgorithmName()
    {
        return "MD5";
    }

    public int getDigestSize()
    {
```

```
        return DIGEST_LENGTH;
    }

    protected void processWord(
        byte[]  in,
        int     inOff)
    {
        X[xOff++] = (in[inOff] & 0xff) | ((in[inOff + 1] & 0xff) << 8)

        | ((in[inOff+2]&0xff)<<16) | ((in[inOff+3]&0xff)<<24);
        if (xOff == 16)
        {
            processBlock();
        }
    }

    protected void processLength(
        long    bitLength)
    {
        if (xOff > 14)
        {
            processBlock();
        }

        X[14] = (int)(bitLength & 0xffffffff);
        X[15] = (int)(bitLength >>> 32);
    }

    private void unpackWord(
        int     word,
        byte[]  out,
        int     outOff)
    {
        out[outOff]     = (byte)word;
        out[outOff + 1] = (byte)(word >>> 8);
        out[outOff + 2] = (byte)(word >>> 16);
        out[outOff + 3] = (byte)(word >>> 24);
    }

    public int doFinal(
        byte[]  out,
        int     outOff)
    {
        finish();

        unpackWord(H1, out, outOff);
        unpackWord(H2, out, outOff + 4);
        unpackWord(H3, out, outOff + 8);
        unpackWord(H4, out, outOff + 12);

        reset();
```

```
        return DIGEST_LENGTH;
    }

    /**
     * reset the chaining variables to the IV values.
     */
    public void reset()
    {
        super.reset();

        H1 = 0x67452301;
        H2 = 0xefcdab89;
        H3 = 0x98badcfe;
        H4 = 0x10325476;

        xOff = 0;

        for (int i = 0; i != X.length; i++)
        {
            X[i] = 0;
        }
    }

    //
    // round 1 left rotates
    //
    private static final int S11 = 7;
    private static final int S12 = 12;
    private static final int S13 = 17;
    private static final int S14 = 22;

    //
    // round 2 left rotates
    //
    private static final int S21 = 5;
    private static final int S22 = 9;
    private static final int S23 = 14;
    private static final int S24 = 20;

    //
    // round 3 left rotates
    //
    private static final int S31 = 4;
    private static final int S32 = 11;
    private static final int S33 = 16;
    private static final int S34 = 23;

    //
    // round 4 left rotates
    //
    private static final int S41 = 6;
```

```
private static final int S42 = 10;
private static final int S43 = 15;
private static final int S44 = 21;

/*
 * rotate int x left n bits.
 */
private int rotateLeft(
    int x,
    int n)
{
    return (x << n) | (x >>> (32 - n));
}

/*
 * F, G, H and I are the basic MD5 functions.
 */
private int F(
    int u,
    int v,
    int w)
{
    return (u & v) | (~u & w);
}

private int G(
    int u,
    int v,
    int w)
{
    return (u & w) | (v & ~w);
}

private int H(
    int u,
    int v,
    int w)
{
    return u ^ v ^ w;
}

private int K(
    int u,
    int v,
    int w)
{
    return v ^ (u | ~w);
}

protected void processBlock()
{
```

```
 int a = H1;
 int b = H2;
 int c = H3;
 int d = H4;

//
// Round 1 - F cycle, 16 times.
//
a = rotateLeft((a + F(b, c, d) + X[ 0] + 0xd76aa478), S11) + b;
d = rotateLeft((d + F(a, b, c) + X[ 1] + 0xe8c7b756), S12) + a;
c = rotateLeft((c + F(d, a, b) + X[ 2] + 0x242070db), S13) + d;
b = rotateLeft((b + F(c, d, a) + X[ 3] + 0xc1bdceee), S14) + c;
a = rotateLeft((a + F(b, c, d) + X[ 4] + 0xf57c0faf), S11) + b;
d = rotateLeft((d + F(a, b, c) + X[ 5] + 0x4787c62a), S12) + a;
c = rotateLeft((c + F(d, a, b) + X[ 6] + 0xa8304613), S13) + d;
b = rotateLeft((b + F(c, d, a) + X[ 7] + 0xfd469501), S14) + c;
a = rotateLeft((a + F(b, c, d) + X[ 8] + 0x698098d8), S11) + b;
d = rotateLeft((d + F(a, b, c) + X[ 9] + 0x8b44f7af), S12) + a;
c = rotateLeft((c + F(d, a, b) + X[10] + 0xffff5bb1), S13) + d;
b = rotateLeft((b + F(c, d, a) + X[11] + 0x895cd7be), S14) + c;
a = rotateLeft((a + F(b, c, d) + X[12] + 0x6b901122), S11) + b;
d = rotateLeft((d + F(a, b, c) + X[13] + 0xfd987193), S12) + a;
c = rotateLeft((c + F(d, a, b) + X[14] + 0xa679438e), S13) + d;
b = rotateLeft((b + F(c, d, a) + X[15] + 0x49b40821), S14) + c;

//
// Round 2 - G cycle, 16 times.
//
a = rotateLeft((a + G(b, c, d) + X[ 1] + 0xf61e2562), S21) + b;
d = rotateLeft((d + G(a, b, c) + X[ 6] + 0xc040b340), S22) + a;
c = rotateLeft((c + G(d, a, b) + X[11] + 0x265e5a51), S23) + d;
b = rotateLeft((b + G(c, d, a) + X[ 0] + 0xe9b6c7aa), S24) + c;
a = rotateLeft((a + G(b, c, d) + X[ 5] + 0xd62f105d), S21) + b;
d = rotateLeft((d + G(a, b, c) + X[10] + 0x02441453), S22) + a;
c = rotateLeft((c + G(d, a, b) + X[15] + 0xd8a1e681), S23) + d;
b = rotateLeft((b + G(c, d, a) + X[ 4] + 0xe7d3fbc8), S24) + c;
a = rotateLeft((a + G(b, c, d) + X[ 9] + 0x21e1cde6), S21) + b;
d = rotateLeft((d + G(a, b, c) + X[14] + 0xc33707d6), S22) + a;
c = rotateLeft((c + G(d, a, b) + X[ 3] + 0xf4d50d87), S23) + d;
b = rotateLeft((b + G(c, d, a) + X[ 8] + 0x455a14ed), S24) + c;
a = rotateLeft((a + G(b, c, d) + X[13] + 0xa9e3e905), S21) + b;
d = rotateLeft((d + G(a, b, c) + X[ 2] + 0xfcefa3f8), S22) + a;
c = rotateLeft((c + G(d, a, b) + X[ 7] + 0x676f02d9), S23) + d;
b = rotateLeft((b + G(c, d, a) + X[12] + 0x8d2a4c8a), S24) + c;

//
// Round 3 - H cycle, 16 times.
//
a = rotateLeft((a + H(b, c, d) + X[ 5] + 0xfffa3942), S31) + b;
d = rotateLeft((d + H(a, b, c) + X[ 8] + 0x8771f681), S32) + a;
c = rotateLeft((c + H(d, a, b) + X[11] + 0x6d9d6122), S33) + d;
```

```
        b = rotateLeft((b + H(c, d, a) + X[14] + 0xfde5380c), S34) + c;
        a = rotateLeft((a + H(b, c, d) + X[ 1] + 0xa4beea44), S31) + b;
        d = rotateLeft((d + H(a, b, c) + X[ 4] + 0x4bdecfa9), S32) + a;
        c = rotateLeft((c + H(d, a, b) + X[ 7] + 0xf6bb4b60), S33) + d;
        b = rotateLeft((b + H(c, d, a) + X[10] + 0xbebfbc70), S34) + c;
        a = rotateLeft((a + H(b, c, d) + X[13] + 0x289b7ec6), S31) + b;
        d = rotateLeft((d + H(a, b, c) + X[ 0] + 0xeaa127fa), S32) + a;
        c = rotateLeft((c + H(d, a, b) + X[ 3] + 0xd4ef3085), S33) + d;
        b = rotateLeft((b + H(c, d, a) + X[ 6] + 0x04881d05), S34) + c;
        a = rotateLeft((a + H(b, c, d) + X[ 9] + 0xd9d4d039), S31) + b;
        d = rotateLeft((d + H(a, b, c) + X[12] + 0xe6db99e5), S32) + a;
        c = rotateLeft((c + H(d, a, b) + X[15] + 0x1fa27cf8), S33) + d;
        b = rotateLeft((b + H(c, d, a) + X[ 2] + 0xc4ac5665), S34) + c;

        //
        // Round 4 - K cycle, 16 times.
        //
        a = rotateLeft((a + K(b, c, d) + X[ 0] + 0xf4292244), S41) + b;
        d = rotateLeft((d + K(a, b, c) + X[ 7] + 0x432aff97), S42) + a;
        c = rotateLeft((c + K(d, a, b) + X[14] + 0xab9423a7), S43) + d;
        b = rotateLeft((b + K(c, d, a) + X[ 5] + 0xfc93a039), S44) + c;
        a = rotateLeft((a + K(b, c, d) + X[12] + 0x655b59c3), S41) + b;
        d = rotateLeft((d + K(a, b, c) + X[ 3] + 0x8f0ccc92), S42) + a;
        c = rotateLeft((c + K(d, a, b) + X[10] + 0xffeff47d), S43) + d;
        b = rotateLeft((b + K(c, d, a) + X[ 1] + 0x85845dd1), S44) + c;
        a = rotateLeft((a + K(b, c, d) + X[ 8] + 0x6fa87e4f), S41) + b;
        d = rotateLeft((d + K(a, b, c) + X[15] + 0xfe2ce6e0), S42) + a;
        c = rotateLeft((c + K(d, a, b) + X[ 6] + 0xa3014314), S43) + d;
        b = rotateLeft((b + K(c, d, a) + X[13] + 0x4e0811a1), S44) + c;
        a = rotateLeft((a + K(b, c, d) + X[ 4] + 0xf7537e82), S41) + b;
        d = rotateLeft((d + K(a, b, c) + X[11] + 0xbd3af235), S42) + a;
        c = rotateLeft((c + K(d, a, b) + X[ 2] + 0x2ad7d2bb), S43) + d;
        b = rotateLeft((b + K(c, d, a) + X[ 9] + 0xeb86d391), S44) + c;
         H1 += a;
         H2 += b;
         H3 += c;
         H4 += d;

        //
        // reset the offset and clean out the word buffer.
        //
        xOff = 0;
        for (int i = 0; i != X.length; i++)
        {
            X[i] = 0;
        }
    }
}
```

Message Authentication Codes

A special type of message digest is known as the *message authentication code* (MAC). A MAC is a message digest that is computed by using as input a given message *and* some secret data; this secret data is some kind of authentication data such as a key:

```
MAC = hashFunction(msg, secret-data); // MAC is a digest using secret data
```

There are four types of MACs: 1) unconditionally secure (the message authenticates itself), 2) hash function-based, 3) block cipher-based, and 4) stream cipher-based. As with basic message digests, a MAC is a unique number that faithfully represents a message, but its value cannot be forged without knowing the secret data (MACs are computed and verified using the same single key). As with a message digest, we use a MAC to detect whether the message has been altered—but we have additional security because of the secret data. Protocols such as SSL and TLS leverage MACs on every message that is exchanged.

Digital Signatures

Digital signatures prove the authenticity of a message or document by using public key encryption (two keys) and message digests. The goal of digital signatures is to create a data signature that can be authenticated to ensure the origin and the integrity of a message or document. As in MAC, secret data is used to encrypt the hash value, but this time the secret data is the private key, which can be used to validate the sender itself:

```
DigitalSig = hashFunction(msg, private-key); // compute dig. signature
```

Because a private key is used to encode the hash value, only recipients who have access to the public key can verify the signature. By encrypting the message digest itself using our private key, we have created a digital signature that ensures message integrity, user authentication, and non-repudiation.

In theory, signing a document can be accomplished by just encrypting the document using public key cryptography, where the sender uses his or her private key to encrypt a message. Successfully decrypting the message by using the sender's public key is in theory the same as verifying the sender's signature. But in practice, this approach is expensive (slow), so instead of signing the whole document by encrypting it using a private key, a message digest or hash value that represents the document is produced by using a one-way hash function and is signed by using the private key. On the receiving side, the recipient uses the sender's public key to decrypt the hash value and to verify the integrity and origin of the message. The recipient recomputes the hash value for the received document and compares it to the decrypted hash value that was sent with the document. If they match, the message is valid and the user is identified. As a side note, not all algorithms can be used for both digital signatures and data encryption—RSA being an example of a public-key algorithm that can be used for both signatures and encryption (and DSA being one that does not).

Digital signatures satisfy many important security needs. They are faster than signing the whole document; the signature is unforgettable because the document and hash value were encrypted by using a private key; the signature is proven authentic because the message was successfully decrypted by using the sender's public key; the signature cannot be reused because the encryption and the hash value is a function of the document itself; and the document cannot be altered because modifying the document will yield an error when the hash values are compared.

Secure Socket Layer (SSL) and the Transport Layer Security (TLS) Protocols

In the early 1990s, Netscape created the *Secure Socket Layer* (SSL) to provide secure socket communication. SSL is the basis for HTTPS, the standard security protocol of the Internet. SSL has evolved into the *Transport Layer Security* (TLS) protocol, as documented on RFC 2246 and RFC 2819 (HTTP over TLS). Please refer to these RFCs for more information.

The goal of SSL/TLS is to protect information that flows over the Internet. SSL/TLS sessions enable true end-to-end security between the client and the server. SSL/TLS assumes a connection-oriented transport, which on the wired network is typically TCP. With SSL/TLS, message tampering can be detected.

An SSL/TLS session has four phases:

1. *Handshake and cipher negotiation.*

   "Exchange hello messages to agree on algorithms, exchange random values, and check for session resumption." (From RFC 2246)

   Both parties agree on the encryption algorithms or ciphers to use. The client sends a "*Client hello*" message to the server with the client's random value and supported cipher suites. Block ciphers supported by SSL/TLS include DES, RC2, RSA, IDEA, and ECC. Stream ciphers include RC4 for MAC SHA-1 and MD5. For signatures, DSS and RSA are supported. Next, the server responds by sending a "*Server hello*" message to the client with the server's random value.

Block versus Stream Ciphers

A *block cipher* is a type of symmetric-key encryption algorithm that transforms a fixed-length block of *plaintext* (unencrypted text) data into a block of *ciphertext* (encrypted text) data of the same length. A *stream cipher* is a type of symmetric encryption that can be much faster than block ciphers. While block ciphers operate on large blocks of data, stream ciphers typically operate on smaller units of plaintext, usually bits. The encryption of plaintext with a block cipher generates the same ciphertext when the same key is used. With a stream cipher, the output from the transformation of plaintext will vary, depending on when bit patterns are encountered during the encryption process.

2. *Authentication.*

   "Exchange the necessary cryptographic parameters to allow the client and server to agree on a premaster secret. Exchange certificates and cryptographic information to allow the client and server to authenticate themselves." (From RFC 2246)

   The server (and optionally, the client) is authenticated by using digital certificates (public keys) and private keys. Next, the server sends its certificate to the client for authentication, and the server can request a certificate from the client. Next, the server sends the *"Server hello done"* message. If the server has requested a certificate from the client, the client must respond with one.

3. *Key exchange.*

   "Generate a master secret from the premaster secret and exchanged random values. Provide security parameters to the record layer. Allow the client and server to verify that their peer has calculated the same security parameters and that the handshake occurred without tampering by an attacker." (From RFC 2246)

   The client creates the premaster secret and encrypts it with the server's public key before sending it to the server. Once received by the server, the server and client each generate the master secret and session keys based on the premaster secret. Next, the client sends a "*Change cipher spec*" message to the server to indicate that the client will start using the new session keys for hashing and encrypting messages. Then, the client sends a "*Client finished*" message. The server receives a "*Change cipher spec*" message, indicating "symmetric encryption state" by using the session keys. Finally, the server sends a "*Server finished*" message to the client. The client and the server are now ready to exchange messages securely.

4. *Application data exchange.*

   Once a secure (symmetric) session has been established, the Record protocol or layer is ready to secure messages by using the keys created during the first three phases, known collectively as the handshake protocol. The record protocol is responsible for fragmenting outgoing messages as appropriate and reassembling incoming messages; optionally compressing and decompressing messages; applying MAC to outgoing messages and verifying incoming messages by using the MAC; and finally encrypting outgoing messages and decrypting incoming messages.

Once a secure session has been established, you are guaranteed that your sensitive data is protected by public key cryptography.

Typical Wireless Network Operation

Wireless devices typically communicate with a gateway run by the network carrier. The gateway is connected to the Internet and makes the ultimate connection to the Web server:

```
             Wireless network                             Internet      |(Firewall)
        [MIDP] <------------------>[Wireless Gateway]<------------->[Web server]
      [device]  GPRS, CDMA, etc.                         HTTP/TCP/IP     |
           |<---------------------------SSL/TLS--------------------->|
                                         or
           |<------------encrypted using other cryptosystem-------->|
```

To the Web server, a request from a wireless device is just like any other request from a conventional Web client, such as a desktop Web browser. The gateway might limit the amount of data that can be transferred in a single request/response cycle or might only allow access to certain well-known TCP/IP ports. These kinds of details are not addressed by the MIDP specification. Apart from such restrictions, however, the HTTP communication must appear to be seamless and direct. If supported, the wireless device can initiate a secure connection by using HTTPS, which is HTTP over SSL/TLS, to guarantee end-to-end security between the client and the destination server.

Note that wireless networks provide some level of encryption between a wireless device and the gateway. You should not rely on this encryption, however, and assume that everything you send over the air can be read by anyone who wants to read it.

MIDP Security

Version 1.0 of the MIDP does not define any communication security. This situation is a problem because security is very important in mobile applications where sensitive information is transmitted over the air. The good news is that this limitation is being addressed by the MIDP Expert Group, which is currently working on extending the MIDP to natively support HTTPS. Device manufacturers have recognized this limitation and also are shipping HTTPS support with their devices. If support is available, securing your communication should be a matter of changing the protocol in your URLs to use `https` instead of `http`, unless a brand new connection class is introduced by the next version of the MIDP, in which case you also would use the new connection class. Note that a new connection class for HTTPS might be introduced by the MIDP Expert Group to handle things such as the management of digital certificates. We will not know the exact approach until the next specification is published.

Ideally, then, you will use HTTPS to protect your sensitive data. If HTTPS is not available, however, or you want to send data by using datagrams or some other method of communication, you will need to use your own cryptographic routines such as the classes from the Legion of Bouncy Castle at `www.bouncy-castle.org`.

Opening an HTTPS Connection

Assuming that `https` in supported by the `HttpConnection` class, let's revisit the sequence of steps that an HTTPS-enabled MIDP device goes through when requesting a secure session with a server:

1. The client requests a secure session with a server.
2. The server provides the client with its server certificate.

3. The client authenticates the server by confirming (through signatures) that a valid certificate authority issued the certificate.
4. The client uses the public key stored in the certificate to encrypt a shared secret key.
5. The client sends the encrypted shared secret key to the server.
6. The private key is used to encrypt the rest of the transmissions.

The following code fragment shows how to open a secure connection by using HTTPS (and, if the device does not support this protocol, fallback to unsecure HTTP):

```
HttpConnection conn = null;
String         path = "//www.j2medeveloper.com/index.html";

try {
    conn = (HttpConnection) Connector.open( "https:" + path );
}
catch( ConnectionNotFoundException cne ){
    try {
        conn = (HttpConnection) Connector.open( "http:" + path );
    }
    catch( IOException e ){
    }
}
catch( IOException ioe ){
}
```

If you cannot fall back to another protocol, be sure to inform the user about it instead of just reporting an input/output (I/O) exception. Also, always notify the user before automatically switching from a secure connection to an unsecured one.

Alternatives to HTTPS in the MIDP

There will be cases where HTTPS is not available to us, or maybe we are not using HTTP for our communications. There are a number of pure Java cryptography solutions, but not many have been adapted to CLDC-based profiles. The Legion of Bouncy Castle (`www.bouncycastle.org`) is an open source project that has created a pure Java cryptographic API that is freely available and that has been adapted to CLDC-based profiles such as the MIDP. Let's look at a code fragment from their lightweight cryptography API adapted to the MIDP:

```
//
// Copyright (c) 2000 The Legion Of The Bouncy Castle
//  (http://www.bouncycastle.org)
//
package org.bouncycastle.crypto.examples;

import java.io.*;
import java.lang.*;
```

```
import javax.microedition.midlet.MIDlet;
import javax.microedition.lcdui.*;

import org.bouncycastle.util.test.*;
import org.bouncycastle.util.encoders.*;

import org.bouncycastle.crypto.*;
import org.bouncycastle.crypto.engines.*;
import org.bouncycastle.crypto.modes.*;
import org.bouncycastle.crypto.params.*;

/**
 * MIDPTest is a simple graphics application for the J2ME CLDC/MIDP.
 *
 * It has hardcoded values for the key and plain text. It also
 * performs the standard testing for the chosen cipher, and
 * displays the results.
 *
 * This example shows how to use the light-weight API and
 * a symmetric cipher.
 *
 */
public class MIDPTest extends MIDlet
{
    private Display d = null;

    private boolean doneEncrypt = false;

    private String key = "0123456789abcdef0123456789abcdef";
    private String plainText = "www.bouncycastle.org";
    private byte[] keyBytes = null;
    private byte[] cipherText = null;
    private BufferedBlockCipher cipher = null;

    private String[] cipherNames = { "DES", "DESede", "IDEA",
                                     "Rijndael", "Twofish" };

    private Form output = null;

    public void startApp()
    {
        Display.getDisplay(this).setCurrent(output);
    }

    public void pauseApp()
    {

    }

    public void destroyApp(boolean unconditional)
    {
```

```
}

public MIDPTest()
{
     output = new Form("BouncyCastle");
     output.append("Key: "+key.substring(0,7)+"...\n");
     output.append("In : "+plainText.substring(0,7)+"...\n");

     cipherText = performEncrypt(Hex.decode(key.getBytes()),
                                    plainText);
     String ctS = new String(Hex.encode(cipherText));

     output.append("\nCT : "+ctS.substring(0,7)+"...\n");

     String decryptText =
             performDecrypt(Hex.decode(key.getBytes()),
                            cipherText);
     output.append("PT : "+decryptText.substring(0,7)+"...\n");

     if (decryptText.compareTo(plainText) == 0)
     {
          output.append("Success");
     }
     else
     {
          output.append("Failure");
          message("["+plainText+"]");
          message("["+decryptText+"]");
     }

}

private final byte[] performEncrypt(byte[] key, String plainText)
{
     byte[] ptBytes = plainText.getBytes();

     cipher = new PaddedBlockCipher(
                    new CBCBlockCipher(getEngineInstance()));

     String name =
             cipher.getUnderlyingCipher().getAlgorithmName();
     message("Using "+name);

     cipher.init(true, new KeyParameter(key));

     byte[] rv = new byte[cipher.getOutputSize(ptBytes.length)];

     int oLen = cipher.processBytes(ptBytes,0,ptBytes.length,rv, 0);
     try
     {
          cipher.doFinal(rv, oLen);
```

```
        }
        catch (CryptoException ce)
        {
            message("Ooops, encrypt exception");
            status(ce.toString());
        }
        return rv;
    }

    private final String performDecrypt(byte[] key,
                                        byte[] cipherText)
    {
        cipher.init(false, new KeyParameter(key));

        byte[] rv = new
                byte[cipher.getOutputSize(cipherText.length)];
        int oLen = cipher.processBytes(cipherText, 0,
                                        cipherText.length, rv, 0);
        try
        {
            cipher.doFinal(rv, oLen);
        }
        catch (CryptoException ce)
        {
            message("Ooops, decrypt exception");
            status(ce.toString());
        }
        return new String(rv).trim();
    }

    private int whichCipher()
    {
        return 4; // DES
    }
    private final BlockCipher getEngineInstance()
    {
        // returns a block cipher according to the current
        // state of the radio button lists.  This is only
        // done prior to encryption.
        BlockCipher rv = null;

        switch (whichCipher())
        {
            case 0:
                rv = new DESEngine();
                break;
            case 1:
                rv = new DESedeEngine();
                break;
            case 2:
                rv = new IDEAEngine();
```

```
                    break;
                case 3:
                    rv = new RijndaelEngine();
                    break;
                case 4:
                    rv = new TwofishEngine();
                    break;
                default:
                    rv = new DESEngine();
                    break;
            }
            return rv;
        }

        public void message(String s)
        {
            System.out.println("M:"+s);
        }

        public void status(String s)
        {
            System.out.println("S:"+s);
        }

    }
```

This example uses hard-coded keys, which is not practical. Let's look at a code fragment that generates a key for DES. Recall that DES is symmetric and hence requires a single key. As a side note, the Legion of Bouncy Castle lightweight cryptography API also supports the creation of Diffie-Hellman, RSA, and Elliptic Curve and DSA key *pairs* (private and public keys):

```
//
// Copyright (c) 2000 The Legion Of The Bouncy Castle
//  (http://www.bouncycastle.org)
//
try
  {
   /*
    * The process of creating a new key requires a
    * number of steps.
    *
    * First, create the parameters for the key generator
    * which are a secure random number generator, and
    * the length of the key (in bits).
    */
   SecureRandom sr = null;
   try
     {
      sr = new SecureRandom();
```

```
            /*
             * This following call to setSeed() makes the
             * initialisation of the SecureRandom object
             * _very_ fast, but not secure AT ALL.
             *
             * Remove the line, recreate the class file and
             * then run DESExample again to see the difference.
             *
             * The initialisation of a SecureRandom object
             * can take 5 or more seconds depending on the
             * CPU that the program is running on.  That can
             * be annoying during unit testing.
             * - jon
             */
           sr.setSeed("www.bouncycastle.org".getBytes());
        }
        catch (Exception nsa){
          System.err.println("Hmmm, no SHA1PRNG, you need the "+
            "Sun implementation");
        }
        KeyGenerationParameters kgp = new KeyGenerationParameters(
                           sr,
                           DESedeParameters.DES_EDE_KEY_LENGTH*8);

        /*
         * Second, initialise the key generator with the parameters
         */
        DESedeKeyGenerator kg = new DESedeKeyGenerator();
        kg.init(kgp);

        /*
         * Third, and finally, generate the key
         */
        key = kg.generateKey();
        ..... // use and/or store the generated key
    }
```

In practice, you would generate your symmetric key (or key pairs if you decide to use public key encryption) on the server and distribute the appropriate key by storing it in the JAR file for your MIDlet suite. The MIDlets in the suite could then use this key to encrypt or decrypt data sent to and received from the server.

Configuring HTTPS in the J2ME Wireless Toolkit

Support for HTTPS is provided in version 1.0.2 and higher of Sun's Java 2 Micro Edition (J2ME) Wireless Toolkit. The toolkit already comes with support for Verisign e-certificates. But to use other certificate authorities, you must manually install their public keys by following these steps:

1. Import the certificate of the CA that issued the certificate you want to verify into a Java 2 Standard Edition (J2SE) keystore by using the J2SE `keytool` command. Assign the certificate an appropriate alias. For example:

```
keytool -import -keystore keystore -storepass password -file
ca_cert.txt -alias alias
```

2. Import the public key of the CA from the J2SE keystore into the MIDP public keystore by using the MIDP `keytool`. For example:

```
java -jar bin/MEKeyTool.jar -import -keystore keystore -alias alias  -
storepass password
```

3. Check the keys in the MIDP public keystore by using the following command:

```
java -jar bin/MEKeyTool.jar -list
```

Full HTTPS support should be enabled when you next run the toolkit's simulator. For more information, please refer to the toolkit documentation.

Summary

In this chapter, we have covered the basic concepts of security and how authentication with public key encryption satisfies most security needs. Supporting SSL-based security on the MIDP is as easy as changing your source code to use `https` instead of `http`, assuming that the MIDP implementation supports HTTPS as an extension, plus installing a server certificate on your Web server. We also covered how to leverage pure Java cryptosystems for cases where we are not using HTTP for communications or where HTTPS is not available to us. There also are a number of XML-based security projects that are of interest but are not covered here. These are the W3C XML Signature and Encryption, OASIS SAML, and AuthXML. These XML-based security technologies are new and not yet adopted but are worth understanding. For mobile devices, Smart cards also will play an important role in security and in implementing PKI solutions. We will leave security now and move on to another topic of interest to many MIDP application developers: XML.

CHAPTER 9

Using XML in MIDP Applications

Extensible Markup Language (XML) is a very important tool for the exchange of information on the Internet and is becoming as important in the area of wireless applications. When combined with network protocols such as HTTP, the result is easy integration with existing servers on the network. In this chapter, we will cover using XML in Mobile Information Device Profile (MIDP) applications. Note that this chapter is not meant to be an exhaustive look at XML—a topic beyond the scope of this book—but rather to teach you enough about XML to get you started.

XML: Extensible Markup Language

XML is many things. It is an extensible text-based *meta-language* used to describe other languages or grammars. It is a *specification* with rules and guidelines that define how XML documents are described, structured, and processed. It is a *family* of related specifications, some of which are still under development, that include DTD, XML transformations (XSL/XSLT), namespaces, XML schemas, and XML-based presentation (XHTML). It is a *standard* for the exchange of structured information.

The development of XML started around 1996, but its foundation is much older than that. XML is based on the *Standard Generalized Markup Language* (SGML), which is circa early 1980s as well as in HTML, which is circa early 1990s. Please refer to the World Wide Web Consortium (W3C) Web site for more information about XML development work.

XML Basics

XML is a broad and complex subject. In this chapter, we will cover the basic XML concepts that enable us to use XML for integration and data exchange with servers on the Internet.

The contents of an XML document are similar to that of an HTML document—both grammars are tag-based. In the case of HTML, the tags are used for presentation (UI), but in XML we use tags to represent any data our application requires. XML is extensible by nature because developers can define their own grammar, or set of tags. XML is really a tag language that enables you to define data elements by name as well as defining the document's organization or structure. For example, you can define `NAME` as an element that is composed of two subelements: `FIRSTNAME` and `LASTNAME`, as in the following example (note that the numbers to the left are for reference only):

```
SAMPLE XML (name.xml)
1       <?xml version="1.0" encoding="utf-8" ?>
2       <!DOCTYPE NAME SYSTEM "name.dtd">
3       <NAME primarykey="true">
4         <FIRSTNAME>Carol</FIRSTNAME>
5         <LASTNAME>Long</LASTNAME>
6       </NAME>
```

In XML, the basic unit of data is known as an *element*. Elements consist of a *start tag*, embedded *data/text*, and an *end tag* (for example, `<FIRSTNAME>Carol</FIRSTNAME>`). Note that elements can contain other elements. In this sample, the `NAME` tag encloses the `FIRSTNAME` and `LASTNAME` tags. *Tags* are the text within angle brackets, as we can see starting at line 3. On line 3, we also define an element *attribute*. An attribute is a parameter to a tag consisting of a name and a value. In our example, the attribute `primarykey` with a value of `true` indicates that `NAME` is a primary key.

As a side note, when you define your own XML grammar or dialect, you will encounter situations where a given piece of information could be defined as either an element or as an attribute. What you decide is completely based on your application, but here are some guidelines about when to use elements versus attributes. Use attributes when:

- You want to constrain (validate) a value—for example, `primarykey` to true or false
- You want to assign default values—for example, `primarykey` equal to false
- You want better performance, as attributes are less verbose than elements

On the other hand, use elements when:

- Other data is contained—for example, `NAME` contains `FIRSTNAME` and `LASTNAME`
- Representing repetitive name/value pairs—for example `<PROPERTY name="name" value="value"/>` or `<BUTTON name="name" label="value"/>`
- Required by other XML technologies such as XPath

In XML, content is either character data or markup. Character data is everything that is not markup. Within XML elements, character data is the text within the element's start and end tags. Within CDATA sections, which contain a sequence of characters that are ignored and not parsed, character data is any sequence of characters not including the CDATA section closing delimiter sequence "]]>". Markup includes tags, comments, XML and text declarations, processing instructions, and others.

The first line of any valid XML document is the prolog (lines 1–2), which precedes the XML data (lines 3–6). The prolog declares the document an XML document and identifies the version of XML being used. The minimal valid declaration is `<?xml version="1.0"?>`. Other information usually found on this same line is the declaration of the document's character encoding or the standalone attribute.

The second line in our example `name.xml` is the optional part of the prolog known as the document type declaration, which defines the root element or node (in our example, `NAME`), as well as the Document Type Definition (DTD) for this document. DTDs themselves can be local or external to the document. In our example, we use an external DTD called `name.dtd`. You must specify the `DOCTYPE` if you want to validate your XML document by using a validating parser. DTDs are used to define and constrain the XML document by defining the grammar tags, attribute values and constraints, and document structure. Let's look at the DTD for the `name.xml`:

```
Name.dtd DTD for name.xml
1       <!ELEMENT NAME (FIRSTNAME, LASTNAME)>
2       <!ATTLIST NAME primarykey  (true | false) "false">
3       <!ELEMENT FIRSTNAME (#PCDATA)>
4       <!ELEMENT LASTNAME  (#PCDATA)>
```

If we were to define a DTD with a DOCTYPE and we use a validating XML parser, this DTD would tell the validating parser that this XML document has three valid tags/elements: `NAME` (the root element), `FIRSTNAME`, and `LASTNAME`. The DTD also defines a hierarchy; that `NAME` has two subelements within it: `FIRSTNAME` and `LASTNAME`. Last, but not least, the DTD also indicates that `NAME` has an attribute, `primarykey`, with valid values of true and false, with false being the default value. If we were to add a new line to our XML document, let's say `<MIDDLENAME>Sarylda</MIDDLENAME>`, our XML document would become non-valid unless we change the DTD and indicate that the middle name is a valid tag/element. To perform this task, we would change line 1 and add a new element definition (line 4):

```
1       <!ELEMENT NAME (FIRSTNAME, MIDDLENAME, LASTNAME)>
2       <!ATTLIST NAME primarykey  (true | false) "false">
3       <!ELEMENT FIRSTNAME EMPTY>
4       <!ELEMENT MIDDLENAME EMPTY>
5       <!ELEMENT LASTNAME EMPTY>
```

Because DTDs have a number of limitations–for example, lack of namespaces, limited data-typing, and limited hierarchical organization–the W3C is developing an alternate form of defining XML documents known as *schemas*. Still, DTD is the most predominant method used to describe XML documents. Please refer to the W3C Web site for more information on XML schemas.

XML Parsers

An XML processor is commonly referred to as an XML *parser*. An XML parser takes an input stream and parses it into XML elements that the application understands and expects. Note that there is no magic to what the application expects from an XML parser because the application is usually tightly coupled to a specific XML grammar.

XML parsers are either validating or non-validating. Validating parsers require a DTD that describes the XML document syntax and structure. Validating parsers process the whole XML document and report any violations if the document is not well formed. Non-validating parsers ignore the DTD and simply ensure that the XML document is relatively well-formed and that it follows the basic XML rules.

XML parsers can be tree-based or event-driven. Tree-based parsers parse an XML document completely into memory, creating a tree-like representation with nodes that represents the document. This model uses more memory than event-driven parsers because the entire document tree resides in memory. Event-driven parsers parse the XML stream and generate events as they are encountered. Event-driven parsers are either push-based or pull-based. With push-based, event-driven parsers, you register event-handler callbacks that the parser invokes as it parses the document. This method is how *Simple API for XML* (SAX) parsers work. With pull-based, event-driven parsers, you request the events one at a time, and your application is in control. This method is how the kXML parser for J2ME works. With kXML, you traverse the XML document recursively by requesting events as they occur. Event-driven parsers are usually more efficient for parsing XML documents, but if you need to manipulate an entire XML document, a tree-based parser might be a better choice.

XML by Example

Let's now explore the XML grammar used in the e-mail client developed in Chapter 5, "User Interface Examples." Here is the grammar that it uses:

Simple XML grammar for our sample email application (emailmessages.xml)

```
1    <?xml version="1.0" encoding="utf-8"?>
2    <!DOCTYPE emailmessages SYSTEM "messages.dtd">
3    <emailmessages count="1">
4      <emailmessage>
5        <msgid>3</msgid>
6        <date>Fri.Mar09.11:49:10.CST 2001</date>
7        <from>eric@ericgiguere.com</from>
8        <subject>Code Review</subject>
9        <body>Please review chapter 6 code</body>
10     </emailmessage>
11   </emailmessages>
```

The numbers to the left are for reference and are not part of the actual XML document. The first line is the XML `prolog`, as we have previously described. Line 2, part of the prolog and optional, must be included if you want to validate the XML stream/document by using a validating XML parser. Lines 3–11 are the set of tags/elements and attributes that describe the e-mail messages. Let's now take a look at the DTD for this e-mail messaging XML grammar:

Document Type Definition for emailmessages.xml

```
<!ELEMENT emailmessages (emailmessage*)>
<!ATTLIST emailmessages count CDATA "">
<!ELEMENT emailmessage (msgid, date, from, to?, subject, body)>
```

```
4       <!ELEMENT msgid (#PCDATA)>
5       <!ELEMENT date (#PCDATA)>
6       <!ELEMENT from (#PCDATA)>
7       <!ELEMENT to (#PCDATA)>
8       <!ELEMENT subject (#PCDATA)>
9       <!ELEMENT body (#PCDATA)>
```

Note the "*" in line 1 and the "?"in line 3. These are element qualifiers and indicate whether the element is required or optional and how many elements of the same kind are allowed to happen within the XML document. Valid qualifiers are as follows:

- No qualifier indicates that *only one* such element is valid.
- The ? (question mark) qualifier indicates that the element can appear at most once.
- The * (asterisk) qualifier indicates that zero or more elements are valid.
- The + (plus sign) qualifier indicates that one or more elements are valid.

The first line of this DTD also describes the relationship between the elements (in this case, emailmessages and emailmessage). The first line indicates that emailmessage is a subelement of emailmessages and that zero or more emailmessage are valid. The second line in our DTD defines the optional attribute count for the element emailmessages. To make this attribute required, add the qualifier #REQUIRED instead of "", for example, <!ATTLIST messages count CDATA #REQUIRED>. Line 3 is similar to line 1 because it defines the relationship between emailmessage and its sub-elements msgid, date, from, to, subject, and body. Line 3 also indicates that the emailmessage element has an optional subelement (to element). Line 4–9 defines the rest of the valid elements for our e-mail message XML dialect, indicating that they are made of *parsed character data* (PCDATA), which means text with no subelements.

XML Parsers for MIDP

Currently, the MIDP has no native support for XML parsing. In other words, your application must include an XML parser if you want to read XML documents. But this approach is expensive, because it forces all MIDP applications that use XML to include a parser—wasting the device's memory. The good news is that the MIDP Expert Group is currently considering adding an XML parser to the next version of the MIDP specification.

There are a number of small XML parsers available on the Web. In this chapter, we will cover two of the most widely used open source XML parsers for J2ME: *NanoXML* and *kXML*. Links to both parsers can be found on the book's Web site.

NanoXML

NanoXML is an open source, small implementation of a tree-based XML parser with an optional SAX API. NanoXML was created by Marc De Scheemaecker and adapted for the CLDC by Eric Giguère. NanoXML is not 100 percent XML 1.0 compliant, and its first version is non-validating. It does not support mixed elements (containing both CDATA and subelements). By including a separate JAR file, a SAX-compatible API is available for performing event-driven parsing—although it still stores and parses the document as a tree. The second version of NanoXML is more robust because it includes support for DTDs (a validating parser), mixed element content, and a faster parser. Of course, all of these goodies come at a price: A larger footprint.

Although NanoXML supports a SAX API, it increases NanoXML's footprint. The code samples that follow use the NanoXML non-SAX API to minimize the application memory footprint. NanoXML licensing is flexible, enabling you to use the parser for any commercial or non-commercial purpose. The only requirement is to disclose the origin of the parser.

kXML

kXML is a pull-based, event-driven XML parser. kXML was created by Stefan Haustein and is part of the Enhydra family of open source projects. As we described earlier in this chapter, pull-based, event-driven parsers give the application control over how and when to process parsing events. Instead of registering callbacks, as in the case of SAX parsers, kXML-based applications enter a recursive loop, pulling events. Applications can keep their own state as necessary, creating a good balance between the parser's complexity (because some of the state management is handled by the application) and size. kXML also provides a DOM-like API, known as kDOM. It is recommended that you use the pull-based parser, because it is more efficient from the point of view of memory utilization and speed and satisfies most of the XML parsing applications' requirements. kXML supports namespaces and the binary encoding of XML according to WAP standards. The licensing terms for kXML are a *little bit* more restrictive than NanoXML, and the parser is bigger than NanoXML. The typical footprint varies from 23KB to 40KB, depending on what is included. Haustein also has created `kSOAP`, a small SOAP framework for J2ME that also is part of the Enhydra family of open source projects. kSOAP uses kXML. If your application requires SOAP, you should then use the kXML parser over NanoXML.

XML And Mobile Applications

In our e-mail application, we use XML over HTTP to exchange e-mail messages between the MIDP device and a server. In other words, we implemented our own XML API over HTTP. XML over HTTP is a very flexible approach to network-based applications and services and is rapidly becoming the standard way to integrate mobile devices with existing server infrastructure and to leverage network-based services. Although XML/HTTP will perform less than binary protocols over TCP or UDP, the ease of integration and the availability of open XML technologies and services overcome such concerns. Note that high performance is not usually an issue in resource-constrained devices.

Let's revisit the diagram that describes the interactions between our MIDP application and the Web server that serves as our gateway to the e-mail server. The diagram is shown in Figure 9.1.

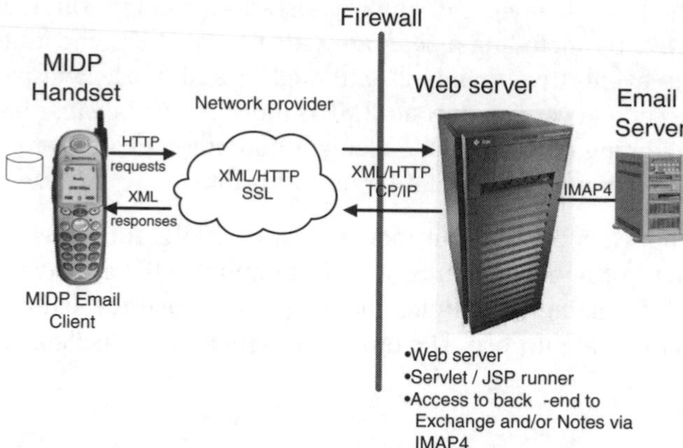

Figure 9.1 Typical flow of XML in a network-aware MIDlet.

The MIDP client makes an HTTP request to a Web server. This server interacts with an e-mail server in the back end. The server packages any results from the e-mail server as an XML document for transmittal back to the MIDP client over HTTP.

XML in the E-Mail Client

When parsing XML, you can use either kXML or NanoXML. The simplest way to compare the two is to look at some actual code—code from the e-mail client that we started building in Chapter 5.

The EmailMessage Class

The `EmailMessage` class represents an e-mail message. This class stores the following attributes about a message—message ID, sender, recipient, data, subject, and the message body. Its definition is as follows:

```
package com.j2medeveloper.email;

public class EmailMessage {

    private String id;
    private String to;
    private String from;
    private String date;
    private String subject;
    private String body;

    /**
     * Creates a new instance.
     * @param none
```

```
 */
public EmailMessage() {
    id      = null;
    from    = null;
    to      = null;
    date    = null;
    subject = null;
    body    = null;
}

/**
 * Creates a new email instance
 * @param message id
 * @param date
 * @param from
 * @param message body
 * @param subject
 */
public EmailMessage( String idArg,
                     String dateArg,
                     String fromArg,
                     String bodyArg,
                     String subjectArg ) {

    id      = idArg;
    date    = dateArg;
    from    = fromArg;
    body    = bodyArg;
    subject = subjectArg;
}

/**
 * returns the message id property
 * @param none
 */
public String getId() {
    return id;
}

/**
 * Returns the to property.
 * @param none
 */
public String getTo() {
    return to;
}

/**
 * Returns the from property.
 * @param none
 */
```

```
public String getFrom() {
    return from;
}

/**
 * Returns the date property.
 * @param none
 */
public String getDate() {
    return date;
}

/**
 * Returns the message body property.
 * @param none
 */
public String getBody() {
    return body;
}

/**
 * Returns the subject property.
 * @param none
 */
public String getSubject() {
    return subject;
}

/**
 * Sets the message id property.
 * @param message id
 */
public void setId(String idArg) {
    this.id = idArg;
}

/**
 * Sets the date property.
 * @param Date
 */
public void setDate(String datearg) {
    this.date = datearg;
}

/**
 * Sets the to property.
 * @param from
 */
public void setTo(String toarg) {
    this.to = toarg;
```

```
    }

    /**
     * Sets the from property.
     * @param from
     */
    public void setFrom(String fromarg) {
        this.from = fromarg;
    }

    /**
     * Sets the body property.
     * @param Email body
     */
    public void setBody(String bodyarg) {
        this.body = bodyarg;
    }

    /**
     * Sets the subject property.
     * @param Subject
     */
    public void setSubject(String subjectarg) {
        this.subject = subjectarg;
    }

    /**
     * Dump the object
     */
    public void dump() {
        System.out.println("Msg. Id.  :" + id);
        System.out.println("Date      :" + date);
        System.out.println("To        :" + to);
        System.out.println("From      :" + from);
        System.out.println("Subject   :" + subject);
        System.out.println("Body      :" + body);
    }
}
```

As you can see, there is nothing special about the `EmailMessage` class.

Sending XML over HTTP

The following code fragment sends an XML document to the server by using HTTP. We use the `HttpConnectionHelper` class from Chapter 6. The POST method is used, and the message body is contained within a CDATA block to avoid having to handle special characters that would otherwise confuse an XML parser. The code is as follows:

```
/*
 * Build XML request
```

```
 */
StringBuffer xmlReq = new StringBuffer();
xmlReq.append("<?xml version=\"1.0\" ?>");
xmlReq.append("<emailmessages count=\"1\">");
xmlReq.append("<emailmessage>");
xmlReq.append("<to>");
xmlReq.append(toField.getString());
xmlReq.append("</to>");
xmlReq.append("<from>");
xmlReq.append(from);
xmlReq.append("</from>");
xmlReq.append("<subject>");
xmlReq.append(subjectField.getString());
xmlReq.append("</subject>");
xmlReq.append("<body><![CDATA[");
xmlReq.append(bodyField.getString());
xmlReq.append("]]></body>");
xmlReq.append("</emailmessage>");
xmlReq.append("</emailmessages>");

/*
 * Build request parameters (name:value pairs)
 */
Hashtable params = new Hashtable();
params.put("username", username);
params.put("password", password);
params.put("action",   "send_message");

/*
 * try sending the request and getting the response
 */
try {
   String targetURL = "http://"+serverURL+":"+serverPort;
   hch = new HttpConnectionHelper(targetURL,
                                  EMAIL_CONTROLLER,
                                  params);
   hch.setContentBody(xml);
   // send request, wait for response
   response = hch.sendReceive();
   ...... // parse the response, etc.
}
catch (Exception e) {
   ...... // handle the exception
}
finally {
    xmlReq = null;
}
```

Notice that while this example sends a single e-mail at a time—the count attribute of `emailmessages` is set to 1—it could easily be adapted to send multiple messages.

Receiving XML over HTTP

The following code fragment is almost identical to the previous one except that it sends a different action to the server. The server sends back an XML document as the response, which we then parse to obtain the list of e-mail messages in the user's inbox:

```
/*
 * Build get message query string
 */
params = new Hashtable();
params.put("username", username);
params.put("password", password);
params.put("action",    "get_messages");

/*
 * Clean up existing UI list of email messages.
 * Send HTTP request and wait for response.
 * Then parse the response and re-build UI list.
 */
try {

   int i, sz;

   // clean up the emailMsgs List
   sz = emailMsgs.size();
   for (i=0; i<sz; i++) {
      emailMsgs.delete(0);
   }

   /*
    * set/compose targetURL and send HTTP request,
    * wait for response.
    */
   String targetURL = "http://"+serverURL+":"+serverPort;
   hch = new HttpConnectionHelper(targetURL,
                                  EMAIL_CONTROLLER,
                                  params);
   response = hch.sendReceive();

   /*
    * Parse the response using either XML parser.
    */
   emailVector = EmailParser_NanoXML.parse(response.trim());
// emailVector = EmailParser_kXML.parse(response.trim());

   /*
    * re-build UI list of email subjects
    */
   for (i = 0; i < emailVector.size(); i++) {
      EmailMessage em = (EmailMessage) emailVector.elementAt(i);
```

```
        emailMsgs.append(em.getSubject(), null);
    }
    catch (Exception e) {
        ....
    }
    finally {
        params = null;
    }
```

This time, we do not send any body content. Rather, all we send are some parameters that the server uses to log into the correct e-mail account and fetch the waiting mail. Of course, this operation and the preceding operation also could be combined into a single operation. Recall that credentials should not be passed in the URL itself but rather as part of the encrypted HTTP body.

Parsing XML by Using NanoXML

The following code fragment parses the XML-based e-mail responses by using the NanoXML parser. The e-mail messages are returned by using a vector of `EmailMessage` objects:

```
package com.j2medeveloper.email;

import com.j2medeveloper.nanoxml.*;
import java.util.*;

/**
 * Uses NanoXML to parse Email HTTP responses represented in XML
 * into collections / vector of EmailMessages
 */

//
// Example of Email XML response
//
// <?xml.version="1.0" encoding ="UTF-8"?>
// <emailmessages count="1">
//    <emailmessage>
//        <msgid>3</msgid>
//        <date>Fri.Mar09.11:49:10.CST 2001</date>
//        <from>eric@giguere.com</from>
//        <subject>Code Review</subject>
//        <body>Please review chapter 6 code</body>
//    </emailmessage>
// </emailmessages>

/**
 * EmailParser parses Email HTTP responses represented in XML,
 * into a collection of EmailMessages objects
 */
public class EmailParser_NanoXML {
```

```
/**
 * Parses the received email information in XML format
 * @param HTTP XML response
 * @throws Exception Signals an error occurred while parsing XML
 * Email.
 */
public static Vector parse(String xml) throws Exception {

    EmailMessage em = null;
    String count = "zero";

    // create element for 1st (root) element (emailmessages), parse
    kXMLElement parser = new kXMLElement();
    parser.parseString(xml);

    // create the vector that will hold Individual emailmessage
    Vector emailMessages  = new Vector(parser.countChildren());

    if ("emailmessages".equals(parser.getTagName())) {
       // extract count attribute
       count = parser.getProperty("count");
    }

    // get enumeration of all children under emailmessages
    Enumeration outterenum = parser.enumerateChildren();

    // for each emailmessage
    while (outterenum.hasMoreElements()) {

        // create element for emailmessage
        kXMLElement outterchild =
           (kXMLElement)(outterenum.nextElement());

        String outterTagName  = outterchild.getTagName();
        String outterContents = outterchild.getContents();

        if ("emailmessage".equals(outterTagName)) {

            // start tag for new emailmessage; allocate an email
            // message object
            em = new EmailMessage();

            // enumeration children's children (msgid, from, to,
            etc.)
            Enumeration innerenum = outterchild.enumerateChildren();

            // For each child within emailmessage(msgid, from, etc.)
            while (innerenum.hasMoreElements()) {
                // create element for emailmessage sub-elements
                kXMLElement innerchild =
```

```
                    (kXMLElement)(innerenum.nextElement());

                    String innerTagName  = innerchild.getTagName();
                    String innerContents = innerchild.getContents();

                    // for each element extract all information
                    if ("msgid".equals(innerTagName)) {
                        em.setId(innerContents);
                    }
                    else
                    if ("to".equals(innerTagName)) {
                        em.setTo(innerContents);
                    }
                    else
                    if ("from".equals(innerTagName)) {
                        em.setFrom(innerContents);
                    }
                    else
                    if ("date".equals(innerTagName)) {
                        em.setDate(innerContents);
                    }
                    else
                    if ("subject".equals(innerTagName)) {
                        em.setSubject(innerContents);
                    }
                    else
                    if ("body".equals(innerTagName)) {
                        em.setBody(innerContents);
                    }
                } // while

                // add just created emailmessage Into collection
                emailMessages.addElement(em);
            }
            else {
                System.out.println("Second tag not expected EMAIL");
            }
        } // while (outterenum.hasMoreElements())

        return emailMessages;
    } // parse
}
```

Using NanoXML is fairly simple. First, you create a `kXMLElement` instance (`kXMLElement` is a version of NanoXML's `XMLElement` class that is modified to work in a CLDC environment). Then, you call its `parseString` method with the raw XML document to parse. This action builds a tree of `kXMLElement` nodes that reflect the structure of the document. The tree is rooted at the `kXMLElement` instance that you created. You then traverse the tree by using the various methods exposed by `kXMLElement`.

Parsing XML by Using kXML

The following code fragment also parses the XML response from the server, but this time by using the kXML parser:

```
package com.j2medeveloper.email;

import java.io.*;
import java.util.*;
import org.kxml.*;
import org.kxml.parser.*;

/**
 * Uses kXML to parse Email HTTP responses represented in XML
 * into collections / vector of EmailMessages
 */

//
// Example of Email XML response
//
// <?xml.version="1.0" encoding ="UTF-8"?>
// <emailmessages count="1">
//    <emailmessage>
//        <msgid>3</msgid>
//        <date>Fri.Mar09.11:49:10.CST 2001</date>
//        <from>eric@giguere.com</from>
//        <subject>Code Review</subject>
//        <body>Please review chapter 6 code</body>
//    </emailmessage>
// </emailmessages>

/**
 * EmailParser parses Email HTTP responses represented in XML,
 * into collections of EmailMessages objects
 */
public class EmailParser_kXML {

    private static String elem          = null;
    private static Vector emailMessages = null;
    private static EmailMessage em      = null;

    /**
     * parse the Input XML stream, Invoke traverse recursively
     */
    public static Vector parse (String xml) throws IOException {

        XmlParser parser = new XmlParser
            (new InputStreamReader
            (new ByteArrayInputStream (xml.getBytes ())));
```

```
        return( traverse (parser, "") );

    }

    /**
     * Traverses the XML document, recursively pulling one
     *  parsing event at a time.
     *
     * @param parser A kXML XmlParser.
     * @param indent Indentention character(s), for debugging.
     * @throws IOException If an error parsing has ocurred
     */
    private static Vector traverse (XmlParser parser,
                                    String indent)
        throws IOException {

        boolean debug     = false;
        boolean leave     = false;
        Attribute attrib = null;
        String count      = null;

        do {
            // extract / pull a parser event
            ParseEvent event = parser.read ();

            switch (event.getType ()) {

                /*
                 * Start of element event
                 */
                case Xml.START_TAG:

                    /*
                     * If Start of Document (root element).
                     *   Create a Vector to hold email messages
                     */
                    if ("emailmessages".equals( event.getName () )) {

                        // get attribute, and create collection/vector
                        // that will hold the email messages
                       count = event.getAttribute("count").getValue();
                        emailMessages  = new Vector();
                    }
                    else
                    /*
                     * Start of email message element.
                     *   Create a new email message object
                     */
                    if ("emailmessage".equals( event.getName () )) {
```

```
        // allocate an email message object
        em = new EmailMessage();

    }

    elem = event.getName();
    // go to / parse next element
    traverse (parser, indent + "."); // recursion

    break;

/*
 * End of element event
 */
case Xml.END_TAG:

    /*
     * End of email message element.
     *  Add email message to Vector of email messages
     */
    if ("emailmessage".equals( event.getName () )) {
        emailMessages.addElement(em);
    }

    leave = true;
    break;

/*
 * End of document event
 */
case Xml.END_DOCUMENT:

    leave = true;
    break;

/*
 * Element text event (the actual data)
 */
case Xml.TEXT:

    /*
     * get text Into appropriate emailmessage
       attribute
     */
    try  {
    if ("msgid".equals( elem )) {
        em.setId(event.getText());
    }
    else
```

```
                    if ("to".equals( elem )) {
                        em.setTo(event.getText());
                    }
                    else
                    if ("from".equals( elem )) {
                        em.setFrom(event.getText());
                    }
                    else
                    if ("date".equals( elem )) {
                        em.setDate(event.getText());
                    }
                    else
                    if ("subject".equals( elem )) {
                        em.setSubject(event.getText());
                    }
                    else
                    if ("body".equals( elem )) {
                        em.setBody(event.getText());
                    }
                    }
                    catch (Exception e) {
                        System.out.println(indent+"
                                    Exception parsing:" + e);
                    }

                    break;

                /*
                 * Ignore the following events
                 */
                case Xml.WHITESPACE:
                default:
                    break;
            } // switch

        } while (!leave);

        return (emailMessages);
    }
}
```

Notice the use of recursion to traverse the XML document and to build the message vector. Unlike NanoXML, kXML does not build a tree in memory but rather returns the next piece of XML in the document. The application keeps track of the document state itself, which is most easily done by using recursive method calls.

Other Important XML Technologies

XML is being used by different technologies, such as those that describe services on a network (WSDL) or that represent data to synchronize (SyncML) or that make remote procedure calls (SOAP). The W3C has a number of projects related to XML, as do other consortiums and development groups. Much of the development is being released as open source for the benefit of the general programming population. Although it is not specifically oriented at MIDP or even J2ME, you can leverage this use of XML in building your MIDP applications. Before we leave this chapter, let's take a look at two of the XML technologies that are particularly appropriate for use by MIDP applications—the Web Services Definition Language (WSDL) and the Simple Object Access Protocol (SOAP). A third important technology, briefly covered in this chapter, is the *Universal Description Discovery and Integration* (UDDI) specification, which provides a platform-independent way of describing services (by using WSDL), discovering businesses, and integrating business services by using the Internet.

Web Services Definition Language (WSDL)

WSDL is an XML grammar for describing the interfaces (API), protocol bindings, and deployment details of network-based services such as SOAP-based network services. WSDL is a W3C draft note that consolidates similar concepts found in NASSL, SCL, and SDL. The main/original contributors to WSDL are Ariba, IBM, and Microsoft. WSDL complements UDDI by providing a consistent way of describing the network services found in UDDI registries or repositories.

WSDL mainly revolves around the concepts of *endpoints* (services), *operations*, *messages*, and *bindings*. WSDL allows for the definition of services independently from the network protocols and/or message formats used by the service. The WSDL specification describes network bindings for SOAP 1.1, HTTP GET/POST, and MIME types and uses XML schemas to describe data types. A fully described WSDL document uses the following elements to describe a given service:

1. *Types*: Group-related data type definitions
2. *Message*: An abstract, typed definition of a message
3. *Operation*: An abstract description of an action supported by the service
4. *Port Type*: An abstract set of operations supported by one or more endpoints
5. *Binding*: A concrete protocol and data format for a particular port type
6. *Port*: An endpoint (a combination of a binding and a network address)
7. *Service*: A collection of related endpoints

WSDL defines four transmission primitives (operations) that an endpoint can support:

1. *One-way*: Message sent to an endpoint
2. *Request-response*: The endpoint receives a message and sends a response message
3. *Solicit-response*: The endpoint sends a message and receives a message
4. *Notification*: The endpoint sends a message

These operations follow their own format, as described by the specification. In addition, the format of the messages can vary depending on the protocol bindings. In the following section, let's explore how a WSDL XML document looks. This particular WSDL file defines a SOAP-based e-mail service available on the network:

```
WSDL DEFINITION FOR SOAP BASED EMAIL SERVICE
<?xml version="1.0"?>
<definitions

DEFINE APPROPRIATE NAMESPACES (SOAP, XML SCHEMA, SOAP ENCODING, SERVICE)
targetNamespace="http://www.borland.com/soapServices/"
xmlns:xs="http://www.w3.org/2001/XMLSchema" name="IEmailServiceservice"
xmlns="http://schemas.xmlsoap.org/wsdl/"
xmlns:xsd="http://www.w3.org/1999/XMLSchema"
xmlns:soap="http://schemas.xmlsoap.org/wsdl/soap"
xmlns:soapenc="http://schemas.xmlsoap.org/soap/encoding/">

DEFINE THE MESSAGES
     <message name="SendMailRequest">
          <part name="To" type="string"/>
          <part name="From" type="string"/>
          <part name="Subject" type="string"/>
          <part name="Message" type="string"/>
     </message>
     <message name="SendMailResponse">
          <part name="return" type="int"/>
     </message>

DEFINE THE OPERATIONS
     <portType name="IEmailService">
          <operation name="SendMail">
               <input message="SendMailRequest"/>
               <output message="SendMailResponse"/>
          </operation>
     </portType>

DEFINE THE BINDINGS (SOAP)
     <binding name="IEmailServicebinding" type="IEmailService">
          <soap:binding style="rpc"
              transport="http://schemas.xmlsoap.org/soap/http"/>
          <operation name="SendMail">
               <soap:operation soapAction=
                    "urn:EmailIPortTypeInft-IEmailService#SendMail"/>
               <input>
                    <soap:body use="encoded"
                       encodingStyle=
                       "http://schemas.xmlsoap.org/soap/encoding/"
                       namespace="urn:EmailIPortTypeInft-IEmailService"/>
               </input>
               <output>
                    <soap:body use="encoded"
                      encodingStyle=
                      "http://schemas.xmlsoap.org/soap/encoding/"
                      namespace="urn:EmailIPortTypeInft-IEmailService"/>
               </output>
          </operation>
     </binding>
```

```
DEFINE THE SERVICE (PORT/ENDPOINT)
     <service name="IEmailServiceservice">
          <port name="IEmailServicePort" binding="IEmailServicebinding">
               <soap:address location=
"http://webservices.matlus.com/scripts/emailwebservice.dll/soap/IEmailse
rvice"/>
          </port>
     </service>

</definitions>
```

Using the information contained in this definition, we can now build an MIDP client that accesses the Web service by using the SOAP protocol.

Simple Object Access Protocol (SOAP)

SOAP is a specification for exchanging structured and typed information based on XML. SOAP is based on XML-RPC, which as the name implies is an XML-based mechanism for performing *remote procedure calls* (RPCs). The XML-RPC Web site (`www.xmlrpc.com`) defines XML-RPC as follows: "a set of implementations that allow software running on disparate operating systems, running in different environments to make procedure calls over the Internet. It's remote procedure calling using HTTP as the transport and XML as the encoding. XML-RPC is designed to be as simple as possible, while allowing complex data structures to be transmitted, processed and returned." XML-RPC came from a set of individuals who used to work at Microsoft and who later worked on SOAP: Dave Winer, Don Box, Bob Atkinson, and Mohsen Al-Ghosein. In 1999, UserLand Software (Dave Winer), DevelopMentor (Don Box), and Microsoft together submitted the SOAP specification to the *Internet Engineering Task Force* (IETF). In May 2000, SOAP was submitted to the W3C together with IBM and Lotus, and its current status is a W3C working draft, version 1.2, created by the W3C XML Protocol Working Group. As a side note, the XML Protocol working group has been chartered with creating an abstract model (called the XML Protocol abstract model, currently a W3C working draft) for XML-based messaging that is not tied to any particular approach or implementation. This abstract model is a layered architecture or framework on top of an extensible and simple (XML) messaging format, like SOAP.

SOAP is an extensible, simple/lightweight protocol to exchange information in a decentralized or distributed environment. It provides the low-level messaging plumbing—the data packaging, encoding, and transportation (protocol bindings) of messages, enabling applications to concentrate on application-level functionality. SOAP itself does not provide any semantics to what it transports, however; semantics are the responsibility of the application. SOAP is mainly an RPC mechanism. SOAP messages are mainly one-way, from a sender to a receiver, but messages can be combined to implement two-way request/responses. SOAP consists of three parts:

1. The *SOAP envelope*, which defines an overall framework for expressing the contents of a message, who should deal with it, whether the message is optional, and so on

2. The *SOAP encoding rules*, which define a serialization and encoding mechanism and rules to exchange application-defined data types
3. The *SOAP RPC* defines a convention to represent remote procedure calls and responses. The SOAP specification also defines how to use SOAP for messaging and RPCs by using HTTP as the protocol binding, but SOAP is not limited to HTTP.

Fortunately, there is an implementation for J2ME that takes care of these details. For example, there is kSOAP, created by Stefan Haustein, who is the same author of kXML. kSOAP is a very good implementation of SOAP that has a memory footprint of about 24KB, not counting the kXML footprint.

The following class, `SOAPEmailComposerTask`, uses kSOAP to communicate with the e-mail service described in the previous section:

```
class SOAPEmailComposerTask extends TimerTask {

    private Thread  th;

    /**
     * Constructor
     */
    SOAPEmailComposerTask() {

        th = new Thread(this);
    }

    /**
     * Start the email composer task
     */
    public void go() {
        th.start();
    }

    /**
     * This Runnable's run method.
     *
     * This methods sends email using a SOAP service available
     *   thru webservices.matlus.com.  For more Information go to:
     *     http://www.xmethods.net/detail.html?id=97
     *
     *   Service Owner: Shiv Kumar
     *
     *   SOAP Endpoint URL:
     *     http://webservices.matlus.com/scripts/
     *          emailwebservice.dll/soap/IEmailservice
     *
     *   SOAPAction: urn:EmailIPortTypeInft-IEmailService#SendMail
     *
     *   Method Namespace URI: urn:EmailIPortTypeInft-IEmailService
     *
```

```
 *   Method Name(s): SendMail
 *
 *   WSDL URL:
 *      http://webservices.matlus.com/
 *         scripts/emailwebservice.dll/wsdl/IEmailService
 *
 *   Instructions:
 *
 *     Method: SendMail
 *
 *     Parameters:
 *
 *        ToAddress: string
 *        FromAddress: string
 *        ASubject: string
 *        MsgBody: string (The email message)
 *
 *     Returns: integer (0 = success anything else is an error)
 */
public void run() {
    try {
        // get 'from' from JAD file
       String from = midlet.getAppProperty("UserEmail");

        /*
         * Dispatch ProgressGauge thread
         */
        ProgressGauge pg =
          new ProgressGauge("Sending Email", display);
        ByteArrayOutputStream bos = new ByteArrayOutputStream ();
        /*
         * Create request SOAP object and set properties for
         *  this request.
         */
        SoapObject request = new SoapObject (
            "urn:EmailIPortTypeInft-IEmailService",
                  "SendMail");
        request.addProperty ("ToAddress",   toField.getString() );
        request.addProperty ("FromAddress", from );
        request.addProperty ("ASubject",
                             subjectField.getString() );
        request.addProperty ("MsgBody",bodyField.getString() );

        // create SOAP envelop an set the request (SOAPObject)
        SoapEnvelope envelope = new SoapEnvelope ();
        envelope.setBody (request);

        XmlWriter xw = new XmlWriter
          (new OutputStreamWriter (bos));
        envelope.write (xw);
        xw.flush ();
```

```
        /*
         *  Make the request over HTTP
         */
        HttpConnectionHelper connection = new
                HttpConnectionHelper(
                    "http://webservices.matlus.com",
                    "/scripts/emailwebservice.dll/soap/IEmailservice",
                    null);

        // set SOAPAction HTTP header
        Hashtable headers = new Hashtable();
        headers.put("SOAPAction",
        "urn:EmailIPortTypeInft-IEmailService#SendMail");
        connection.setMessageHeaders(headers);

        // set message body and set HTTP request to POST
        connection.setMessageBody(bos.toString());
        connection.setRequestMethod (HttpConnection.POST);

        /*
         * Process the response; parse it
         */
        String response = connection.sendReceive();

        Reader reader = new InputStreamReader
            (new ByteArrayInputStream (response.getBytes ()));

        XmlParser parser = new XmlParser (reader);

        SoapEnvelope resultEnvelope = new SoapEnvelope ();
        resultEnvelope.parse (parser);

        // display email choices
        display.setCurrent(emailChoices);

    }
    catch (Exception e) {
        System.out.println("Error while sending email via SOAP");
    }
    finally {
        try {
            reader.close ();
            connection.close ();
            pg.stop();  // notify progress gauge to quit
            display.setCurrent(emailChoices);
        }
        catch(IOException ioe) {
          ..... // handle the exception
        }
    }
```

```
        }
    }
```

Because it is difficult to see what is happening just by looking at code, let's take a look at the contents of the HTTP request and response and the XML documents that are embedded within them. The HTTP request, a SOAP action that is sent by using the POST method, invokes the `SendMail` method published by the `EmailIPortType-Inft-IemailService` WSDL service as described previously:

```
POST /scripts/emailwebservice.dll/soap/IEmailservice HTTP/1.1
SOAPAction: urn:EmailIPortTypeInft-IEmailService#SendMail
User-Agent: Profile/MIDP-1.0 Configuration/CLDC-1.0
Accept: text/xml
Host: webservices.matlus.com:80
Content-Type: application/x-www-form-urlencoded
Connection: close
Content-Length: 764
Content-Language: en-US
<SOAP-ENV:Envelope xmlns:xsd="http://www.w3.org/1999/XMLSchema"
                   xmlns:SOAP-
ENV="http://schemas.xmlsoap.org/soap/envelope/"
                   xmlns:xsi="http://www.w3.org/1999/XMLSchema-instance"
                   xmlns:SOAP-
ENC="http://schemas.xmlsoap.org/soap/encoding/"
                   SOAP-
ENV:encodingStyle="http://schemas.xmlsoap.org/soap/encoding/">
     <SOAP-ENV:Body>
       <SendMail xmlns="urn:EmailIPortTypeInft-IEmailService" id="o0"
root="1">
          <ToAddress xmlns=""
xsi:type="xsd:string">eric@j2medeveloper.com</ToAddress>
          <FromAddress xmlns=""
xsi:type="xsd:string">eortiz@j2medeveloper.com</FromAddress>
          <ASubject xmlns="" xsi:type="xsd:string">Email over
SOAP</ASubject>
          <MsgBody xmlns="" xsi:type="xsd:string">This email is
transported over SOAP</MsgBody>
       </SendMail>
   </SOAP-ENV:Body>
</SOAP-ENV:Envelope>
```

The HTTP response, a SOAP response, is an integer that is equal to 0 for success or 1 for failure:

```
HTTP/1.1 200 OK
Server: Microsoft-IIS/5.0
Date: Mon, 11 Jun 2001 07:09:52 GMT
Connection: close
Content-Type: text/xml
Content-Length: 531
```

```
Content:0A 0D 0A
<?xml.version="1.0" encoding='UTF-8'?>
<SOAP-ENV:Envelope xmlns:SOAP-
ENV="http://schemas.xmlsoap.org/soap/envelope/"
                   xmlns:xsd="http://www.w3.org/1999/XMLSchema"
                   xmlns:xsi="http://www.w3.org/1999/XMLSchema-instance"
                   xmlns:SOAP-
ENC="http://schemas.xmlsoap.org/soap/encoding/">
  <SOAP-ENV:Body>
     <NS1:SendMailResponse xmlns:NS1="urn:EmailIPortTypeInft-
IEmailService"
         SOAP-
ENV:encodingStyle="http://schemas.xmlsoap.org/soap/encoding/">
         <NS1:return xsi:type="xsd:int">0</NS1:return>
      </NS1:SendMailResponse>
     </SOAP-ENV:Body>
</SOAP-ENV:Envelope>
```

The client parses the response to extract the return code and report success or failure.

kSOAP is still new and under development. If you are interested in contributing to kSOAP or any of the other J2ME Enhydra projects (kXML, kJMS, kSync, kUDDI and others), visit `http://me.enhydra.org`.

A Quick Note on UDDI

UDDI (`www.uddi.org`) is a specification and an XML schema that defines a SOAP-based API for registering and discovering distributed network services. The motivation behind UDDI is to provide for a consistent method to discover Web/network-based services. UDDI uses SOAP for its API and "transport" and WSDL for the definition of abstract interfaces and network bindings. UDDI provides two sets of APIs—an Inquiry API and a Publishers' API. From the MIDP perspective, we are only concerned with the Inquiry API, which is further divided into two parts—one to search and browse information found in a UDDI registry and the other to handle failures. Once a WSDL definition for a given service has been created and registered into a UDDI repository, we can retrieve the WSDL definition for a particular service by parsing the `overviewDoc` element and `overviewURL` subelement as follows:

```
<tModel authorizedName="..." operator="..." tModelKey="...">
  <name>Email Service</name>
  <description xml:lang="en">
    WSDL description of a simple email service interface
  </description>
  <overviewDoc>
    <description xml:lang="en">WSDL source document.</description>
    <overviewURL> http://email-definitions/email.wsdl </overviewURL>
  </overviewDoc>
  <categoryBag>
```

```
    <keyedReference tModelKey="uuid:C1ACF26D-9672-4404-9D70-
39B756E62AB4"
      keyName="uddi-org:types" keyValue="wsdlSpec"/>
  </categoryBag>
</tModel>
```

In a nutshell, we can leverage UDDI from within our MIDP applications to discover network services by querying UDDI registries by using SOAP, discovering the details of the service by parsing its associated WSDL definition. Be sure to visit `http://me.enhydra.org` for information on kUDDI, an open source UDDI client for J2ME in the early development stages as this book is being written.

Summary

XML is a powerful tool that needs to be added to every programmer's toolbox. For J2ME environments, XML is the key to building mobile applications that leverage network services. Both Sun's Open Network Environment and Microsoft's .NET initiatives rely on XML as the way to discover and use network-based services. Even if you are not using either initiative, you can also define your own services by using XML and SOAP. This chapter has given you some XML fundamentals and some examples of what you can do with XML, but there is much more to cover than what is presented here. In the next chapter, we will move away from XML and concentrate instead on writing efficient and portable applications.

CHAPTER 10

Techniques for Writing Better MIDP Applications

At this point in the book, we can turn our attention to the techniques that you can use to write better, more portable MIDP applications. These are suggestions, not absolute rules, and they are not necessarily appropriate for all applications. Writing truly portable code—code that runs on all three editions of Java—can make an application larger than it would be if it were targeted at a single edition of Java or a single J2ME profile (or even an individual device). It is your call as to which techniques are appropriate for the applications that you write.

Writing Better Code

Good software is efficient, maintainable, reusable, and extensible. Efficiency is important for any application, but especially for MIDP applications, which can run on extremely limited devices. These devices have limits on the application's footprint—the amount of memory required to install in the device—as well as on its runtime performance and capabilities. As always, the goal is to find an acceptable balance between application size and application performance, while trying to keep the code reusable and extensible.

Follow Coding Conventions

Good coding conventions make for readable, consistent, and maintainable code. Software developers use coding guidelines or standards as "communications tools" to be more efficient by documenting a common, consistent way to write software. Recall that the lifecycle of your code continues even after deployment: your code must be maintained, perhaps by someone else, maybe months after you wrote it. Adhering to coding conventions makes the maintainer's life much easier, even if that maintainer is you.

A good place to start is with Sun's "Code Conventions For the Java Programming Language," which you can find on Sun's Web Site at `http://java.sun.com/docs/codeconv/html/CodeConvTOC.doc.html`.

Use Patterns and Frameworks

Writing code that can be reused and extended should always be your goal. A design that allows you to easily support future implementations not even being considered today will minimize the amount of code that you have to throw away and rewrite. A good example of this is the user interface for your applications. The MIDP defines its own set of user interface classes. By all accounts, the PDAP will define a different set of user interface classes. But non-user interface code is likely to run on both profiles unchanged. A good design, therefore, will separate the user interface from the actual business logic, allowing you to switch implementations as needed. *Design patterns*, *anti-patterns*, and *frameworks* are all tools you can use to create good designs.

A design pattern allows software designers to share knowledge (using consistent terminology) about a design they have come across. *Patterns* are an abstraction created from a concrete design. Patterns are recurring and applicable to other software applications. Patterns are usually concerned with the architecture or organization of components (subsystems) that when put together produce greater systems like frameworks.

An *anti-pattern* is a design pattern that demonstrates a bad solution to a problem. A good *anti-pattern* also tells you why the solution is bad, why it works in some situations, and which good design patterns should be used instead.

A framework, on the other hand, provides architectural guidance by putting together patterns, components, and abstract classes and defining their responsibilities and collaborations. In contrast to patterns, which are applicable to many software applications, frameworks usually have a particular application domain. In other words, d*esign patterns are smaller architectural elements than frameworks, but frameworks are more specialized.*

There are many excellent resources available on design patterns. The classic text is Design Patterns: Elements of Reusable Object-Oriented Software by Erich Gamma, Richard Helm, Ralph Johnson, and John Vlissides. Another good book on this subject is *Pattern-Oriented Software Architecture* by Frank Buschmann, Regine Meunier, Hans Rohnert, Peter Sommerlad, and Michael Stal. For design patterns in Java, see *Patterns in Java, Volume 1* by Mark Grand.

Simplify the Application

Bloatware is a term used to describe software that is excessively large and complex. Bloatware often occurs when features are added to an application in order to broaden its appeal beyond its core customer base or to make use of new technologies and capabilities, even if the improvements to the application are marginal. Bloatware is tolerated on desktop and server computers because the total storage capacities of those devices—the available amount of memory and offline storage—continually increases. The storage capacities of handheld devices are also growing, but at much slower rates. In fact, these devices are often closed systems that lack the capability to quickly and easily increase their storage capacity the way desktop and server computers do. Also, the user of a device tends to load it with games and other non-critical applications, reducing the amount of memory available for the applications you create.

The easiest way to avoid writing bloatware is to simplify the application by removing unnecessary and/or optional features. Strip the flesh off the application to expose the skeleton underneath. Only add features if they are actually required for the application to work correctly or in response to actual user feedback.

Be creative with your MIDlet packaging, as well. MIDlets that have classes in common should be part of the same MIDlet suite to avoid unnecessary class duplication. Remember that in the MIDP, there is no concept of building libraries or other facilities for sharing common classes. On the other hand, it might make sense to provide different versions of a MIDlet suite—versions with or without specific MIDlets. Users could then choose to install the MIDlet suite that best meets their needs.

Move Functionality to the Server

Although the whole point of smart-client computing is to move some application logic onto the client, it is also important to realize that not everything can be moved onto the client. Things that are computationally expensive to perform or that require resources that are not available on the device should be left on the server. Make the application "smart," but keep it simple.

Remember, though, that the server is not always available. Whenever possible, your application should *degrade gracefully* and handle the specific situation where the server is unavailable. You might be able to simply queue a request, for example, and submit it later when the server is available again. Or you might choose to only enable certain functionalities when the server is unavailable. Having the application freeze or crash because the server is not available is simply unacceptable.

Use Threads

MIDP applications can be multithreaded, just like J2SE applications. The usual warnings and recommendations for J2SE apply. In particular, be sure to move long-lasting operations off the event thread (the thread that the system uses to call into your application—for example, when a command is triggered) and onto a separate thread. All HTTP communication should be done this way, as was shown with the email client example earlier in this book.

When you use threads, however, you will need to synchronize access to shared data. Synchronizing threads will slow your application, so you should minimize the points of contention whenever possible. Remember that the standard utility classes such as

Clean Up Objects When the MIDlet Is Paused

A good place to clean up the application's use of objects is to free unnecessary objects whenever the application is paused. For example, objects that are allocated by using lazy instantiation are often good candidates for cleanup.

`Vector` and `Hashtable` are synchronized, which makes them candidates for replacement with your own similar classes if you can guarantee that only a single thread will access such objects.

Avoid Unnecessary Object Creation

Keep the number of objects that the application creates down to a minimum. The more objects you create, the more work the garbage collector has to do, which steals processor cycles away from the application. Also, the memory heap can get quite fragmented, making it harder for the VM to find memory blocks for allocating new objects.

All the usual J2SE rules for efficient object creation apply to J2ME, as well. For example, avoid using the concatenation operator ("+") to combine `String` objects. Instead, create a `StringBuffer` object and call its `append` method. Otherwise, the compiler generates code that creates numerous `String` and `StringBuffer` objects for you (more than is necessary).

Another way to avoid unnecessary object creation is to perform *lazy instantiation* of objects. In other words, do not create an object until you actually need it. This situation is particularly useful with client applications, because the path through a set of user interface screens can vary greatly. Allocate as you go along.

Class Variable Initialization (Initialize Your Variables Once)

You can improve performance some by not initializing your *class member* variables twice. Recall that when an object's constructor is called, Java by default initializes all *class* variables to a known value or state as follows:

- All **reference types** (objects) are set to **null**.
- **Boolean** are set to **false**.
- **Integers** (byte, short, int, long) are set to **0**.
- **Float** and **doubles** (not supported by CLDC) are set to **0.0**.
- **char** are set to **null character, '\u0000'**.

Also, recall that when an object extends other objects, their constructors are chained and automatically called at creation time, so you can see how initializing your *class* variables twice can degrade performance.

Local variables are also defaulted as explained above; but their initialization occurs when the statement that declares the variable is executed. Good coding practices initialize *local* variables where they're declared, for example:

```
void myMethod() {
    int int1 = 0;           // beginning of method block

    if (condition) {
        int int2 = 0;       // beginning of "if" block
        ...
    }

    for (int i = 0; i < maxLoops; i++) { ... }
}
```

Be Smart about Arithmetic Operations

Remember to use bit shifting if possible when doing multiplication and/or division. For example, instead of multiplying a number by let's say 4, bit shift the value twice to the left (<<2) to accomplish the same result. Recall that in binary arithmetic, shifting left once is the same as multiplying by a factor of 2. Same with division, where shifting right once is the same as dividing by a factor of 2, for example:

```
x = y * 4, is the same as x = y << 2;
x = y / 2, is the same as x = y >> 1;
```

Some compilers will do this kind of optimization for you automatically, but it never hurts to help the compiler in making such decisions.

Stack Is Faster than Heap

Maximize the use of local variables. Local variables (as opposed to static or new objects) are stored on the stack, which is faster than the heap.

Make Classes Final Whenever Possible

You define your classes `final` to prevent the class from being extended. Defining the class `final` also means that all its methods are `final` as well. This allows the compiler to apply optimization techniques by making all the methods inline, which improves performance.

Obfuscate the Code

A Java class file contains a lot of information about the original source code, including the names and parameters of all methods and classes used. Combine this information with the byte code and you can easily reconstruct the original source from a set of class files, especially if debugging information is also present in the class files. Several tools are available, both open source and commercial products, to remedy this situation by processing the source files to remove and rename as much of the symbolic information as possible—a process known as *obfuscation*. These tools, referred to as *obfuscators*, cannot prevent you from decompiling a set of class files, but the resulting source code is extremely hard to read and might offer some protection from casual snoopers.

A side effect of obfuscation, however, is that the resulting class files are usually smaller than the original class files, due primarily to the shortening or outright replacement of class and method names by the obfuscation process. Also, the obfuscator prunes unused methods and data members. The size reduction is not enormous, usually in the 10 to 20 percent range, but it is still significant enough to be worth investigating when you are ready to deploy your MIDlet suite. Any size reduction helps reduce the time (and expense, if done wirelessly) required to download and install your applications on a user's device. Obfuscation does complicate the dynamic loading of classes, however, so it might require changes to your code. A good obfuscator to look at is RetroGuard, an open source obfuscator available from `www.retrologic.com`.

If you are using an obfuscator, be sure to help it as much as you can. Make as many classes, methods, and data members `final` and/or `private` as possible. The obfuscator can then make better decisions about what code can be left out of the obfuscated application.

Writing Portable Code

Portability is important because it enables you to write code that you can use and reuse across different Java implementations, whether it is a J2ME environment or a J2EE environment. You cannot expect your J2EE or J2SE applications to run unchanged in a J2ME environment, but it is possible for some code to move transparently between these different platforms.

Platform Detection

There are several techniques you can use to detect the platform on which your code is running; for example, whether it is CLDC-based, CDC-based, or J2SE-based. You can then use this information at runtime to decide which methods or classes to call. Many early applet developers used similar techniques to detect whether Java 1.02 or Java 1.1 support was available in a browser and to act accordingly. Note, however, that `NoSuchMethodException` is not available on CLDC-based platforms, so you cannot portably detect whether specific methods in a class are available or not.

Platform detection is performed in two ways. The first way is to simply query a system property to see whether a particular configuration or profile is supported. For example, here is how you detect whether the platform is CLDC-based:

```
boolean isCLDC = false;
String config = System.getProperty( "microedition.configuration" );

if( config != null ){
    isCLDC = ( config.indexOf( "CLDC-" ) != -1 );
}
```

Similar code can detect whether the MIDP profile is available:

```
boolean isMIDP = false;
String  config = System.getProperty( "microedition.profiles" );

if( config != null ){
    isMIDP = ( config.indexOf( "MIDP-" ) != -1 );
}
```

This code works because the CLDC and MIDP specifications require that the `microedition.configuration` and `microedition.profiles` properties be defined for those platforms. You can combine this sequence into a single utility class:

```
package com.j2medeveloper.util;

public class Platform {

    public static final boolean isCLDC;
    public static final boolean isMIDP;

    static {
        String config = System.getProperty(
                               "microedition.configuration" );
        if( config != null ){
            isCLDC = ( config.indexOf( "CLDC-" ) != -1 );
        } else {
            isCLDC = false;
        }

        config = System.getProperty( "microedition.profiles" );
        if( config != null ){
            isMIDP = ( config.indexOf( "MIDP-" ) != -1 );
        } else {
            isMIDP = false;
        }
    }
}
```

You can then do things differently based on the values of `Platform.isCLDC` and `Platform.isMIDP`, as follows:

```
if( Platform.isCLDC ){
    .... // do it the CLDC way...
} else {
    .... // do it the CDC/J2SE way....
}
```

Note that the `Platform` class uses a static initializer to initialize the values of its `final` data members. Because the values are not actually known at compile time, the class files will include unnecessary code that cannot be removed by the compiler or by the obfuscator. You can avoid this situation by using a technique similar to the debugging technique presented in Chapter 3. Instead of having a single `Platform` class that detects the platform at runtime, you create different versions (in different directories) of the class with different hard-coded values—one for each platform of interest. You then compile this class and include the appropriate version of the class in the classpath for your application. This action gives the compiler the opportunity to "haul out" the unused code.

The second way to perform platform detection is to obtain information about which classes are available. You can perform this task easily enough by using the normal `Class.forName` construct to detect whether a class is missing or present:

```
boolean useSocketAPI = true;
try {
    Class.forName( "java.net.Socket" );
}
catch( ClassNotFoundException e ){
    useSocketAPI = false;
}
```

The absence of a class is usually a clear indication of a particular platform. As well, you can use this technique in order to take advantage of vendor-specific classes. In other words, check to see whether a vendor-specific class is available, and if it is, use it; otherwise, fall back on a more standard implementation.

Object Serialization

The CLDC does not support serialization, but it can be simulated to a certain degree (as we indicated in Chapter 7). You will need to build helper classes to serialize and deserialize standard classes, but ideally, you can build serialization methods into your own classes. The sample `serialize` and `deserialize` methods in Chapter 7 serialized objects to and from byte arrays, but you could instead use hashtables to store and retrieve the internal state of objects, serializing those hashtables into byte form. While this extra step adds some overhead, it makes the serialization a bit simpler to implement. Consider, for example, the following classes:

```
class A {
    private int a;
    private String b;
```

```
    public A( int a, String b ){
        this.a = a;
        this.b = b;
    }
}

class B extends A {
    private String c;

    public B( int a, String b, String c ){
        super( a, b );
        this.c = c;
    }
}
```

Modify the first class as follows:

```
import java.util.Hashtable;

class A {
    private int a;
    private String b;

    private A(){
    }

    public A( int a, String b ){
        this.a = a;
        this.b = b;
    }

    public static A create( Hashtable props ){
        A a = new A();
        a.deserialize( props );
        return a;
    }

    protected void deserialize( Hashtable props ){
        try {
            a.a = Integer.parseInt( props.get( "A.a" ) );
            a.b = props.get( "A.b" );
        }
        catch( Exception e ){
            ..... // do something here
        }
    }

    public void serialize( Hashtable props ){
        props.put( "A.a", Integer.toString( a ) );
        props.put( "A.b", b );
```

```
        }
    }
```

The second class is modified in a similar fashion, except that its `create` method returns an instance of `B` and its `serialize` and `deserialize` methods first call the `superclass` method in order to properly initialize the superclass.

Dealing with Missing Classes

Detecting whether a specific platform is being used is not always enough because your application might depend on the functionality of a specific J2SE class that is not available. If you cannot recode the application to use other classes, you will have to develop your own equivalent classes to provide the required functionality. Just adding the missing J2SE classes into your application is not good enough. Even if it were legal, the J2ME implementation you are targeting should ignore any classes you include that are in the `java` package namespace. As well, those classes might themselves depend on other missing classes and on unimplemented native methods.

Writing your own classes does not have to be very hard. Take the `java.util.Properties` class, for example, which is missing from CLDC-based profilessuch as the MIDP. Instead of referring directly to the `Properties` class, make your classes use a class that you develop called `MyProperties`. Build two versions of the class: one for the CDC/J2SE where `Properties` is supported:

```
public class MyProperties extends java.util.Properties {
    public MyProperties(){
    }
}
```

and one for the CLDC:

```
public class MyProperties extends java.util.Hashtable {
    public MyProperties(){
    }

    public String getProperty( String key ){
        return (String) super.get( key );
    }

    public String getProperty( String key, String defVal ){
        String val = getProperty( key );
        return( val != null ? val : defVal );
    }

    ...... // other methods you need
}
```

By adjusting the classpath, you control which version the application uses. Note that all versions of the application can use the second form of `MyProp-erties`, but it makes more sense to use the existing `Properties` class if it is available.

Subclassing existing classes as such is not always possible, though,because the classes you are interested in might be declared final. For those cases, you will have to build your own classes. But again, you can build two versions: one that is basically just a wrapper that forwards method calls to the "real" J2SE class and one that is a special implementation for CLDC-based platforms. Another approach is to take an existing utility class and split it into two classes, one class extending the other. The base class can be CLDC-compliant—no floating-point support, for example—and the subclass can be meant for J2SE. At runtime, you use platform detection to decide which class to instantiate and which methods you can call.

Internationalization and Localization

Any widely deployed application should be written with internationalization and localization in mind. *Internationalization* is the process of designing and developing your software to work in multiple locales. A *locale* is a set of conventions defined by a particular geo-political region. Internationalization means writing code that works well in any locale. *Localization* is the process of adapting and modifying your software to work in a particular locale by displaying text in the appropriate language and dealing with formatting and input issues.

The CLDC (and hence the MIDP) offers little support for the internationalization and the localization of applications. This situation is mostly due to size restrictions. There is *some* support, though:

- Character data can be transformed to and from Unicode by using at least one default encoding that is appropriate for the device. The default encoding is stored in the `microedition.encoding` system property.
- Strings can be written and read in UTF-8 format by using the `DataInputStream` and `DataOutputStream` classes.
- Although there is no `Locale` class, the device has an implicit locale—and classes such as `Calendar` and `DateField` adjust themselves accordingly. The implicit locale is stored in the `microedition.locale` system property.

Anything else, though, is at the discretion of the implementation (which might supply additional locale information and supporting classes) or must be supplied by the application.

For example, it is easy enough to write a class that simulates the J2SE `java.util.ResourceBundle` class. The example below is drawn from a J2ME Tech Tip written by one of the authors and republished here with the permission of Sun Microsystems.

```
package com.j2medeveloper.util;

import java.util.Hashtable;
```

```
/**
 * Simulates a J2SE ResourceBundle for CLDC-based platforms.
 */

public class ResourceBundle {

    private static Hashtable groups = new Hashtable();

    public static Object getObject( String group, String key ) {
        ResourceBundle bundle;

        synchronized( groups ){
            bundle = (ResourceBundle) groups.get( group );
            if( bundle == null ){
                bundle = loadBundle( group );
            }
        }

        return bundle.getResource( key );
    }

    public static String getString( String group, String key ) {
        return (String) getObject( group, key );
    }

    public static ResourceBundle loadBundle( String name ) {
        ResourceBundle bundle = null;
        Locale         locale = Locale.getDefaultLocale();
        String         language = locale.getLanguage();
        String         country = locale.getCountry();

        try {
            bundle = (ResourceBundle)
                     Class.forName( name ).newInstance();
        }
        catch( Exception e ){
        }

        if( language != null ){
            ResourceBundle child;

            try {
                child = (ResourceBundle) Class.forName(
                            name + '_' + language ).newInstance();
                child.setParent( bundle );
                bundle = child;
            }
            catch( Exception e ){
            }

            if( country != null ){
                try {
```

```
                child = (ResourceBundle) Class.forName(
                        name + '_' + language +
                          '_' + country ).newInstance();
                child.setParent( bundle );
                bundle = child;
            }
            catch( Exception e ){
            }
        }
    }

    if( bundle == null ){
        bundle = new ResourceBundle();
    }

    groups.put( name, bundle );
    return bundle;
}

protected Hashtable resources = new Hashtable();
private   ResourceBundle parent;

protected ResourceBundle() {
}

protected void setParent( ResourceBundle parent ) {
    this.parent = parent;
}

protected Object getResource( String key ) {
    Object obj = null;

    if( resources != null ){
        obj = resources.get( key );
    }

    if( obj == null && parent != null ){
        obj = parent.getResource( key );
    }

    return obj;
}

/**
 * Inner class that simulates java.util.Locale
 */

public static class Locale {
    private String language = "en";
    private String country = "US";
```

```
        public Locale( String language, String country ) {
            this.language = language;
            this.country = country;
        }

        public Locale( String locale ) {
            if( locale != null ){
                int pos = locale.indexOf( '-' );
                if( pos != -1 ){
                    language = locale.substring( 0, pos );
                    locale = locale.substring( pos+1 );

                    pos = locale.indexOf( '-' );
                    if( pos == -1 ){
                        country = locale;
                    } else {
                        country = locale.substring( 0, pos );
                    }
                }
            }
        }

        public String getLanguage() {
            return language;
        }

        public String getCountry() {
            return country;
        }

        private static Locale defaultLocale = new Locale(
                    System.getProperty( "microedition.locale" ) );

        public static Locale getDefaultLocale() {
            return defaultLocale;
        }

        public static void setDefaultLocale( Locale locale ) {
            defaultLocale = locale;
        }
    }
}
```

You use this `ResourceBundle` replacement just like the original by first defining the appropriate classes to hold the resources, as in this example:

```
// Default locale (base name)

public class Test extends ResourceBundle {
    public Test() {
        resources.put( "hello", "Hello!" );
```

```
            resources.put( "goodbye", "Goodbye!" );
            resources.put( "stop", "Stop!" );
            resources.put( "notranslation", "This is English." );
        }
    }

    // French (fr) language, no specific country

    public class Test_fr extends ResourceBundle {
        public Test_fr() {
            resources.put( "hello", "Bonjour!" );
            resources.put( "goodbye", "Aurevoir!" );
        }
    }

    // French (fr) language, Canada (CA) country

    public class Test_fr_CA extends ResourceBundle {
        public Test_fr_CA() {
            resources.put( "stop", "Arretez!" );
        }
    }
```

Obtaining and using a resource at runtime is quite simple. The following code snippet uses a `ResourceBundle` called `MsgCat` to retrieve the title and elements for a `List` in a locale-independent fashion:

```
String msgCatName = "MsgCat"; // should be a config. value from JAD
List list = new List( ResourceBundle.getString(
        msgCatName, "listTitle" ), List.EXCLUSIVE );
list.append( ResourceBundle.getString( msgCatName, "Item1" ),
             null );
list.append( ResourceBundle.getString( msgCatName, "Item2" ),
             null );
Command nextCmd = new Command(
        ResourceBundle.getString( msgCatName, "nextCmdLabel" ),
        Command.OK, 1 );
list.addCommand(nextCmd);
```

Resource bundles rely on naming conventions to find the bundle for the active locale. Resource bundle names have two parts: a base name and a locale suffix. The base name is anything you want, in our example above `MsgCat`. The locale suffix indicates the locale's language (as specified by ISO 639) and country (as specified by ISO 3166), for example `en_US` for English (U.S.) or `fr_FR` for French (France) and `fr_CA` for French (Canada).

What about deployment? In order to reduce code size, separate versions of the MIDlet suite are typically built, one for each supported locale. Only the MIDlet suite that best matches the locale is installed on each target device.

You could also modify the ResourceBundle class to read the resources from a record store that you populate by downloading the appropriate resources from a Web server.

Summary

Writing portable, efficient code should always be your goal—even if you are targeting a specific device or a family of devices. Sooner or later, you will want to move some of that code over to another platform. If you have coded with portability and efficiency in mind, that job will be a lot easier. We are now at the end of the book, and we will conclude with a few final thoughts on the future of MIDP programming.

CHAPTER 11

Final Thoughts

We conclude this book with some thoughts on the future of the MIDP and J2ME itself and a look at alternatives you might wish to consider using instead of or in conjunction with the MIDP.

The Future of the MIDP and J2ME

With J2ME, Sun Microsystems extends the reach of Java down to small devices that were previously ignored by the efforts put into J2SE and J2EE. The MIDP might become the preferred development platform for the low end of the handheld device spectrum, while the Personal Profile and other CDC-based profiles will provide the same functionality for higher-end devices. Still, nothing is certain in life, and you would be wise to consider some of the alternatives to J2ME discussed in the next section before starting to develop your mission-critical software.

The MIDP is in the early stages of its development. It has some important limitations, some of which will be addressed in the next version of the specification, but it also has the support of major device manufacturers. They, together with Sun Microsystems, have committed to promoting and shipping J2ME implementations in all kinds of devices. J2ME technology, and the MIDP in particular, will only get better. What is really lacking right now, of course, is a critical mass in terms of J2ME-compliant devices. Only a few devices are shipping right now, and features such as over-the-air provisioning, security, push, sound, and enhanced networking are in the early stages of development. The business case for writing J2ME applications might not be obvious at this stage, but it will only get better once other profiles such as the Personal Profile and the PDA Profile are finalized. The fact that a MIDP implementation is now available for Palm devices is a good step forward, because it greatly increases the potential customer base for MIDP applications.

Not all applications need to be written in Java, of course. Many applications are intrinsically online in nature and might not necessarily benefit from local data storage and the local execution of logic. For those applications, a thin-client model is more than adequate. You need to weigh the alternatives and come up with the solution that is best for you. Java is no panacea, despite what anyone else might claim. It is a good programming language that has a lot of industry support. Writing client applications in Java lets you reuse many of your J2SE and J2EE skills; the ramp-up time is fairly short if you already know Java. Java also hides a lot of the messy details of handheld device programming, letting you concentrate on the application and not on how the application interacts with the device. Also, as devices gain in power and capability, the Java implementations on those devices can only benefit. J2ME is here to stay, but it is still leading-edge technology. It will settle down fairly quickly, though, so now is the time to consider doing J2ME development. And now that you have read this book, you know just how to do that.

If performance is an issue, there are development tools available for some platforms that will compile J2ME applications into native code or that claim to offer better performance in general. Please refer to Appendix B for a list.

Alternatives to Consider

There are alternatives to J2ME and the MIDP that you should be aware of. Some of these alternatives might be better suited for your project, so be sure to investigate them:

- The Binary Runtime Environment for Wireless (BREW) is a platform for the development of applications for handsets with QUALCOMM CDMA chipsets. BREW attempts to address many of the same issues J2ME addresses. Even though BREW is mainly C/C++ based, support for CLDC and MIDP (via Hewlett-Packard's MicroChai VM) has been announced but not released yet. As of the writing of this book, none of the major cell phone manufacturers that support J2ME (such as Nokia and Motorola) have announced support for BREW. See `www.qualcomm.com/brew` for FAQ and other details.
- IBM has a platform for writing Palm, Linux, and QNX applications in Java called Visual Age Micro Edition. It is not yet CLDC or MIDP compliant, but it does offer access to native APIs. See `www.embedded.oti.com` for details. It is expected to offer CLDC and MIDP compatibility by the time you read this.
- There are full-fledged PersonalJava and J2SE implementations to consider, as well. See Appendix B for a list.
- Open source developers can consider using the Waba VM, which enables you to run Java applications on a variety of devices. It has some severe limitations (no threads in the base edition, for example), but it can be an option for Java

development on handheld devices where it is not possible for you to install a proper Java runtime environment. Check it out at `www.wabasoft.com`.

There might be no real alternatives, though, if you are trying to build applications for closed systems such as cell phones that only support J2ME. In that case, you will have to decide whether the system's performance is good enough or whether you should move to a thinner, browser-based application model. Only you can decide what the answer should be. Good luck, and let us know how your development goes.

APPENDIX A

MIDP/CLDC Quick Reference

This appendix lists the complete set of classes and interfaces defined by the MIDP and the CLDC. They are listed in alphabetical order based on the name of the class or interface. The methods and fields within a class or interface are sorted alphabetically for easier reading.

Alert

Defined by the MIDP 1.0 specification

Description

Displays a message for the user before automatically switching to another screen. The message can be displayed for a specified amount of time or until it is dismissed by the user. An optional image can be displayed with the alert, and a sound can be associated with it as well.

Class Definition

```
package javax.microedition.lcdui;

public class Alert
    extends Screen {
    // Constructors
    public Alert( String title );
    public Alert( String title, String alertText, Image alertImage,
            AlertType alertType );

    // Methods
    public void addCommand( Command cmd );
```

```
        public int getDefaultTimeout();
        public Image getImage();
        public String getString();
        public int getTimeout();
        public AlertType getType();
        public void setCommandListener( CommandListener l );
        public void setImage( Image img );
        public void setString( String str );
        public void setTimeout( int time );
        public void setType( AlertType type );

        // Fields
        public static final int FOREVER = -2;
    }
```

All Superclasses: Screen, Displayable, Object

AlertType

Defined by the MIDP 1.0 specification

Description

Defines the type of an alert and provides a static playSound method that can be used to play a set of predefined sounds.

Class Definition

```
package javax.microedition.lcdui;

public class AlertType {
    // Constructors
    protected AlertType();

    // Methods
    public boolean playSound( Display display );

    // Fields
    public static final AlertType ALARM;
    public static final AlertType CONFIRMATION;
    public static final AlertType ERROR;
    public static final AlertType INFO;
    public static final AlertType WARNING;
}
```

All Superclasses: Object

ArithmeticException

Defined by the CLDC 1.0 specification

Description

Thrown when an arithmetic operation fails, such as when a division by zero occurs.

Class Definition

```
package java.lang;

public class ArithmeticException
    extends RuntimeException {
    // Constructors
    public ArithmeticException();
    public ArithmeticException( String s );
}
```

All Superclasses: RuntimeException, Exception, Throwable, Object

ArrayIndexOutOfBoundsException

Defined by the CLDC 1.0 specification

Description

Thrown whenever an element outside the array is accessed. The index value is either negative or greater than or equal to the array size. Unchanged from J2SE 1.3.

Class Definition

```
package java.lang;

public class ArrayIndexOutOfBoundsException
    extends IndexOutOfBoundsException {
    // Constructors
    public ArrayIndexOutOfBoundsException();
    public ArrayIndexOutOfBoundsException( int index );
    public ArrayIndexOutOfBoundsException( String s );
}
```

All Superclasses: IndexOutOfBoundsException, RuntimeException, Exception, Throwable, Object

ArrayStoreException

Defined by the CLDC 1.0 specification

Description

Thrown to indicate that an incompatible object type is being stored into an array of objects; unchanged from J2SE 1.3.

Class Definition

```
package java.lang;

public class ArrayStoreException
     extends RuntimeException {
     // Constructors
     public ArrayStoreException();
     public ArrayStoreException( String s );
}
```

All Superclasses: RuntimeException, Exception, Throwable, Object

Boolean

Defined by the CLDC 1.0 specification

Description

An object representation of the primitive boolean type. Major differences from J2SE 1.3: The TRUE, FALSE, and TYPE static fields are not defined, nor are the valueOf, toBoolean, and getBoolean static methods.

Class Definition

```
package java.lang;

public final class Boolean {
     // Constructors
     public Boolean( boolean value );

     // Methods
     public boolean booleanValue();
     public boolean equals( Object obj );
     public int hashCode();
     public String toString();
}
```

All Superclasses: Object

Byte

Defined by the CLDC 1.0 specification

Description

An object representation of the primitive byte type. Major differences from J2SE 1.3: No TYPE static field, no toString(byte) or valueOf methods (use the methods on the Integer class instead), and none of the primitive value methods other than byteValue.

Class Definition

```
package java.lang;

public final class Byte {
    // Constructors
    public Byte( byte value );

    // Methods
    public byte byteValue();
    public boolean equals( Object obj );
    public int hashCode();
    public static byte parseByte( String s )
            throws NumberFormatException;
    public static byte parseByte( String s, int radix )
            throws NumberFormatException;
    public String toString();

    // Fields
    public static final byte MAX_VALUE = 127;
    public static final byte MIN_VALUE = -128;
}
```

All Superclasses: Object

ByteArrayInputStream

Defined by the CLDC 1.0 specification

Description

Defines an input stream that reads from an in-memory array of bytes; unchanged from J2SE 1.3.

Class Definition

```
package java.io;

public class ByteArrayInputStream
    extends InputStream {
    // Constructors
    public ByteArrayInputStream( byte[] buf );
    public ByteArrayInputStream( byte[] buf, int offset, int length );

    // Methods
    public synchronized int available();
    public synchronized void close() throws IOException;
    public void mark( int readAheadLimit );
    public boolean markSupported();
    public synchronized int read();
    public synchronized int read( byte[] b, int off, int len );
```

```
    public synchronized void reset();
    public synchronized long skip( long n );

    // Fields
    protected byte buf;
    protected int count;
    protected int mark;
    protected int pos;
}
```

All Superclasses: InputStream, Object

ByteArrayOutputStream

Defined by the CLDC 1.0 specification

Description

Defines an output stream for writing data into an in-memory byte array, growing the byte array as necessary. Unchanged from J2SE 1.3 except for the removal of the toString methods.

Class Definition

```
package java.io;

public class ByteArrayOutputStream
    extends OutputStream {
    // Constructors
    public ByteArrayOutputStream();
    public ByteArrayOutputStream( int size );

    // Methods
    public synchronized void close() throws IOException;
    public synchronized void reset();
    public int size();
    public synchronized byte[] toByteArray();
    public synchronized void write( int b );
    public synchronized void write( byte[] b, int off, int len );

    // Fields
    protected byte buf;
    protected int count;
}
```

All Superclasses: OutputStream, Object

Calendar

Defined by the CLDC 1.0 specification

Description

Manipulates dates by using human-oriented representations rather than the internal milliseconds-based format used by the Date class. Major changes from J2SE 1.3: No methods related to determining the first day of the week, no methods to retrieve the ranges of individual fields, and only limited ability to set and get the values of the fields.

Class Definition

```
package java.util;

public abstract class Calendar {
    // Constructors
    protected Calendar();

    // Methods
    public boolean after( Object when );
    public boolean before( Object when );
    public boolean equals( Object obj );
    public final int get( int field );
    public static synchronized Calendar getInstance();
    public static synchronized Calendar getInstance( TimeZone zone );
    public final Date getTime();
    protected long getTimeInMillis();
    public TimeZone getTimeZone();
    public final void set( int field, int value );
    public final void setTime( Date date );
    protected void setTimeInMillis( long millis );
    public void setTimeZone( TimeZone value );

    // Fields
    public static final int AM = 0;
    public static final int AM_PM = 9;
    public static final int APRIL = 3;
    public static final int AUGUST = 7;
    public static final int DATE = 5;
    public static final int DAY_OF_MONTH = 5;
    public static final int DAY_OF_WEEK = 7;
    public static final int DECEMBER = 11;
    public static final int FEBRUARY = 1;
    public static final int FRIDAY = 6;
    public static final int HOUR = 10;
    public static final int HOUR_OF_DAY = 11;
    public static final int JANUARY = 0;
    public static final int JULY = 6;
    public static final int JUNE = 5;
    public static final int MARCH = 2;
    public static final int MAY = 4;
    public static final int MILLISECOND = 14;
    public static final int MINUTE = 12;
    public static final int MONDAY = 2;
```

```
        public static final int MONTH = 2;
        public static final int NOVEMBER = 10;
        public static final int OCTOBER = 9;
        public static final int PM = 1;
        public static final int SATURDAY = 7;
        public static final int SECOND = 13;
        public static final int SEPTEMBER = 8;
        public static final int SUNDAY = 1;
        public static final int THURSDAY = 5;
        public static final int TUESDAY = 3;
        public static final int WEDNESDAY = 4;
        public static final int YEAR = 1;
    }
```

All Superclasses: Object

Canvas

Defined by the MIDP 1.0 specification

Description

Defines a screen object that has access to the low-level input events generated by the device and that has complete access to the display. A canvas is entirely responsible for painting its contents on the display and for reacting appropriately to user input. The only high-level user-interface objects that can be associated with a canvas are Command objects. A canvas is typically used in games or to draw graphs and other custom business graphics.

Class Definition

```
package javax.microedition.lcdui;

public abstract class Canvas
    extends Displayable {
    // Constructors
    protected Canvas();

    // Methods
    public int getGameAction( int keyCode );
    public int getHeight();
    public int getKeyCode( int gameAction );
    public String getKeyName( int keyCode );
    public int getWidth();
    public boolean hasPointerEvents();
    public boolean hasPointerMotionEvents();
    public boolean hasRepeatEvents();
    protected void hideNotify();
    public boolean isDoubleBuffered();
```

```
    protected void keyPressed( int keyCode );
    protected void keyReleased( int keyCode );
    protected void keyRepeated( int keyCode );
    protected abstract void paint( Graphics g );
    protected void pointerDragged( int x, int y );
    protected void pointerPressed( int x, int y );
    protected void pointerReleased( int x, int y );
    public final void repaint();
    public final void repaint( int x, int y, int width, int height );
    public final void serviceRepaints();
    protected void showNotify();

    // Fields
    public static final int DOWN = 6;
    public static final int FIRE = 8;
    public static final int GAME_A = 9;
    public static final int GAME_B = 10;
    public static final int GAME_C = 11;
    public static final int GAME_D = 12;
    public static final int KEY_NUM0 = 48;
    public static final int KEY_NUM1 = 49;
    public static final int KEY_NUM2 = 50;
    public static final int KEY_NUM3 = 51;
    public static final int KEY_NUM4 = 52;
    public static final int KEY_NUM5 = 53;
    public static final int KEY_NUM6 = 54;
    public static final int KEY_NUM7 = 55;
    public static final int KEY_NUM8 = 56;
    public static final int KEY_NUM9 = 57;
    public static final int KEY_POUND = 35;
    public static final int KEY_STAR = 42;
    public static final int LEFT = 2;
    public static final int RIGHT = 5;
    public static final int UP = 1;
}
```

All Superclasses: Displayable, Object

Character

Defined by the CLDC 1.0 specification

Description

An object representation of the primitive char type. Major changes from J2SE 1.3: No support for Unicode subsets or blocks, and most of the isXXXX static methods are omitted.

Class Definition

```
package java.lang;

public final class Character {
    // Constructors
    public Character( char value );

    // Methods
    public char charValue();
    public static int digit( char ch, int radix );
    public boolean equals( Object obj );
    public int hashCode();
    public static boolean isDigit( char ch );
    public static boolean isLowerCase( char ch );
    public static boolean isUpperCase( char ch );
    public static char toLowerCase( char ch );
    public String toString();
    public static char toUpperCase( char ch );

    // Fields
    public static final int MAX_RADIX = 36;
    public static final char MAX_VALUE = '\uffff';
    public static final int MIN_RADIX = 2;
    public static final char MIN_VALUE = '\u0000';
}
```

All Superclasses: Object

Choice

Defined by the MIDP 1.0 specification

Description

Defines common methods for user interface components that enable the user to select individual items from a list of items. Each item consists of a string and an optional image. See the List and ChoiceGroup components for more details.

Interface Definition

```
package javax.microedition.lcdui;

public interface Choice {
    // Methods
    int append( String stringElement, Image imageElement );
    void delete( int elementNum );
    Image getImage( int elementNum );
```

```
    int getSelectedFlags( boolean[] selectedArray_return );
    int getSelectedIndex();
    String getString( int elementNum );
    void insert( int elementNum, String stringElement,
            Image imageElement );
    boolean isSelected( int elementNum );
    void set( int elementNum, String stringElement,
            Image imageElement );
    void setSelectedFlags( boolean[] selectedArray );
    void setSelectedIndex( int elementNum, boolean selected );
    int size();
    // Fields
    int EXCLUSIVE = 1;
    int IMPLICIT = 3;
    int MULTIPLE = 2;
}
```

ChoiceGroup

Defined by the MIDP 1.0 specification

Description

Defines a form item consisting of a group of selectable strings (with optional images). The user can select either a single string (using a radio button type of interface) or multiple strings (using a check box type of interface), depending on the mode of the group.

Class Definition

```
package javax.microedition.lcdui;

public class ChoiceGroup
    extends Item
    implements Choice {
    // Constructors
    public ChoiceGroup( String label, int choiceType );
    public ChoiceGroup( String label, int choiceType,
            String[] stringElements, Image[] imageElements );

    // Methods
    public int append( String stringElement, Image imageElement );
    public void delete( int index );
    public Image getImage( int i );
    public int getSelectedFlags( boolean[] selectedArray_return );
    public int getSelectedIndex();
    public String getString( int i );
    public void insert( int index, String stringElement,
            Image imageElement );
```

```
        public boolean isSelected( int index );
        public void set( int index, String stringElement,
                Image imageElement );
        public void setSelectedFlags( boolean[] selectedArray );
        public void setSelectedIndex( int index, boolean selected );
        public int size();
    }
```

All Superclasses: Item, Object

Class

Defined by the CLDC 1.0 specification

Description

A run-time representation of a class or interface in a Java application. Each class or interface has an associated Class object, as do arrays of the same element type and dimension number. Major changes from J2SE 1.3: No reflection methods and no methods that involve class loaders or security other than the static forName method.

Class Definition

```
package java.lang;

public final class Class {
    // Methods
    public static Class forName( String className )
            throws ClassNotFoundException;
    public String getName();
    public java.io.InputStream getResourceAsStream( String name );
    public boolean isArray();
    public boolean isAssignableFrom( Class cls );
    public boolean isInstance( Object obj );
    public boolean isInterface();
    public Object newInstance() throws InstantiationException,
                IllegalAccessException;
    public String toString();
}
```

All Superclasses: Object

ClassCastException

Defined by the CLDC 1.0 specification

Description

Thrown whenever an object instance is casted to a class or interface that it does not extend or implement; unchanged from J2SE 1.3

Class Definition

```
package java.lang;

public class ClassCastException
     extends RuntimeException {
     // Constructors
     public ClassCastException();
     public ClassCastException( String s );
}
```

All Superclasses: RuntimeException, Exception, Throwable, Object

ClassNotFoundException

Defined by the CLDC 1.0 specification

Description

Thrown when a class could not be loaded at application runtime. Major changes from J2SE 1.3: No support for tracking the underlying exception that caused the class loading to fail.

Class Definition

```
package java.lang;

public class ClassNotFoundException
     extends Exception {
     // Constructors
     public ClassNotFoundException();
     public ClassNotFoundException( String s );
}
```

All Superclasses: Exception, Throwable, Object

Command

Defined by the MIDP 1.0 specification

Description

Defines the semantic information associated with an action. This feature enables the device to choose how to best display and trigger the action. The semantic information includes a label, an action type, and an action priority. The application is responsible for performing the action when the command is triggered.

Class Definition

```
package javax.microedition.lcdui;

public class Command {
    // Constructors
    public Command( String label, int commandType, int priority );

    // Methods
    public int getCommandType();
    public String getLabel();
    public int getPriority();

    // Fields
    public static final int BACK = 2;
    public static final int CANCEL = 3;
    public static final int EXIT = 7;
    public static final int HELP = 5;
    public static final int ITEM = 8;
    public static final int OK = 4;
    public static final int SCREEN = 1;
    public static final int STOP = 6;
}
```

All Superclasses: Object

CommandListener

Defined by the MIDP 1.0 specification

Description

The listener interface for objects that wish to be notified whenever a Command object is triggered.

Interface Definition

```
package javax.microedition.lcdui;

public interface CommandListener {
    // Methods
    void commandAction( Command c, Displayable d );
}
```

Connection

Defined by the CLDC 1.0 specification

Description

The base interface for all connection types defined by the Generic Connection Framework; mostly a marker interface, because it only defines one method. See Chapter 6, "Network Communicaton," for more details.

Interface Definition

```
package javax.microedition.io;

public interface Connection {
    // Methods
    void close() throws java.io.IOException;
}
```

ConnectionNotFoundException

Defined by the CLDC 1.0 specification

Description

Thrown when a connection could not be opened because the requested connection protocol is not supported by the implementation. Part of the Generic Connection Framework. See Chapter 6 for more details.

Class Definition

```
package javax.microedition.io;

public class ConnectionNotFoundException
    extends java.io.IOException {
    // Constructors
    public ConnectionNotFoundException();
    public ConnectionNotFoundException( String s );
}
```

All Superclasses: java.io.IOException, Exception, Throwable, Object

Connector

Defined by the CLDC 1.0 specification

Description

Defines the factory methods that are used to obtain connections by using the Generic Connection Framework. A URL describing the connection is passed to one of the methods, which then attempts to create the appropriate kind of connection. If the connection could not be created, a `ConnectionNotFound-Exception` is thrown. See Chapter 6 for more details.

Class Definition

```
package javax.microedition.io;

public class Connector {
    // Methods
    public static Connection open( String name )
             throws java.io.IOException;
    public static Connection open( String name, int mode )
             throws java.io.IOException;
    public static Connection open( String name, int mode,
            boolean timeouts ) throws java.io.IOException;
    public static java.io.DataInputStream openDataInputStream(
            String name ) throws java.io.IOException;
    public static java.io.DataOutputStream openDataOutputStream(
            String name ) throws java.io.IOException;
    public static java.io.InputStream openInputStream( String name )
             throws java.io.IOException;
    public static java.io.OutputStream openOutputStream(
            String name ) throws java.io.IOException;
    // Fields
    public static final int READ = 1;
    public static final int READ_WRITE = 3;
    public static final int WRITE = 2;
}
```

All Superclasses: Object

ContentConnection

Defined by the CLDC 1.0 specification

Description

Defines a two-way stream connection that returns information about the content that can be read from it. Part of the Generic Connection Framework. Note that the `HttpConnection` interface defined by the MIDP extends this interface. See Chapter 6 for more details.

Interface Definition

```
package javax.microedition.io;

public interface ContentConnection
    extends StreamConnection {
    // Methods
    String getEncoding();
    long getLength();
    String getType();
}
```

All Superinterfaces: StreamConnection, InputConnection, Connection, OutputConnection

DataInput

Defined by the CLDC 1.0 specification

Description

Defines an interface for reading Java data types from a raw input stream. Unchanged from J2SE 1.3 except for the removal of the methods to read floating-point values.

Interface Definition

```
package java.io;

public interface DataInput {
    // Methods
    boolean readBoolean() throws IOException;
    byte readByte() throws IOException;
    char readChar() throws IOException;
    void readFully( byte[] b ) throws IOException;
    void readFully( byte[] b, int off, int len ) throws IOException;
    int readInt() throws IOException;
    long readLong() throws IOException;
    short readShort() throws IOException;
    String readUTF() throws IOException;
    int readUnsignedByte() throws IOException;
    int readUnsignedShort() throws IOException;
    int skipBytes( int n ) throws IOException;
}
```

DataInputStream

Defined by the CLDC 1.0 specification

Description

An input stream that implements the DataInput interface to allow the reading of Java data types from the stream. Major changes from J2SE 1.3: No readLine method and no support for floating-point.

Class Definition

```
package java.io;

public class DataInputStream
    extends InputStream
    implements DataInput {
    // Constructors
```

```
    public DataInputStream( InputStream in );

    // Methods
    public int available() throws IOException;
    public void close() throws IOException;
    public synchronized void mark( int readlimit );
    public boolean markSupported();
    public int read() throws IOException;
    public final int read( byte[] b ) throws IOException;
    public final int read( byte[] b, int off, int len )
           throws IOException;
    public final boolean readBoolean() throws IOException;
    public final byte readByte() throws IOException;
    public final char readChar() throws IOException;
    public final void readFully( byte[] b ) throws IOException;
    public final void readFully( byte[] b, int off, int len )
           throws IOException;
    public final int readInt() throws IOException;
    public final long readLong() throws IOException;
    public final short readShort() throws IOException;
    public final String readUTF() throws IOException;
    public static final String readUTF( DataInput in )
           throws IOException;
    public final int readUnsignedByte() throws IOException;
    public final int readUnsignedShort() throws IOException;
    public synchronized void reset() throws IOException;
    public long skip( long n ) throws IOException;
    public final int skipBytes( int n ) throws IOException;

    // Fields
    protected InputStream in;
}
```

All Superclasses: InputStream, Object

DataOutput

Defined by the CLDC 1.0 specification

Description

An interface for writing Java data types to a raw output stream. Unchanged from J2SE 1.3 except for the methods related to floating-point data.

Interface Definition

```
package java.io;

public interface DataOutput {
    // Methods
    void write( int b ) throws IOException;
    void write( byte[] b ) throws IOException;
```

```
    void write( byte[] b, int off, int len ) throws IOException;
    void writeBoolean( boolean v ) throws IOException;
    void writeByte( int v ) throws IOException;
    void writeChar( int v ) throws IOException;
    void writeChars( String s ) throws IOException;
    void writeInt( int v ) throws IOException;
    void writeLong( long v ) throws IOException;
    void writeShort( int v ) throws IOException;
    void writeUTF( String str ) throws IOException;
}
```

DataOutputStream

Defined by the CLDC 1.0 specification

Description

Defines an output stream that implements the DataOutput interface. Unchanged from J2SE 1.3 except for the floating-point write methods.

Class Definition

```
package java.io;

public class DataOutputStream
    extends OutputStream
    implements DataOutput {
    // Constructors
    public DataOutputStream( OutputStream out );

    // Methods
    public void close() throws IOException;
    public void flush() throws IOException;
    public void write( int b ) throws IOException;
    public void write( byte[] b, int off, int len )
           throws IOException;
    public final void writeBoolean( boolean v ) throws IOException;
    public final void writeByte( int v ) throws IOException;
    public final void writeChar( int v ) throws IOException;
    public final void writeChars( String s ) throws IOException;
    public final void writeInt( int v ) throws IOException;
    public final void writeLong( long v ) throws IOException;
    public final void writeShort( int v ) throws IOException;
    public final void writeUTF( String str ) throws IOException;

    // Fields
    protected OutputStream out;
}
```

All Superclasses: OutputStream, Object

Datagram

Defined by the CLDC 1.0 specification

Description

Defines a datagram-a holder for data sent or received by using DatagramConnection. Part of the Generic Connection Framework. Note that the MIDP 1.0 specification does not require devices to include datagram support, but vendors might provide it as an extension. See Chapter 6 for more details.

Interface Definition

```
package javax.microedition.io;

public interface Datagram
     extends java.io.DataInput,
             java.io.DataOutput {
     // Methods
     String getAddress();
     byte[] getData();
     int getLength();
     int getOffset();
     void reset();
     void setAddress( String addr ) throws java.io.IOException;
     void setAddress( Datagram reference );
     void setData( byte[] buffer, int offset, int len );
     void setLength( int len );
}
```

All Superinterfaces: java.io.DataInput, java.io.DataOutput

DatagramConnection

Defined by the CLDC 1.0 specification

Description

Defines a connection that is capable of sending or receiving datagrams. Part of the Generic Connection Framework. Note that the MIDP 1.0 specification does not require devices to support datagram connections, but vendors might provide them as extensions. See Chapter 6 for more details.

Interface Definition

```
package javax.microedition.io;

public interface DatagramConnection
     extends Connection {
     // Methods
     int getMaximumLength() throws java.io.IOException;
     int getNominalLength() throws java.io.IOException;
```

```
    Datagram newDatagram( int size ) throws java.io.IOException;
    Datagram newDatagram( byte[] buf, int size )
            throws java.io.IOException;
    Datagram newDatagram( int size, String addr )
            throws java.io.IOException;
    Datagram newDatagram( byte[] buf, int size, String addr )
            throws java.io.IOException;
    void receive( Datagram dgram ) throws java.io.IOException;
    void send( Datagram dgram ) throws java.io.IOException;
}
```

All Superinterfaces: Connection

Date

Defined by the CLDC 1.0 specification

Description

Defines a moment in time with a millisecond granularity. Moments are represented as offsets relative to January 1, 1970 at 00:00:00 GMT. Major changes from J2SE 1.3: Most methods are gone, but the same information is available by using the `get` and `set` methods of the Calendar class.

Class Definition

```
package java.util;

public class Date {
    // Constructors
    public Date();
    public Date( long date );

    // Methods
    public boolean equals( Object obj );
    public long getTime();
    public int hashCode();
    public void setTime( long time );
}
```

All Superclasses: Object

DateField

Defined by the MIDP 1.0 specification

Description

Displays an editable field for entering date and time information.

Class Definition

```
package javax.microedition.lcdui;

public class DateField
    extends Item {
    // Constructors
    public DateField( String label, int mode );
    public DateField( String label, int mode,
            java.util.TimeZone timeZone );

    // Methods
    public java.util.Date getDate();
    public int getInputMode();
    public void setDate( java.util.Date date );
    public void setInputMode( int mode );
    public String toString();

    // Fields
    public static final int DATE = 1;
    public static final int DATE_TIME = 3;
    public static final int TIME = 2;
}
```

All Superclasses: Item, Object

Display

Defined by the MIDP 1.0 specification

Description

Provides access to the device's display, including setting and getting the current screen object.

Class Definition

```
package javax.microedition.lcdui;

public class Display {
    // Methods
    public void callSerially( Runnable r );
    public Displayable getCurrent();
    public static Display getDisplay(
            javax.microedition.midlet.MIDlet c );
    public boolean isColor();
    public int numColors();
    public void setCurrent( Displayable next );
    public void setCurrent( Alert alert,
```

```
                Displayable nextDisplayable );
}
```

All Superclasses: Object

Displayable

Defined by the MIDP 1.0 specification

Description

Defines an object that can be displayed on the device's screen. The root class for alerts, forms, canvases, and other top-level window objects.

Class Definition

```
package javax.microedition.lcdui;

public abstract class Displayable {
    // Methods
    public void addCommand( Command cmd );
    public boolean isShown();
    public void removeCommand( Command cmd );
    public void setCommandListener( CommandListener l );
}
```

All Superclasses: Object

EOFException

Defined by the CLDC 1.0 specification

Description

Thrown when the end of file or end of stream has been reached during input. Unchanged from J2SE 1.3.

Class Definition

```
package java.io;

public class EOFException
    extends IOException {
    // Constructors
    public EOFException();
    public EOFException( String s );
}
```

All Superclasses: IOException, Exception, Throwable, Object

EmptyStackException

Defined by the CLDC 1.0 specification

Description

Thrown whenever a stack is empty and an operation requiring a non-empty stack is attempted. Unchanged from J2SE 1.3.

Class Definition

```
package java.util;

public class EmptyStackException
     extends RuntimeException {
     // Constructors
     public EmptyStackException();
}
```

All Superclasses: RuntimeException, Exception, Throwable, Object

Enumeration

Defined by the CLDC 1.0 specification

Description

Defines a generic interface to obtain the individual elements in a series of elements. Unchanged from J2SE 1.3.

Interface Definition

```
package java.util;

public interface Enumeration {
     // Methods
     boolean hasMoreElements();
     Object nextElement();
}
```

Error

Defined by the CLDC 1.0 specification

Description

The base class for all non-recoverable exceptions. Errors are unexpected indications of abnormal conditions and are not normally caught by an application. Unchanged from J2SE 1.3.

Class Definition

```
package java.lang;

public class Error
    extends Throwable {
    // Constructors
    public Error();
    public Error( String s );
}
```

All Superclasses: Throwable, Object

Exception

Defined by the CLDC 1.0 specification

Description

Indicates that an exceptional but not necessarily fatal condition has occurred. The application can catch the exception and deal with it in a graceful manner. Unchanged from J2SE 1.3.

Class Definition

```
package java.lang;

public class Exception
    extends Throwable {
    // Constructors
    public Exception();
    public Exception( String s );
}
```

All Superclasses: Throwable, Object

Font

Defined by the MIDP 1.0 specification

Description

Defines the properties and metrics of a font, including methods to obtain the width of character strings. Fonts are predefined by the system.

Class Definition

```
package javax.microedition.lcdui;

public final class Font {
    // Methods
    public int charWidth( char ch );
    public int charsWidth( char[] ch, int offset, int length );
```

```
        public int getBaselinePosition();
        public static Font getDefaultFont();
        public int getFace();
        public static Font getFont( int face, int style, int size );
        public int getHeight();
        public int getSize();
        public int getStyle();
        public boolean isBold();
        public boolean isItalic();
        public boolean isPlain();
        public boolean isUnderlined();
        public int stringWidth( String str );
        public int substringWidth( String str, int offset, int len );
        // Fields
        public static final int FACE_MONOSPACE = 32;
        public static final int FACE_PROPORTIONAL = 64;
        public static final int FACE_SYSTEM = 0;
        public static final int SIZE_LARGE = 16;
        public static final int SIZE_MEDIUM = 0;
        public static final int SIZE_SMALL = 8;
        public static final int STYLE_BOLD = 1;
        public static final int STYLE_ITALIC = 2;
        public static final int STYLE_PLAIN = 0;
        public static final int STYLE_UNDERLINED = 4;
    }
```

All Superclasses: Object

Form

Defined by the MIDP 1.0 specification

Description

Defines a screen object that can contain and display an arbitrary collection of user interface components that extend the Item class. The form is responsible for allowing the user to navigate between the items and for scrolling the items as necessary.

Class Definition

```
package javax.microedition.lcdui;

public class Form
    extends Screen {
    // Constructors
    public Form( String title );
    public Form( String title, Item[] items );
```

```
    // Methods
    public int append( Image image );
    public int append( Item item );
    public int append( String str );
    public void delete( int index );
    public Item get( int index );
    public void insert( int index, Item item );
    public void set( int index, Item item );
    public void setItemStateListener( ItemStateListener iListener );
    public int size();
}
```

All Superclasses: Screen, Displayable, Object

Gauge

Defined by the MIDP 1.0 specification

Description

A user-interface component that displays a value within a range of values by using a bar graph. The user can optionally set the value interactively.

Class Definition

```
package javax.microedition.lcdui;

public class Gauge
    extends Item {
    // Constructors
    public Gauge( String label, boolean interactive, int maxValue,
            int initialValue );

    // Methods
    public int getMaxValue();
    public int getValue();
    public boolean isInteractive();
    public void setMaxValue( int maxValue );
    public void setValue( int value );
}
```

All Superclasses: Item, Object

Graphics

Defined by the MIDP 1.0 specification

Description

Defines the two-dimensional drawing capabilities of a canvas or an offscreen image. An object of this type is passed to the application whenever the application must draw on the display. The application can also obtain an object that enables it to draw directly on an offscreen image buffer.

Class Definition

```
package javax.microedition.lcdui;

public class Graphics {
    // Methods
    public void clipRect( int x, int y, int width, int height );
    public void drawArc( int x, int y, int width, int height,
            int startAngle, int arcAngle );
    public void drawChar( char character, int x, int y, int anchor );
    public void drawChars( char[] data, int offset, int length,
            int x, int y, int anchor );
    public void drawImage( Image img, int x, int y, int anchor );
    public void drawLine( int x1, int y1, int x2, int y2 );
    public void drawRect( int x, int y, int width, int height );
    public void drawRoundRect( int x, int y, int width, int height,
            int arcWidth, int arcHeight );
    public void drawString( String str, int x, int y, int anchor );
    public void drawSubstring( String str, int offset, int len,
            int x, int y, int anchor );
    public void fillArc( int x, int y, int width, int height,
            int startAngle, int arcAngle );
    public void fillRect( int x, int y, int width, int height );
    public void fillRoundRect( int x, int y, int width, int height,
            int arcWidth, int arcHeight );
    public int getBlueComponent();
    public int getClipHeight();
    public int getClipWidth();
    public int getClipX();
    public int getClipY();
    public int getColor();
    public Font getFont();
    public int getGrayScale();
    public int getGreenComponent();
    public int getRedComponent();
    public int getStrokeStyle();
    public int getTranslateX();
    public int getTranslateY();
    public void setClip( int x, int y, int width, int height );
    public void setColor( int RGB );
    public void setColor( int red, int green, int blue );
    public void setFont( Font font );
    public void setGrayScale( int value );
    public void setStrokeStyle( int style );
```

```
    public void translate( int x, int y );
    // Fields
    public static final int BASELINE = 64;
    public static final int BOTTOM = 32;
    public static final int DOTTED = 1;
    public static final int HCENTER = 1;
    public static final int LEFT = 4;
    public static final int RIGHT = 8;
    public static final int SOLID = 0;
    public static final int TOP = 16;
    public static final int VCENTER = 2;
}
```

All Superclasses: Object

Hashtable

Defined by the CLDC 1.0 specification

Description

Implements a hashtable to efficiently map keys to values. Unchanged from J2SE 1.3 except for the lack of cloning and serialization support and the fact that it inherits directly from Object instead of from Dictionary.

Class Definition

```
package java.util;

public class Hashtable {
    // Constructors
    public Hashtable();
    public Hashtable( int initialCapacity );

    // Methods
    public synchronized void clear();
    public synchronized boolean contains( Object value );
    public synchronized boolean containsKey( Object key );
    public synchronized Enumeration elements();
    public synchronized Object get( Object key );
    public boolean isEmpty();
    public synchronized Enumeration keys();
    public synchronized Object put( Object key, Object value );
    protected void rehash();
    public synchronized Object remove( Object key );
    public int size();
    public synchronized String toString();
}
```

All Superclasses: Object

HttpConnection

Defined by the MIDP 1.0 specification

Description

Defines an HTTP 1.1 connection in terms of the Generic Connection Framework. The MIDP specification requires support for HTTP and defines this interface to expose all the features of the HTTP protocol beyond the few simple methods defined by ContentConnection and its superinterfaces. See Chapter 6 for more details.

Interface Definition

```
package javax.microedition.io;

public interface HttpConnection
    extends ContentConnection {
    // Methods
    long getDate() throws java.io.IOException;
    long getExpiration() throws java.io.IOException;
    String getFile();
    String getHeaderField( int n ) throws java.io.IOException;
    String getHeaderField( String name ) throws java.io.IOException;
    long getHeaderFieldDate( String name, long def )
             throws java.io.IOException;
    int getHeaderFieldInt( String name, int def )
             throws java.io.IOException;
    String getHeaderFieldKey( int n ) throws java.io.IOException;
    String getHost();
    long getLastModified() throws java.io.IOException;
    int getPort();
    String getProtocol();
    String getQuery();
    String getRef();
    String getRequestMethod();
    String getRequestProperty( String key );
    int getResponseCode() throws java.io.IOException;
    String getResponseMessage() throws java.io.IOException;
    String getURL();
    void setRequestMethod( String method )
             throws java.io.IOException;
    void setRequestProperty( String key, String value )
             throws java.io.IOException;
    // Fields
    String GET = "GET";
    String HEAD = "HEAD";
    int HTTP_ACCEPTED = 202;
    int HTTP_BAD_GATEWAY = 502;
    int HTTP_BAD_METHOD = 405;
    int HTTP_BAD_REQUEST = 400;
```

```
    int HTTP_CLIENT_TIMEOUT = 408;
    int HTTP_CONFLICT = 409;
    int HTTP_CREATED = 201;
    int HTTP_ENTITY_TOO_LARGE = 413;
    int HTTP_EXPECT_FAILED = 417;
    int HTTP_FORBIDDEN = 403;
    int HTTP_GATEWAY_TIMEOUT = 504;
    int HTTP_GONE = 410;
    int HTTP_INTERNAL_ERROR = 500;
    int HTTP_LENGTH_REQUIRED = 411;
    int HTTP_MOVED_PERM = 301;
    int HTTP_MOVED_TEMP = 302;
    int HTTP_MULT_CHOICE = 300;
    int HTTP_NOT_ACCEPTABLE = 406;
    int HTTP_NOT_AUTHORITATIVE = 203;
    int HTTP_NOT_FOUND = 404;
    int HTTP_NOT_IMPLEMENTED = 501;
    int HTTP_NOT_MODIFIED = 304;
    int HTTP_NO_CONTENT = 204;
    int HTTP_OK = 200;
    int HTTP_PARTIAL = 206;
    int HTTP_PAYMENT_REQUIRED = 402;
    int HTTP_PRECON_FAILED = 412;
    int HTTP_PROXY_AUTH = 407;
    int HTTP_REQ_TOO_LONG = 414;
    int HTTP_RESET = 205;
    int HTTP_SEE_OTHER = 303;
    int HTTP_TEMP_REDIRECT = 307;
    int HTTP_UNAUTHORIZED = 401;
    int HTTP_UNAVAILABLE = 503;
    int HTTP_UNSUPPORTED_RANGE = 416;
    int HTTP_UNSUPPORTED_TYPE = 415;
    int HTTP_USE_PROXY = 305;
    int HTTP_VERSION = 505;
    String POST = "POST";
}
```

All Superinterfaces: ContentConnection, StreamConnection, InputConnection, Connection, OutputConnection

IOException

Defined by the CLDC 1.0 specification

Description

Thrown when a general input/output exception occurs. Unchanged from J2SE 1.3.

Class Definition

```
package java.io;

public class IOException
    extends Exception {
    // Constructors
    public IOException();
    public IOException( String s );
}
```

All Superclasses: Exception, Throwable, Object

IllegalAccessException

Defined by the CLDC 1.0 specification

Description

Thrown when an application attempts to load a class or create an instance of a class to which it does not have proper access. Unchanged from J2SE 1.3.

Class Definition

```
package java.lang;

public class IllegalAccessException
    extends Exception {
    // Constructors
    public IllegalAccessException();
    public IllegalAccessException( String s );
}
```

All Superclasses: Exception, Throwable, Object

IllegalArgumentException

Defined by the CLDC 1.0 specification

Description

Thrown when a method is passed an illegal or otherwise inappropriate argument. Unchanged from J2SE 1.3.

Class Definition

```
package java.lang;

public class IllegalArgumentException
    extends RuntimeException {
    // Constructors
    public IllegalArgumentException();
```

```
        public IllegalArgumentException( String s );
    }
```

All Superclasses: RuntimeException, Exception, Throwable, Object

IllegalMonitorStateException

Defined by the CLDC 1.0 specification

Description

Thrown when a thread calls wait, notify, or notifyAll on an object whose monitor it does not own. Unchanged from J2SE 1.3.

Class Definition

```
package java.lang;

public class IllegalMonitorStateException
    extends RuntimeException {
    // Constructors
    public IllegalMonitorStateException();
    public IllegalMonitorStateException( String s );
}
```

All Superclasses: RuntimeException, Exception, Throwable, Object

IllegalStateException

Defined by the MIDP 1.0 specification

Description

Thrown when a method is inappropriately invoked, usually due to the internal state of the object. Unchanged from J2SE 1.3.

Class Definition

```
package java.lang;

public class IllegalStateException
    extends RuntimeException {
    // Constructors
    public IllegalStateException();
    public IllegalStateException( String s );
}
```

All Superclasses: RuntimeException, Exception, Throwable, Object

IllegalThreadStateException

Defined by the CLDC 1.0 specification

Description

Thrown when an invalid operation is performed on a thread. In a CLDC environment, this situation will only occur when an attempt is made to start the same thread twice. Unchanged from J2SE 1.3.

Class Definition

```
package java.lang;

public class IllegalThreadStateException
    extends IllegalArgumentException {
    // Constructors
    public IllegalThreadStateException();
    public IllegalThreadStateException( String s );
}
```

All Superclasses: IllegalArgumentException, RuntimeException, Exception, Throwable, Object

Image

Defined by the MIDP 1.0 specification

Description

Defines a graphical image. Images can also be used as offscreen drawing buffers. Images can be created from external data stored in the *Portable Network Graphics* (PNG) format.

Class Definition

```
package javax.microedition.lcdui;

public class Image {
    // Methods
    public static Image createImage( Image image );
    public static Image createImage( String name )
            throws java.io.IOException;
    public static Image createImage( int width, int height );
    public static Image createImage( byte[] imagedata,
            int imageoffset, int imagelength );
    public Graphics getGraphics();
```

```
        public int getHeight();
        public int getWidth();
        public boolean isMutable();
    }
```

All Superclasses: Object

ImageItem

Defined by the MIDP 1.0 specification

Description

Defines a user interface component that displays an image and an optional text label.

Class Definition

```
    package javax.microedition.lcdui;

    public class ImageItem
        extends Item {
        // Constructors
        public ImageItem( String label, Image img, int layout,
                String altText );

        // Methods
        public String getAltText();
        public Image getImage();
        public int getLayout();
        public void setAltText( String altText );
        public void setImage( Image img );
        public void setLayout( int layout );

        // Fields
        public static final int LAYOUT_CENTER = 3;
        public static final int LAYOUT_DEFAULT = 0;
        public static final int LAYOUT_LEFT = 1;
        public static final int LAYOUT_NEWLINE_AFTER = 512;
        public static final int LAYOUT_NEWLINE_BEFORE = 256;
        public static final int LAYOUT_RIGHT = 2;
    }
```

All Superclasses: Item, Object

IndexOutOfBoundsException

Defined by the CLDC 1.0 specification

Description

Thrown when an index is out of range for a particular data structure. Unchanged from J2SE 1.3.

Class Definition

```
package java.lang;

public class IndexOutOfBoundsException
    extends RuntimeException {
    // Constructors
    public IndexOutOfBoundsException();
    public IndexOutOfBoundsException( String s );
}
```

All Superclasses: RuntimeException, Exception, Throwable, Object

InputConnection

Defined by the CLDC 1.0 specification

Description

Defines an input stream connection. Part of the Generic Connection Framework. Note that the MIDP 1.0 specification defines support for HTTP connections through the `HttpConnection` interface, which extends this interface, but any other input connection stream is a vendor extension. See Chapter 6 for more details.

Interface Definition

```
package javax.microedition.io;

public interface InputConnection
    extends Connection {
    // Methods
    java.io.DataInputStream openDataInputStream()
              throws java.io.IOException;
    java.io.InputStream openInputStream()
              throws java.io.IOException;
}
```

All Superinterfaces: Connection

InputStream

Defined by the CLDC 1.0 specification

Description

Defines an abstraction for reading bytes of data from a stream. Unchanged from J2SE 1.3.

Class Definition

```
package java.io;

public abstract class InputStream {
     // Constructors
     public InputStream();

     // Methods
     public int available() throws IOException;
     public void close() throws IOException;
     public synchronized void mark( int readlimit );
     public boolean markSupported();
     public abstract int read() throws IOException;
     public int read( byte[] b ) throws IOException;
     public int read( byte[] b, int off, int len )
               throws IOException;
     public synchronized void reset() throws IOException;
     public long skip( long n ) throws IOException;
}
```

All Superclasses: Object

InputStreamReader

Defined by the CLDC 1.0 specification

Description

A reader for reading character data from a byte-oriented input stream. Unchanged from J2SE 1.3 except that there is no support for getting the byte encoding.

Class Definition

```
package java.io;

public class InputStreamReader
     extends Reader {
     // Constructors
     public InputStreamReader( InputStream is );
     public InputStreamReader( InputStream is, String enc )
               throws UnsupportedEncodingException;

     // Methods
     public void close() throws IOException;
     public void mark( int readAheadLimit ) throws IOException;
```

```
        public boolean markSupported();
        public int read() throws IOException;
        public int read( char[] cbuf, int off, int len )
                 throws IOException;
        public boolean ready() throws IOException;
        public void reset() throws IOException;
        public long skip( long n ) throws IOException;
    }
```

All Superclasses: Reader, Object

InstantiationException

Defined by the CLDC 1.0 specification

Description

Thrown when the application attempts to create an instance of a Class object but that Class object represents an interface or an abstract class. Unchanged from J2SE 1.3.

Class Definition

```
package java.lang;

public class InstantiationException
    extends Exception {
    // Constructors
    public InstantiationException();
    public InstantiationException( String s );
}
```

All Superclasses: Exception, Throwable, Object

Integer

Defined by the CLDC 1.0 specification

Description

An object representation of the primitive int type. Major differences from J2SE 1.3: No TYPE static field, no getInteger, compareTo, and decode methods and no support for floating-point conversions.

Class Definition

```
package java.lang;

public final class Integer {
    // Constructors
    public Integer( int value );
```

```
    // Methods
    public byte byteValue();
    public boolean equals( Object obj );
    public int hashCode();
    public int intValue();
    public long longValue();
    public static int parseInt( String s )
            throws NumberFormatException;
    public static int parseInt( String s, int radix )
            throws NumberFormatException;
    public short shortValue();
    public static String toBinaryString( int i );
    public static String toHexString( int i );
    public static String toOctalString( int i );
    public String toString();
    public static String toString( int i );
    public static String toString( int i, int radix );
    public static Integer valueOf( String s )
            throws NumberFormatException;
    public static Integer valueOf( String s, int radix )
            throws NumberFormatException;

    // Fields
    public static final int MAX_VALUE = 2147483647;
    public static final int MIN_VALUE = -2147483648;
}
```

All Superclasses: Object

InterruptedException

Defined by the CLDC 1.0 specification

Description

Thrown when a thread is interrupted, which can only be done in a CLDC environment by the virtual machine itself and not under programmatic control. Unchanged since J2SE 1.3.

Class Definition

```
package java.lang;

public class InterruptedException
    extends Exception {
    // Constructors
    public InterruptedException();
    public InterruptedException( String s );
}
```

All Superclasses: Exception, Throwable, Object

InterruptedIOException

Defined by the CLDC 1.0 specification

Description

Thrown when an input/output operation is interrupted. Unchanged from J2SE 1.3.

Class Definition

```
package java.io;

public class InterruptedIOException
    extends IOException {
    // Constructors
    public InterruptedIOException();
    public InterruptedIOException( String s );

    // Fields
    public int bytesTransferred;
}
```

All Superclasses: IOException, Exception, Throwable, Object

InvalidRecordIDException

Defined by the MIDP 1.0 specification

Description

Thrown when a record store operation fails due to an invalid record ID.

Class Definition

```
package javax.microedition.rms;

public class InvalidRecordIDException
    extends RecordStoreException {
    // Constructors
    public InvalidRecordIDException();
    public InvalidRecordIDException( String message );
}
```

All Superclasses: RecordStoreException, Exception, Throwable, Object

Item

Defined by the MIDP 1.0 specification

Description

The base class for user interface components that can be placed on and contained by a form. Each item can define a text label.

Class Definition

```
package javax.microedition.lcdui;

public abstract class Item {
    // Methods
    public String getLabel();
    public void setLabel( String label );
}
```

All Superclasses: Object

ItemStateListener

Defined by the MIDP 1.0 specification

Description

A listener interface for notification of changes to the state of the items on a form.

Interface Definition

```
package javax.microedition.lcdui;

public interface ItemStateListener {
    // Methods
    void itemStateChanged( Item item );
}
```

List

Defined by the MIDP 1.0 specification

Description

A predefined top-level window that lets the user select one or more strings from a list of strings.

Class Definition

```
package javax.microedition.lcdui;

public class List
    extends Screen
    implements Choice {
    // Constructors
    public List( String title, int listType );
    public List( String title, int listType,
            String[] stringElements, Image[] imageElements );

    // Methods
    public int append( String stringElement, Image imageElement );
    public void delete( int index );
    public Image getImage( int index );
    public int getSelectedFlags( boolean[] selectedArray_return );
    public int getSelectedIndex();
    public String getString( int index );
    public void insert( int index, String stringElement,
            Image imageElement );
    public boolean isSelected( int index );
    public void set( int index, String stringElement,
            Image imageElement );
    public void setSelectedFlags( boolean[] selectedArray );
    public void setSelectedIndex( int index, boolean selected );
    public int size();

    // Fields
    public static final Command SELECT_COMMAND;
}
```

All Superclasses: Screen, Displayable, Object

Long

Defined by the CLDC 1.0 specification

Description

An object representation of the primitive long type. Major changes from J2SE 1.3: No TYPE static field, no support for converting to hex/octal/binary strings, and no value methods other than longValue.

Class Definition

```
package java.lang;

public final class Long {
    // Constructors
    public Long( long value );
```

```
    // Methods
    public boolean equals( Object obj );
    public int hashCode();
    public long longValue();
    public static long parseLong( String s )
            throws NumberFormatException;
    public static long parseLong( String s, int radix )
            throws NumberFormatException;
    public String toString();
    public static String toString( long i );
    public static String toString( long i, int radix );

    // Fields
    public static final long MAX_VALUE = 9223372036854775807;
    public static final long MIN_VALUE = -9223372036854775808;
}
```

All Superclasses: Object

MIDlet

Defined by the MIDP 1.0 specification

Description

Defines the entry point to a Mobile Information Device Profile application. Each application, or MIDlet, must extend this class. The subclass must provide a no-argument constructor and implementations of the startApp, pauseApp, and destroyApp methods according to the rules described in Chapter 3, "The MIDlet Lifecycle."

Class Definition

```
package javax.microedition.midlet;

public abstract class MIDlet {
    // Constructors
    protected MIDlet();

    // Methods
    protected abstract void destroyApp( boolean unconditional )
            throws MIDletStateChangeException;
    public final String getAppProperty( String key );
    public final void notifyDestroyed();
    public final void notifyPaused();
    protected abstract void pauseApp();
    public final void resumeRequest();
    protected abstract void startApp()
            throws MIDletStateChangeException;
}
```

All Superclasses: Object

MIDletStateChangeException

Defined by the MIDP 1.0 specification

Description

Thrown by a MIDlet when it is requested to change its state but the MIDlet cannot or does not want to change its state. See Chapter 3 for more details.

Class Definition

```
package javax.microedition.midlet;

public class MIDletStateChangeException
    extends Exception {
    // Constructors
    public MIDletStateChangeException();
    public MIDletStateChangeException( String s );
}
```

All Superclasses: Exception, Throwable, Object

Math

Defined by the CLDC 1.0 specification

Description

Defines static methods for mathematical operations. Major changes from J2SE 1.3: Only the abs, min, and max methods are defined, and only for integer and long types.

Class Definition

```
package java.lang;

public final class Math {
    // Methods
    public static int abs( int a );
    public static long abs( long a );
    public static int max( int a, int b );
    public static long max( long a, long b );
    public static int min( int a, int b );
    public static long min( long a, long b );
}
```

All Superclasses: Object

NegativeArraySizeException

Defined by the CLDC 1.0 specification

Description

Thrown if an application creates an array with negative size. Unchanged from J2SE 1.3.

Class Definition

```
package java.lang;

public class NegativeArraySizeException
    extends RuntimeException {
    // Constructors
    public NegativeArraySizeException();
    public NegativeArraySizeException( String s );
}
```

All Superclasses: RuntimeException, Exception, Throwable, Object

NoSuchElementException

Defined by the CLDC 1.0 specification

Description

Thrown when there are no more elements in an enumeration. Unchanged from J2SE 1.3.

Class Definition

```
package java.util;

public class NoSuchElementException
    extends RuntimeException {
    // Constructors
    public NoSuchElementException();
    public NoSuchElementException( String s );
}
```

All Superclasses: RuntimeException, Exception, Throwable, Object

NullPointerException

Defined by the CLDC 1.0 specification

Description

Thrown when an application uses a null object reference when a non-null object reference is required. Unchanged from J2SE 1.3.

Class Definition

```
package java.lang;

public class NullPointerException
    extends RuntimeException {
    // Constructors
    public NullPointerException();
    public NullPointerException( String s );
}
```

All Superclasses: RuntimeException, Exception, Throwable, Object

NumberFormatException

Defined by the CLDC 1.0 specification

Description

Thrown when a string cannot be converted to a number. Unchanged from J2SE 1.3.

Class Definition

```
package java.lang;

public class NumberFormatException
    extends IllegalArgumentException {
    // Constructors
    public NumberFormatException();
    public NumberFormatException( String s );
}
```

All Superclasses: IllegalArgumentException, RuntimeException, Exception, Throwable, Object

Object

Defined by the CLDC 1.0 specification

Description

The root of the Java class hierarchy. All objects explicitly or implicitly extend this class. Major changes from J2SE 1.3: no clone or finalize methods.

Class Definition

```
package java.lang;
```

```
public class Object {
    // Constructors
    public Object();

    // Methods
    public boolean equals( Object obj );
    public final Class getClass();
    public int hashCode();
    public final void notify();
    public final void notifyAll();
    public String toString();
    public final void wait() throws InterruptedException;
    public final void wait( long timeout )
            throws InterruptedException;
    public final void wait( long timeout, int nanos )
            throws InterruptedException;
}
```

OutOfMemoryError

Defined by the CLDC 1.0 specification

Description

Thrown when the virtual machine runs out of memory, even after running the garbage collector. Unchanged from J2SE 1.3.

Class Definition

```
package java.lang;

public class OutOfMemoryError
    extends VirtualMachineError {
    // Constructors
    public OutOfMemoryError();
    public OutOfMemoryError( String s );
}
```

All Superclasses: VirtualMachineError, Error, Throwable, Object

OutputConnection

Defined by the CLDC 1.0 specification

Description

Defines an output stream connection. Part of the Generic Connection Framework. Note that the MIDP 1.0 specification defines support for HTTP connections through the `HttpConnection` interface, which extends this interface, but any other output connection stream is a vendor extension. See Chapter 6 for more details.

Interface Definition

```
package javax.microedition.io;

public interface OutputConnection
    extends Connection {
    // Methods
    java.io.DataOutputStream openDataOutputStream()
              throws java.io.IOException;
    java.io.OutputStream openOutputStream()
              throws java.io.IOException;
}
```

All Superinterfaces: Connection

OutputStream

Defined by the CLDC 1.0 specification

Description

Defines an abstraction for writing bytes of data to an output stream. Unchanged from J2SE 1.3.

Class Definition

```
package java.io;

public abstract class OutputStream {
    // Constructors
    public OutputStream();

    // Methods
    public void close() throws IOException;
    public void flush() throws IOException;
    public abstract void write( int b ) throws IOException;
    public void write( byte[] b ) throws IOException;
    public void write( byte[] b, int off, int len )
              throws IOException;
}
```

All Superclasses: Object

OutputStreamWriter

Defined by the CLDC 1.0 specification

Description

A writer for writing character data to a byte-oriented output stream. Unchanged from J2SE 1.3 except for the capability to get the byte encoding.

Class Definition

```
package java.io;

public class OutputStreamWriter
    extends Writer {
    // Constructors
    public OutputStreamWriter( OutputStream os );
    public OutputStreamWriter( OutputStream os, String enc )
            throws UnsupportedEncodingException;

    // Methods
    public void close() throws IOException;
    public void flush() throws IOException;
    public void write( int c ) throws IOException;
    public void write( char[] cbuf, int off, int len )
            throws IOException;
    public void write( String str, int off, int len )
            throws IOException;
}
```

All Superclasses: Writer, Object

PrintStream

Defined by the CLDC 1.0 specification

Description

An output stream that has convenience methods for writing data values to the underlying byte stream. Unchanged from J2SE 1.3 except for the removal of the autoflush capability and methods related to floating point values.

Class Definition

```
package java.io;

public class PrintStream
    extends OutputStream {
    // Constructors
    public PrintStream( OutputStream out );

    // Methods
    public boolean checkError();
    public void close();
    public void flush();
    public void print( boolean b );
    public void print( char c );
    public void print( int i );
    public void print( long l );
```

```
        public void print( Object obj );
        public void print( char[] s );
        public void print( String s );
        public void println();
        public void println( boolean x );
        public void println( char x );
        public void println( int x );
        public void println( long x );
        public void println( char[] x );
        public void println( String x );
        public void println( Object x );
        protected void setError();
        public void write( int b );
        public void write( byte[] buf, int off, int len );
    }
```

All Superclasses: OutputStream, Object

Random

Defined by the CLDC 1.0 specification

Description

Generates a pseudo-random number. Major changes from J2SE 1.3: No support for Gaussian distributions or for types other than int or long.

Class Definition

```
package java.util;

public class Random {
    // Constructors
    public Random();
    public Random( long seed );

    // Methods
    protected synchronized int next( int bits );
    public int nextInt();
    public long nextLong();
    public synchronized void setSeed( long seed );
}
```

All Superclasses: Object

Reader

Defined by the CLDC 1.0 specification

Description

An abstract reader for reading character streams as opposed to byte streams. Unchanged from J2SE 1.3.

Class Definition

```
package java.io;

public abstract class Reader {
    // Constructors
    protected Reader();
    protected Reader( Object lock );

    // Methods
    public abstract void close() throws IOException;
    public void mark( int readAheadLimit ) throws IOException;
    public boolean markSupported();
    public int read() throws IOException;
    public int read( char[] cbuf ) throws IOException;
    public abstract int read( char[] cbuf, int off, int len )
            throws IOException;
    public boolean ready() throws IOException;
    public void reset() throws IOException;
    public long skip( long n ) throws IOException;

    // Fields
    protected Object lock;
}
```

All Superclasses: Object

RecordComparator

Defined by the MIDP 1.0 specification

Description

An interface for user-defined record comparison. Because records are just arrays of bytes, only the application can determine the relative sort order of two records. When the `compare` method is called, it should return EQUIVALENT if the two records are equivalent, PRECEDES if the first record precedes the second record, or FOLLOWS if the first record follows the second record.

Interface Definition

```
package javax.microedition.rms;

public interface RecordComparator {
```

```
    // Methods
    int compare( byte[] rec1, byte[] rec2 );
    // Fields
    int EQUIVALENT = 0;
    int FOLLOWS = 1;
    int PRECEDES = -1;
}
```

RecordEnumeration

Defined by the MIDP 1.0 specification

Description

Defines an enumeration of a record store's records or a subset of those records. The enumeration is bidirectional and can optionally be updated on the fly as the record store changes.

Interface Definition

```
package javax.microedition.rms;

public interface RecordEnumeration {
    // Methods
    void destroy();
    boolean hasNextElement();
    boolean hasPreviousElement();
    boolean isKeptUpdated();
    void keepUpdated( boolean keepUpdated );
    byte[] nextRecord() throws InvalidRecordIDException,
                    RecordStoreNotOpenException,
                    RecordStoreException;
    int nextRecordId() throws InvalidRecordIDException;
    int numRecords();
    byte[] previousRecord() throws InvalidRecordIDException,
                    RecordStoreNotOpenException,
                    RecordStoreException;
    int previousRecordId() throws InvalidRecordIDException;
    void rebuild();
    void reset();
}
```

RecordFilter

Defined by the MIDP 1.0 specification

Description

Defines a filter for determining whether a record in a record store matches application-defined criteria. Used to build enumerations that contain a subset of the records in a record store.

Interface Definition

```
package javax.microedition.rms;

public interface RecordFilter {
    // Methods
    boolean matches( byte[] candidate );
}
```

RecordListener

Defined by the MIDP 1.0 specification

Description

Defines a listener interface for tracking changes to a record store. Anyone who registers a listener with a record store is notified when records are changed, added, or deleted.

Interface Definition

```
package javax.microedition.rms;

public interface RecordListener {
    // Methods
    void recordAdded( RecordStore recordStore, int recordId );
    void recordChanged( RecordStore recordStore, int recordId );
    void recordDeleted( RecordStore recordStore, int recordId );
}
```

RecordStore

Defined by the MIDP 1.0 specification

Description

Implements a record-oriented persistent data store. Records are byte arrays of arbitrary length whose contents are understood only by the application (or applications, because data stores can be shared by MIDlets within a MIDlet suite) that creates them. Each record is assigned a unique record ID-an integer greater than or equal to 1. Record IDs are not reused when records are deleted. The contents of a record are read or written in their entirety as atomic operations to avoid data corruption when two or more threads attempt to read or write the same record. Enumerations are used to traverse the records in the record store, and the application can provide callbacks for filtering and sorting the records to return only the records that match specific criteria and/or to return them in a specific order.

Class Definition

```
package javax.microedition.rms;

public class RecordStore {
    // Methods
    public int addRecord( byte[] data, int offset, int numBytes )
             throws RecordStoreNotOpenException,
                    RecordStoreException,
                    RecordStoreFullException;
    public void addRecordListener( RecordListener listener );
    public void closeRecordStore()
             throws RecordStoreNotOpenException,
                    RecordStoreException;
    public void deleteRecord( int recordId )
             throws RecordStoreNotOpenException,
                    InvalidRecordIDException,
                    RecordStoreException;
    public static void deleteRecordStore( String recordStoreName )
             throws RecordStoreException,
                    RecordStoreNotFoundException;
    public RecordEnumeration enumerateRecords( RecordFilter filter,
            RecordComparator comparator, boolean keepUpdated )
             throws RecordStoreNotOpenException;
    public long getLastModified()
             throws RecordStoreNotOpenException;
    public String getName() throws RecordStoreNotOpenException;
    public int getNextRecordID() throws RecordStoreNotOpenException,
                    RecordStoreException;
    public int getNumRecords() throws RecordStoreNotOpenException;
    public byte[] getRecord( int recordId )
             throws RecordStoreNotOpenException,
                    InvalidRecordIDException,
                    RecordStoreException;
    public int getRecord( int recordId, byte[] buffer, int offset )
             throws RecordStoreNotOpenException,
                    InvalidRecordIDException,
                    RecordStoreException;
    public int getRecordSize( int recordId )
             throws RecordStoreNotOpenException,
                    InvalidRecordIDException,
                    RecordStoreException;
    public int getSize() throws RecordStoreNotOpenException;
    public int getSizeAvailable()
             throws RecordStoreNotOpenException;
    public int getVersion() throws RecordStoreNotOpenException;
```

```
    public static String[] listRecordStores();
    public static RecordStore openRecordStore(
            String recordStoreName, boolean createIfNecessary )
             throws RecordStoreException,
                    RecordStoreFullException,
                    RecordStoreNotFoundException;
    public void removeRecordListener( RecordListener listener );
    public void setRecord( int recordId, byte[] newData, int offset,
            int numBytes ) throws RecordStoreNotOpenException,
                    InvalidRecordIDException,
                    RecordStoreException,
                    RecordStoreFullException;
}
```

All Superclasses: Object

RecordStoreException

Defined by the MIDP 1.0 specification

Description

Thrown when a record store operation fails. The base class for all record store exceptions.

Class Definition

```
package javax.microedition.rms;

public class RecordStoreException
    extends Exception {
    // Constructors
    public RecordStoreException();
    public RecordStoreException( String message );
}
```

All Superclasses: Exception, Throwable, Object

RecordStoreFullException

Defined by the MIDP 1.0 specification

Description

Thrown when an operation could not be completed because there is no more room to grow the record store

Class Definition

```
package javax.microedition.rms;

public class RecordStoreFullException
    extends RecordStoreException {
```

```
    // Constructors
    public RecordStoreFullException();
    public RecordStoreFullException( String message );
}
```

All Superclasses: RecordStoreException, Exception, Throwable, Object

RecordStoreNotFoundException

Defined by the MIDP 1.0 specification

Description

Thrown when an operation is attempted on a non-existent record store.

Class Definition

```
package javax.microedition.rms;

public class RecordStoreNotFoundException
    extends RecordStoreException {
    // Constructors
    public RecordStoreNotFoundException();
    public RecordStoreNotFoundException( String message );
}
```

All Superclasses: RecordStoreException, Exception, Throwable, Object

RecordStoreNotOpenException

Defined by the MIDP 1.0 specification

Description

Thrown when an operation is attempted on a record store that is not open.

Class Definition

```
package javax.microedition.rms;

public class RecordStoreNotOpenException
    extends RecordStoreException {
    // Constructors
    public RecordStoreNotOpenException();
    public RecordStoreNotOpenException( String message );
}
```

All Superclasses: RecordStoreException, Exception, Throwable, Object

Runnable

Defined by the CLDC 1.0 specification

Description

Defines a single method that is invoked to execute an action on an object. What happens when the method is invoked is up to the object. An object that implements this interface can be run on a separate thread. Unchanged from J2SE 1.3.

Interface Definition

```
package java.lang;

public interface Runnable {
    // Methods
    void run();
}
```

Runtime

Defined by the CLDC 1.0 specification

Description

Provides access to the application's run-time environment. Major changes from J2SE 1.3: No finalization support, no tracing support, and no capability to load native code libraries or to execute external applications. As well, the exit method throws an exception when called because the MIDP specification forbids its use.

Class Definition

```
package java.lang;

public class Runtime {
    // Methods
    public void exit( int status );
    public long freeMemory();
    public void gc();
    public static Runtime getRuntime();
    public long totalMemory();
}
```

All Superclasses: Object

RuntimeException

Defined by the CLDC 1.0 specification

Description

The superclass for unchecked exceptions (exceptions that can be thrown as a program runs but that do not need to be declared in the throws clause of methods that throw them). Unchanged from J2SE 1.3.

Class Definition

```
package java.lang;

public class RuntimeException
    extends Exception {
    // Constructors
    public RuntimeException();
    public RuntimeException( String s );
}
```

All Superclasses: Exception, Throwable, Object

Screen

Defined by the MIDP 1.0 specification

Description

The base class for all top-level windows except for canvases. Screens have optional titles and tickers.

Class Definition

```
package javax.microedition.lcdui;

public abstract class Screen
    extends Displayable {
    // Methods
    public Ticker getTicker();
    public String getTitle();
    public void setTicker( Ticker ticker );
    public void setTitle( String s );
}
```

All Superclasses: Displayable, Object

SecurityException

Defined by the CLDC 1.0 specification

Description

Thrown to indicate some kind of security violation, such as calling System.exit from within a MIDlet. Unchanged from J2SE 1.3.

Class Definition

```
package java.lang;

public class SecurityException
    extends RuntimeException {
```

```
        // Constructors
        public SecurityException();
        public SecurityException( String s );
    }
```

All Superclasses: RuntimeException, Exception, Throwable, Object

Short

Defined by the CLDC 1.0 specification

Description

An object representation of the primitive short type. Major changes from J2SE 1.3: No static TYPE field, missing string conversion methods (use those in the Integer class instead), and no floating point support.

Class Definition

```
    package java.lang;

    public final class Short {
        // Constructors
        public Short( short value );

        // Methods
        public boolean equals( Object obj );
        public int hashCode();
        public static short parseShort( String s )
                throws NumberFormatException;
        public static short parseShort( String s, int radix )
                throws NumberFormatException;
        public short shortValue();
        public String toString();

        // Fields
        public static final short MAX_VALUE = 32767;
        public static final short MIN_VALUE = -32768;
    }
```

All Superclasses: Object

Stack

Defined by the CLDC 1.0 specification

Description

Implements a simple stack. Unchanged from J2SE 1.3.

Class Definition

```
package java.util;

public class Stack
    extends Vector {
    // Constructors
    public Stack();

    // Methods
    public boolean empty();
    public synchronized Object peek();
    public synchronized Object pop();
    public Object push( Object item );
    public synchronized int search( Object o );
}
```

All Superclasses: Vector, Object

StreamConnection

Defined by the CLDC 1.0 specification

Description

Defines a two-way stream with input and output capabilities. Part of the Generic Connection Framework. Note that the MIDP 1.0 specification requires support only for HTTP connections via the `HttpConnection` interface, which extends this interface-but any other stream connections are vendor extensions. See Chapter 6 for more details.

Interface Definition

```
package javax.microedition.io;

public interface StreamConnection
    extends InputConnection,
            OutputConnection {
}
```

All Superinterfaces: InputConnection, Connection, OutputConnection

StreamConnectionNotifier

Defined by the CLDC 1.0 specification

Description

Defines the interface for a stream connection notifier, a connection type that waits for incoming stream connections. Part of the Generic Connection Framework. See Chapter 6 for more details.

Interface Definition

```
package javax.microedition.io;

public interface StreamConnectionNotifier
    extends Connection {
    // Methods
    StreamConnection acceptAndOpen() throws java.io.IOException;
}
```

All Superinterfaces: Connection

String

Defined by the CLDC 1.0 specification

Description

Defines the class used to store immutable (read-only) strings. Major differences from J2SE 1.3: Some alternate constructors are missing, no equalsIgnoreCase method, and no intern method.

Class Definition

```
package java.lang;

public final class String {
    // Constructors
    public String();
    public String( StringBuffer buffer );
    public String( byte[] bytes );
    public String( String value );
    public String( char[] value );
    public String( byte[] bytes, String enc )
            throws java.io.UnsupportedEncodingException;
    public String( byte[] bytes, int off, int len );
    public String( char[] value, int offset, int count );
    public String( byte[] bytes, int off, int len, String enc )
            throws java.io.UnsupportedEncodingException;

    // Methods
    public char charAt( int index );
    public int compareTo( String anotherString );
    public String concat( String str );
    public boolean endsWith( String suffix );
    public boolean equals( Object anObject );
    public byte[] getBytes();
    public byte[] getBytes( String enc )
            throws java.io.UnsupportedEncodingException;
    public void getChars( int srcBegin, int srcEnd, char[] dst,
           int dstBegin );
```

```
    public int hashCode();
    public int indexOf( int ch );
    public int indexOf( String str );
    public int indexOf( int ch, int fromIndex );
    public int indexOf( String str, int fromIndex );
    public int lastIndexOf( int ch );
    public int lastIndexOf( int ch, int fromIndex );
    public int length();
    public boolean regionMatches( boolean ignoreCase, int toffset,
            String other, int ooffset, int len );
    public String replace( char oldChar, char newChar );
    public boolean startsWith( String prefix );
    public boolean startsWith( String prefix, int toffset );
    public String substring( int beginIndex );
    public String substring( int beginIndex, int endIndex );
    public char[] toCharArray();
    public String toLowerCase();
    public String toString();
    public String toUpperCase();
    public String trim();
    public static String valueOf( boolean b );
    public static String valueOf( char c );
    public static String valueOf( char[] data );
    public static String valueOf( int i );
    public static String valueOf( long l );
    public static String valueOf( Object obj );
    public static String valueOf( char[] data, int offset,
            int count );
}
```

All Superclasses: Object

StringBuffer

Defined by the CLDC 1.0 specification

Description

Defines the class used to store mutable (read-write) strings. Major changes from J2SE 1.3: Removal of serialization and floating point support.

Class Definition

```
package java.lang;

public final class StringBuffer {
    // Constructors
    public StringBuffer();
    public StringBuffer( int length );
    public StringBuffer( String str );
```

```
    // Methods
    public StringBuffer append( boolean b );
    public synchronized StringBuffer append( char c );
    public StringBuffer append( int i );
    public StringBuffer append( long l );
    public synchronized StringBuffer append( Object obj );
    public synchronized StringBuffer append( String str );
    public synchronized StringBuffer append( char[] str );
    public synchronized StringBuffer append( char[] str, int offset,
            int len );
    public int capacity();
    public synchronized char charAt( int index );
    public synchronized StringBuffer delete( int start, int end );
    public synchronized StringBuffer deleteCharAt( int index );
    public synchronized void ensureCapacity( int minimumCapacity );
    public synchronized void getChars( int srcBegin, int srcEnd,
            char[] dst, int dstBegin );
    public StringBuffer insert( int offset, boolean b );
    public synchronized StringBuffer insert( int offset, char c );
    public StringBuffer insert( int offset, int i );
    public StringBuffer insert( int offset, long l );
    public synchronized StringBuffer insert( int offset, Object obj );
    public synchronized StringBuffer insert( int offset, String str );
    public synchronized StringBuffer insert( int offset, char[] str );
    public int length();
    public synchronized StringBuffer reverse();
    public synchronized void setCharAt( int index, char ch );
    public synchronized void setLength( int newLength );
    public String toString();
}
```

All Superclasses: Object

StringIndexOutOfBoundsException

Defined by the CLDC 1.0 specification

Description

Thrown to indicate that an index is outside the valid bounds of a string. Unchanged from J2SE 1.3.

Class Definition

```
package java.lang;

public class StringIndexOutOfBoundsException
    extends IndexOutOfBoundsException {
    // Constructors
    public StringIndexOutOfBoundsException();
```

```
    public StringIndexOutOfBoundsException( int index );
    public StringIndexOutOfBoundsException( String s );
}
```

All Superclasses: IndexOutOfBoundsException, RuntimeException, Exception, Throwable, Object

StringItem

Defined by the MIDP 1.0 specification

Description

Defines a form item that consists of a single string, with an optional label. The string is non-editable.

Class Definition

```
package javax.microedition.lcdui;

public class StringItem
    extends Item {
    // Constructors
    public StringItem( String label, String text );

    // Methods
    public String getText();
    public void setText( String text );
}
```

All Superclasses: Item, Object

System

Defined by the CLDC 1.0 specification

Description

Provides access to system-related information and capabilities. Major changes from J2SE 1.3: No System.in static field or any way to reassign the standard streams, no security manager, and no access to system properties except as individual values, plus the same restrictions as the Runtime class.

Class Definition

```
package java.lang;

public final class System {
    // Methods
    public static void arraycopy( Object src, int src_position,
            Object dst, int dst_position, int length );
    public static long currentTimeMillis();
```

```
    public static void exit( int status );
    public static void gc();
    public static String getProperty( String key );
    public static int identityHashCode( Object x );
    // Fields
    public static final java.io.PrintStream err;
    public static final java.io.PrintStream out;
}
```

All Superclasses: Object

TextBox

Defined by the MIDP 1.0 specification

Description

A screen that allows the user to enter and edit text.

Class Definition

```
package javax.microedition.lcdui;

public class TextBox
    extends Screen {
    // Constructors
    public TextBox( String title, String text, int maxSize,
            int constraints );

    // Methods
    public void delete( int offset, int length );
    public int getCaretPosition();
    public int getChars( char[] data );
    public int getConstraints();
    public int getMaxSize();
    public String getString();
    public void insert( String src, int position );
    public void insert( char[] data, int offset, int length,
            int position );
    public void setChars( char[] data, int offset, int length );
    public void setConstraints( int constraints );
    public int setMaxSize( int maxSize );
    public void setString( String text );
    public int size();
}
```

All Superclasses: Screen, Displayable, Object

TextField

Defined by the MIDP 1.0 specification

Description

A form item that enables the user to enter and edit text.

Class Definition

```
package javax.microedition.lcdui;

public class TextField
     extends Item {
     // Constructors
     public TextField( String label, String text, int maxSize,
             int constraints );

     // Methods
     public void delete( int offset, int length );
     public int getCaretPosition();
     public int getChars( char[] data );
     public int getConstraints();
     public int getMaxSize();
     public String getString();
     public void insert( String src, int position );
     public void insert( char[] data, int offset, int length,
             int position );
     public void setChars( char[] data, int offset, int length );
     public void setConstraints( int constraints );
     public int setMaxSize( int maxSize );
     public void setString( String text );
     public int size();

     // Fields
     public static final int ANY = 0;
     public static final int CONSTRAINT_MASK = 65535;
     public static final int EMAILADDR = 1;
     public static final int NUMERIC = 2;
     public static final int PASSWORD = 65536;
     public static final int PHONENUMBER = 3;
     public static final int URL = 4;
}
```

All Superclasses: Item, Object

Thread

Defined by the CLDC 1.0 specification

Description

Defines and controls a thread of execution. Major changes from J2SE 1.3: No daemon threads, no thread names, and no methods for stopping or interrupting threads.

Class Definition

```
package java.lang;

public class Thread
    implements Runnable {
    // Constructors
    public Thread();
    public Thread( Runnable target );

    // Methods
    public static int activeCount();
    public static Thread currentThread();
    public final int getPriority();
    public final boolean isAlive();
    public final void join() throws InterruptedException;
    public void run();
    public final void setPriority( int newPriority );
    public static void sleep( long millis )
            throws InterruptedException;
    public synchronized void start();
    public String toString();
    public static void yield();

    // Fields
    public static final int MAX_PRIORITY = 10;
    public static final int MIN_PRIORITY = 1;
    public static final int NORM_PRIORITY = 5;
}
```

All Superclasses: Object

Throwable

Defined by the CLDC 1.0 specification

Description

The base class for all errors and exceptions. Only objects that extend Throwable can be thrown and caught by using Java's exception-handling mechanisms. Major changes from J2SE 1.3: No support for localized messages and no stack tracing.

Class Definition

```
package java.lang;

public class Throwable {
    // Constructors
    public Throwable();
    public Throwable( String message );

    // Methods
    public String getMessage();
```

```
        public void printStackTrace();
        public String toString();
    }
```

All Superclasses: Object

Ticker

Defined by the MIDP 1.0 specification

Description

Displays a string by using a scrolling marquee. The string is displayed continuously until the ticker is removed or the screen to which the ticker is attached is hidden. The implementation controls the speed and direction of the text scrolling and the look and placement of the ticker.

Class Definition

```
package javax.microedition.lcdui;

public class Ticker {
    // Constructors
    public Ticker( String str );

    // Methods
    public String getString();
    public void setString( String str );
}
```

All Superclasses: Object

Timer

Defined by the MIDP 1.0 specification

Description

Defines a way to schedule tasks for later execution by a background thread. Unchanged from J2SE 1.3 except that there is no way to make the timer a daemon thread because the CLDC does not support daemon threads.

Class Definition

```
package java.util;

public class Timer {
    // Constructors
    public Timer();
```

```
    // Methods
    public void cancel();
    public void schedule( TimerTask task, long delay );
    public void schedule( TimerTask task, Date time );
    public void schedule( TimerTask task, long delay, long period );
    public void schedule( TimerTask task, Date firstTime,
            long period );
    public void scheduleAtFixedRate( TimerTask task, long delay,
            long period );
    public void scheduleAtFixedRate( TimerTask task, Date firstTime,
            long period );
}
```

All Superclasses: Object

TimerTask

Defined by the MIDP 1.0 specification

Description

A task that can be scheduled for execution by a Timer; unchanged from J2SE 1.3.

Class Definition

```
package java.util;

public abstract class TimerTask
    implements Runnable {
    // Constructors
    protected TimerTask();

    // Methods
    public boolean cancel();
    public abstract void run();
    public long scheduledExecutionTime();
}
```

All Superclasses: Object

TimeZone

Defined by the CLDC 1.0 specification

Description

Represents a time zone offset from *Greenwich Mean Time* (GMT) for use in date and time calculations. Major changes from J2SE 1.3: No support for setting the time zone ID or for determining whether a particular date falls in the daylight savings time period.

Class Definition

```
package java.util;

public abstract class TimeZone {
    // Constructors
    public TimeZone();

    // Methods
    public static String[] getAvailableIDs();
    public static synchronized TimeZone getDefault();
    public String getID();
    public abstract int getOffset( int era, int year, int month,
            int day, int dayOfWeek, int millis );
    public abstract int getRawOffset();
    public static synchronized TimeZone getTimeZone( String ID );
    public abstract boolean useDaylightTime();
}
```

All Superclasses: Object

UnsupportedEncodingException

Defined by the CLDC 1.0 specification

Description

Thrown if the requested character encoding is not supported. Unchanged from J2SE 1.3.

Class Definition

```
package java.io;

public class UnsupportedEncodingException
    extends IOException {
    // Constructors
    public UnsupportedEncodingException();
    public UnsupportedEncodingException( String s );
}
```

All Superclasses: IOException, Exception, Throwable, Object

UTFDataFormatException

Defined by the CLDC 1.0 specification

Description

Thrown when a malformed UTF-8 string is read by using any class that implements the DataInput interface. Unchanged from J2SE 1.3.

Class Definition

```
package java.io;

public class UTFDataFormatException
    extends IOException {
    // Constructors
    public UTFDataFormatException();
    public UTFDataFormatException( String s );
}
```

All Superclasses: IOException, Exception, Throwable, Object

Vector

Defined by the CLDC 1.0 specification

Description

Implements a growable array of objects. Major changes from J2SE 1.3: removal of the clone method.

Class Definition

```
package java.util;

public class Vector {
    // Constructors
    public Vector();
    public Vector( int initialCapacity );
    public Vector( int initialCapacity, int capacityIncrement );

    // Methods
    public synchronized void addElement( Object obj );
    public int capacity();
    public boolean contains( Object elem );
    public synchronized void copyInto( Object[] anArray );
    public synchronized Object elementAt( int index );
    public synchronized Enumeration elements();
    public synchronized void ensureCapacity( int minCapacity );
    public synchronized Object firstElement();
    public int indexOf( Object elem );
    public synchronized int indexOf( Object elem, int index );
    public synchronized void insertElementAt( Object obj, int index );
    public boolean isEmpty();
    public synchronized Object lastElement();
    public int lastIndexOf( Object elem );
    public synchronized int lastIndexOf( Object elem, int index );
    public synchronized void removeAllElements();
    public synchronized boolean removeElement( Object obj );
```

```
        public synchronized void removeElementAt( int index );
        public synchronized void setElementAt( Object obj, int index );
        public synchronized void setSize( int newSize );
        public int size();
        public synchronized String toString();
        public synchronized void trimToSize();

        // Fields
        protected int capacityIncrement;
        protected int elementCount;
        protected Object elementData;
    }
```

All Superclasses: Object

VirtualMachineError

Defined by the CLDC 1.0 specification

Description

Thrown when the virtual machine has encountered a fatal error and cannot continue to operate. Unchanged from J2SE 1.3.

Class Definition

```
    package java.lang;

    public abstract class VirtualMachineError
        extends Error {
        // Constructors
        public VirtualMachineError();
        public VirtualMachineError( String s );
    }
```

All Superclasses: Error, Throwable, Object

Writer

Defined by the CLDC 1.0 specification

Description

An abstract writer for writing character streams as opposed to byte streams. Unchanged from J2SE 1.3.

Class Definition

```
    package java.io;

    public abstract class Writer {
        // Constructors
```

```
    protected Writer();
    protected Writer( Object lock );

    // Methods
    public abstract void close() throws IOException;
    public abstract void flush() throws IOException;
    public void write( int c ) throws IOException;
    public void write( char[] cbuf ) throws IOException;
    public void write( String str ) throws IOException;
    public abstract void write( char[] cbuf, int off, int len )
            throws IOException;
    public void write( String str, int off, int len )
            throws IOException;

    // Fields
    protected Object lock;
}
```

All Superclasses: Object

APPENDIX B

Resources

This appendix lists J2ME and MIDP resources that might be of interest to MIDP application developers. For updates to this information, consult the book's Web site at `www.wiley.com/compbooks/ortiz`.

J2ME Specifications

Table B.1 lists the *Java Specification Requests* (JSR) that pertain to J2ME at the time this book was written. A JSR is a formal specification developed through the *Java Community Process* (JCP). For information about the JCP and the latest about the specifications, see `www.jcp.org`.

Table B.1 J2ME Java Specification Requests

Number	Title	Description
1	Real-Time Specification for Java	The Real-Time Specification for Java extends the Java platform to support both current practice and advanced real-time systems application programming. www.jcp.org/jsr/detail/1.jsp
7	Factory Floor Automation Extension	The Factory Floor Automation specification will result in an industry standard for industrial automation that is based on the Java and Jini technologies. www.jcp.org/jsr/detail/7.jsp

Table B.1 Continued

Number	Title	Description
30	J2ME Connected, Limited Device Configuration	This specification defines a standard platform configuration of the Java 2 platform, Micro Edition (J2ME) for small, resource-limited, connected devices. www.jcp.org/jsr/detail/30.jsp
36	J2ME Connected Device Configuration	The J2ME Connected Device Configuration (CDC) provides the basis of the Java 2 platform, Micro Edition for devices that have a sufficient 32-bit microprocessor and ample memory. www.jcp.org/jsr/detail/36.jsp
37	Mobile Information Device Profile for the J2ME Platform	This specification defines a profile that will extend and enhance the "J2ME Connected, Limited Device Configuration" (JSR-000030), enabling application development for mobile information appliances and voice communication devices. www.jcp.org/jsr/detail/37.jsp
46	J2ME Foundation Profile	The J2ME Foundation Profile is a set of APIs meant for applications running on small devices that have some type of network connection. www.jcp.org/jsr/detail/46.jsp
50	Distributed Real-Time Specification	The Distributed Real-Time Specification for Java extends RMI in the Real-Time Specification for Java, to provide support for predictability of end-to-end timeliness of trans-node activities. www.jcp.org/jsr/detail/50.jsp
62	Personal Profile Specification	The J2ME Personal Profile provides the J2ME environment for those devices with a need for a high degree of Internet connectivity and web fidelity. www.jcp.org/jsr/detail/62.jsp
66	J2ME RMI Profile	The J2ME RMI Profile provides Java platform to Java platform remote method invocation for Java devices and interoperates with J2SE RMI. www.jcp.org/jsr/detail/66.jsp

Table B.1 Continued

Number	Title	Description
68	J2ME Platform Specification	This specification will define the next major revision of the Java 2 platform, Micro Edition. www.jcp.org/jsr/detail/68.jsp
75	PDA Profile for the J2ME Platform	This profile will provide user interface and data storage APIs for small, resource-limited handheld devices. It is based on the Connected, Limited Device Configuration (CLDC). www.jcp.org/jsr/detail/75.jsp
80	Java USB API	This specification provides a Java API for communicating with devices that are attached via the USB (Universal Serial Bus). It will allow Java applications to communicate with and manipulate USB devices attached to the bus. www.jcp.org/jsr/detail/80.jsp
82	Java APIs for Bluetooth	Bluetooth is an important emerging standard for wireless integration of small devices. The specification will standardize a set of Java APIs to allow these Java-enabled devices to integrate into a Bluetooth environment. www.jcp.org/jsr/detail/82.jsp
113	Java Speech API 2.0	This JSR extends the work of the 1.0 Java Speech API, which allows developers to incorporate speech technology into user interfaces for their Java programming language applets and applications. This API specifies a cross-platform interface to support command and control recognizers, dictation systems, and speech synthesizers. www.jcp.org/jsr/detail/113.jsp
118	Mobile Information Device Next Generation	This specification will define a profile that will extend and enhance the "J2ME Mobile Information Device Profile" (JSR-000037). www.jcp.org/jsr/detail/118.jsp

Table B.1 Continued

Number	Title	Description
120	Wireless Telephony Communication APIs (WTCA)	The purpose of this JSR is to define a set of optional APIs that provides standard access to wireless communication resources. This will allow third-party developers to build intelligent connected Java applications. The WTCA is designed to run on J2ME configurations and to enhance J2ME profiles with unique functionality. The intention of this JSR is to offer a set of reusable components that can be used singly or in any combination within any J2ME profile. www.jcp.org/jsr/detail/120.jsp
129	Personal Basis Profile Specification	The J2ME Personal Basis Profile provides a J2ME application environment for network-connected devices supporting a basic level of graphical presentation. www.jcp.org/jsr/detail/129.jsp
133	Java Memory Model and Thread Specification Revision	The proposed specification describes the semantics of threads, locks, volatile variables, and data races. This includes what has been referred to as the Java memory model. www.jcp.org/jsr/detail/133.jsp
134	Java Game Profile	Defines a J2ME Profile for the purpose of game development targeting high-end consumer game devices and desktops. www.jcp.org/jsr/detail/134.jsp
135	J2ME Multimedia API	The proposed JSR specifies a Multimedia API for J2ME. This small-footprint API allows easy and simple access and control of basic audio and multimedia resources but also addresses scalability and support of more sophisticated features. www.jcp.org/jsr/detail/135.jsp

Table B.1 Continued

Number	Title	Description
138	DMS—Dynamic Monitoring Service	Will specify an API and semantics for instrumenting and subsequently monitoring Java programs. Instrumentation will be low cost to allow production applications to retain instrumentation. Statistics can be output using any appropriate API, including Java logging and Management API's. www.jcp.org/jsr/detail/138.jsp
	Java Card	The Java Card Specification http://java.sun.com/products/javacard

J2ME Development Tools

Table B.2 lists the most popular J2ME development tools that were available at the time this book was written.

Table B.2 J2ME Development Tools

Vendor	Description
Sun Java Wireless Toolkit	A set of tools that provides Java developers with the emulation environment, documentation, and examples needed to develop MIDP compliant applications http://java.sun.com/products/j2mewtoolkit/
RIM Java IDE	The BlackBerry Java Development Environment (JDE) is a complete application development environment for building J2ME applications. http://developers.rim.net/tools/jde/index.shtml
Metrowerks CodeWarrior	CodeWarrior Java tools support J2SE(tm), PersonalJava™ and J2ME™ http://www.codewarrior.com/
Borland JBuilder	JBuilder MobileSet is a J2ME compliant environment, fully integrated with JBuilder 5, to support software development in Java-enabled devices. www.borland.com/jbuilder/mobileset/

Table B.2 Continued

Vendor	Description
JBuilder Handheld Express	JBuilder Handheld Express provides support for developing solutions using the Java 2 Platform, Micro Edition (J2ME) Software Development Kit (SDK) Version 1.0 currently targeted at the Palm OS. In addition, JBuilder provides features that dynamically adapt to any J2ME profile, including the Mobile Information Device Profiles (MIDP) currently being developed through the Java Community Process. www.borland.com/jbuilder/hhe
WHITEboard SDK	The WHITEboardSDK provides a complete development environment for creating and testing wireless Java applications for J2ME-compliant mobile devices. The kit complies with the J2ME configuration and profile for mobile devices (CLDC and MIDP). www.zucotto.com
Esmertec's Jbed	Esmertec's Jbed product line "the only real choice for Java technology - small, fast, and hard real-time". www.esmertec.com
Kada Systems Kada Mobile	Kada Mobile is "the industry's smallest, fastest, most complete and easily ported Java application platform for mobile devices." www.kadasystems.com

Web Sites of Interest

Table B.3 lists a number of Web sites that are of interest to MIDP application developers.

Table B.3 Web Sites of Interest

Resource	Description
J2ME FAQ	Managed by Bill Day, the J2ME FAQ addresses the networked consumer and embedded devices, from smart cards, pagers, and mobile phones, to set-top boxes and automobile navigation systems. This FAQ also addresses technologies used to connect J2ME-enabled devices to consumer and enterprise services, including standard wireless data formats and protocols. www.jguru.com/faq/J2ME
World Wide Web consortium	The World Wide Web Consortium (W3C). www.w3c.org
Bill Day's J2ME archive	Bill Day is an evangelist with Sun Microsystems and has compiled an extensive list of links and resources for J2ME. www.billday.com/j2me/index.html
IETF	The Internet Engineering Task Force. www.ietf.org/
Micro Java Network	Java news related to mobile and wireless devices. www.microjava.com
XML security	A discussion of security issues and XML. www.nue.et-inf.uni-siegen.de/~geuer-pollmann/xml_security.html
JDC J2ME Tech Tips	Contains tips, techniques, and sample code on various topics of interest to developers using the Java programming language in Java 2 Platform, Micro Edition (J2ME). Written by Eric Giguère, one of the authors of this book. http://developer.java.sun.com/developer/J2METechTips
Sun's page for wireless	Information and resources for wireless developers. developers http://developer.java.sun.com/developer/products/wireless/
Java Developer Connection	A central place for developers to learn about the latest Java technologies. http://developer.java.sun.com/developer/
OnJava wireless	Includes the Java 2 Micro Edition (J2ME), Java Wireless Toolkit, Personal Java, Embedded Java, Java Card, KVM, CLDC, CDC, MIDP.

Table B.3 Continued

Resource	Description
XML developers news	XML news for developers. http://xmlhack.com/
OASYS Open	Industry standards for interoperability based on XML. www.oasis-open.org

Index

A

B

C

S

T

U

V

W

X